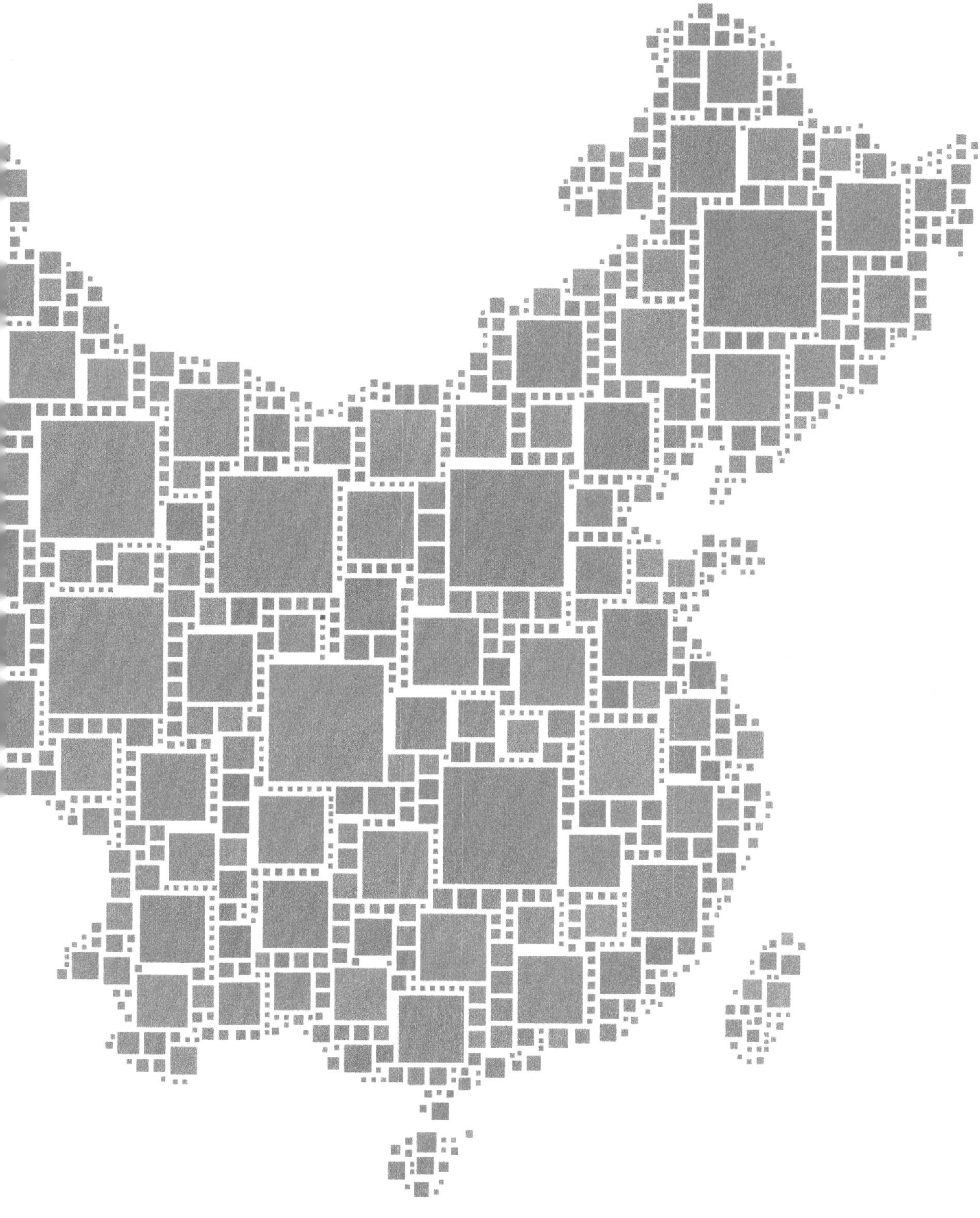

Structural Reform in China's Regional Governments

Structural Reform in China's Regional Governments

Volume 2

Guo Qingwang and Jia Junxue

Enrich Professional Publishing

Honolulu • Hong Kong • Beijing • Singapore

Published by

Enrich Professional Publishing, Inc.
Suite 208
Davies Pacific Center
841 Bishop Street
Honolulu, HI, 96813
Website: www.enrichprofessional.com
A Member of Enrich Culture Group Limited

Hong Kong Head Office:
11/F, Benson Tower, 74 Hung To Road, Kwun Tong, Kowloon, Hong Kong, China

China Office:
Rm 309, Building A, Central Valley, 16 Hai Dian Middle Street, Haidian District, Beijing, China

Singapore Office:
16L, Enterprise Road, Singapore 627660

Chapter 6 translated by Vivien Lee
Chapters 7–9 & Annex translated by W.H. Hau

Edited by Glenn Griffith and W.H. Hau

ISBN (Hardback) 978-1-62320-042-8
ISBN (ebook) 978-1-62320-063-3

Enrich Professional Publishing is an independent globally-minded publisher focusing on the economic and financial developments that have revolutionized new China. We aim to serve the needs of advanced degree students, researchers, and business professionals who are looking for authoritative, accurate, and engaging information on China.

Printed in Hong Kong with woodfree paper from Japan

Contents

6

Chapter

Optimization of the Size and Structure of Regional Governments from the Perspective of Economic Growth

Chapters 3 to 5 in Volume 1 examined the determining factors in the size and structure of regional governments and explored in detail the mechanisms of effect for fiscal decentralization and government organizational structure on the size and structure of regional governments. What, then, are the existing inadequacies in the current size and structure of China's regional governments? How do they affect social-economic development in the country? What is the optimal size and structure of regional governments for achieving a balanced social-economic development? These are the questions that the following chapters in this volume aim to address.

Modern fiscal decentralization theories address the focuses of the central government and regional governments in the handling of resource allocation, maintaining macroeconomic stability, and income distribution. It is generally accepted that regional governments assume a significant information advantage over the central government, since they have greater access to the preferences of the residents and the costs of the provision of public services in their jurisdictions. Therefore, they should be assigned greater responsibilities in resource allocation.[1] In the real-world economy, however, factors such as the degree of heterogeneity of regional preferences, economies of scale, factor mobility, and the budget constraint of regional governments need to be considered.[2]

The traditional view is that regional governments have little effect on maintaining macroeconomic stability due to the lack of available monetary measures and that the high degree of economic openness limits the effectiveness of regional fiscal policies. This view, however, has been challenged by many who view macroeconomic fluctuations as more of a regional phenomenon than a national one, and so maintaining macroeconomic stability and achieving regional economic stability depends on regional governments coordinating their policies.[3]

As for their role in income distribution, it is generally believed that mobility of factors and externalities of welfare policies limit the effectiveness of the income distribution policies of regional governments,[4] such that income distribution policies are essentially national policies.[5] Other theories point out that certain items of redistribution are more suitably assumed by regional governments.[6] In fact, regional governments do assume a large share of responsibility for income distribution items such as social welfare expenses.

It can be seen that a thorough understanding of the effects of the size and structure of regional governments on economic growth, economic stability, income distribution, and social welfare would offer a comprehensive evaluation of the actual size and structure of regional governments. Chapters 6 to 9 will thus systematically and comprehensively evaluate the size and structure of regional governments through the perspectives of economic growth, economic stability, income distribution and social welfare, in order to find the optimal way of sizing and structuring regional governments.

This chapter will proceed to examine the size and structure of regional governments from the perspective of economic growth, in order to analyze the problems underlying the current state of regional governments and find measures for optimizing the size and structure of regional governments.

Effects of the Size and Structure of Provincial Governments on Economic Growth

There is no academic consensus as to the exact nature of the effects of the size and structure of governments on economic growth: one view believes that an increase in the government size would crowd out private economic resources and exert a negative wealth effect, which does not favor economic growth, while another view is that government expenditure — especially the economic expenditure on infrastructure and transportation and social expenditure on education, healthcare, and public hygiene — can help improve the efficiency of private production, thereby stimulating economic growth.

Relevant empirical studies also fail to offer consistent conclusions. Some studies have found that a sizeable government expenditure and production expenditure such as infrastructure constrains economic growth,[7] while on the other hand, other studies find that the negative impacts of these factors are not significant, and may in some cases be favorable to economic growth.[8]

The Chinese academia has also conducted some interesting research on this topic. For instance, Zhuang and Zou analyzed provincial data for the period 1980 to 1999, finding that the widespread existence of "adjustment costs" directly causes the expenditure of regional governments to have a clear constraining effect on economic growth.[9] Zhang and Duan conducted an empirical analysis from a regional economics perspective of the effects of size and structure of expenditure on economic growth for the Eastern, Central, and Western regions, finding that administrative expenditure, infrastructure expenditure, and capital funding for enterprises has a negative effect on the Eastern economy but has a promoting effect in the Central and Western economies, while the opposite is the case for expenditure on education, science, culture and healthcare as well as that for agricultural development, and that an unreasonable structure of expenditure of regional governments suppresses the effects of the expenditure on economic growth.[10]

Liao and Yu used a dynamic panel data model and system GMM to examine the effects of the size and structure of regional governments on the basis of panel data of 31 provinces over 1995 to 2004, finding that the expenditure of regional governments has significant short-term and long-term effects. Of which, production expenditures such as agricultural development, infrastructure, and capital funding do not promote long-term economic growth, while some non-production expenditures such as administrative expenditure have a significantly promoting effect on long-term economic growth.[11] Jia et al. examined the effects of capital expenditure decentralization and the composition of regional investment in public capital on long-term economic growth, concluding that the structure of regional public capital investment is unreasonable: the proportion of regional public investment in physical capital was too low, which constrained long-term economic growth. This, to a large extent, was due to the fact that the assignment of authority over public capital investments between the central government and regional government was unreasonable.[12]

This section will examine the effects of the size and structure of regional governments on economic growth and the fiscal competition mechanism, using a spatial econometric model and actual data of the 29 provinces of the country for the period 1986 to 2006. Additionally, considering that central fiscal transfer payments are a major part of the fiscally decentralized institution, inevitably affecting the behavior of regional governments and the consequent effects on the economy, and further taking into account the importance of the public investment in physical and human capital, a dynamic panel data model and system GMM are also used to evaluate the effects of public capital investment of regional governments on economic growth, as well as the mechanism of constraint arising from the central fiscal transfer payment system.

Effects of fiscal competition and the size and structure of regional governments on economic growth

Two opposing views exist as to whether fiscal competition promotes economic growth: public choice theorists believe that regional governments follow a Leviathan model in pursuing maximization of their own sizes. In this model, fiscal competition is seen to be capable of effectively constrain the behavior of regional governments, prompting them to pay greater attention to the preferences of the residents, improve the efficiency of government expenditure, and optimize the government expenditure structure, ultimately stimulating economic growth.[13] Traditional public sector theorists, on the other hand, think that overly intense fiscal competition drives the maximal-public interest-seeking regional governments towards a race to the bottom, leading to an inefficient size and distorted structure of expenditure, which hinders economic growth.[14]

Academics have also shown a keen interest in the situation of China after the start of the Chinese Economic Reform. Qian and Weingast, and Qian and Roland, proposed the theory of market-preserving federalism, which argues that the arrangements in the decentralized system can help reduce regional government intervention in the microeconomic sector and promote marketization, which in turn stimulates regional economic growth.[15] Zhou Li'an examined the effects of political promotion on the competitive behavior of regional governments and in turn economic growth, finding that while competition in political promotion is an important stimulant in rapid economic growth, it also brings about a series of negative effects ranging from regional protectionism, infrastructure repetition to vicious competition among regional governments.[16]

Using a game model, Zhou Ye'an finds that the vertical administrative structure and limitations in mobility of resources lead to regional governments adopting protective and predatory strategies, decreasing efficiency in resource allocation and hindering economic growth.[17] Qiao et al. considers fiscal decentralization in China as essentially a type of central government appointment framework, and given the limitations to population mobility, regional governments are more orientated towards economic growth in the regional economic competition, which hinders the promotion of social welfare levels.[18] Guo and Jia also used a game model to demonstrate that under the double incentives of financial benefits and political promotion, regional governments are strongly motivated to practice irregular policies, leading to huge shocks on macroeconomic stability and is unfavorable for long-term stability in economic growth.[19]

Model framework

Taking into account the strong mutual interactions among regional economies resulting from trade and resource mobility, the following spatial econometrics model is constructed:

$$Gy = \rho WGy + \alpha Fe + \beta FeDum94 + \gamma X + \varepsilon \tag{6.1}$$

Of which, Gy is the vector of actual provincial per capita output growth rate, W is the spatial weights matrix, WGy is the spatially lagged term of Gy, and ρ is the influence coefficient, measuring the mutual influence between economic growths of different provinces. Fe is the core explanatory variable, which is the variable in provincial fiscal expenditure, for which total fiscal expenditure (both budgetary and extra-budgetary) and the various types of expenditure (economic, social, and administrative) are taken into consideration, taking natural logarithms of the actual per capita values. *FeDum94* is the tax sharing system dummy variable in provincial fiscal expenditure (*Fe* times 0 before 1994; *Fe* times 1 in and after 1994), measuring the effects of the changes in the strategic interactions among regional governments on regional economic growth after the introduction of the tax sharing system in 1994. ε is the error term.

For the spatial weights matrix W, four settings are considered: geographical proximity spatial weights matrix, i.e. if province i and province j share a common boundary, the spatial weights W_{ij} is set as 1, otherwise it is set as 0; per capita output spatial weights matrix, i.e. using the extent of similarity of the provincial per capita output levels to set the matrix, defined as $w_{ij} = 1 / |Ry_i - Ry_j|$, where Ry_i and Ry_j are the per capita output of province i and province j; population mobility spatial weights matrix, based on the size of interprovincial population movement, defined as $w_{ij} = PM_{ij}$, where PM_{ij} is the total movement of population between province i and province j; FDI spatial weights matrix, i.e. using the extent of similarity between the foreign direct investment (FDI) value and output ratio of the province to set the matrix, defined as $w_{ij} = 1 / |Fdir_i - Fdir_j|$, where $Fdir_i$ is the average ratio of FDI to output for province i in the sample period. In the actual calculation, the spatial weights matrix is standardized so that the total value of the elements of the matrix equals to 1.

For the control variable X, the main variables considered are: physical capital investment rate, i.e. ratio of physical capital investment to output; level of investment in human capital, measured using the ratio of the total number of students in secondary and tertiary education institutions to the labor force, and a five-year lagged moving average is taken in order to reflect the long-term economic effect of human capital investment;[20] variables in labor, measuring the labor market performance, including the effects of the changes in the employment rate and labor force participation rate on the per capita output. Due to the lack of available data on the unemployment rate and labor force participation rate of the provinces, the ratio of the labor force to total population is used instead; level of economic development, taking the natural logarithm of the five-year moving average value of the actual per capita output, measuring potentially existing economic convergence effects;[21] degree of economic openness, measured by the ratio of the total import and export to total output; ratio of employees in the non-public sector, used to measure the effects of marketization; and fiscal revenue ratio, i.e. ratio of fiscal revenue to total output, measuring the economic burden of each province. To ensure that the effects of the 1994 tax sharing system are captured, the tax sharing system dummy variable in fiscal revenue ratio is also taken into consideration.

Estimation results

Two technical problems need to be addressed in performing the model calculations: one, endogeneity in WG_y, i.e. possible correlation between the spatially lagged term and the error term; and two, spatial autocorrelation in the error term. In the real-world economy, the expenditure policies of regional governments would suffer common shocks and be influenced by the changes in the national fiscal policies, leading to spatial autocorrelation in the error term in Model 6.1, i.e. $\varepsilon = \lambda W\varepsilon + \upsilon$, of which λ is the spatial autocorrelation coefficient and υ is the independent and identically distributed error term. These two spatial correlation issues can lead to inconsistencies and deviations in the OLS regression results.[22] In fact, from the Moran's I spatial autocorrelation and the LM spatial error correlation tests, it can be seen that the two types of spatial correlation exist in every model within the sample period. Therefore, spatial GMM is used for correction.[23] Also, considering the possible mutual influence between government expenditure and economic growth, two-step regression is used to correct for potential endogeneity. First, the reaction function of the fiscal expenditure of provincial governments is estimated as follows:

$$LG = \rho WLG + X\beta + \varepsilon \tag{4.1}$$

The estimated value of the fiscal expenditure variable derived from the model is introduced into Model 6.1. Furthermore, to eliminate endogeneity in other explanatory variables, the one-phase lagged value of all explanatory variables is used in Model 6.1.[24] Table 6.1 shows the results of test and estimations of various models.

Table 6.1 Estimation results of the effects of the size and structure of provincial government expenditure on the growth of per capita output using spatial GMM

	Spatial model for the effect of total fiscal expenditure on economic growth				Spatial model for the effect of the expenditure items on economic growth			
Explanatory variable	Model 1a	Model 1b	Model 1c	Model 1d	Model 2a	Model 2b	Model 2c	Model 2d
Constant term	0.062 (0.030)*	0.056 (0.040)	-0.001 (0.030)	0.035 (0.040)	0.023 (0.040)	-0.048 (0.06)	-0.018 (0.040)	-0.041 (0.080)
Spatial lag term of the growth of per capita output	0.074 (0.180)	0.152 (0.150)	0.567 (0.150)***	0.369 (0.170)**	0.242 (0.130)*	0.115 (0.140)	0.504 (0.140)***	0.405 (0.150)***

Table 6.1 Estimation results of the effects of the size and structure of provincial government expenditure on the growth of per capita output using spatial GMM (Cont'd)

		Spatial model for the effect of total fiscal expenditure on economic growth				Spatial model for the effect of the expenditure items on economic growth			
Explanatory variable		Model 1a	Model 1b	Model 1c	Model 1d	Model 2a	Model 2b	Model 2c	Model 2d
(natural logarithm)	Budgetary expenditure	-0.029 (0.010)***	-0.026 (0.010)**	-0.021 (0.010)**	-0.020 (0.010)**	—	—	—	—
(natural logarithm)	Extra-budgetary expenditure	0.019 (0.020)	0.012 (0.020)	0.021 (0.010)	0.013 (0.014)	-0.049 (0.030)*	-0.039 (0.020)*	-0.029 (0.020)	-0.032 (0.020)
(natural logarithm)	Economic expenditure	—	—	—	—	-0.008 (0.020)	-0.030 (0.020)	-0.003 (0.020)	-0.025 (0.030)
(natural logarithm)	Social expenditure	—	—	—	—	0.140 (0.070)**	0.175 (0.070)***	0.106 (0.060)*	0.148 (0.080)*
(natural logarithm)	Administrative expenditure	—	—	—	—	-0.103 (0.030)***	-0.102 (0.030)***	-0.082 (0.030)***	-0.086 (0.030)***
Tax sharing system dummy variable	Budgetary expenditure	0.018 (0.010)	0.014 (0.010)	0.019 (0.010)**	0.016 (0.010)	—	—	—	—
Tax sharing system dummy variable	Extra-budgetary expenditure	-0.025 (0.010)*	-0.021 (0.010)	-0.027 (0.010)**	-0.022 (0.010)*	0.048 (0.030)	0.044 (0.030)	0.034 (0.030)	0.026 (0.020)
Tax sharing system dummy variable	Economic expenditure	—	—	—	—	-0.028 (0.010)**	-0.035 (0.010)***	-0.049 (0.020)***	-0.032 (0.010)***
Tax sharing system dummy variable	Social expenditure	—	—	—	—	-0.112 (0.070)	-0.101 (0.050)*	-0.052 (0.070)	-0.075 (0.050)
Tax sharing system dummy variable	Administrative expenditure	—	—	—	—	0.115 (0.040)***	0.120 (0.040)***	0.102 (0.040)***	0.090 (0.030)***
Per capita output (natural logarithm)		0.017 (0.010)*	0.019 (0.010)**	0.012 (0.010)	0.015 (0.010)*	0.006 (0.010)	-0.007 (0.020)	-0.001 (0.020)	-0.003 (0.020)
Physical capital investment rate		0.081 (0.020)***	0.080 (0.020)***	0.086 (0.020)***	0.076 (0.020)***	0.077 (0.020)***	0.087 (0.020)***	0.087 (0.020)***	0.091 (0.020)***
Level of investment in human capital		-0.139 (0.110)	-0.140 (0.110)	-0.138 (0.110)	-0.150 (0.090)	-0.078 (0.100)	-0.098 (0.100)	-0.094 (0.100)	-0.105 (0.100)
Labor force participation rate		-0.0002 (0.070)	-0.0006 (0.050)	0.007 (0.050)	-0.014 (0.050)	0.001 (0.050)	0.003 (0.050)	0.017 (0.050)	-0.016 (0.050)
Degree of economic openness		0.003 (0.010)	0.003 (0.010)	-0.006 (0.010)	0.001 (0.010)	0.016 (0.010)	0.029 (0.010)**	0.017 (0.010)	0.021 (0.020)
Ratio of employees in the non-public sector		0.127 (0.030)***	0.120 (0.030)***	0.095 (0.030)***	0.104 (0.030)***	0.102 (0.040)**	0.059 (0.050)	0.053 (0.040)	0.066 (0.060)
Fiscal revenue ratio		-0.331 (0.080)***	-0.322 (0.060)***	-0.285 (0.070)***	-0.299 (0.070)***	-0.425 (0.080)***	-0.416 (0.080)***	-0.388 (0.080)***	-0.391 (0.080)***

Table 6.1 Estimation results of the effects of the size and structure of provincial government expenditure on the growth of per capita output using spatial GMM

(Cont'd)

	Spatial model for the effect of total fiscal expenditure on economic growth				Spatial model for the effect of the expenditure items on economic growth			
Explanatory variable	Model 1a	Model 1b	Model 1c	Model 1d	Model 2a	Model 2b	Model 2c	Model 2d
Tax sharing system dummy variable of fiscal revenue ratio	-0.302 (0.180)*	-0.297 (0.160)*	-0.215 (0.150)	-0.286 (0.150)**	-0.072 (0.160)	-0.131 (0.160)	-0.097 (0.160)	-0.085 (0.160)
Spatial autocorrelation coefficient	0.068 (0.020)***	-0.049 (0.030)*	-0.011 (0.050)	-0.144 (0.010)***	-0.034 (0.020)**	-0.045 (0.020)**	-0.006 (0.070)	-0.168 (0.010)***
Moran's I spatial correlation test	4.210***	1.030	5.540***	1.240	3.640***	0.670	4.730***	1.200
LM spatial error correlation test	77.300***	0.570	51.800***	0.880	35.600***	0.120	73.900***	1.310
Effective sample size	580	580	580	580	580	580	580	580
R^2	0.179	0.166	0.091	0.103	0.202	0.213	0.180	0.105

Notes: (1) Models a, b, c, and d uses the geographical proximity spatial weights matrix, per capita output spatial weights matrix, population flow spatial weights matrix, and FDI spatial weights matrix, respectively.
(2) *, **, and *** indicate confidence levels of 10%, 5%, and 1%, respectively.
(3) Bracketed values are standard deviations.

From Table 6.1, it can be seen that during 1986 to 2006, provincial economic growth had a significant spatial positive spillover effect, of which the mobility of the labor force and foreign capital played an important role. During the sample period, there were no trends of convergence or divergence seen in regional economic growth, as represented by the ambiguous effects of per capita output on economic growth.

Physical capital investment had a significant effect in promoting regional economic growth. Marketization had a similar effect, but lacks robust significance. The size of regional government expenditure significantly constrained regional economic growth, although this unfavorable impact has significantly weakened since the introduction of the tax sharing system in 1994. Other factors, including human capital investment, the performance of the labor force market, and the level of economic openness, did not have statistically significant effects on regional economic growth.

During the sample period, the regression coefficient of budgetary expenditure remained negative (within -0.020 to -0.029) and statistically significant. This shows that budgetary expenditure had a significant constraining effect on regional economic growth. Since the 1994 introduction of the tax sharing system, as the mode of the strategic interactions among regional governments changes, the effects of budgetary expenditure on regional economic growth also change significantly: the regression coefficient of budgetary expenditure became positive, although having poor statistical significance. The effects of extra-budgetary expenditure on regional economic growth are unclear: the regression coefficients of the functions of the effects of extra-budgetary expenditure on economic growth are positive, but that for the functions of the effect of the expenditure items on economic growth are negative and not statistically significant. The introduction of the tax sharing system in 1994 did not improve the situation much.

As for the various types of expenditure, during the sample period, economic expenditure exhibits a constraining but not statistically significant effect on regional economic growth, while administrative expenditure exhibits a prominent constraining and statistically significant effect. Since the introduction of the tax sharing system in 1994, the effects of the different types of expenditure have changed significantly: the constraining effect of economic expenditure has become stronger and more statistically significant, and the effect of social expenditure has become constraining although not statistically significant, while administrative expenditure has exerted a promoting effect on regional economic growth.

The above analysis shows that the fiscal competition mechanism has important impacts on the effects of the size and structure of regional governments on economic growth. During the time when the fiscal contract system was in play, interregional fiscal expenditure competition was unfavorable for economic growth. The situation improved when the tax sharing system was implemented in 1994. This may be attributed to how the fiscal contracting system had strengthened the position of regional governments in fiscal revenue, such that in fiscal competition, they have a tendency to adopt the strategy of racing to the bottom, leading to inefficiency in total fiscal expenditure, which in turn suppressed regional economic growth.[25] The 1994 tax sharing system acknowledged the existence of regional intergovernmental fiscal competition, and so focused on standardizing and regulating the interest relationships between the central government and regional governments, which effectively curtailed excessive competition and raised the efficiency of fiscal expenditure, promoting economic growth. It may thus be seen that the mechanism of effect of fiscal competition on the economy that is emphasized by public sector theorists has to a large extent played a dominant role, although this theory still needs corroboration through further empirical analysis. However, it should also be noted that the system has also excessively curbed the competitive behavior of regional governments regarding social expenditure and economic expenditure, which led to a drop in the efficiency of expenditure and thus undesirable effects on regional economies.

Effects of the central fiscal transfer payments and the structure of regional public capital investment on economic growth

As discussed in Chapter 4, the central fiscal transfer payments have a significant impact on the strategic interactions and in turn the size and structure of regional governments, and so it is necessary to examine the effects of transfer payments, as a crucial part of the institutional arrangement in the fiscally decentralized system, on the size and structure of regional governments. Moreover, as a lot of research has pointed out, public physical capital investment and public human capital investment are two important government expenditure items in terms of their significance to long-term sustainable economic growth.[26] However, these two types of public capital investment have different economic effect mechanisms. Under financial constraints, governments often find it difficult to balance the two types of investment, leading to a disparity in the effects on long-term economic growth. This warrants an in-depth analysis of the structure of public capital investment of regional governments — the mechanism of how the allocation of public physical capital investment and public human capital investment impact economic growth, and how it promotes the optimization of the regional government expenditure structure and the resulting economic growth, especially in developing countries such as China, which has limited financial power and economic and social infrastructure with the primary goal of promoting economic growth.

This section will employ a dynamic panel data model and system GMM, using actual data from the 30 provinces of the country within the period 1995 to 2006, in examining the effect of composition of public capital investment of regional governments on economic growth, as well as the constraining effects of central fiscal transfer payments, under a multi-tier government framework of analysis. The data comes from past year publications of *China Statistical Yearbook*, *Fiscal Yearbook of China*, and *China Educational Finance Statistical Yearbook*.

Model framework

Actual economic growth is a dynamic process, dependent on both current and past factors, and so endogeneity problems may exist in the dynamic structure of data, leading to inconsistencies in estimation.[27] Furthermore, the behavior of regional governments and regional economic growth mutually influence each other, and so endogeneity may also exist in the explanatory variables. In view of this, the following dynamic panel data model is constructed to correct possible endogeneity:

$$Gy_{it} = \sum^{M} \alpha_j Gy_{it-j} + \beta X_{it} + \gamma Z_{it} + \mu_i + \lambda_t + \varepsilon_{it} \quad (6.2)$$

Of which Gy_{it-j} is the lagged term of the growth rate of per capita output, and M is the largest lag order. X_{it} is the exogenous explanatory variable (satisfying $\forall t$, $E(X_{it}\varepsilon_{it}) = 0$). Z_{it} includes the predetermined explanatory variable (satisfying $s < t$, $E(X_{it}\varepsilon_{is}) \neq 0$ and $s \geq t$, $E(X_{it}\varepsilon_{is}) = 0$) and the endogenous explanatory variable (satisfying $\forall t$, $E(X_{it}\varepsilon_{it}) \neq 0$). μ_i is the regional effect, λ_t the temporal effect, and ε_{it} the random disturbance, satisfying $E(\mu_i) = E(\varepsilon_{it}) = E(\mu_i\varepsilon_{it}) = 0$, $E(\varepsilon_{it}\varepsilon_{is}) = 0$ ($\forall i, t, s, t \neq s$), and $E(\mu_i D.\varepsilon_{is}) = 0$.

The model mainly examines three policy variables: the regional public investment in physical capital ratio [Regional infrastructure expenditure/ (Regional infrastructure expenditure + Regional public education expenditure)], regional fiscal revenue ratio (the proportion of local regional fiscal revenue of the governments to the total regional GDP, measuring the effect of revenue size of regional governments), and the ratio of central fiscal transfer payments (the proportion of the central fiscal transfer payments to the local regional fiscal revenue).[28] Also, in order to capture the regional differences in the economic growth effect of the policy variables, the regional dummy variable is introduced, i.e. for the Eastern provinces, the regional public investment in physical capital ratio, the regional fiscal revenue ratio, and the central fiscal transfer payments ratio are multiplied by 1; and that of the remaining provinces are multiplied by 0.

The income tax reform implemented in 2002 abandoned the income tax sharing method based on the hierarchical relationships of the central government and regional governments, instituting a standard sharing ratio, and directed all extra central revenue resulting from the tax sharing system reform to central fiscal transfer payments. To capture the effects of this reform, the temporal dummy variable is introduced, i.e. the regional public capital investment ratio, regional fiscal revenue ratio, and the transfer payments before 2002 are multiplied by 1, and those after 2002 multiplied by 0.

The other explanatory variables considered are: level of economic development, measured by taking natural logarithms of the five-year moving average value of the actual per capita output of each province, in order to capture potential economic convergence effect; physical capital investment rate, measured with the ratio of investment in fixed assets to the total regional output, examining the effects of physical capital accumulation; labor force variable, measured with the ratio of the employed urban population to total population of each province, capturing the double effects of the labor force market and the degree of urbanization; and degree of economic openness, measured by total imports and exports to the regional output of each province.

Estimation results

In performing the calculations for Model 6.2, the IPS unit root test for panel data was first used to examine the serial features of each variable.[29] The results in Table 6.2 show that it is not possible to reject the assumption of an order of I(1) for the ratio of central fiscal transfer payments, proportion of regional public physical capital investment, physical capital investment rate, variables in labor, and the fiscal revenue ratio. Thus, system GMM is used instead of difference GMM to overcome the problem of weak instrumental variables.[30]

Table 6.2 IPS unit root test of the main explanatory variables

Variable	Ratio of central fiscal transfer payments	Structure of regional public physical capital investment	Physical capital investment rate	Variables in labor	Degree of economic openness	Fiscal revenue ratio
T Statistic (P)	-1.473 (0.570)	-1.671 (0.180)	-1.415 (0.690)	-1.080 (0.990)	-3.287 (0.000)	-1.091 (0.990)

Additionally, the largest lagged order of the per capita output growth rate and the nature of the explanatory variables, especially the variables in policy, needs to be determined. Comparing the Arellano-Bond second-differenced autocorrelation tests for model calculations with different lagged orders, it is determined that the largest lagged order of the per capita output growth rate is 1. Although mutual influence may exist among the proportion of public investment of physical capital of regional governments, the regional fiscal revenue ratio, and regional economic growth, in the real-world economy, the regional public capital investment policies will also be affected by all kinds of non-economic factors. Therefore, the analysis cannot exclude the possibility of the proportion of public investment in physical capital and the regional fiscal revenue ratio being exogenous variables.

Similarly, existing studies have not come up with a definite conclusion about the nature of the other explanatory variables, so different hypothetical situations are considered. In Model a, all explanatory variables are set as exogenous variables. In Model b, the proportion of regional public investment in physical capital, regional fiscal revenue ratio, and the ratio of central fiscal transfer payments are set as exogenous explanatory variables, while the level of economic development, physical capital investment ratio, variables in labor, and the degree of economic openness are set as predetermined explanatory variables. In Model c, all the variables mentioned in Model b are set as predetermined explanatory variables, and in Model d, they are set as endogenous variables. The regional and temporal dummy variables in proportion of regional public investment in physical capital, regional fiscal revenue ratio, and the central fiscal transfer payments ratio are consistently set as exogenous explanatory variables. Table 6.3 gives the estimation and tests results of each model.

Table 6.3 Estimation results of the system GMM of the economic growth effect of regional public capital investment

	Model 1a	Model 1b	Model 1c	Model 1d
Constant term	0.051 (0.018)***	0.037 (0.014)**	0.037 (0.014)**	0.038 (0.014)**
L1.Per capita output growth rate	0.452 (0.068)***	0.434 (0.041)***	0.436 (0.041)***	0.436 (0.042)***
Level of economic development	0.149 (0.082)*	0.246 (0.088)***	0.246 (0.088)***	0.235 (0.084)***
L1.Level of economic development	-0.140 (0.082)*	-0.238 (0.088)**	-0.239 (0.088)**	-0.227 (0.084)**
Physical capital investment ratio	0.151 (0.050)***	0.124 (0.026)***	0.123 (0.026)***	0.137 (0.030)***
L1.Physical capital investment ratio	-0.130 (0.057)**	-0.094 (0.026)***	-0.094 (0.026)***	-0.107 (0.030)***
Variables in labor	0.361 (0.125)*	0.204 (0.081)**	0.203 (0.080)**	0.205 (0.085)**
L1.Variables in labor	-0.343 (0.129)**	-0.184 (0.081)**	-0.183 (0.080)**	-0.184 (0.086)**
Degree of economic openness	0.004 (0.014)	-0.005 (0.010)	-0.005 (0.010)	-0.004 (0.010)
L1.Degree of economic openness	-0.009 (0.019)	0.008 (0.008)	0.008 (0.008)	0.007 (0.008)
Proportion of regional public investment in physical capital	-0.040 (0.026)	-0.032 (0.015)**	-0.030 (0.014)**	-0.036 (0.014)**
Regional fiscal revenue ratio	-0.090 (0.148)	-0.092 (0.092)	-0.099 (0.088)	-0.075 (0.089)
Central fiscal transfer payments ratio	0.002 (0.001)*	0.0006 (0.0006)	0.0005 (0.0005)	0.0007 (0.0006)

Table 6.3 Estimation results of the system GMM of the economic growth effect of regional public capital investment

(Cont'd)

		Model 1a	Model 1b	Model 1c	Model 1d
Regional dummy variables	Proportion of regional public investment in physical capital	-0.091 (0.034)**	0.055 (0.023)**	0.053 (0.022)**	0.060 (0.035)**
	Regional fiscal revenue ratio	-0.474 (0.136)***	-0.344 (0.086)***	-0.333 (0.081)***	-0.360 (0.092)***
	Central fiscal transfer payments ratio	-0.006 (0.007)	-0.001 (0.005)	-0.001 (0.005)	-0.001 (0.005)
Temporal dummy variables	Proportion of regional public investment in physical capital	0.022 (0.023)	0.016 (0.017)	0.015 (0.016)	0.020 (0.015)
	Regional fiscal revenue ratio	0.032 (0.129)	0.051 (0.092)	0.057 (0.090)	0.032 (0.084)
	Central fiscal transfer payments ratio	-0.002 (0.001)*	-0.001 (0.001)	-0.001 (0.001)	-0.001 (0.001)*
Arellano-Bond AR(1) test		-3.770***	-3.720***	-3.710***	-3.710***
Arellano-Bond AR(2) test		0.790	0.640	0.650	0.660
Hansen overidentification test		21.150	18.040	10.110	14.870
Diff-in-Hansen GMM-style test		–0.530	0.000	0.000	–0.000
Diff-in-Hansen IV-style test		5.520	4.580	–0.250	7.020
Effective sample size		330	330	330	330
F value		245.390***	316.430***	365.760***	301.610***

Notes: (1) L1 is the first-order lagged operator.
(2) Diff-in-Hansen GMM style test is a validity test for the GMM-style instrumental variables, including endogenous and predetermined variables. Diff-in-Hansen IV style test is a validity test for the IV-style instrumental variables, including the exogenous variables.
(3) *, **, and *** indicate confidence levels of 10%, 5%, and 1%, respectively.
(4) Bracketed value are standard deviations.

It can be seen from the Arellano-Bond AR(1) and AR(2) tests given in Table 6.3 that the remainder sequences of each model exhibit significant first-order autocorrelation but not second-order autocorrelation, so the model settings are on the whole acceptable. Also, the results of the Hansen overidentification test and the Difference-in-Hansen GMM and IV style tests show that the constructions of the instrumental variables for the models are effective. However, it should be noted that the number of instrumental variables are high relative to the sample size, which will cause a relatively larger loss in degrees of freedom and may weaken to a certain extent the results of the Hansen tests; but as Bond and Roodman pointed out, endogeneity will cause the OLS estimations to deviate upwards and the SSW estimations to deviate downwards,[31] meaning that the actual value of the effect coefficient for the one-phase lagged per capita output growth rate should lie between the OLS estimate and SSW estimate. Using this as a benchmark, it can be seen that the estimation results of Model 1a are overall relatively poor, meaning that not all explanatory variables should be set as exogenous variables.[32]

From the estimation results of Models 1b, 1c, and 1d, it can be seen that increase in the proportion of regional public investment in physical capital significantly constrains regional economic growth, meaning that in exercising tradeoffs between public investment in physical and human capital, regional governments tend to be biased towards the former, such that public investment in human capital is clearly inadequate, and so constraining long-term economic growth; it would thus be prudent to increase the input in human capital investment in the future, in order to achieve better long-term economic growth.

The situation varies for specific regions and sub-periods: in the Eastern provinces, the proportion of regional public investment in physical capital has a significant and positive effect on the regional economic growth. Since the 2002 income tax reform, increase in the proportion of regional public investment in physical capital has helped to promote regional economic growth, although this is not statistically significant. Increase in the size of autonomous fiscal revenue of regional governments does not favor regional economic growth, although the effect is also statistically insignificant; this could be due to the fact that the autonomous financial power of provincial governments is significantly weaker. The economic growth effect of the size of autonomous fiscal revenue of regional governments varies across different regions and periods: in particular, it has a significant constraining effect on regional economic growth in the Eastern provinces, while post-2002 income tax reform, it has helped to promote economic growth, although this effect is not statistically significant.

The central fiscal transfer payments have a positive but statistically insignificant effect on regional economic growth. The situation varies in different regions, however: central fiscal transfer payments have a relatively strong but not statistically significant constraining effect on the regional economic growth in the Eastern provinces. Post-2002 income tax reform, the central fiscal transfer payments have a relatively strong constraining effect on regional economic growth in general, although the statistical significant of this is rather poor. This may be attributed to that post-2002 income tax reform, the additional revenue resulting from the reform has all been directed to general transfer payments, the purpose of which is for equalization of finances, such that the incentivizing role of the transfer payments on the behavior of regional governments is weakened, leading to a constraining effect on regional economic growth. This may also mean that from the perspective of economic growth, the current size of central fiscal transfer payments is overly large, exceeding the optimal levels for maximizing growth, and so does not favor regional economic growth.[33]

Constraining effects of central fiscal transfer payments

To further reveal the constraining effects of the central fiscal transfer payments on the composition of public capital investment of regional governments and on the economic growth effects of the fiscal revenue size, the product terms of the policy variables (the product term of the proportion of regional public investment in physical capital and the ratio of the central fiscal transfer payments, the product term of the regional government fiscal revenue ratio and the ratio of the central fiscal transfer payments, and the product term of the above three variables) are introduced in order to capture their mutual influence. Additionally, considering that a large part of regional fiscal revenue is still extra-budgetary, it was attempted to include extra-budgetary budget in the local regional fiscal revenue.[34]

Estimation results

Table 6.4 gives the estimation results, of which Model 2 is based on Model 1 (given in Table 6.3) with the product terms of policy variables introduced. Model 3 adds in consideration for the extra-budgetary funds of regional governments. Model 4 is based on Model 3 with the introduction of the product terms of policy variables. For each model, only the results of setting all variables as predetermined (Model a) and as endogenous (Model b) are shown.

It can be seen from Table 6.4 that, taking into consideration the mutual influence of regional extrabudgetary revenue and the variables in policy, there are significant changes in the regression results. After introducing the product terms of the variables in policy, there is no significant change in the constraining effect of proportion of regional public investment in physical capital on regional economic growth, but the promoting effect on regional economic growth in the Eastern provinces is strengthened. The promoting effect is also more prominent and significant after the 2002 income tax reform (the regression coefficients of the proportion of regional public investment in physical capital and the regional and temporal dummy variables are between -0.031 and 0.039, -0.027 and 0.10, and 0.017 and 0.059 respectively), while the constraining effect of increase in size of

Table 6.4 Constraining effects of central fiscal transfer payments on the economic growth effect of the composition of public capital investment of regional governments

Explanatory variables	Model 2a	Model 2b	Model 3a	Model 3b	Model 4a	Model 4b
Constant term	0.032 (0.020)**	0.032 (0.020)**	0.041 (0.010)***	0.039 (0.010)***	0.037 (0.020)**	0.034 (0.020)**
L1.Per capita output growth rate	0.429 (0.050)***	0.432 (0.050)***	0.444 (0.050)***	0.448 (0.050)***	0.427 (0.050)***	0.429 (0.050)***
Level of economic development	0.230 (0.090)**	0.230 (0.090)**	0.253 (0.090)***	0.256 (0.090)***	0.235 (0.090)**	0.239 (0.090)**
L1.Level of economic development	-0.224 (0.090)**	-0.225 (0.090)**	-0.247 (0.090)***	-0.250 (0.080)***	-0.230 (0.090)**	-0.233 (0.090)**
Physical capital investment ratio	0.119 (0.030)***	0.118 (0.030)***	0.118 (0.030)***	0.117 (0.030)***	0.113 (0.030)***	0.112 (0.030)***
L1.Physical capital investment ratio	-0.091 (0.030)***	-0.091 (0.030)***	-0.087 (0.030)***	-0.087 (0.030)***	-0.080 (0.030)***	-0.080 (0.030)***
Variables in labor	0.214 (0.090)**	0.213 (0.080)**	0.171 (0.090)*	0.168 (0.090)*	0.203 (0.080)**	0.199 (0.080)**
L1.Variables in labor	-0.182 (0.080)**	-0.183 (0.080)**	-0.163 (0.080)*	-0.162 (0.08)*	-0.183 (0.080)**	-0.181 (0.080)**
Degree of economic openness	-0.009 (0.010)	-0.009 (0.010)	-0.003 (0.010)	0.003 (0.01)	0.001 (0.010)	0.001 (0.010)
L1.Degree of economic openness	0.008 (0.010)	0.008 (0.010)	0.002 (0.010)	0.001 (0.01)	-0.000 (0.010)	-0.001 (0.010)
Proportion of regional public investment in physical capital	-0.039 (0.020)**	-0.035 (0.02)**	-0.033 (0.020)**	-0.031 (0.01)**	-0.039 (0.020)*	-0.038 (0.020)*
Regional fiscal revenue ratio	0.073 (0.130)	0.052 (0.12)	-0.110 (0.070)	-0.091 (0.06)	-0.003 (0.080)	0.029 (0.080)
Ratio of central fiscal transfer payments	0.013 (0.010)	0.011 (0.01)	0.0004 (0.001)	0.0004 (0.001)	0.016 (0.020)	0.017 (0.020)
Regional public physical capital investment x Ratio of central fiscal transfer payments	-0.018 (0.020)	-0.015 (0.02)	—	—	-0.023 (0.030)	-0.023 (0.030)
Regional fiscal revenue ratio x Ratio of central fiscal transfer payments	-0.341 (0.310)	-0.293 (0.30)	—	—	-0.315 (0.260)	-0.316 (0.270)
Proportion of regional public investment in physical capital x Regional fiscal revenue ratio x Ratio of central fiscal transfer payments	0.516 (0.500)	0.432 (0.50)	—	—	0.476 (0.450)	0.466 (0.460)

Table 6.4 Constraining effects of central fiscal transfer payments on the economic growth effect of the composition of public capital investment of regional governments

(Cont'd)

Explanatory variables		Model 2a	Model 2b	Model 3a	Model 3b	Model 4a	Model 4b
Regional dummy variables	Proportion of regional public investment in physical capital	-0.117 (0.040)***	0.115 (0.040)***	-0.027 (0.020)	0.025 (0.020)	0.096 (0.040)**	0.100 (0.030)***
	Regional fiscal revenue ratio	-0.6 71 (0.170)***	-0.656 (0.160)***	-0.116 (0.060)*	-0.116 (0.060)*	-0.382 (0.120)***	-0.405 (0.110)***
	Ratio of central fiscal transfer payments	-0.046 (0.020)**	-0.048 (0.020)**	-0.002 (0.010)	-0.001 (0.010)	-0.128 (0.040)***	-0.138 (0.040)***
	Regional public physical capital investment x Ratio of central fiscal transfer payments	-0.028 (0.070)	-0.029 (0.070)	—	—	0.111 (0.120)	0.125 (0.120)
	Regional fiscal revenue ratio x Ratio of central fiscal transfer payments	1.659 (0.490)**	1.694 (0.480)***	—	—	2.374 (0.580)***	2.593 (0.530)***
	Proportion of regional public investment in physical capital x Regional fiscal revenue ratio x Ratio of central fiscal transfer payments	-2.207 (0.840)**	-2.213 (0.820)**	—	—	-3.833 (1.460)**	-4.236 (1.380)***
Temporal dummy variables	Proportion of regional public investment in physical capital	0.033 (0.020)	0.031 (0.020)	0.018 (0.020)**	0.017 (0.020)	0.058 (0.030)**	0.059 (0.030)**
	Regional fiscal revenue ratio	-0.027 (0.110)	-0.017 (0.100)	0.010 (0.070)	0.012 (0.070)	-0.136 (0.110)	-0.145 (0.100)
	Ratio of central fiscal transfer payments	-0.007 (0.010)	-0.001 (0.120)	-0.001 (0.001)*	-0.001 (0.001)	-0.022 (0.020)	-0.021 (0.020)
	Regional public physical capital investment x Ratio of central fiscal transfer payments	0.016 (0.020)	0.013 (0.020)	—	—	0.044 (0.030)	0.043 (0.030)
	Regional fiscal revenue ratio x Ratio of central fiscal transfer payments	0.236 (0.260)	0.201 (0.260)	—	—	0.453 (0.270)*	0.442 (0.260)
	Proportion of regional public investment in physical capital x Regional fiscal revenue ratio x Ratio of central fiscal transfer payments	-0.532 (0.480)	-0.467 (0.480)	—	—	-0.944 (0.490)*	-0.932 (0.480)*

Table 6.4 Constraining effects of central fiscal transfer payments on the economic growth effect of the composition of public capital investment of regional governments

(Cont'd)

Explanatory variables	Model 2a	Model 2b	Model 3a	Model 3b	Model 4a	Model 4b
Arellano-Bond AR(1) test	-3.690***	-3.690***	-3.750**	-3.740***	-3.730***	-3.730***
Arellano-Bond AR(2) test	0.310	0.330	0.600	0.640	0.230	0.240
Hansen overidentification test	1.570	1.370	16.850	14.260	8.020	0.650
Diff-in-Hansen GMM style test	0.000	-0.000	-0.000	-0.000	-0.000	-0.000
Diff-in-Hansen IV style test	-3.510	-2.550	2.790	-4.260	7.740	-1.110
Effective sample size	330	330	330	330	330	330
F value	2,175.780***	2,126.360***	301.590***	263.110***	1,389.100***	2,316.510***

Notes: (1) L1 is the first-order lagged operator.
(2) Diff-in-Hansen GMM style test is a validity test for the GMM-style instrumental variables, including endogenous and predetermined variables. Diff-in-Hansen IV style test is a validity test for the IV-style instrumental variables, including the exogenous variables.
(3) *, **, and *** indicate confidence levels of 10%, 5%, and 1%, respectively.
(4) Bracketed values are standard deviations.

autonomous revenue of regional governments on economic growth is no longer significant except in the Eastern provinces, where the constraining effect is clearly strengthened (the regression coefficient of the regional dummy variable in fiscal revenue ratio is between -0.382 and -0.116).

The effect of central fiscal transfer payments on regional economic growth is significantly stronger (the regression coefficients of the proportion of the central fiscal transfer payments and its regional and temporal dummy variables are between 0.011 and 0.017, -0.046 and -0.138, and -0.001 and -0.022 respectively). The results are in general very consistent: central fiscal transfer payments has a promoting but not significant effect on regional economic growth, and has a constraining effect on the regional economic growth in the Eastern provinces, while the 2002 income tax reform has been unfavorable to regional economic growth.

It can further be seen from Models 2a, 2b, 4a, and 4b that the central fiscal transfer payment policies affects to a certain extent the economic growth effect from the size and structure of regional government, in general strengthening the constraining effect of the proportion of regional public investment in physical capital and the size of fiscal revenue on economic growth, exhibited in the negative values of the regression coefficients of the product term of the proportion of regional public investment in physical capital and the central fiscal transfer payments, as well as the product term of the regional fiscal revenue ratio and the central fiscal transfer payments. This means that in the provinces which receive more central fiscal transfer payments, the constraining effect of the proportion of regional public investment in physical capital and the size of fiscal revenue would be greater although not statistically significant.

For the Eastern provinces, there are no significant differences in the effect of central fiscal transfer payments on the economic growth effects from regional policies in public investment in physical capital, relative to that for the entire country. On the other hand, the promoting effect on economic growth from the size of regional fiscal revenue is strengthened.

Since the 2002 income tax reform, the central fiscal transfer payments has no significant effects on the economic growth effects from regional public investment policies and fiscal revenue policies. Additionally, there exists significant mutual influence among the transfer payment policies, regional fiscal revenue policies, and regional public capital investment policies. In particular, when the intertemporal and interregional differences in the economic growth effects of extrabudgetary fiscal revenue and the size and structure of regional governments are taken into consideration, this mutual influence weakens the promoting effect of the increase in the proportion of regional public investment in physical capital and the size of fiscal revenue on economic growth in the Eastern provinces, as well as the positive effect from the 2002 income tax reform on economic growth, exhibited in the negative and statistically significant regressive coefficients of the product terms of the proportion of the central fiscal transfer payments, proportion of regional public investment in physical capital, and regional fiscal revenue ratio.

Effects of the Size and Structure of County-Level Governments on Economic Growth

As discussed in previous chapters, there are significant differences in the behavior of provincial governments and county-level governments. Thus, in order to reveal the differences in the effects of the size and structure of different levels of governments on economic growth, this section proceeds to examine, from the perspective of county-level economies, the effects of size and structure of regional governments on economic growth, based on actual data from the 1938 counties and county-level cities for the period 1997 to 2005.

Model framework

Taking into consideration that path dependence problems may exist in county-level economic growth, the following dynamic panel data model is constructed:

$$g_{it} = \sum_{j=1}^{M} \alpha_j g_{it-j} + \beta Fiscal_{it} + \delta Z_{it} + f_i + f_t + \varepsilon_{it} \quad (6.3)$$

Of which, g_{it} is the actual per capita GDP growth rate of province i during time period t. $Fiscal_{it}$ is the core explanatory variable, which includes the size and structure of both fiscal expenditure and revenue. The size of fiscal expenditure is measured by the ratio of the local fiscal expenditure of county-level governments to GDP, while the structure of fiscal expenditure is measured by the proportions of economic expenditure, administrative expenditure, and social expenditure. Economic expenditure is approximated by infrastructure expenditure, agricultural and forestry expenditure and hydrometeorology expenditure; administrative expenditure by administration expenditure and public security expenditure; and social expenditure by education expenditure and social security expenditure. The size of fiscal revenue is measured with the ratio of the total of fiscal revenue of county-level governments and fund revenue to GDP,[35] while fiscal revenue structure is measured with the proportion of tax revenue and fund revenue.

Z_{it} is the control variable, consisting of the following variables: level of economic development, measured by the actual per capita output, in order to capture the potentially existing economic convergence effect; population density, measured by dividing the total population by the total area of the province; degree of economic openness, measured by the ratio of total volume of exports and imports to GDP; degree of urbanization, measured by the proportion of the urban population to total population; physical capital investment ratio, i.e. the proportion of total physical capital investment to the annual GDP; variables in labor, measured by the ratio of total labor force to total population, measuring the effects of employment rate, labor force participation rate, and labor force mobility on economic growth.

Taking into consideration that the economic environment and the economic events differ for different provinces in different years, individual fixed effects term f_i and temporal effects term f_t are introduced to capture the effects of regional and temporal heterogeneities. ε_{it} is the error term. Other than the explained variables and their respective lagged terms, natural logarithms are taken for all variables.

Data

Unbalanced panel data of 30 provinces, autonomous regions and municipal-level cities, and 1,938 counties and county-level cities, is used for the model in this section. The data comes from past year publications of the *National Statistics of Prefectures and Counties*, *China's Regional Economic Statistics Yearbook*, and the Statistical Yearbook of the provinces. Table 6.5 shows the basic statistic description of the main economic variables.

Table 6.5 Statistic description of the main economic variables

Variable	Sample size	Mean value	Standard deviation	Minimum value	Maximum value
Actual GDP growth rate (%)	15,467	11.36	15.10	-65.99	575.07
Size of fiscal revenue (%)	17,409	14.03	11.68	0.98	178.59
Size of fiscal expenditure (%)	17,413	12.81	11.21	0.89	162.22
Proportion of tax revenue to fiscal revenue (%)	17,429	27.89	14.21	0.83	85.11
Proportion of fund revenue to fiscal revenue (%)	12,689	3.75	4.66	0.00	50.29
Proportion of economic expenditure (%)	17,413	1.87	3.05	0.07	94.23
Proportion of administrative expenditure (%)	17,413	2.80	2.89	0.10	34.08
Proportion of social expenditure (%)	15,487	3.40	2.54	0.02	27.84
Level of economic development, with 1978 as base period (CNY)	17,414	1581.99	1458.18	104.20	29605.27
Population density (%)	17,433	289.64	278.56	0.15	4698.80
Degree of urbanization (%)	17,119	17.88	12.51	0.27	95.83
Physical capital investment rate (%)	13,881	26.60	18.09	0.01	99.93
Variables in labor (%)	9,367	50.59	17.88	0.23	631.55

From Table 6.5, it can be seen that the dispersion coefficient of the size of the fiscal revenue and fiscal expenditure of county-level governments are 0.83 (116.8/14.03) and 0.88 (11.21/12.81) respectively. This shows that the degree of heterogeneity is smaller in the size of fiscal revenue. The dispersion coefficient of the proportion of tax revenue to fiscal revenue is smaller than that of the proportion of fund revenue to fiscal revenue, which shows that the degree of heterogeneity is smaller in the proportion of tax revenue. For the expenditure structure, the mean of social expenditure is the highest, followed by administrative expenditure and then economic expenditure. The dispersion coefficients of economic, administrative, and social expenditures are 1.63, 1.03, and 0.75, respectively, showing that heterogeneity is greatest in economic expenditure and smallest in social expenditure.

Estimation results

Taking the multicolinearity of fiscal variables into consideration, Models 1a, 1b, and 1c are constructed to examine the economic growth effects of the size of fiscal revenue, fiscal revenue structure, and fiscal expenditure structure respectively. From the Arellano-Bond AR(1) and AR(2) tests for remainder autocorrelation, it can be determined that the largest lagged order M for the lagged term of the explained variable g_{it-j} is 1. To avoid SSW estimation bias, cluster correction is applied to county-level governments under the same secondary-level government (i.e. prefecture-level or provincial governments). Additionally, in Models 1a(2), 1b(2), and 1c(2), the size fiscal revenue, level of economic development, variables in labor, and the lagged term of the dependent variables are set as endogenous variables; the size of fiscal expenditure, degree of economic openness, physical capital investment rate, and the degree of urbanization are set as predetermined variables; and population density is set as the exogenous variable. The estimations results are compared to those in Models 1a(1), 1b(1), and 1c(1) where all explanatory variables except the lagged terms of the dependent variables are set as exogenous variables. The estimation and test results are given in Table 6.6.[36]

Table 6.6 Estimation results of the dynamic panel data model for economic growth effect of the size and structure of county-level governments (system GMM)

Explanatory variable	Model 1a(1)	Model 1a(2)	Model 1b(1)	Model 1b(2)	Model 1c(1)	Model 1c(2)
Constant term	-43.212 (7.660)***	-46.645 (14.390)***	-31.332 (5.230)***	-23.121 (11.700)**	-40.227 (7.370)***	-25.983 (14.940)*
L1.Actual per capita GDP growth rate	-0.004 (0.030)	-0.115 (0.030)***	0.012 (0.030)	-0.019 (0.030)	0.009 (0.030)	-0.125 (0.030)***
Size of fiscal revenue	13.058 (5.010)***	45.101 (11.040)***	—	—	—	—
Size of fiscal expenditure	-10.457 (4.640)**	-48.989 (11.090)***	—	—	—	—
Proportion of tax revenue	—	—	-2.358 (0.740)***	-4.776 (1.070)***	—	—
Proportion of fund revenue	—	—	-0.107 (0.160)	0.394 (0.410)	—	—

Table 6.6 Estimation results of the dynamic panel data model for economic growth effect of the size and structure of county-level governments (system GMM)

(Cont'd)

Explanatory variable	Model 1a(1)	Model 1a(2)	Model 1b(1)	Model 1b(2)	Model 1c(1)	Model 1c(2)
Proportion of economic expenditure	—	—	—	—	0.970 (0.430)**	3.308 (1.070)***
Proportion of administrative expenditure	—	—	—	—	-1.345 (1.130)	-13.991 (3.380)***
Proportion of social expenditure	—	—	—	—	1.933 (1.060)*	-4.811 (2.550)*
Level of economic development	8.764 (0.800)***	10.284 (1.400)***	8.966 (0.880)***	10.159 (1.190)***	9.044 (0.910)***	10.128 (1.590)***
Population density	-1.264 (0.390)***	-4.457 (0.950)***	-1.664 (0.360)***	-1.627 (0.500)***	-1.439 (0.410)***	-6.990 (1.410)***
Degree of urbanization	-4.403 (0.620)***	-10.416 (2.160)***	-4.313 (0.640)***	-4.522 (0.880)***	-4.297 (0.620)***	-12.051 (2.560)***
Physical capital investment rate	0.680 (0.380)*	3.379 (0.890)***	1.045 (0.330)***	-0.379 (0.700)	0.962 (0.360)***	4.571 (1.140)***
Variables in labor	0.412 (0.820)	8.147 (2.510)***	0.890 (0.860)	-0.268 (2.390)	0.623 (0.800)	9.385 (2.610)***
Arellano-Bond AR(1)	-6.500***	-6.860***	-5.790***	-5.310***	-6.200***	-5.110***
Arellano-Bond AR(2)	1.220	0.420	1.140	0.570	1.070	-1.470
Hansen overidentification test	44.100**	258.440	42.330**	202.600	41.870**	255.070
Diff-in-Hansen GMM test	8.550	30.250	7.470	38.040	6.410	16.920
Diff-in-Hansen IV test	18.530**	1.210	16.470**	4.010	17.680**	0.690
Effective sample size	7,808	7,808	7,367	7,367	7,808	7,808
OLS (L1.g_{it})	-0.004	-0.004	0.015	0.015	0.008	0.008
SSW (L1.g_{it})	-0.376	-0.376	-0.382	-0.382	-0.375	-0.375

Notes: (1) "—" indicates that the variable is absent in that model.
(2) L1 is the first-order lagged operator.
(3) Diff-in-Hansen GMM style test is a validity test for the GMM style instrumental variables, including endogenous and predetermined variables. Diff-in-Hansen IV style test is a validity test for the IV style instrumental variables, including the exogenous variables.
(4) *, **, and *** indicate confidence levels of 10%, 5%, and 1%, respectively.
(5) The bracketed figures are the robust standard deviations after the application of cluster correction.

It can be seen from Table 6.6 that the P-values of the Hansen overidentification test and the Difference-in-Hansen IV-style test for Models 1a(1), 1b(1), and 1c(1) are all smaller than 0.05, showing that overidentification exists in all three models, and that the instrumental variables constructed in these models are ineffective, both in general and as an IV-style collection, meaning that it is unreasonable to set all explanatory variables as exogenous. Models 1a(2), 1b(2), and 1c(2) pass the Arellano-Bond (1) and (2) autocorrelation tests as well as the Hansen overidentification test, and the regression coefficients of the one phase-lagged dependent variables lie between the OLS and SSW estimations, showing that the settings of these three models are acceptable.

In Model 1a(2), the regression coefficients of the size of fiscal revenue and fiscal expenditure were 45.101 and -48.989 respectively and statistically significant, showing that the size of the revenue and expenditure of county-level governments have significant promoting and constraining effects respectively on economic growth. However, the promoting effect is significantly smaller than the constraining effect. This result is strangely inconsistent with the situation in the provincial economies of the country, and might very well be that since the introduction of the tax sharing system in 1994, sub-provincial level regional governments mirror the central government's arrangements tendencies in assuming more financial responsibilities and less administrative responsibilities, such that county-level governments assume excessive terms of expenditure with seriously inadequate financial powers; thus, the size of fiscal expenditure may have already far exceeded the optimal level, while the size of fiscal revenue may be far below the optimal level, and so increase in size of fiscal expenditure has a significantly constraining effect on economic growth, while increase in size of fiscal revenue promotes economic growth.

It may further be seen from the estimation results of Model 1b(2) that the regression coefficient of the proportion of tax revenue is negative, showing that increase in the proportion of tax revenue has a significantly constraining effect on county-level economic growth, while the proportion of fund revenue has no significant effects.

For fiscal expenditure structure, it can be seen from the estimation results of Model 1c(2) that increase in the proportion of economic expenditure has a significant and positive economic effect, but increase in the proportions of administrative and social expenditures have significant and negative effects. This result is also inconsistent with the situation in the provincial economies of the country. (Since the introduction of the tax sharing system in 1994, the constraining effect of provincial economic expenditure on regional economic growth has been strengthened with excellent statistical significance; that of social expenditure is similar but not statistically significant; while administrative expenditure has a significant and positive effect on regional economic growth.) This may be attributed to that the expenditure terms in administrative and social responsibilities assumed by county-level governments exceed the optimal level by a far greater extent relative to prefecture-level governments, but the expenditure terms in economic responsibilities they assume are relatively less, and so increase in social or administrative expenditure is unfavorable for regional economic growth, but increase in economic expenditure promotes economic growth.

Optimal Size and Structure of Regional Governments for Promoting Economic Growth

As China's fiscal decentralization reforms continue to take effect, the role played by regional governments in the vertical organization structure of China's government becomes increasingly prominent. Optimization of the size and structure of regional governments for promoting regional and national economic growth is thus of crucial significance to a developing country such as China, where economic growth looks set to be the top priority for China's government for a long time to come.

Existing studies argue that the relationship between economic growth and the size and structure of regional governments is an inverted U-shaped curve rather than a simple linear relationship, such that there does exist an optimal point of size and structure of government expenditure for maximized growth.[37] This allows for an evaluation of whether the expenditure size and structure of governments is reasonable, based on their effects on economic growth, and from there propose a direction of adjustment for optimizing the expenditure size and structure: for example, if the size of (a certain term of) expenditure has a positive effect on economic growth, i.e. the (term of) expenditure lies on the left side of the inverted-U curve, then it may be argued that the (term of) expenditure is lower than the optimal level for maximized growth, and so the (term of) expenditure should be moderately increased.

The model results in this chapter has shown that, from the perspective of economic growth, the current size and structure of regional governments exhibit a high degree of inadequacy. Not only is it not playing a role in promoting regional economic growth, it is even hindering to a certain extent economic growth in the country. The inadequacy is exhibited in the following aspects:

- The size of provincial expenditure and administrative expenditure is clearly too large, exceeding the optimal level for maximized growth, which does not favor regional economic growth; provincial social expenditure size is clearly too small, lower than the optimal level for maximized growth; extrabudgetary expenditure and economic expenditure sizes are close to optimal level, and so their effects on regional economic growth is unclear;

- The structure of provincial public capital investment is less than reasonable. In juggling between public investment in physical capital, such as infrastructure expenditure, and public investment in human capital, such as education expenditure, there is a clear preference towards favoring physical capital investment, such that input into human capital investment such as public education is significantly inadequate, leading to constraints on long-term economic growth. This situation is especially prominent in the Central and Western provinces;
- The size of county-level expenditure and administrative expenditure is also significantly too large, far exceeding the optimal level, which does not favor economic growth; in contrast to provincial-level governments, county-level governments assume a significantly heavier share of social expenditure terms and a lighter share of economic expenditure terms.

From the perspective of promoting economic growth, then, in order to optimize the size and structure of regional governments, the government should take into consideration the following areas for improvement:

1. Moderate down the expenditure terms assumed by regional (especially county-level) governments, in order to effectively stem the trend of inflation in the size of provincial and county-level governments;
2. Actively promote function change in provincial-level governments, such that they will tend to take better care of social public services such as education and healthcare in exercising fiscal allocation, while reducing the strength of input on administrative expenses;
3. Regional governments, especially Central and Western provincial-level governments, need to moderately reduce public investment in physical capital, and instead devote more fiscal resources to public education expenditure, in order to optimize the composition of public capital investment for promoting long-term economic growth;
4. County-level governments should have their assumed share of public expenditure terms reduced; in particular, social expenditure terms such as public education, and administrative expenditure terms such as law enforcement, while increasing their share of responsibilities for economic expenditure terms.

It should be pointed out, however, that if the above points are to be effectively achieved, it is clearly insufficient to tinker with provincial and county-level governments. What is truly important is to promote fiscal decentralization reforms that will reasonably divide and assign the expenditure responsibilities between the central and the various levels of regional governments, with the central government assuming more administrative expenditure terms, assigning more social expenditure terms such as public education and healthcare upwards to provincial-level governments, and grant more autonomy to county-level governments on economic expenditure terms.[38] At the same time, more fiscal powers should be granted to regional and especially county-level governments, in order to reduce their reliance on central fiscal transfer payments and strengthen rational behavior in regional governments.

Summary

This chapter examined the economic growth effect of the size and structure of different levels of government, using data from the 29 provinces of the country over the period 1986 to 2006, and the 1938 counties and county-level cities over the period 1997 to 2005 as the basis for models of analysis. The study reveals the existing problems with the size and structure of regional governments, and finds the adjustment measures in the size and structure of regional governments for promoting economic growth:

- Fiscal expenditure competition is in general detrimental to provincial regional governments, causing budgetary and administrative expenditure to have a significantly constraining effect on regional economic growth, economic expenditure to have a constraining but not statistically significant effect, while social expenditure has a significantly promoting effect, and the effect of extrabudgetary expenditure is unclear;
- The introduction of the tax sharing system in 1994 significantly altered the strategic interactions among regional governments, effectively reversing the situation of excessive interregional competition, and so helps to promote regional economic growth; but in excessively weakening the competitive behavior in economic expenditure terms, it also aggravates the negative impact of economic expenditure on regional economic growth;
- Increase in the proportion of provincial public investment in physical capital has a significantly constraining effect on regional economic growth, meaning that provincial governments currently favor investment in physical capital over human capital, leading to significant inadequacies in input to human capital such as education expenditure, which constrains long-term economic growth. For specific regions and periods, the situation is slightly different: increase in public investment in physical capital has a significantly

promoting effect on regional economic growth in the Eastern provinces; since the introduction of the income tax reform in 2002, such an increase also helps to promote regional economic growth, although here the effect is not significant;

- Increase in the size of autonomous fiscal revenue of regional governments does not favor regional economic growth, although this effect is not statistically significant, since regional governments have significantly low autonomous fiscal powers. The economic growth effect of the size of autonomous fiscal revenue of regional governments have clear interregional and intertemporal differences: it has a significantly constraining effect on regional economic growth in the Eastern provinces; since the introduction of the income tax reform in 2002, it helps to promote regional economic growth, although here the effect is not significant;
- Central fiscal transfer payments have a relatively significant effect on the economic growth effect of the composition of provincial public capital investment and the size of fiscal revenue. In general, it has strengthened their constraining effects on economic growth; for the Eastern provinces, it has strengthened the promoting effect of the size of fiscal revenue on economic growth; since the introduction of the income tax reform in 2002, its impacts have weakened;
- The economic growth effects of the size and structure of county-level governments are significantly different from that of provincial-level governments: increase in the size of county-level revenue and expenditure have significant promoting and constraining effects respectively on economic growth, and increase in the proportion of county-level economic, social and administrative expenditure have significantly positive, negative and highly negative effects respectively on county-level economic growth. This may be attributed to that the expenditure responsibilities, especially social and administrative expenditure terms, that county-level governments assume far exceed the optimal levels, while the fiscal powers available to them are extremely limited, far below the optimal level.

Thus, from the perspective of economic growth, it may be argued that there are clear flaws in the current size and structure of China's regional governments. It is prudent that in the near future, China's government takes effective measures to reasonably divide and assign expenditure responsibilities between the central and the various levels of regional governments, adequately increasing the fiscal powers of regional governments, refining the mechanisms of incentives and restraints of fiscal decentralization on regional governments, in order to encourage rational behavior in regional governments and promote regional economic growth through an optimal size and structure of regional governments.

7

Chapter

Optimization of the Size and Structure of Regional Governments from the Perspective of Economic Stability

The previous chapter examined the effect of size and structure of regional governments on regional economic growth. That alone, however, is insufficient for revealing all the existing problems with or for facilitating the optimization of the size and structure of regional governments. The fact is, regional governments have been the source of economic fluctuations in the provincial, regional and national economies, and is thus a major factor behind the historical development of China's macroeconomy.[1] The aim of this chapter, then, is to study the size and structure of regional governments from the perspective of economic stability, by examining both the economic stabilization effect of the size and structure of regional governments, as well as the constraints imposed by fiscal decentralization and governance arrangements, under a meta-analysis framework. This will reveal existing problems and the institutional arrangements behind them, and suitable measures may be adopted to optimize the size and structure of regional governments to promote economic stability.

Economic Stability Effect of the Size and Structure of Regional Governments and Its Institutional Causes

The traditional academic belief is that, since macroeconomic stabilization policies are essentially national policies, regional governments have little control over currency policy and economic openness, and as such, their impact in promoting macroeconomic stability is very limited.[2] With fiscal decentralization reform gradually taking effect, however, regional governments have an increasingly strong effect on the vertical structure of the government. The incentive mechanisms and policy choices of regional governments, as well as the consequent effects on economic stability, are gradually attracting attention from academia and political circles.

For example, Guo and Jia proposed a hypothesis concerning the behavior of regional governments in regard to macroeconomic fluctuations, arguing that the presence of fiscal and political incentives provide strong motivations for regional governments to adopt irregular policies in attracting investors, in order to promote investment growth, which ultimately causes shocks on macroeconomic stability.[3] Fang and Zhang stressed that with fiscal and political incentives, the expenditure of regional governments tends to expand, and that soft constraints on budgets further encourage this expansion.[4] Li and Shen argued that short-termism in the behavior of regional governments is a main contributor to economic fluctuations in China, although the short-termism itself may be blamed on corrupt practices, while the effects of fiscal and political incentives are not significant.[5]

Brandt and Zhu, Bennett and Dixon, and Feltenstein and Iwata pointed out that China's fiscal decentralization reform simultaneously increased the self-interests and budget constraints on regional governments, and this prompts regional governments to adopt irregular measures such as implicit guarantee and credit intervention to support inefficient state-owned enterprises, leading to credit expansion and inflation.[6] Zhao and Zhou found that fiscal decentralization intensifies the fiscal expenditure competition among regional governments, resulting in excessive expansion of the size of expenditure of regional governments, which does not favor price stability.[7]

The above studies have helped shed light on the effect mechanisms of fiscal and political incentives brought about by fiscal decentralization and governance systems on regional government behavior and macroeconomic stability. These studies, however, often choose to focus on a single aspect of the mechanism, and thus do not cover an analysis of the entire effect mechanism chain (i.e. Financial system and governance system → Regional government behavior → Macroeconomic stability).

More importantly, the existing literature has yet to consider how, under the unique financial and governance systems of a multi-tier government structure in China, maintaining macroeconomic stability is a matter of collective behavior, dependent on the balancing of conflicting interests between the central and regional governments,[8] which subsequently affects regional government behavior as well as regional and national economic stability.[9] Under a multi-tier government structure, China's fiscal decentralization reform and a cadre evaluation system based mainly on the criterion of economic growth may have strengthened self-interests in regional governments, but it should also be noted that the central government still retains its dominant role both in determining budget allocation and in direct administrative relationships, such that it still wields substantial fiscal power and administrative authority in regulating the behavior of regional governments.

It is under such circumstances that regional governments assume a double identity of being both a relatively independent entity with its own interests and as an administrative extension of the central government. The need to balance pursuits in regional self-interest and protection of national interests, therefore, causes the behavior of regional governments to display periodic features on both regional and national levels, which in turn leads to different impacts on regional and national economic stability. This is called the periodic regional government behavior paradox.

For the convenience of analysis, this study will focus on regional government expenditure behavior, examining through a unified analysis framework, the periodic features, macroeconomic stability effect, and the institutional roots of regional government expenditure, taking into account conflicting interests between regional and national government: first, the periodic regional government behavior paradox is formulated based on the real world situation in China, in order to examine the formation mechanisms and systematic causes of the regional and national periodic features in the expenditure behavior of regional governments; second, a multi-dynamic-factor model using provincial data is used to differentiate between provincial and national periodic features; third, spatial econometric models are used to examine the effects of fiscal decentralization and governance system on the periodic features; finally, a breakdown of the expenditure structure is conducted for further analysis on the periodic features and their institutional causes.

Periodic regional government behavior paradox: A hypothesis

Macroeconomic stability has never been purely an economic problem. Extensive political economics literature points out that a key feature in macroeconomic stability is collective consumption goods, since the core of macroeconomics is collective behavior.[10] Decentralization not only increases the number of interest entities, but also encourages them to take 'free rides', which is unfavorable for macroeconomic stability.[11] On the other hand, political centralization, in the forms of direct administrative relationships and a strong single-party system, can help resolve collective behavior problems and promote macroeconomic stability.[12] This effect is especially prominent in developing countries.[13]

Since the start of the Chinese Economic Reform, a number of reforms, including the fiscal contract system reform from 1978 to 1993 and the tax sharing system introduced in 1994, have granted greater financial autonomy to regional governments and increased regional financial interests. At the same time, as focus of the national development strategy switches to economic development, the evaluation criteria of the cadre evaluation system also change from being political achievements-heavy to economic achievements-heavy, which helps to align the political and economic interests of regional governments.

Owing to its single-party system, China's fiscal decentralization reforms have not granted legislative powers to regional governments in fiscal policies. The high degree of political centralization also means that the central government wields strong influence over the promotions of regional government officials. Thus, not only does the central government possess effective fiscal measures (e.g. arrangements of fiscal revenue responsibilities, fiscal transfer payment) to influence the fiscal behavior of regional governments; it can also do so by optimizing the governance system and performance evaluation of regional government officials, in order to encourage regional governments to act in accordance with the intentions of the central government and protect national interests.

This unique political system thus contributes to creating the double identity of the regional governments, both as relatively independent entities with their own concerns of self-interests, and as administrative agents of the central government with the responsibility of protecting national interests. The balancing of the potential conflicts of interests is the key to understanding the periodic features of the expenditure behavior of regional governments and its impact on the stabilization of the country's macroeconomy (see Fig. 7.1).

Fig. 7.1 Theoretical framework for the periodic regional government behavior paradox

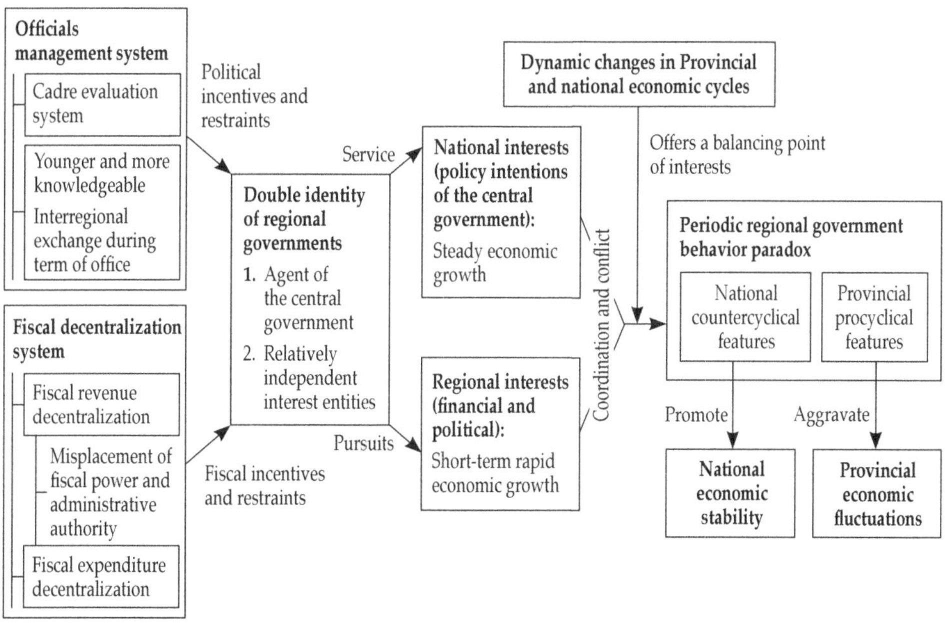

Normally, the interests of regional governments and the central government are aligned in the active promotion of economic growth. However, under the intense pressure of fiscal and political competition, regional governments tends to be more focused on short-term economic performance, such that even in periods of relative economic prosperity, regional governments are strongly motivated to promote faster economic growth through expansionary expenditure behavior, and such fast economic expansion over a short period of time is bound to lead to economic overheating. On the other hand, during periods of economic downturn, constraints in fiscal revenue in the face of economic uncertainties means that regional governments are more inclined to adopt conservative fiscal expenditure policies in order to reduce risk and avoid being in an uncompetitive fiscal and political position. All these contribute to the relatively significant provincial procyclical features in the expenditure behavior of provincial governments, i.e. fiscal expenditure of provincial governments are aligned to be consistent with the periodic dynamics of the provincial economic cycle, causing a negative impact on provincial economic stability.

If this negative impact becomes a nationwide phenomenon, however, the stability of the national economy may come under question, and this situation will be in conflict with the central government's goal of long-term stable national economic growth. In such a scenario, the central government would intervene to regulate the expenditure behavior of regional governments through fiscal and administrative measures, in order to stabilize the national economy. This prospect of central intervention, coupled with motivation to increase individual political competitiveness through positive evaluation from central authorities, often means that regional governments can be encouraged to carry out policies that help in regulating the country's macroeconomy, especially in fiscal expenditure policies that are openly observable, such that their expenditure behavior exhibits relatively significant national countercyclical features, i.e. fiscal expenditure of provincial governments are aligned to the opposite of the periodic dynamics of the national economic cycle.

Of course, in the real-world scenario, the provincial economic cycle is not synchronized with the national economic cycle (see Fig. 7.2).[15] In theory, this provides a point of balance for regional governments to both preserve regional self-interest and protect national interests, giving rise to a paradox in the periodic behavior of regional government expenditure: the simultaneous existence of procyclical features in the provincial economy and countercyclical features in the national economy aggravates fluctuations in the provincial economy but contributes to national economic stability. In reality, however, due to the difficulties in ascertaining precisely the dynamic trends in regional and national economic periods, especially the inability to predict the timing of the shift in central macroeconomic regulation policies, it is difficult for regional governments to locate the point of balance that allows them to both preserve regional self-interest and protect national interests.[16] This is compounded by the significant differences in the impact of central government regulations on provincial policies for the various provinces, such that there is a significant disparity in the strength of the provincial procyclical and national countercyclical features in expenditure behavior across the various provinces. The asynchrony between provincial and national economic cycles are most pronounced in underdeveloped provinces, which are heavily reliant on fiscal transfer payments from central authorities and are thus more open to influence from central policy intentions, such that their expenditure behavior will display relatively more significant provincial procyclical and national countercyclical features (see Fig 7.2c).

Fig. 7.2 (a) Dynamic changes of the fiscal expenditure, provincial GDP, and national GDP in Shanghai, Hunan Province, and Shaanxi Province

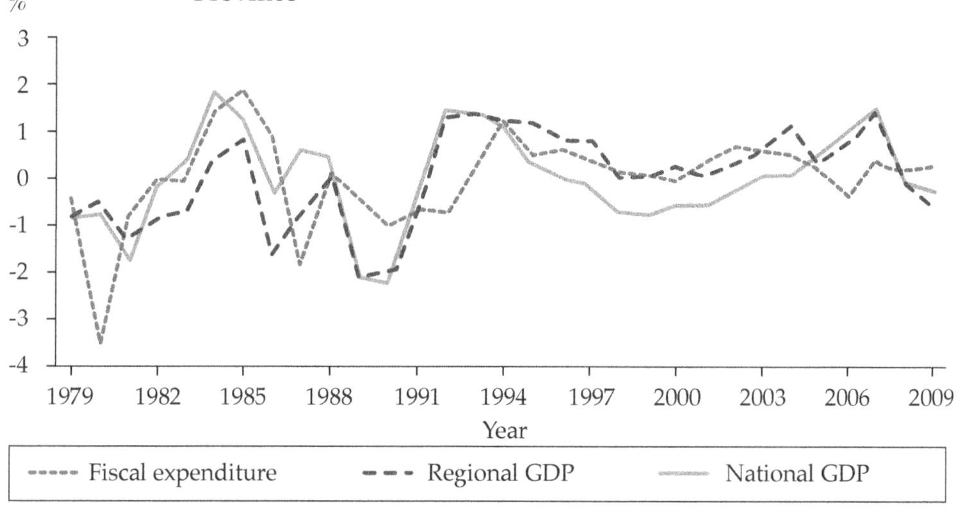

Fig. 7.2 (b) Dynamic changes of the fiscal expenditure, provincial GDP, and national GDP in Hunan

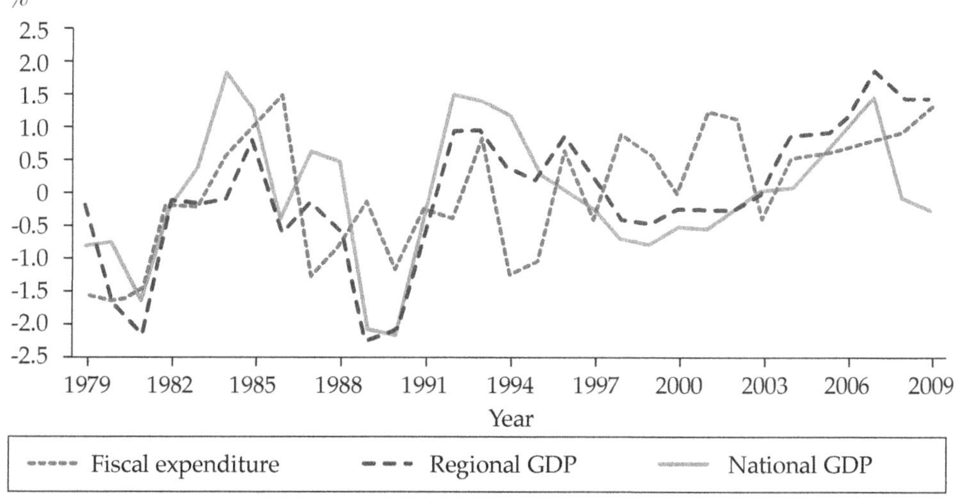

Fig. 7.2 (c) Dynamic changes of the fiscal expenditure, provincial GDP, and national GDP in Shaanxi

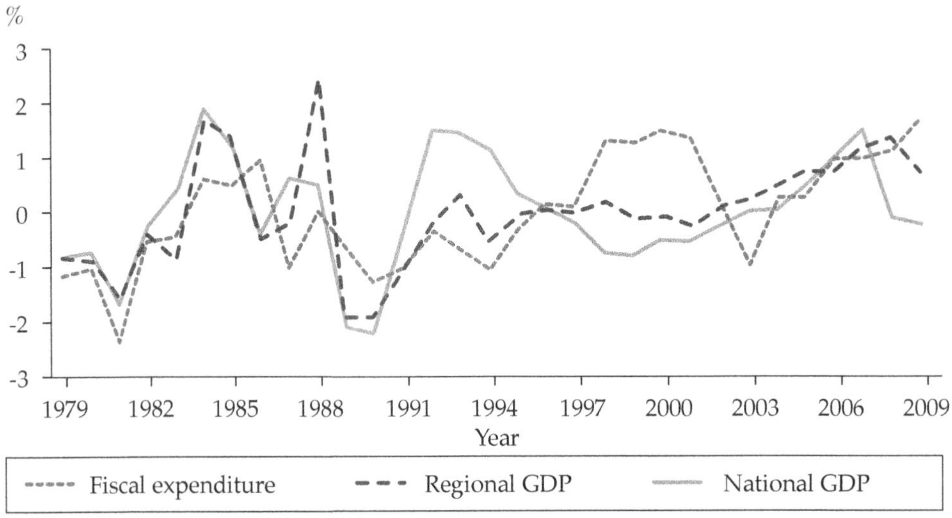

From the theoretical analysis above, the first proposition for the paradox of periodic regional government behavior may be formulated as follows:

Proposition 1: Under China's unique fiscal decentralization and governance system, regional governments assume double identities as both a relatively independent entity and an extension of the central government, necessitating a balancing of regional and national interests that emerge as the key in determining the periodic features of the expenditure behavior of regional governments. The asynchrony between the provincial and national economic cycles provide a relatively suitable balancing point for regional governments to both preserve regional self-interest and protect national interests, thus forming a paradox for the periodic nature in the expenditure behavior of regional governments: The expenditure behavior of regional governments generally exhibits relatively significant provincial procyclical and national countercyclical features, and this is especially prominent in underdeveloped provinces.

It should be noted that empirical studies based on national data show that current national fiscal expenditure policies is in general directed to be contradirectional to periodic fluctuations in the national economy, making an important impact in promoting macroeconomic stability.[17] On the other hand, studies based on provincial panel data find that current fiscal expenditure policies are unfavorable for economic stability.[18] The difference in the findings may be attributed to the inconsistency between the regional and national cycles, and the stabilization effect of regional fiscal expenditure policy on the regional and national economy. Proposition 1, however, is actually capable of organically unifying these two seemingly opposing findings: provincial fiscal expenditure policies are unfavorable for provincial economic stability, consistent with the findings of Fang and Zhang, and Zhao and Zhou;[19] provincial fiscal expenditure policies are also favorable for national economic stability, which explains the findings of Guo et al.[20] The findings from these studies, in turn, help to establish the the paradox proposed in Proposition 1.

Additionally, existing literature on the impact of fiscal decentralization generally often fail to address important features present in the decentralized fiscal institution. As Fig. 7.1 shows, fiscal incentives and restraints and their impact on the periodic features of the expenditure behavior of regional governments are also, to a large extent, dependent on a special feature in the decentralized fiscal institution: since the start of the Chinese Economic Reform, there has been an acute problem of misplacement and asymmetry between fiscal power and administrative authority, as well as significant vertical fiscal imbalance in regional governments.[21] These lead to differentiations in the mechanisms of incentives and restraints in the decentralized fiscal institution and their impacts on the periodic features of expenditure behavior. Vertical fiscal imbalance softens the budget constraints of regional governments,[22] strengthening the procyclical features in regional governments behavior,[23] and exacerbating ethical risk problems such as common-pool and central resource assistance.[24] On the other hand, where the central government has to invoke common-pool and central resources to compensate for regional vertical fiscal imbalance, it would also use the fiscal transfer payments involved to regulate the expenditure behavior of regional governments in alignment with the central government's policy intentions, strengthening the national countercyclical features in regional government behavior.

Of course, fiscal revenue decentralization helps to alleviate the problem of vertical fiscal imbalance and the consequential ethical risk problems, and so helps to constrain the provincial procyclical expenditure behavior of regional governments while promoting national countercyclical expenditure behavior. But fiscal revenue decentralization also adds fiscal incentives for regional governments, encouraging them to focus more attention on regional self-interest, which strengthens the provincial procyclical features in expenditure behavior and weakens the national countercyclical features. At the same time, the alleviation of vertical fiscal imbalance in fiscal revenue decentralization leads to a reduced dependence of fiscal transfer payments from the central government, weakening the influence of the central government on the fiscal restraints to regional governments, as well as the national countercyclical features in the expenditure behavior of regional governments.

It can thus be seen that the effects of fiscal revenue decentralization on the provincial procyclical features of expenditure behavior of regional governments are rather unclear, while there is a weakening effect on the national countercyclical features, although to a lesser extent. On the other hand, fiscal expenditure decentralization aggravates vertical fiscal imbalance, strengthening the provincial procyclical features in the expenditure behavior of regional governments while weakening the national countercyclical features. Summarizing the above, a second proposition may be derived:

Proposition 2: The misplacement of fiscal power and administrative authority causes fiscal decentralization to have an asymmetric impact on the periodic features of the expenditure behavior of regional governments: fiscal expenditure decentralization weakens the national countercyclical features in the expenditure behavior of regional governments, while strengthening the provincial procyclical features; fiscal revenue decentralization has a negative but relatively weak impact on the national countercyclical features, and the impact on provincial procyclical features are unclear.[25]

One more factor to take note of is political advancement incentives. Current studies normally emphasize the effect of a cadre evaluation system with growth numbers as its core criterion of judgment, but in reality, the situation is more complex: the career prospects of government officials depend not only on achievements in growth numbers, but also to a large extent on other arrangements in the country's governance system. Since the start of the Chinese Economic Reform, the central government has been exploring reforms in the cadre human resource system, with an official directive issued in 1982 to emphasize youth, knowledge, and professionalism, and establish new systems for cadre retirement, terms of office, and interregional exchange for officials.[26] This reform direction has meant that attributes of age, education level, and administrative experience in individual officials also play a major role in their career prospects, such that it ultimately has an important effect on the behavior of regional governments.[27]

The push towards youth and knowledge is driven by the desire of the central committee to optimize the age and intellectual composition in the cadre leadership, in order to bring in new ways of political thinking and perspectives, and thus raise the overall quality of cadre leadership and decision-making.[28] By ensuring that younger government officials with higher education levels and cultural training have a much more competitive edge in the prospects of their political careers, it can also ensure more rational behavior in regional governments, correcting the short-termist thinking behind provincial procyclical expenditure behavior.

The interregional exchange of officials has also gradually become an important feature of central policy on governance management and cadre training, and was officially institutionalized in 1990 as part of the human resource management system for cadres. Interregional exchange not only involves cross-regional postings of regional officials, but also the postings of central officials to regional appointments (colloquially known as *jingguan* 京官, literally 'capital officials'). The latter is intended as an important part of the training of cadres, but in reality, *jingguan* themselves often see such arrangements as a transitory posting, and so tends to place more focus on short-term economic performances;[29] they also seek to obtain as much local support as possible, and so has a tendency to help regional governments maximize regional self-interest. All these contribute to strengthen the provincial procyclical features in the expenditure behavior of regional governments.

Aside from cadre retirement and interregional exchange of officials, limited terms of office have also been implemented for regional government officials. However, since regional officials may be 'exchanged' to a different region or even promoted to a more senior position within their term, this institution is relatively unobservable and unstable.[30] The length of the terms of office, then, becomes an important factor affecting regional officials in their career advancement considerations, e.g. relatively long term of office increases the urgency in advancement for regional officials, increasing their focus on regional short-term economic performance and strengthening the provincial procyclical features in the expenditure behavior of regional governments.

It should be noted, though, that the factors discussed above has no clear mechanism of effect on the fiscal and administrative restraining powers of the central authorities on the expenditure behavior of regional governments through the country's unique fiscal and administration system. Thus, their impact on the national countercyclical features of the expenditure behavior of regional governments may yet be unclear. From the above analysis, a third proposition may be derived as follows:

Proposition 3: The governance system has a significant effect on political incentives and restraints for regional governments and, by extension, the periodic features in the expenditure behavior of regional governments: promoting a younger and knowledge-based cadre body helps to weaken the provincial procyclical features in the expenditure behavior of regional governments, while longer terms of office and central appointments (*jingguan*) have an opposite effect; but the impact of these factors on the national countercyclical features are rather unclear.

Periodic features in the expenditure behavior of regional governments: Empirical analysis

This segment will perform an empirical analysis to test Proposition 1, using provincial panel data from 1979 to 2009 and a multi-dynamic-factor model, to examine the co-movements between regional fiscal expenditure and periodic fluctuations in the provincial economy, and identify the national and provincial periodic features in the expenditure behavior of regional governments.

Model framework

In order to examine the national and provincial periodic features of the expenditure behavior of regional governments, it is necessary to identify the co-movements between provincial fiscal expenditure and the national and provincial economic cycles, within an integrated measurement and analysis framework. Additionally, macroeconomic fluctuations not only involve factors of real economy but also of nominal economy. A multi-dynamic-factor model is employed, as it has been proven to be capable of measuring the co-movements between multiple variables in multiple economic bodies.[31] The 29 provinces of the country are grouped into 3 regions (Eastern, Central, and Western).[32] For each province, 6 economic indicators (production, inflation rate, employment, consumption, investment, and fiscal expenditure) are chosen, with inflation rate measured as the rate of change in the Consumer Price Index (CPI). Due to a lack of data, the total retail volume of consumption goods is used to give an approximation for consumption. To ensure that the various variables remain in stationary sequence, and to avoid the size of economy from affecting estimation results, natural logarithms are taken for all variables, and processed with first difference and mean subtraction, deriving the multi-dynamic-factor model as follows:

$$x_{it} = a_i^{na} f_t^{na} + a_i^{re} f_t^{re} + a_i^{pr} f_t^{pr} + \varepsilon_{it} \quad (7.1)$$

Of which, x_{it} (i = 1, 2, ... , 39 x 6) are the provincial production, employment, inflation rate, consumption, investment, and fiscal expenditure respectively. f_t^{na} (1 value), f_t^{re} (3 values), f_t^{pr} (29 values) are the national, regional, and provincial common factors respectively, measuring the periodic dynamics of the national, regional, and provincial economies. a_i^{na}, a_i^{re}, and a_i^{pr} are the corresponding loading factors, demonstrating the co-movements between x_{it} and the periodic fluctuations in the national, regional, and provincial economies. The sign for the loading coefficients of the provincial fiscal expenditure and the national and provincial common factors will identify the national and provincial periodic features of the expenditure behavior of regional governments (negative indicates countercyclical features, positive indicates procyclical features). ε_{it} is the error term, following a autocorrelation function of the order p: $\varepsilon_{it} = \phi_{i1}\varepsilon_{it-1} + \cdots + \phi_{ip}\,\varepsilon_{it-p} + \mu_{it}$, of which ϕ_{ij} is the autocorrelation coefficient, and $u_{it} \sim (0, \sigma_i^2)$ is an error term. It is also assumed that the national, regional, and provincial dynamic factor changes follow an autocorrelation function of the order q: $f_{mt} = \varphi_{m1} f_{mt-1} + \cdots + \varphi_{mq}\varepsilon_{mt-q} + v_{mt}$, where φ_{kj} is the autocorrelation coefficient, and $v_{mt} \sim (0, \sigma_{fm}^2)$ is an error term.

Since the number of parameters involved in this model is relatively high (522 loading coefficients, 621 autocorrelation coefficients, 207 innovation variations, and 33 groups of dynamic factor sequences), Bayesian estimation is used to better resolve the estimation complexity caused by the relatively high number of parameters.[33] Following the autocorrelogram of the simulation data, the lagged order number $p = q = 3$ is taken, and the Gibbs sampling version of the Metropolis-Hastings algorithm is used. From experimental sampling, it can be seen that the Markov chain converges when the sampling size reaches 5000; thus a sample size of 55000 is used with the first 5000 samples discarded, in order to ensure the reliability of the estimation results.

Estimation results

Table 7.1 gives the estimation results for the loading coefficients of fiscal expenditure and national and provincial common factor for the 29 provinces of the country, for the period 1979 to 2009.[34] To better reveal the effects of the tax sharing system reforms of 1994, the estimation results for 1979 to 1993 and 1994 to 2009 are also given. Additionally, considering that there still exists relatively sizeable extrabudgetary expenditure in regional governments, the estimation results for provincial extrabudgetary expenditure and the loading coefficients of national and provincial common factor for 1994 to 2008 are also given.

From Table 7.1, it can be seen that, for the period 1979 to 2009, there are 27 provinces with loading coefficients of fiscal expenditure and national economic cycles that are less than zero (negative), showing that the expenditure behavior of regional governments generally exhibits clear national countercyclical features, favoring national economic stability. On the other hand, there are 21 provinces with loading coefficients of fiscal expenditure and provincial economic cycles that are larger than zero (positive), showing that the expenditure behavior of regional governments exhibits relatively clear codirectionality with the periodic dynamics of the provincial economy, which does not favor provincial economic stability.

Table 7.1 Co-movements of fiscal expenditure and periodic fluctuations in national and provincial economies (loading coefficients)

		Periodic fluctuation of national economy				Periodic fluctuation of provincial economy			
		1979-2009	1979-1993	1994-2009	1994-2008#	1979-2009	1979-1993	1994-2009	1994-2008#
Eastern Region	Beijing	-0.73	-0.59	-0.02	0.70	0.70	0.35	0.15	-0.74
	Tianjin	-0.38	-0.47	-0.004	1.27	0.59	-0.05	0.63	0.08
	Hebei	-0.72	0.05	-0.04	0.97	0.88	1.56	0.15	0.16
	Liaoning	-0.01	0.43	0.004	-0.19	0.09	0.23	0.23	-0.51
	Shanghai	0.31	0.20	0.02	0.37	0.22	-0.04	0.12	0.33
	Jiangsu	-0.39	0.26	-0.04	1.64	-0.88	-0.10	0.03	-0.43
	Zhejiang	-0.20	0.46	-0.06	1.16	-0.24	0.20	-0.07	0.90
	Fujian	-0.18	0.76	-0.06	0.67	-0.08	0.21	0.38	0.02
	Shandong	-0.18	0.84	-0.02	1.20	0.11	0.32	-0.08	-0.26
	Guangdong	0.10	0.47	-0.05	0.55	-0.28	-0.32	-0.06	0.19
	Hainan	-0.52	0.38	-0.03	1.65	0.55	0.42	0.29	0.09
Central Region	Shanxi	-0.71	-0.05	-0.02	1.33	0.95	1.25	-0.07	-1.37
	Jilin	-0.60	0.39	-0.06	0.57	0.16	-0.03	0.67	-0.45
	Heilongjiang	-0.60	0.08	-0.07	0.79	-0.06	-0.24	-0.05	0.29
	Anhui	-0.32	0.01	-0.03	1.40	-0.11	-0.03	0.30	0.67
	Jiangxi	-0.61	0.39	-0.09	0.55	0.91	0.91	1.02	0.34
	Henan	-0.63	0.42	-0.03	0.69	-0.77	-1.02	0.49	0.12
	Hubei	-0.23	0.53	-0.05	0.90	0.34	0.24	0.57	-0.24
	Hunan	-0.46	0.77	-0.07	1.17	0.12	0.35	0.86	0.15
Western Region	Sichuan	-0.02	0.39	-0.04	0.73	0.42	0.49	0.24	0.14
	Guizhou	-0.95	-0.28	-0.07	1.15	0.59	0.96	0.53	0.07
	Yunnan	-0.50	0.30	-0.06	0.79	0.47	-0.17	-0.004	-0.04
	Shaanxi	-0.36	0.44	-0.10	-0.27	0.51	0.53	0.46	-0.28
	Gansu	-0.51	-0.02	0.004	0.16	0.23	0.37	-0.32	-0.01
	Qinghai	-0.91	-0.38	-0.10	0.44	0.72	0.62	0.09	-0.04
	Ningxia	-1.07	0.20	-0.09	0.23	1.25	1.60	-0.02	-0.57
	Xinjiang	-0.71	0.03	-0.05	0.87	-0.18	0.37	-0.24	-0.20
	Guangxi	-1.27	-0.55	-0.08	0.84	0.38	0.36	0.53	0.28
	Inner Mongolia	-1.41	-0.57	-0.08	0.38	0.98	1.03	0.57	0.20

Note: # indicates extrabudgetary expenditure. Due to limitations in data, only provincial extrabudgetary expenditure for 1994 to 2008 is considered.

Additionally, as shown by Table 7.1, the fiscal expenditures of underdeveloped provinces exhibits even more prominent provincial procyclical and national countercyclical features, with the highest absolute value for the loading coefficient of provincial fiscal expenditure and national economic cycle being that for Inner Mongolia (-1.41), and that for the loading coefficient of provincial fiscal expenditure and provincial economic cycle being that for Ningxia (1.25). On the other hand, the periodic features for the provincial fiscal expenditure of developed provinces such as Shanghai, Jiangsu, Zhejiang, and Guangdong are relatively weak in general, and some even display different periodic modes. In particular, the fiscal expenditure of Shanghai exhibits relatively significant provincial and national procyclical features (with loading coefficients for fiscal expenditure and provincial and national economic cycles as 0.22 and 0.31 respectively), which does not favor both the regional and national economic stability; but this is also consistent with the view that Shanghai is a major contributor to the periodic fluctuations in the national economy.[35] Overall, the results obtained are very much consistent with the theoretical expectations, thus helping to establish Proposition 1.

The situation is slightly different for particular sub-periods. For the period 1979 to 1993, the expenditure behavior of regional governments exhibits relatively significant national procyclical features. This may be mainly attributed to the reforms in the fiscal contract system, which established the positions of regional governments as 'surplus holders' and placed the central fiscal authority at a clearly disadvantaged position, such that the central government lacked fiscal restraining measures to deal with regional governments, and was unable to effectively ensure regional governments would fully execute the central government's macroeconomic regulation policies.

The tax sharing system reforms of 1994, on the other hand, fundamentally reversed this situation, establishing the central fiscal authority in the dominant position for the entire fiscal distribution system, greatly strengthening the restraining powers of the central authority on the expenditure behavior of regional governments, and so helps to strengthen the national countercyclical features in the expenditure behavior of regional governments; this is shown from the negative value in the loading coefficients for almost all the provinces.

On the other hand, economic system reforms, especially the reforms in the fiscal contract system, significantly strengthened regional fiscal interests. Thus, similar to the case for the entire sample period, the expenditure behavior of regional governments for 1994 to 2009 and, to a larger extent, 1979 to 1993, exhibits significant provincial procyclical features, which does not favor provincial economic stability. Unlike the case for budgetary expenditure, the extrabudgetary expenditure for regional governments since 1994 exhibits significant provincial and, to a larger extent, national procyclical features, intensifying fluctuations in the provincial and especially the national economy. This may be due to the lack of effective control for the central government on the extrabudgetary expenditure of regional governments, and that regional governments have a tendency to make use of this to covertly look out for regional self-interest. Thus, even though there are differences in results for the particular sub-periods, the situation very much consistent with Proposition 1.

Periodic features in the expenditure behavior of regional governments: Institutional causes

This segment will test Propositions 2 and 3 by examining the impact of fiscal decentralization and governance system of regional officials on the periodic features of the expenditure behavior of regional governments, in order to show the institutional causes for the periodic features.

Model framework

The loading coefficients for provincial fiscal expenditure and periodic fluctuations of national and provincial economies, obtained in the previous section, is set as the explanatory variable, and variables in fiscal revenue decentralization and governance as the core explanatory variable. Taking into consideration that in the real-life regional economy, much of the decision-making and management powers lie with the top-ranking regional official (i.e. provincial committee secretary), for the variables in governance, the main factors under consideration are the age, education level, term of office, and central office appointment history of the provincial committee secretary.[36] To ensure the robustness in the results of the main conclusions, the actual GDP per capita (using 1978 as the base period), the ratio the total volume of provincial imports and exports to the GDP, and the provincial population number, are also taken into consideration as controls for the effects of economic development level, economic openness, and population size. Additional consideration is given to the relatively significant fiscal expenditure competition amongst provinces, and the following spatial econometrics model is derived:

$$a_i = \rho Wa_i + \beta dec_i + \phi off_i + \gamma X_i + \eta Wdec_i + \kappa Woff_i + \varphi WX_i + \varepsilon_i \tag{7.2}$$

Of which, the loading coefficients a_i (i = 1, 2, ⋯ , 29) are the dependent variables, taking into consideration the loading coefficients of the provincial fiscal expenditure and the periodic fluctuations of the provincial and national economies; *Wa* is the spatially lagged term of the dependent variable. *W* is the spatial weights matrix, set apriori: taking into consideration that there is a higher degree of capital and labor force movements and technical exchanges between geographically neighboring provinces, such that the interactive effects of economic and fiscal policies are more significant, a geographical neighboring spatial weight matrix is used, where if provinces *i* and *j* share a border, the spatial weight w_{it} is set as 1; otherwise, it is set as 0.[37] *dec* is the variables in fiscal revenue decentralization; *off* is the variables in governance (age, dummy variables in tertiary education level, term of office and dummy variables in central office appointment history); *X* is the control variables (actual GDP per capita, economic openness and population size); *Wdec*, *Woff*, and *WX* are the spatially lagged terms of the explanatory variable, used to account for potential endogenous problems. ε is the error term.

Estimation results

To account for potential estimation bias problems caused by spatial autocorrelation, maximum likelihood estimation is used.[38] The estimation results for the impact of fiscal decentralization and regional governance on the national and provincial periodic features of the expenditure behavior of regional governments are given in Table 7.2.[39]

Table 7.2 Impact of fiscal decentralization and regional governance on the national and provincial periodic features of the expenditure behavior of regional governments

	National periodic features in expenditure behavior of regional governments				Provincial periodic features in expenditure behavior of regional governments			
	Model 1a (1979–2009)	Model 1b (1979–1993)	Model 1c (1994–2009)	Model 1d (1994–2008)	Model 2a (1979–2009)	Model 2b (1979–1993)	Model 2c (1994–2009)	Model 2d (1994–2008)
Fiscal revenue decentralization	0.651 (0.330)**	0.384 (0.110)***	0.273 (0.130)**	-0.339 (0.190)*	-0.824 (0.240)***	-0.038 (0.110)	-0.054 (0.150)	-0.801 (0.260)***
Fiscal expenditure decentralization	0.980 (0.410)**	-0.892 (0.250)***	0.331 (0.080)***	-0.126 (0.120)	-0.334 (0.300)	-0.658 (0.250)***	0.216 (0.090)**	0.111 (0.160)
Age of official	-0.048 (0.220)	0.426 (0.210)**	-0.011 (0.080)	-0.145 (0.110)	0.562 (0.160)***	-0.255 (0.220)	0.128 (0.080)	0.322 (0.150)**
Tertiary education level of official (Dummy variables)	0.353 (0.210)*	-0.181 (0.150)	-0.563 (0.080)***	0.457 (0.120)***	-0.280 (0.150)*	-0.338 (0.160)**	-0.301 (0.090)***	-0.721 (0.170)***

Table 7.2 Impact of fiscal decentralization and regional governance on the national and provincial periodic features of the expenditure behavior of regional governments

(Cont'd)

	National periodic features in expenditure behavior of regional governments				Provincial periodic features in expenditure behavior of regional governments			
	Model 1a (1979–2009)	Model 1b (1979–1993)	Model 1c (1994–2009)	Model 1d (1994–2008)	Model 2a (1979–2009)	Model 2b (1979–1993)	Model 2c (1994–2009)	Model 2d (1994–2008)
Term of office	-0.239 (0.610)	-1.039 (0.210)***	-0.164 (0.180)	0.251 (0.230)	2.095 (0.440)***	0.190 (0.210)	0.430 (0.200)**	0.552 (0.320)*
Central appointment history (Dummy variables)	0.035 (0.230)	-0.447 (0.240)*	0.025 (0.100)	-0.281 (0.140)**	0.288 (0.170)*	0.471 (0.240)*	0.017 (0.110)	0.217 (0.190)
Economic development level	-0.784 (0.390)**	-0.275 (0.230)	-0.391 (0.130)***	0.116 (0.170)	0.848 (0.290)***	0.492 (0.230)**	-0.457 (0.150)***	0.536 (0.240)**
Economic openness level	-0.217 (0.210)	-0.210 (0.120)*	0.049 (0.110)	-0.257 (0.160)	0.319 (0.150)**	0.154 (0.120)	-0.572 (0.110)***	0.011 (0.230)
Population size	0.026 (0.300)	-0.313 (0.150)**	0.458 (0.140)***	-0.031 (0.190)	0.616 (0.220)***	0.691 (0.150)***	-0.269 (0.160)*	0.601 (0.250)**
W.Fiscal revenue decentralization	-0.437 (0.660)	0.348 (0.250)	0.238 (0.300)	-0.623 (0.440)	0.287 (0.470)	-0.439 (0.240)*	0.451 (0.330)	0.844 (0.590)
W.Fiscal expenditure decentralization	-0.290 (0.790)	2.205 (0.980)**	0.353 (0.270)	-0.187 (0.370)	-0.429 (0.550)	-1.938 (0.980)**	1.174 (0.290)***	-0.213 (0.500)
W.Age of official	-0.283 (0.580)	0.378 (0.500)	0.170 (0.150)	0.827 (0.220)***	1.022 (0.440)**	-1.019 (0.510)**	0.345 (0.170)**	-0.829 (0.310)***
W.Tertiary education level of official (Dummy variables)	0.342 (0.570)	0.459 (0.370)	-0.285 (0.220)	1.001 (0.290)***	-0.834 (0.410)**	-0.999 (0.380)***	-0.093 (0.200)	-1.103 (0.420)***
W.Term of office	-1.215 (1.550)	-1.705 (0.480)***	-0.494 (0.450)	0.574 (0.580)	5.514 (1.140)***	0.022 (0.480)	0.492 (0.490)	1.192 (0.790)
W.Central appointment history (Dummy variables)	-0.591 (0.660)	-0.057 (0.290)	0.235 (0.240)	-0.477 (0.300)	1.866 (0.480)***	1.030 (0.290)***	0.198 (0.260)	0.289 (0.410)
W.Economic development level	0.554 (0.890)	-2.183 (0.780)***	-0.425 (0.320)	0.418 (0.420)	1.007 (0.630)	2.199 (0.790)***	-0.888 (0.370)**	0.027 (0.580)
W.Economic openness level	0.696 (0.630)	-0.737 (0.450)	0.565 (0.250)**	-0.636 (0.390)	0.291 (0.480)	0.640 (0.460)	-0.776 (0.300)***	0.737 (0.550)
W.Population size	0.168 (0.740)	0.365 (0.260)	0.237 (0.300)	0.097 (0.340)	-0.188 (0.550)	0.755 (0.280)***	0.729 (0.320)**	-0.282 (0.470)
ρ	-0.460 (0.270)*	-0.908 (0.230)***	-0.749 (0.230)***	-0.961 (0.190)***	-0.660 (0.230)***	-0.999 (0.220)***	-0.378 (0.250)	-0.377 (0.240)

Table 7.2 Impact of fiscal decentralization and regional governance on the national and provincial periodic features of the expenditure behavior of regional governments

(Cont'd)

	National periodic features in expenditure behavior of regional governments				Provincial periodic features in expenditure behavior of regional governments			
	Model 1a (1979–2009)	Model 1b (1979–1993)	Model 1c (1994–2009)	Model 1d (1994–2008)	Model 2a (1979–2009)	Model 2b (1979–1993)	Model 2c (1994–2009)	Model 2d (1994–2008)
Sample size	28	28	29	29	28	28	29	29
Log-likelihood function maximum value	-19.342	-9.101	3.478	-8.191	-11.248	-10.289	2.410	-14.073
R^2	0.475	0.618	0.884	0.619	0.695	0.491	0.890	0.630

Notes: (1) Models 1d and 2d use the loading coefficients for extrabudgetary expenditure and provincial and national economic cycles as dependent variables.
(2) *, ** and *** indicate regression coefficients significantly above confidence levels of 10%, 5% and 1% respectively.
(3) Bracketed values are standard deviations.

From Table 7.2, it can be seen that the regression coefficients of the spatially lagged terms for the dependent variables in the various models, ρ, are all negative in value, and, with the exception of Models 2c and 2d, are all statistically significant, showing that the periodic features of the expenditure behavior in regional governments exhibit relatively strong contradirectional interactive effects. For Model 1a, the regression coefficients of fiscal decentralization are positive in value and are statistically significant, showing that fiscal decentralization significantly weakens the national countercyclical features in the expenditure behavior of regional governments, which does not favor national economic stability. From Model 2a, however, it can be seen that the regression coefficients are negative in value, showing that fiscal revenue decentralization also significantly restrains the provincial procyclical features in the expenditure behavior of regional governments, which favors provincial economic stability; the effects of fiscal expenditure decentralization are not statistically significant.

The estimation results deviate to a certain extent from theoretical expectations, and this may be mainly attributed to structural changes in the effects of fiscal decentralization, which in turn resulted from changes in the country's fiscal institution since the start of the Chinese Economic Reform. Compared to the fiscal contract system reforms, the tax sharing system reforms of 1994 exhibits significant revenue centralization features, but this did little to change the situation where the responsibilities for affairs of expenditure rely heavily on the division of administrative authority in regional governments (a problem which has existed since the introduction of the fiscal contract system reforms), leading to an increase in the severity of vertical fiscal imbalance in regional governments, and thus changing the mechanism of effect for fiscal decentralization on the expenditure behavior of regional governments.

In fact, for the period 1994 to 2009, serious vertical fiscal imbalance led to the appearance of significant differentiations in the mechanisms of incentives and restraints in the decentralized fiscal institution and its effects on the periodic features in the expenditure behavior of regional governments: fiscal expenditure decentralization further aggravates vertical fiscal imbalance and the consequent ethical risk problems, thus strengthening significantly the provincial procyclical features and weakening the national countercyclical features in the expenditure behavior of regional governments, which does not favor provincial and national economic stability; on the other hand, while fiscal revenue decentralization also weakens the national countercyclical features, the effect is relatively smaller, and its effect on provincial procyclical features are not significant (see Models 1c and 2c). These results are consistent with theoretical expectations, which helps to establish Proposition 2.

In contrast, during the fiscal contract system era when fiscal powers and administrative authority are relatively properly arranged, fiscal expenditure decentralization significantly weakened the provincial and national procyclical features in the expenditure behavior of regional governments, which favored provincial and national economic stability; this also demonstrates the importance of proper arrangement of fiscal powers and administrative authority to maintaining provincial and national economic stability. There is, however, no significant difference in the effect of fiscal revenue decentralization before and after the tax sharing reforms of 1994. Additionally, it can be seen from the estimation results in Models 1d and 2d that post-1994 tax sharing reforms, revenue decentralization has helped to weaken the provincial and national procyclical features in extrabudgetary expenditure of regional governments, while expenditure decentralization has no significant effects.

As for the impact of regional governance, it can be seen from Table 7.2 that the regression coefficients in Model 2a for age and dummy variables in tertiary education levels are positive and negative in value respectively, and are statistically significant. This shows that moving towards a younger and knowledge-based cadre body not only helps in optimizing the age and intellectual composition, raising the general quality of the cadre leadership, but also helps to ensure the security of the career path of officials, thus promoting rationality in the behavior of regional governments, restraining the inclination of regional governments to overzealously pursue self-interest, weakening provincial procyclical features in expenditure behavior, and promote provincial economic stability.

Since the tax sharing reforms of 1994, a younger and knowledge-based cadre body has also helped to mitigate the unfavorable effects of regional extrabudgetary expenditure on provincial economic stability (see Model 2d). Rejuvenation has no significant effect on the national countercyclical features in expenditure behavior in the entire sample period, but it helped to weaken the national procyclical features for the period 1997 to 1993. This may be explained by the fact that the cadre retirement system was only fully established in the early 1990s, such that the problem of an aging cadre body was especially acute for 1997 to 1993, making marginal returns for rejuvenation during this period relatively large. Within the entire sample period, a knowledge-based cadre body weakened to a certain extent the national countercyclical features in expenditure behavior, and after the tax sharing reforms of 1994, higher levels of knowledge and cultural training has helped to optimize regional expenditure in promoting national economic stability, although at the same time it also strengthened national procyclical features in extrabudgetary expenditure behavior.

It can also be seen from Models 1a and 2a that extended terms of office and central appointment history significantly increase the provincial procyclical features in the expenditure behavior of regional governments. Extended term of office aggravates the urgency in advancement for regional officials, increasing the focus on regional short-term economic performance, which may explain the significant strengthening of provincial procyclical features in both budgetary and extrabudgetary expenditure behavior. Central appointment history significantly strengthened the provincial procyclical features in expenditure behavior for 1979 to 1993. Neither terms of office nor central appointment history have any significant effects on the national countercyclical features in the entire sample period, but they help to restraining unfavorable effects of the expenditure behavior of regional governments on national economic stability. Despite the existence of a certain degree of deviation, then, the above results are in general consistent with the theoretical expectations, thus establishing Proposition 3.

Periodic features in the expenditure behavior of regional governments and their institutional causes: Structure of expenditure

Thus far, the analysis for the period features in the expenditure behavior of regional governments and their institutional causes has been performed on the basis of data concerning size of expenditure. This segment furthers the analysis by looking at the structure of expenditure. Tables 7.3 to 7.8 give, for the various periods, the impacts of provincial and national periodic features in provincial economic, social, and administrative expenditure, as well as that of fiscal decentralization and regional governance.[40]

Table 7.3 Co-movements of economic expenditure and periodic fluctuations in national, regional and provincial economies for various periods (loading coefficient)

	Province	Periodic fluctuations (loading coefficient)								
		National economy			Regional economy			Provincial economy		
		1979-2006	1979-1993	1994-2006	1979-2006	1979-1993	1994-2006	1979-2006	1979-1993	1994-2006
Eastern	Beijing	-0.45	-0.03	-0.17	0.27	0.05	-0.92	-0.09	0.44	-0.42
	Tianjin	0.26	-0.13	0.37	0.44	0.12	0.12	-0.12	-0.57	0.85
	Hebei	-0.77	-0.01	-0.25	0.94	0.28	-0.51	1.76	1.81	-0.43
	Liaoning	0.34	0.34	0.50	1.29	0.50	0.20	0.05	-0.005	-0.03
	Shanghai	-0.48	-0.22	0.27	0.62	-0.05	-0.11	0.37	0.07	0.13
	Jiangsu	-0.13	0.28	-0.11	0.97	0.41	0.33	-0.89	-0.28	-0.07
	Zhejiang	-0.90	0.20	-0.74	0.63	-0.31	-1.61	-0.84	-0.33	-0.49
	Fujian	0.05	0.41	-0.26	1.03	0.28	-0.44	-0.46	1.14	-0.02
	Shandong	-0.32	0.27	0.08	0.87	0.16	-0.99	-0.17	0.11	0.17
	Guangdong	0.24	0.20	0.41	1.19	0.56	-1.86	-0.38	0.43	0.35
	Hainan	-0.34	0.21	-1.10	-0.20	0.33	-0.66	1.08	0.49	0.29
Central	Shanxi	-0.79	-0.08	-0.35	0.18	0.38	-0.60	0.63	2.19	-0.48
	Jilin	-0.77	0.45	-0.49	0.84	0.91	-0.64	0.36	0.57	-0.03
	Heilongjiang	-1.05	-0.42	-0.37	-0.27	-0.14	-0.92	0.11	-0.12	-0.11
	Anhui	-0.33	0.15	-0.01	0.47	0.44	-0.25	-0.17	0.01	-0.21
	Jiangxi	-0.61	0.37	-0.21	0.34	0.47	-0.51	0.03	0.29	-0.06
	Henan	-0.44	0.32	-0.66	0.49	0.37	-0.24	-0.70	-0.68	-0.08
	Hubei	-0.65	-0.14	-0.21	0.19	-0.16	-0.40	0.74	-0.22	0.19
	Hunan	-0.64	0.34	-0.32	0.31	0.17	-0.74	-0.15	0.42	0.50
Western	Sichuan	-0.64	-0.01	-0.21	0.28	-0.10	-1.07	0.59	0.62	-0.78
	Guizhou	-0.76	-0.07	-0.24	-0.09	-0.41	-0.64	-0.06	0.28	-0.49
	Yunnan	0.001	0.30	-0.23	0.37	0.33	-0.93	-0.12	0.35	-0.29

Table 7.3 Co-movements of economic expenditure and periodic fluctuations in national, regional and provincial economies for various periods (loading coefficient)

(Cont'd)

	Province	Periodic fluctuations (loading coefficient)								
		National economy			Regional economy			Provincial economy		
		1979-2006	1979-1993	1994-2006	1979-2006	1979-1993	1994-2006	1979-2006	1979-1993	1994-2006
Western	Shaanxi	-0.60	0.16	-0.33	-0.02	0.01	-0.76	0.74	0.32	-0.28
	Gansu	-0.72	-0.13	-0.27	0.15	-0.19	-0.68	0.33	0.61	-0.28
	Qinghai	-0.97	-0.23	-0.24	0.42	0.47	-0.56	1.36	1.97	-0.29
	Ningxia	-0.86	0.15	-0.27	0.18	0.26	-0.80	0.86	1.88	-0.26
	Xinjiang	-0.75	0.17	-0.35	0.29	0.12	-0.75	-0.63	1.34	-0.53
	Guangxi	-0.57	0.14	-0.25	0.26	0.05	-0.76	0.89	1.07	-0.44
	Inner Mongolia	-1.06	-0.01	-0.57	-0.06	-0.02	-0.82	0.47	0.72	-0.18

Table 7.4 Co-movements of social expenditure and periodic fluctuations in national, regional and provincial economies for various periods (loading coefficient)

	Province	Periodic fluctuations (loading coefficient)								
		National economy			Regional economy			Provincial economy		
		1979-2006	1979-1993	1994-2006	1979-2006	1979-1993	1994-2006	1979-2006	1979-1993	1994-2006
Eastern	Beijing	-0.45	-0.04	-0.38	0.20	0.08	0.36	0.68	0.84	-0.03
	Tianjin	-0.58	-0.53	-0.12	-0.04	-0.10	0.01	1.33	0.36	0.02
	Hebei	-0.68	-0.64	-0.32	0.45	0.38	0.19	-0.40	0.18	-0.42
	Liaoning	0.15	0.002	0.25	0.18	0.05	1.16	0.09	-0.07	0.25
	Shanghai	0.61	0.08	0.92	0.38	0.88	-0.60	0.25	0.03	0.01
	Jiangsu	-0.21	-0.45	-0.002	0.26	0.07	-0.30	-0.19	-0.07	-0.08
	Zhejiang	-0.61	-0.36	-0.73	0.34	0.36	-0.38	0.35	0.40	0.18
	Fujian	-0.58	-0.82	-0.35	-0.07	-0.36	-0.79	0.36	0.33	0.29
	Shandong	-0.32	0.91	-0.86	0.75	1.78	-0.47	0.03	0.003	-0.01
	Guangdong	0.57	0.63	0.31	0.61	1.21	0.46	0.44	0.37	0.25
	Hainan	-0.50	-0.34	-0.28	-0.08	-0.18	1.54	0.26	0.17	0.57
Central	Shanxi	-0.35	-0.17	-0.40	0.18	0.38	0.49	0.68	0.94	-0.05
	Jilin	-0.26	-0.20	0.08	0.21	0.23	0.02	0.13	-0.30	0.01
	Heilongjiang	-1.10	0.19	-1.62	-0.08	-0.11	-0.18	0.36	0.56	-0.28

Table 7.4 Co-movements of social expenditure and periodic fluctuations in national, regional and provincial economies for various periods (loading coefficient)

(Cont'd)

	Province	Periodic fluctuations (loading coefficient)								
		National economy			Regional economy			Provincial economy		
		1979-2006	1979-1993	1994-2006	1979-2006	1979-1993	1994-2006	1979-2006	1979-1993	1994-2006
Central	Anhui	-0.12	-0.24	-0.08	0.36	0.53	0.17	0.16	0.09	0.04
	Jiangxi	-0.77	-0.39	-0.81	0.25	0.42	0.29	1.05	0.69	0.25
	Henan	-0.76	-0.25	-0.92	0.15	0.10	0.24	-0.47	-0.25	-0.05
	Hubei	-0.15	-0.14	-0.40	0.56	0.79	0.05	0.25	0.08	-0.08
	Hunan	-0.73	-0.34	-0.85	0.27	0.27	0.11	0.11	0.20	0.18
Western	Sichuan	-0.68	0.16	-0.71	0.21	0.23	-0.63	-0.77	-0.55	-0.18
	Guizhou	-1.11	-0.91	-0.90	0.47	0.07	0.34	-0.03	0.15	-0.35
	Yunnan	-0.27	-0.30	0.06	0.51	0.37	-0.40	0.51	0.34	-0.19
	Shaanxi	-0.84	0.18	-1.05	0.26	0.15	0.08	0.38	0.49	-0.18
	Gansu	-0.07	0.32	-0.38	0.70	0.59	0.38	0.64	0.72	-0.02
	Qinghai	-0.72	-1.10	-0.38	0.29	-0.13	0.38	0.28	0.67	0.32
	Ningxia	-1.58	-0.76	-1.27	0.08	-0.28	-0.41	0.52	0.75	-0.01
	Xinjiang	-0.52	-0.51	-0.23	0.36	-0.03	-0.01	-0.19	0.04	0.04
	Guangxi	-1.30	-1.04	-1.06	0.36	0.26	-0.52	0.24	0.23	0.32
	Inner Mongolia	-1.60	-1.08	-1.34	0.17	-0.29	0.29	0.57	0.64	-0.38

Table 7.5 Co-movements of administrative expenditure and periodic fluctuations in national, regional and provincial economies for various periods (loading coefficient)

	Province	Periodic fluctuations (loading coefficient)								
		National economy			Regional economy			Provincial economy		
		1979-2006	1979-1993	1994-2006	1979-2006	1979-1993	1994-2006	1979-2006	1979-1993	1994-2006
Eastern	Beijing	0.55	0.27	0.27	0.43	0.11	0.52	0.22	-0.06	0.01
	Tianjin	-0.75	-1.22	-0.12	0.47	0.10	0.72	0.16	-0.25	0.76
	Hebei	-1.27	-1.66	-0.64	0.06	0.36	0.80	0.02	1.33	-0.77
	Liaoning	-0.66	-1.07	-0.06	0.34	-0.10	0.05	-0.06	0.40	0.03
	Shanghai	-0.82	-1.07	-0.42	0.69	0.60	-0.06	0.27	0.21	-0.32

Table 7.5 Co-movements of administrative expenditure and periodic fluctuations in national, regional and provincial economies for various periods (loading coefficient)

(Cont'd)

	Province	Periodic fluctuations (loading coefficient)								
		National economy			Regional economy			Provincial economy		
		1979-2006	1979-1993	1994-2006	1979-2006	1979-1993	1994-2006	1979-2006	1979-1993	1994-2006
Eastern	Jiangsu	0.27	-0.25	0.42	0.64	-0.02	1.05	-0.03	0.42	0.30
	Zhejiang	-0.83	-1.02	-0.75	0.72	0.46	-0.04	0.12	0.80	0.52
	Fujian	0.62	0.32	0.47	0.22	-0.38	0.72	0.36	0.31	0.92
	Shandong	-0.42	0.14	-0.66	1.97	1.74	-0.40	0.09	1.14	0.31
	Guangdong	-0.36	-0.36	-0.13	0.38	0.63	-0.56	0.51	0.69	0.12
	Hainan	-0.27	-0.53	0.004	0.27	-0.35	0.48	0.53	0.80	0.25
Central	Shanxi	-0.55	-0.36	-0.42	0.18	0.07	0.40	0.90	1.00	0.14
	Jilin	-0.70	-0.31	-0.81	0.22	0.04	0.13	0.41	0.38	0.53
	Heilongjiang	-0.50	0.67	-1.45	-0.05	-0.37	0.20	1.00	1.66	-0.09
	Anhui	-0.11	0.27	0.09	0.90	0.75	0.04	0.26	0.49	-0.04
	Jiangxi	-0.68	-1.18	-0.52	0.24	0.49	0.22	-0.15	0.15	0.50
	Henan	-0.33	0.19	-0.53	0.36	0.47	0.15	-0.29	0.63	0.01
	Hubei	-0.73	-0.86	-0.71	0.10	0.20	0.48	0.12	-0.06	0.15
	Hunan	-0.94	-1.14	-0.41	0.93	1.01	0.12	0.16	-0.02	0.21
Western	Sichuan	-1.34	-0.66	-1.33	0.68	0.44	-0.64	-1.64	-1.30	-0.39
	Guizhou	-0.25	-0.85	0.05	0.54	0.27	0.80	0.79	0.80	-1.21
	Yunnan	-0.60	-1.04	0.07	0.85	0.79	0.11	0.18	0.01	-0.11
	Shaanxi	-1.35	-1.50	-0.88	0.24	0.29	-0.31	-0.29	-0.21	-0.12
	Gansu	-0.74	-0.83	-0.51	0.12	0.20	-0.08	0.09	0.27	-0.11
	Qinghai	0.14	-0.87	0.56	0.81	0.71	0.52	-0.09	0.38	0.11
	Ningxia	-1.63	-1.34	-1.16	0.17	0.24	-0.02	-0.40	-0.19	-0.03
	Xinjiang	0.004	-0.63	0.15	0.35	-0.06	0.66	0.18	0.66	-0.08
	Guangxi	-0.95	-0.26	-1.22	0.17	0.33	-0.30	0.05	0.02	0.42
	Inner Mongolia	-1.22	-1.07	-0.72	0.57	0.27	-0.07	-0.02	-0.66	0.22

Table 7.6 Effects of fiscal decentralization and regional governance on national and provincial periodic features in provincial economic expenditure

	National periodic features			Provincial periodic features		
	(1979–2009)	(1979–1993)	(1994–2009)	(1979–2009)	(1979–1993)	(1994–2009)
Fiscal revenue decentralization	0.277 (0.248)	-0.053 (0.166)	0.163 (0.259)	-0.440 (0.208)**	0.072 (0.148)	0.306 (0.287)
Fiscal expenditure decentralization	0.516 (0.265)*	0.617 (0.331)*	-0.058 (0.201)	-0.021 (0.224)	-0.349 (0.298)	0.169 (0.224)
Age of official	-0.229 (0.167)	-0.240 (0.264)	0.162 (0.138)	0.438 (0.138)***	0.003 (0.234)	0.217 (0.153)
Tertiary education level of official (Dummy variables)	-0.103 (0.190)	-0.246 (0.214)	-0.329 (0.173)*	-0.194 (0.160)	-0.447 (0.192)**	-0.128 (0.193)
Term of office	-0.276 (0.319)	0.140 (0.289)	-0.311 (0.247)	1.073 (0.267)***	0.563 (0.257)**	-0.198 (0.274)
Central appointment history (Dummy variables)	-0.252 (0.173)	-0.241 (0.316)	-0.353 (0.186)*	0.739 (0.145)***	0.208 (0.282)	-0.511 (0.206)**
Economic development level	0.545 (0.300)*	0.398 (0.323)	0.020 (0.219)	-0.146 (0.248)	0.386 (0.289)	0.105 (0.244)
Economic openness level	-0.415 (0.143)***	-0.031 (0.172)	0.616 (0.223)***	0.023 (0.119)	0.013 (0.156)	0.012 (0.256)
Population size	0.053 (0.240)	0.290 (0.193)	0.197 (0.226)	0.287 (0.201)	0.477 (0.170)***	0.486 (0.250)*
W.Fiscal revenue decentralization	0.354 (0.554)	0.185 (0.358)	0.181 (0.510)	-0.697 (0.466)	0.523 (0.317)*	1.689 (0.566)***
W.Fiscal expenditure decentralization	0.585 (0.451)	-0.450 (1.243)	-0.197 (0.570)	-0.542 (0.387)	-2.049 (1.084)*	1.825 (0.634)***
W.Age of official	0.251 (0.446)	0.401 (0.676)	0.103 (0.296)	1.285 (0.377)***	0.819 (0.604)	-0.334 (0.313)
W.Tertiary education level of official (Dummy variables)	0.219 (0.470)	-0.096 (0.498)	-0.477 (0.345)	-0.540 (0.396)	-1.485 (0.442)***	-0.734 (0.379)*
W.Term of office	-0.697 (0.694)	0.113 (0.690)	-0.873 (0.636)	2.327 (0.572)***	0.612 (0.617)	-0.984 (0.704)
W.Central appointment history (Dummy variables)	-0.292 (0.391)	0.245 (0.533)	0.198 (0.398)	0.860 (0.336)**	-0.461 (0.472)	0.049 (0.442)

Table 7.6 Effects of fiscal decentralization and regional governance on national and provincial periodic features in provincial economic expenditure

(Cont'd)

	National periodic features			Provincial periodic features		
	(1979–2009)	(1979–1993)	(1994–2009)	(1979–2009)	(1979–1993)	(1994–2009)
W.Economic development level	-0.516 (0.709)	0.644 (1.018)	-0.438 (0.391)	-0.139 (0.584)	1.586 (0.917)*	-1.050 (0.456)**
W.Economic openness level	-1.296 (0.460)***	-0.423 (0.577)	0.073 (0.457)	1.337 (0.379)***	-1.092 (0.523)**	-2.040 (0.481)***
W.Population size	0.660 (0.521)	-0.278 (0.512)	-0.453 (0.448)	0.465 (0.446)	0.497 (0.472)	0.470 (0.485)
ρ	-0.871 (0.242)***	-0.570 (0.267)**	-0.602 (0.252)**	-0.998 (0.197)***	-0.414 (0.267)	0.007 (0.242)
Sample size	28	28	29	28	28	29
Log-likelihood function maximum value	-12.438	-14.875	-12.582	-8.447	-10.957	-14.121
R^2	0.603	0.580	0.650	0.525	0.701	0.679

Table 7.7 Effects of fiscal decentralization and regional governance on national and provincial periodic features in provincial social expenditure

	National periodic features			Provincial periodic features		
	(1979–2009)	(1979–1993)	(1994–2009)	(1979–2009)	(1979–1993)	(1994–2009)
Fiscal revenue decentralization	-0.686 (0.239)***	-0.670 (0.106)***	0.516 (0.271)*	0.616 (0.212)***	0.242 (0.085)***	0.081 (0.287)
Fiscal expenditure decentralization	0.470 (0.254)*	0.442 (0.209)**	-0.147 (0.212)	-0.559 (0.217)**	-0.578 (0.174)***	0.351 (0.223)
Age of official	-0.372 (0.157)**	0.492 (0.165)***	-0.264 (0.146)*	0.343 (0.136)**	-0.026 (0.134)	-0.530 (0.153)***
Tertiary education level of official (Dummy variables)	-0.163 (0.184)	0.131 (0.137)	-0.358 (0.182)**	0.458 (0.160)***	0.042 (0.110)	-0.262 (0.193)
Term of office	-0.051 (0.306)	0.138 (0.184)	-0.209 (0.261)	-0.274 (0.257)	0.376 (0.149)**	0.045 (0.273)
Central appointment history (Dummy variables)	0.103 (0.166)	-0.200 (0.200)	-0.209 (0.196)	-0.837 (0.140)***	0.164 (0.161)	-0.454 (0.204)**

Table 7.7 Effects of fiscal decentralization and regional governance on national and provincial periodic features in provincial social expenditure

(Cont'd)

	National periodic features			Provincial periodic features		
	(1979–2009)	(1979–1993)	(1994–2009)	(1979–2009)	(1979–1993)	(1994–2009)
Economic development level	1.650 (0.286)***	-0.228 (0.204)	-0.459 (0.231)**	-0.747 (0.251)***	0.268 (0.174)	0.201 (0.244)
Economic openness level	0.141 (0.137)	0.063 (0.111)	0.575 (0.234)**	0.266 (0.120)**	0.613 (0.088)***	0.199 (0.249)
Population size	0.068 (0.229)	-0.003 (0.121)	0.015 (0.238)	0.086 (0.194)	0.716 (0.097)***	0.371 (0.260)
W.Fiscal revenue decentralization	-0.692 (0.556)	-0.287 (0.270)	1.487 (0.532)***	1.730 (0.489)***	0.860 (0.182)***	-0.164 (0.561)
W.Fiscal expenditure decentralization	0.530 (0.446)	-0.239 (0.824)	-0.223 (0.614)	-0.129 (0.380)	-2.707 (0.622)***	0.458 (0.631)
W.Age of official	-0.646 (0.430)	-0.320 (0.452)	-0.408 (0.300)	0.173 (0.378)	-0.741 (0.350)**	0.093 (0.347)
W.Tertiary education level of official (Dummy variables)	-0.414 (0.451)	-0.730 (0.346)**	-0.878 (0.359)**	0.440 (0.411)	-0.547 (0.263)**	-0.502 (0.393)
W.Term of office	-0.120 (0.661)	0.022 (0.435)	-0.997 (0.680)	-0.211 (0.550)	0.134 (0.353)	0.101 (0.701)
W.Central appointment history (Dummy variables)	0.169 (0.376)	-0.019 (0.344)	0.187 (0.414)	0.189 (0.369)	0.872 (0.272)***	0.307 (0.443)
W.Economic development level	0.462 (0.759)	0.772 (0.676)	-0.957 (0.400)**	-1.445 (0.563)**	2.545 (0.524)***	0.236 (0.422)
W.Economic openness level	-0.481 (0.433)	-0.674 (0.369)*	0.007 (0.480)	-0.452 (0.366)	0.305 (0.303)	-1.161 (0.477)**
W.Population size	0.315 (0.507)	-0.087 (0.321)	-0.872 (0.450)*	0.221 (0.428)	0.820 (0.272)***	1.307 (0.474)***
ρ	-0.750 (0.250)***	-0.994 (0.222)***	-0.388 (0.250)	-0.390 (0.262)	-0.998 (0.191)***	0.185 (0.229)
Sample size	28	28	29	28	28	29
Log-likelihood function maximum value	-10.622	-4.462	-13.165	-4.453	1.329	-14.209
R^2	0.677	0.726	0.686	0.805	0.792	0.679

Table 7.8 Effects of fiscal decentralization and regional governance on national and provincial periodic features in provincial administrative expenditure

	National periodic features			Provincial periodic features		
	(1979–2009)	(1979–1993)	(1994–2009)	(1979–2009)	(1979–1993)	(1994–2009)
Fiscal revenue decentralization	-0.156 (0.290)	-0.138 (0.131)	0.260 (0.298)	0.216 (0.270)	-0.382 (0.196)**	0.258 (0.299)
Fiscal expenditure decentralization	-0.691 (0.310)**	1.092 (0.264)***	0.118 (0.230)	-1.572 (0.280)***	1.110 (0.391)***	0.043 (0.232)
Age of official	-0.486 (0.187)***	0.788 (0.210)***	-0.469 (0.161)***	-0.374 (0.174)**	-0.359 (0.308)	-0.482 (0.160)***
Tertiary education level of official (Dummy variables)	0.036 (0.217)	0.458 (0.170)***	-0.125 (0.198)	0.374 (0.202)*	0.557 (0.254)**	-0.045 (0.201)
Term of office	-1.222 (0.364)***	-1.336 (0.229)***	-0.330 (0.282)	-1.765 (0.336)***	-0.018 (0.348)	0.219 (0.286)
Central appointment history (Dummy variables)	-0.185 (0.196)	-0.882 (0.251)***	-0.299 (0.211)	-0.408 (0.183)**	0.902 (0.373)**	-0.535 (0.212)**
Economic development level	0.490 (0.341)	-1.306 (0.255)***	0.022 (0.251)	-0.133 (0.314)	-0.338 (0.379)	0.740 (0.254)***
Economic openness level	0.223 (0.163)	0.048 (0.139)	0.317 (0.259)	0.296 (0.158)*	0.401 (0.203)**	0.277 (0.264)
Population size	-0.389 (0.274)	-0.184 (0.152)	0.181 (0.257)	-0.774 (0.255)***	0.430 (0.230)*	0.095 (0.265)
W.Fiscal revenue decentralization	-2.326 (0.634)***	-0.658 (0.283)**	-0.980 (0.579)*	1.033 (0.603)*	0.591 (0.438)	-0.199 (0.587)
W.Fiscal expenditure decentralization	2.093 (0.491)***	5.820 (0.983)***	-0.244 (0.653)	0.893 (0.471)*	-2.190 (1.471)	0.774 (0.661)
W.Age of official	-0.256 (0.522)	2.321 (0.568)***	0.424 (0.339)	-1.792 (0.475)***	-1.382 (0.796)*	0.557 (0.336)*
W.Tertiary education level of official (Dummy variables)	0.113 (0.533)	1.834 (0.398)***	-0.698 (0.390)*	-0.495 (0.495)	-0.421 (0.587)	-0.280 (0.395)
W.Term of office	-1.834 (0.773)**	-3.227 (0.545)***	-0.531 (0.724)	-3.499 (0.726)***	-0.964 (0.820)	0.194 (0.733)
W.Central appointment history (Dummy variables)	-1.279 (0.454)***	-2.060 (0.443)***	-0.183 (0.451)	-1.054 (0.416)**	0.242 (0.622)	0.043 (0.470)
W.Economic development level	2.447 (0.780)***	-5.123 (0.837)***	0.254 (0.436)	0.075 (0.718)	1.307 (1.204)	0.194 (0.468)

Table 7.8 Effects of fiscal decentralization and regional governance on national and provincial periodic features in provincial administrative expenditure

(Cont'd)

	National periodic features			Provincial periodic features		
	(1979–2009)	(1979–1993)	(1994–2009)	(1979–2009)	(1979–1993)	(1994–2009)
W.Economic openness level	-2.092 (0.517)***	0.061 (0.456)	0.822 (0.499)*	-3.005 (0.478)***	0.797 (0.677)	-1.493 (0.500)***
W.Population size	0.269 (0.601)	0.600 (0.407)	0.850 (0.489)*	-0.789 (0.553)	-0.601 (0.612)	1.535 (0.495)***
ρ	-0.508 (0.254)**	-0.352 (0.234)	-0.484 (0.255)*	-0.453 (0.225)**	-0.145 (0.261)	0.232 (0.226)
Sample size	28	28	29	28	28	29
Log-likelihood function maximum value	-14.398	-7.455	-15.965	-12.075	-18.159	-15.573
R^2	0.567	0.759	0.559	0.596	0.555	0.638

Tables 7.3 to 7.5 shows that, within the entire sample period, social and administrative expenditure exhibit provincial procyclical features, which does not favor provincial economic stability; provincial procyclical features in economic expenditure are rather unclear, demonstrated by the roughly equal numbers in positive and negative loading coefficients of economic expenditure and provincial economic cycles. On the other hand, economic, social, and administrative expenditures all exhibit national countercyclical features, which favors national economic stability; this is consistent with the results for overall expenditure.

Examining particular sub-periods show different results. For 1979 to 1993, the various expenditures exhibit significant provincial procyclical features; social and administrative expenditures exhibit national countercyclical features, while economic expenditure exhibits national procyclical features, showing that the national procyclical features exhibited in the overall provincial fiscal expenditure during this period may be mainly attributed to economic expenditure. This is consistent with the intuited expectations, i.e. pre-1994 tax sharing reforms, economic expenditure behavior of regional governments is a main contributor to fluctuations in the provincial and national economies. It also shows that during the fiscal contract system period, the incentives and restraining measures on the expenditure behavior of regional governments available to the central authorities were relatively limited. Since the 1994 tax sharing reforms, economic expenditure exhibits significant provincial and national countercyclical features, which favors provincial and national economic stability; this is consistent with the fiscal policy characteristic since the mid-1990s in using economic expenditure to regulate national macroeconomics. It also shows that the tax sharing system reforms effectively strengthens the control for the central authorities over the expenditure behavior of regional governments. Social and administrative expenditure also exhibits national countercyclical features, but the provincial periodic features are rather unclear.[41]

Rejuvenation of the cadre body helps to mitigate the negative effects of economic and social expenditure on provincial economic stability; this is consistent with the results for the overall expenditure. However, rejuvenation also aggravates the negative impact of social expenditure on national economic stability as well as administrative expenditure on provincial and national economic stability, and a knowledge-based cadre body increases the negative impacts of social and administrative expenditure on the provincial economy. Since the tax sharing system reforms of 1994, the negative effects of rejuventation of the cadre body have been especially significant, while the positive effects of a knowledge-based cadre body have been strengthened; this is similar to the results for the overall expenditure. Taking into consideration that economic expenditure is an important means for regional offiicals for the pursuit of regional self-interest and promote rapid short-term economic growth, the results obtained are consistent with the intuited expectations: extended office term and central appointment history strengthens the motivations for short-term interests in regional governments, significantly increasing the negative effects of economic expenditure on provincial economic stability; this also provides good empirical support for the argument in Proposition 3. On the other hand, extended term of office and central appointment history also helps to increase the positive effects of admistrative expenditure on national and especially provincial economic stability. Overall, then, the negative effects of terms of office mainly occured during the fiscal contract system period, and since 1994, with the gradual establishment of the exchange system for officials, the effects of central appointment history have been relatively positive.

Optimizing Size and Structure of Regional Governments for Promoting Economic Stability

China's macroeconomy has for a long time continuously exhibited relatively large fluctuations. It should be noted, however, that under a multi-tier government framework, macroeconomic stability is at its core a collective behavior problem, dependent on the balance of conflicts between national interests and regional self-interests; existing research in general, however, seems to have neglected this important point. Furthermore, the analysis in the previous section shows that, from the perspective of economic stability, it is the current dynamics of the size and structure of regional governments that has a significantly negative impact on the country's macroeconomic stability. It is thus insufficient to attribute the cause of the problems simply to overspending or underspending in the size of expenditure or in certain specific types of expenditure, but also to discover whether the dynamic changes in expenditure as well as in the various types of expenditure actually helps to satisfy the demands of a stable economy (i.e. whether the changes are contradirectional to periodic fluctuations).

To account for this here, provincial data is used as a basis for analysis on the mechanism of balance of conflicts of national and regional interests, formed from China's unique fiscal decentralization and regional governance system, and its impact on the periodic features of the expenditure behavior of regional governments as well as provincial and national economic stability, within a relatively unified framework of analysis. The results are given in Table 7.9.

Table 7.9(a) Provincial and national periodic features in total provincial expenditure and the effects of fiscal decentralization and governance

	National periodic features			Provincial periodic features		
	1997–2009 (Counter)	1979–1993 (Pro)	1994–2006 (Counter)	1997–2009 (Pro)	1979–1993 (Pro)	1994–2006 (Pro)
Fiscal revenue decentralization	0.65***	0.38***	0.27***	0.28	-0.06	0.16
Fiscal expenditure decentralization	0.98***	-0.89***	0.33***	0.52*	0.62*	-0.06
Age of officials	-0.05	0.43**	-0.01	-0.23	-0.24	0.16
Tertiary education level (Dummy variables)	0.35	-0.18	-0.56***	-0.11	-0.24	-0.33*
Term of office	-0.24	-1.04***	-0.16	-0.28	0.14	-0.31
Central appointment history (Dummy variables)	0.04	-0.45***	0.03	-0.25	-0.23	-0.35*

Table 7.9(b) Provincial and national periodic features in provincial economic expenditure and the effects of fiscal decentralization and governance

	National periodic features			Provincial periodic features		
	1997–2009 (Counter)	1979–1993 (Pro)	1994–2006 (Counter)	1997–2009 (Pro)	1979–1993 (Pro)	1994–2006 (Unclear)
Fiscal revenue decentralization	0.28	-0.06	0.16	0.61***	0.24***	0.08
Fiscal expenditure decentralization	0.52*	0.62*	-0.06	-0.56**	-0.58***	0.35
Age of officials	-0.23	-0.24	0.16	0.34**	-0.03	-0.53***
Tertiary education level (Dummy variables)	-0.11	-0.24	-0.33*	0.45***	0.04	-0.26
Term of office	-0.28	0.14	-0.31	-0.27	0.38**	0.04
Central appointment history (Dummy variables)	-0.25	-0.23	-0.35*	-0.84***	0.16	-0.45**

Table 7.9(c) Provincial and national periodic features in provincial social expenditure and the effects of fiscal decentralization and governance

	National periodic features			Provincial periodic features		
	1997–2009 (Counter)	1979–1993 (Counter)	1994–2006 (Counter)	1997–2009 (Pro)	1979–1993 (Pro)	1994–2006 (Unclear)
Fiscal revenue decentralization	-0.69***	-0.67***	0.52*	0.61***	0.24***	0.08
Fiscal expenditure decentralization	0.47*	0.44**	-0.15	-0.56**	-0.58***	0.35
Age of officials	-0.37**	0.49***	-0.26*	0.34**	-0.03	-0.53***
Tertiary education level (Dummy variables)	-0.16	0.13	-0.36**	0.45***	0.04	-0.26
Term of office	-0.05	0.14	-0.21	-0.27	0.38**	0.04
Central appointment history (Dummy variables)	0.10	-0.20	-0.21	-0.84***	0.16	-0.45**

Table 7.9(d) Provincial and national periodic features in provincial administrative expenditure and the effects of fiscal decentralization and governance

	National periodic features			Provincial periodic features		
	1997–2009 (Counter)	1979–1993 (Counter)	1994–2006 (Counter)	1997–2009 (Pro)	1979–1993 (Pro)	1994–2006 (Unclear)
Fiscal revenue decentralization	-0.16	-0.14	0.26	0.22	-0.38*	0.26
Fiscal expenditure decentralization	-0.69**	1.09***	0.12	-1.57***	1.11***	0.04
Age of officials	-0.49***	0.79***	-0.47***	-0.38**	-0.36	-0.48***
Tertiary education level (Dummy variables)	0.04	0.46***	-0.13	0.37*	0.56**	-0.05
Term of office	-1.22***	-1.34***	-0.33	-1.77***	-0.02	0.22
Central appointment history (Dummy variables)	-0.18	-0.88***	-0.30	-0.41**	0.90**	-0.53**

Note: *, ** and *** indicate regression coefficients significantly above confidence levels of 10%, 5% and 1% respectively.

It can thus be seen that the inadequacies in the dynamics of the size and structure of regional governments may be considered in the following four areas:

1. The expenditure behavior of regional governments exhibit in general relatively significant national countercyclical and provincial procyclical features, and while this helps in maintaining national economic stability, it also contributes to provincial economic fluctuations, and this effect is even more prominently exhibited in underdeveloped provinces.
2. Misplacement of fiscal power and administrative authority causes fiscal decentralization to have a significantly assymetrical effect on periodic features in the expenditure behavior of regional governments. Fiscal expenditure decentralization weakens the national countercyclical features and strengthens the provincial procyclical features, which does not favor provincial and national economic stability; fiscal revenue decentralization has a relatively weaker negative impact on national countercyclical features, while its impact on provincial procyclical features are rather unclear.
3. Changes in the governance system also have a significant impact on the periodic features in the expenditure behavior of regional governments. A

younger and knowledge-based cadre body helps to restrain the provincial procyclical features in expenditure behavior, while extended office term and central appointment history have the opposite effect; but the effects of these factors on national countercyclical features are rather unclear.

4. Economic, social, and administrative expenditures of regional governments all exhibit different provincial and national periodic features, resulting in different impacts on provincial and national economic stability, with fiscal decentralization and governance also being major factors affecting this.

From the perspective of promoting macroeconomic stability in the country, then, the key in optimizing the dynamics of the size and structure of regional governments lies in how to effectively manage the mechanisms of incentives and restraints for regional governments, in order to encourage expenditure behavior that satisfies the demands of economic stability:

- The central government should ensure its own awareness of the existence of strong regional self-interests in regional governments under its institution of fiscal and political incentives; while the incentives has helped to regulate activeness in regional governments in realizing rapid economic growth, it has also brought negative effects such as macroeconomic fluctuations. Thus, the central government should consider taking into account regional self-interests while proceeding with reforms in the financial and administration system, so as to allow regional governments to focus attention on the macroeconomy and better protect national interests.
- The central government should also ensure its own awareness of the negative effects from the misplacement of fiscal powers and administrative authority. In the process of drawing up financial system reforms, it should look to ensure that there is sufficient fiscal powers while moderating excess administrative authority, so as to allow fiscal powers and administrative authority to be properly matched in the division of responsibilities. At the same time, it should also implement measures to fully incorporate extrabudgetary capital into the budget, in order to expunge the negative effects of extrabudgetary capital on macroeconomic stability.
- Central and regional governments should all actively contribute to improving the country's human resource institution. In the short-term, it is understandably difficult to fundamentally change the core criterion of growth numbers in the cadre evaluation system, so it becomes even more imperative to promote rationality in pursuing development, encouraging regional governments to adopt the 'right' mindset with regards to pursuing political achievements, in order to avoid negative effects of behavior of regional governments that are unfavorable for economic stability.

- In actively promoting reforms in the cadre institution, interregional exchange of officials, and establishing the term of office system, the central government should keep an eye on the current governance system, especially in how it negatively affects rationality in the behavior of regional governments. It should also consider to gradually introduce a system of external supervision, in order to reinforce political responsibility in regional governments, and fundamentally correct the short-termist behavior in regional governments.

Finally, it should be noted that this chapter has kept its focus of analysis as the periodic features in the expenditure behavior of regional governments and its institutional causes. In the real economy, regional governments may also utilize relatively unobservable irregularities such as land leasing, tax breaks incentives and credit intervention to pursue regional self-interest, thus negatively affecting the stability of the provincial and, by extension, national economies. If it should come to pass that relevant and comprehensive data can be obtained, then an in-depth analysis on the periodic features of the abovementioned irregularities in the behavior of regional governments, under the necessity of balancing the conflicts of regional and national interests, and its effects on provincial and national economic stability, shall make a very valuable contribution to existing research.

Summary

Using provincial data since the start of the Chinese Economic Reform, this chapter first used a multi-dynamic-factor model to examine the co-movements between regional fiscal expenditure as well as various expenditure types, and the periodic fluctuations in the provincial, regional and national economies, demonstrating the periodic features in the expenditure behavior of regional governments and their effects on macroeconomic stability; next, a spatial econometrics model was used to examine the impacts of fiscal decentralization and regional governance on the periodic features in the expenditure behavior of regional governments and the economic stabilizing effect of the size and structure of regional governments; lastly, there was a brief exploration on optimization measures for the dynamics of the size and structure of regional governments that would help promote the country's macroeconomic stability.

The analysis in this chapter has shown the following:

- Since the start of the Chinese Economic Reform, provincial fiscal expenditure has in general exhibited relatively significant national countercyclical and provincial procyclical features, which is favorable for national economic stability but aggravates provincial economic fluctuations, and this is especially prominent in underdeveloped provinces. Viewing the situation through particular sub-periods gives a more detailed picture: in the fiscal contracting system era, provincial fiscal expenditure exhibits relatively strong national and provincial procyclical features, and post-1994 tax sharing reforms era, national countercyclical features strengthened, while provincial procyclical features were still exhibited but were relatively weaker;

- Misplacement of fiscal powers and administrative authority causes fiscal decentralization to have significant and asymmetric effects on the periodic features in the expenditure behavior of regional governments: fiscal expenditure decentralization weakens national countercyclical features and aggravates provincial procyclical features, which does not favor provincial and national economic stability, while fiscal revenue decentralization has a relatively weaker effect on national countercyclical features and rather unclear effects on provincial procyclical features;
- The governance system also has a significant impact on the periodic features in the expenditure behavior of regional governments: a younger and knowledge-based cadre body helps to restrain provincial procyclical features, while extended term of office and central appointment history have the opposite effects, and in general these factors have rather unclear effects on national countercyclical features;
- Economic, social, and administrative expenditure exhibit different provincial and national periodic features, thus having different impacts on provincial and national economic stability, with fiscal decentralization and governance being major factors affecting this.

From the perspective of economic stability, then, it may be seen that there are significant deficiencies in the expenditure behavior of regional governments, which demonstrates the existence of the same deficiencies in the size and structure of regional governments, and that fiscal decentralization and regional governance are major factors in this problem. Thus, China's government should look at measures for improving the mechanisms of incentives and constraints on regional governments, and encourage regional governments to focus attention on the broader regional and national interests, making necessary adjustments in fiscal expenditure policies according to the dynamic changes in the economy, so as to realize optimization in the size and structure of regional governments that promotes the country's macroeconomic stability.

8

Chapter

Optimization of the Size and Structure of Regional Governments from the Perspective of Income Distribution

Chapters 6 and 7 explored the optimization of the size and structure of regional governments from the perspectives of economic growth and stability. This chapter will continue the exercise from the perspective of income distribution, exploring, on the basis of the effects of size and structure of regional governments on income distribution, optimization measures that would promote equitable income distribution.

In studying the effects of size and structure of regional governments on income distribution, census microdata obtained from the China Health and Nutrition Survey (CHNS) was first used as a basis for calculating the Gini coefficient of residents' income in Liaoning and other provinces, for the period between 1989 to 2006. Panel data model and broad torque estimation methods (GMM) were then used to examine the effects of size and structure of regional governments on income distribution disparity in the population.

Special attention is paid to the fact that a major factor affecting individual income and, by extention, income distribution disparity, is the individual's level of education.[1] China's public education policies has been receiving increasing attention in recent years, as both government and civilians come to view education as integral in reducing income distribution disparity. (Basic and vocational education remains the responsibility of regional governments, and there is an increasing directive to move higher education into a mode where teaching responsibilities are tasked to the regional government, while management will be handled hierarchically from central authorities to regional governments.) Given this present and future prominent role of regional government in public education, as a major factor affecting income and distribution disparity, this chapter will devote a section to examine regional public education policies, focusing on the size and structure of the regional government's public education budget, and the effect that admission policy for higher education has on the premium of human capital (i.e. wage differences based on different education levels), in order to provide a more accurate analysis of the effect of size and structure of regional governments on income distribution.

Effect of Size and Structure of Regional Governments on Income Distribution

In the decades since the implementation of the Chinese Economic Reform, China's economic growth has taken the world by storm. At the same time, however, the income distribution disparity of residents continues to grow, fostering increasing social unrest. This not only presents challenges for maintaining social justice, but also threatens to undermine the long-term stability of the entire country. Thus, reducing the income disparity of residents and realising social justice has become a major challenge facing China's government and academia.

There are complex reasons for the increasingly alarming situation of income disparity in China. To a certain extent, market-oriented reforms (including the restructuring of the ownership system, the reform of the wage system etc.) and the "extensive mode" of economic growth have contributed to the problem, but it could be argued that the root of the problem lies with the country's reform of the financial and taxation systems.[2] Effective reversal of the growth in income disparity of residents, then, will involve complex systematic engineering to optimize the structure of the regional governments, such that multiple public policies can be well-coordinated to produce the intended effects.

Fiscal policies will no doubt play a vital role: it has already been shown that progressive income tax and public expenditure on policies benefiting vulnerable groups are effective at narrowing the income gap of residents.[3] Still, this role is limited by the fact that indirect tax, rather than progressive income tax, forms the bulk of China's tax system; this is something that is difficult to conduct reform on, even in the distant future.[4] Therefore, optimizing the structure of fiscal expenditure and increasing the public expenditure on policies benefiting low-income groups is, at the current stage, a strategically important choice to improve the income disparity situation in China.

Of course, whether this choice will achieve its expected results still depends, to a large extent, on how far regional governments would go to administer fiscal policies benefiting low-income groups, especially since regional governments are at the moment shouldering over 70% of the national expenditure.[5] Thus, this section aims to provide in-depth analysis of the history of public expenditure behavior of regional governments, as well as how this behavior affects the income distribution of residents, in the hope of contributing to a better understanding of the role that fiscal policies can play in promoting income distribution justice for residents.

In fact, China's academics have long been aware of the significance of this question. Thus far, however, the studies that have been conducted have limited their scope to how the public expenditure behavior of regional governments affects the income disparity between urban and rural communities; they lack a comprehensive systematic analysis of the effects on income distribution for residents.[6]

For example, Lu and Chen studied panel data of provinces for the period 1987 to 2001 to examine the effect of public expenditure behavior of regional governments on the income disparity between urban and rural communities, and found that increase in financial support for agriculture and rural infrastructure reduces the income disparity, whereas increase in public funding for education, sciences, culture and health increases the income disparity.[7] Li and Shen studied how the fiscal structure of regional governments affects the relative wealth between urban and rural communities, and found that expenditure on social security helps to reduce the relative difference between the wealth of urban and rural communities, while funding for educational and healthcare infrastructure has had negligible effects.[8] Tao and Liu studied panel data of 270 prefecture-level cities for the period 1994 to 2003, and found serious bias in the expenditure behavior of regional governments towards urban communities, which increases the income disparity between the urban and rural populations; fiscal decentralization, on the other hand, was found to help relieve the negative impact that expenditure behavior of regional governments exert on the income disparity.[9]

For the analysis in this section, census data from the China Health and Nutrition Survey (CHNS) is used to calculate the Gini coefficient of the income of provincial residents in general (Fig. 8.1a), the income of urban residents (Fig. 8.1b), the income of rural residents (Fig. 8.1c), and the comparative ratio of income between urban and rural residents (Fig. 8.2). These are then used along with broad torque estimation methods to examine: one, the general and structural effects that the size and structure of the expenditure of regional governments has on the income distribution of residents; two, the constraining influence of fiscal decentralization on these effects.

Evolutionary trend of income distribution disparity in the regional population

Methodology

Following the methodology used in past studies, Gini coefficients are used to measure the income distribution disparity in the regional population. This requires a relatively large and complete sample of multi-provincial microdata, which can often be unavailable for developing nations. The CHNS database, however, allows us to overcome this difficulty. It provides household census data for 9 provinces, namely Liaoning, Heilongjiang, Jiangsu, Shandong, Henan, Hubei, Hunan, Guangxi and Guizhou, for the years of 1989, 1991, 1993, 1997, 2000, 2004, and 2006. The data covers around 4000 rural and urban families, numbering more than 13,000 individuals, along with relatively detailed data on household income, making it a suitable database for obtaining the Gini coefficient of the income of the regional population.[10]

The Gini coefficients are obtained as follows: first, the household income per capita is converted to actual values using the Consumer Price Index (CPI), with

2006 as the base period. This is then weighted with the size of the household, and finally the coefficients are calculated using the formula proposed by Whitehouse (1995).[11] Additionally, the Gini coefficients of the income of urban residents, the income of rural residents, and the comparative ratio of income between urban and rural residents were calculated, in order to better show the distribution structure of the income in the regional population.

Results

The basic statistical calculations are given in Table 8.1. Figure 8.1 shows the Gini coefficients as kernel density graphs, and Figure 8.2 also shows the ratio of income between urban and rural populations as a kernel density graph.

Table 8.1 Statistical description of Gini coefficient for income of regional population

Variables	Sample size	Mean value	Standard devation	Smallest value	Largest value
Overall Gini coefficient of regional population	59	0.42	0.06	0.30	0.56
Gini coefficient of income of urban residents	59	0.37	0.08	0.19	0.58
Gini coefficient of income of rural residents	59	0.43	0.06	0.33	0.55
Income ratio between urban and rural population	54	2.56	0.59	1.66	4.25

As shown in Table 8.1, the mean Gini coefficient of the sample regional population is 0.42, indicating a very significant disparity in income distribution in the regional population. The smallest value obtained, indicating relatively narrow disparity, is 0.3 for Liaoning province in 1991, and the largest value, indicating relatively wide disparity, is 0.56 for Henan province in 2006.

It can further be seen from Fig. 8.1(a) that, from the late 1980s to the late 1990s, there was a significant decrease in income disparity in the regional population, and data across different provinces returned close coefficient levels. This can be seen by the significant shift in the curve representing the Gini coefficient data of the regional population in 1997 to the left of the curve for the data in 1989, along with higher density in smaller Gini coefficient numbers. Thereafter, the income distribution situation in the regional population has steadily deteriorated, with the curve for the data in 2000 and 2006 shifting dramatically to the right, along with

Fig. 8.1(a) Overall Gini coefficient of income of regional population (Epanechnikov kernel)

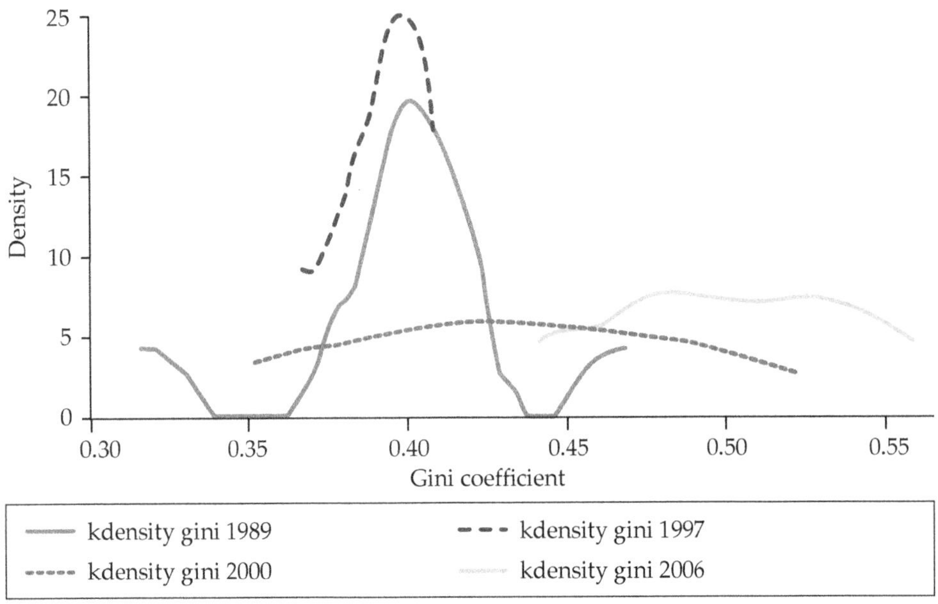

Fig. 8.1(b) Gini coefficient of income of urban population (Epanechnikov kernel)

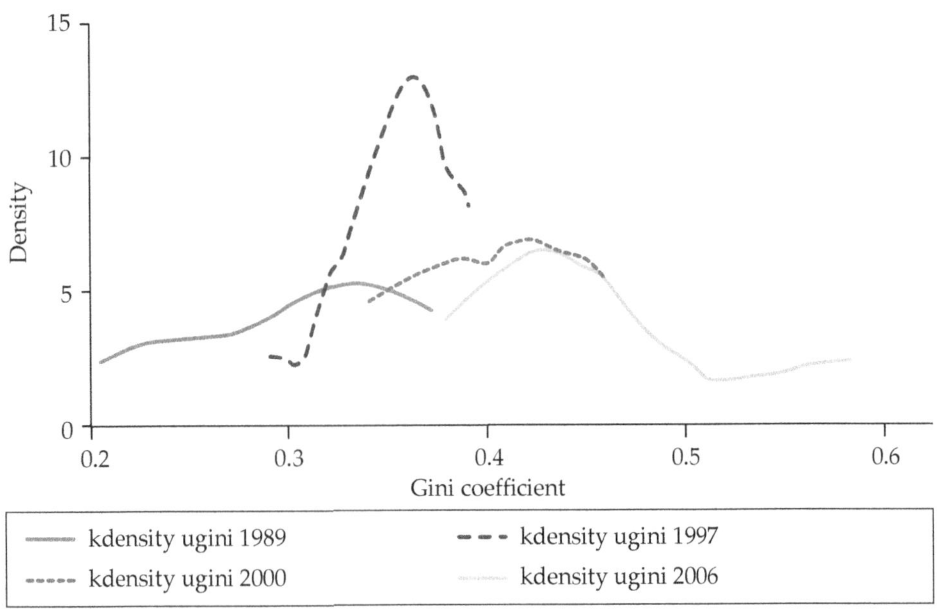

Fig. 8.1(c) Gini coefficient of income of rural population (Epanechnikov kernel)

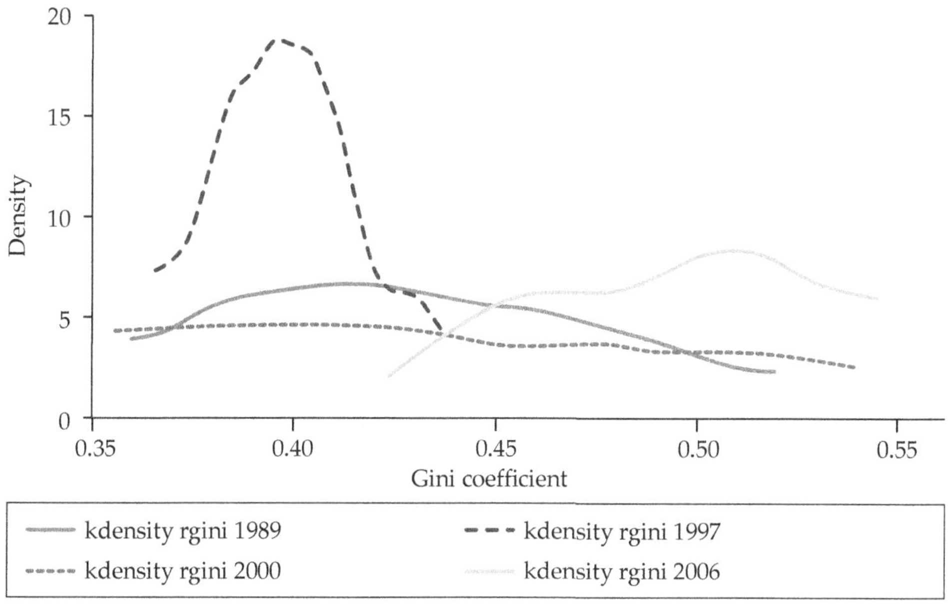

Fig. 8.2 Ratio of income between urban and rural populations

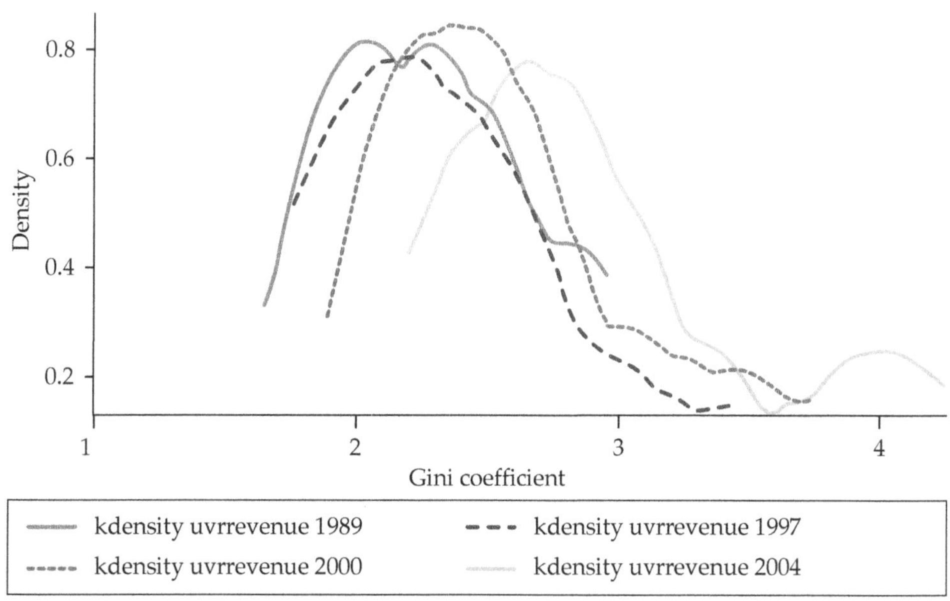

low density in smaller Gini coefficient numbers and relatively higher density in larger Gini coefficient numbers.[12]

Income distribution disparity is wider in the rural population than the urban population, with the mean Gini coefficient of the sample data being 0.43 for the rural population and 0.37 for the urban population (Table 8.1). Income disparity is high between the urban and the rural populations, with the per capita income of the urban population being 2.56 times that of the rural population. Interestingly, though, the income distribution situation for the urban population shows greater variation across different provinces compared to the rural population (variance for the Gini coefficient of urban population is 0.21 and that of the rural population is 0.14).

For the period in which the sample data was collected, income disparity in the urban population and income disparity between the urban and rural populations continued to widen, as shown by the shift of the curves for the respective data to the right [Fig. 8.1(b) and Fig 8.2]. Income disparity in the rural population, on the other hand, showed consistency with the income disparity in the entire regional population: significantly narrowing in the data year of 1989, and rapidly widening after 1997 [Fig. 8.1(a) and (c)].

The analysis in this segment shows that the income distribution situation in China's regional population was, on the whole, stable through the 1990s, but the turn of the century has seen a continued deterioration in the situation, with problems in income distribution most conspicuous in the rural population. What, then, is the role played by regional governments, and just how far does the expenditure behavior of regional governments affect, generally and structurally, the income distribution of the regional population? These are crucial questions that the next segment will attempt to answer, and from there, find out the problems concerning the size and structure of regional governments and their systematic causes, and explore possible reform proposals.

Effect of size and structure of the expenditure of regional governments on income distribution of residents

This segment will use IV-2SLS and HAC-GMM to examine specifically the general and structural effects that size and scale of expenditure of regional governments has on the income disparity of the regional population.[13]

Model framework

Given the vast expanse of China's country, the geographical environment, natural resources and local customs differ vastly amongst different provinces. It is difficult to measure the extent to which these environmental factors affect the income distribution situation of the regional populations. Politically, conflicting policies such as wage system reform and changes in central policy regarding distribution will also impact income distribution. With that in mind, the following formula is adopted as the fixed effects model for panel data:

$$Gini_{it} = \beta Lge_{it} + \delta Z_{it} + f_i + f_t + \varepsilon_{it} \tag{8.1}$$

Of which, $Gini_{it}$ is the explained variable, taking into consideration the distribution structures, i.e. the three Gini coefficients and the income ratio obtained in the previous segment. Lge_{it} is the core explanatory variable, taking into consideration both the size of the expenditure of regional governments (measured as the ratio between provincial fiscal expenditure and GDP), and its structure, measured as economic (infrastructure, support for agriculture, forestry and fisheries), social (welfare, education, culture, science and health), and administrative expenditure.[14] Z_{it} is the controlled variable, f_i is the entity fixed effects, intended to account for variations caused by environmental factors, f_t is the temporal fixed effects, intended to account for effects caused by conflicting policies. ε_{it} is the error term.

For the controlled variable Z_{it}, the following considerations are made based on available literature and the current situation in China: (1) Fiscal revenue ratio (i.e. the ratio between provincial fiscal revenue and GDP), used to measure the effect fiscal burden has on income distribution; (2) Economic development level, measured as actual mean GDP (using 1978 as the base period); (3) Degree of economic openness, measured as the ratio between the total value of provincial imports and exports, and GDP; (4) Physical capital investment ratio (i.e. the ratio between physical capital investment and GDP), used to measure the effects of accumulation of physical capital; (5) Labor force variables, measured as the ratio between the size of the provincial workforce and the total provincial population, for the effects that labor market performance has on income distribution; (6) Level of urbanization, measured as the ratio of urban population number to the total population number in the regional population, for the effects that the urbanization process has on income distribution. Natural logarithms are used for the above variables in order to offset potential heteroscedasticity problems.

Effects on the general regional population

The effects that size and structure of the expenditure of regional governments have on the income distribution of the regional population in general are given in Table

8.2, using the overall Gini coefficient of the income of regional populations as the explained variable. Models 1a and 1b gives the estimated results of the fixed effects models. Models 2a and 2b gives the estimated results of IV-2SLS, setting fiscal revenue ratio and economic development level as endogenous variables, and their one-phase lagged values as instrumental variables.[15] Additionally, the estimated results of HAC-GMM are given in Models 3a and 3b, to account for potential heteroscedasticity and autocorrelation problems, since the Gini coefficients were calculated from microdata.

Table 8.2 Effects of size and structure of expenditure of regional governments on the income distribution in the general regional population

Explanatory variable: Overall Gini coefficient of the income of regional populations						
Explained variable	Model 1a (Fixed effects)	Model 1b (Fixed effects)	Model 2a (IV-2SLS)	Model 2b (IV-2SLS)	Model 3a (HAC-GMM)	Model 3b (HAC-GMM)
Constant term	-3.332 (1.24)**	-5.980 (1.56)***	—	—	—	—
Fiscal expenditure ratio	0.175 (0.12)	—	0.178 (0.11)	—	0.243 (0.10)**	—
Economic expenditure proportion	—	0.232 (0.09)**	—	0.213 (0.09)**	—	0.236 (0.09)**
Administrative expenditure proportion	—	0.136 (0.09)	—	0.135 (0.09)	—	0.088 (0.08)
Social expenditure proportion	—	0.138 (0.26)	—	0.181 (0.17)	—	0.187 (0.14)
Fiscal revenue ratio	0.034 (0.08)	0.108 (0.11)	0.034 (0.08)	0.146 (0.09)	-0.005 (0.07)	0.102 (0.09)
Economic development level	0.148 (0.09)	0.224 (0.11)**	0.143 (0.08)*	0.246 (0.09)***	0.107 (0.07)	0.216 (0.08)**
Economic openness level	-0.074 (0.05)	-0.063 (0.09)	-0.072 (0.05)	-0.078 (0.07)	-0.067 (0.04)	-0.071 (0.07)
Physical capital investment ratio	0.019 (0.05)	0.053 (0.07)	0.026 (0.08)	0.044 (0.08)	0.053 (0.07)	0.047 (0.08)
Labor force variables	0.258 (0.30)	0.459 (0.20)**	0.264 (0.22)	0.458 (0.16)***	0.333 (0.21)	0.421 (0.15)***

Table 8.2 Effects of size and structure of expenditure of regional governments on the income distribution in the general regional population

(Cont'd)

Explanatory variable: Overall Gini coefficient of the income of regional populations						
Explained variable	Model 1a (Fixed effects)	Model 1b (Fixed effects)	Model 2a (IV-2SLS)	Model 2b (IV-2SLS)	Model 3a (HAC-GMM)	Model 3b (HAC-GMM)
Urbanization level	-0.005 (0.06)	-0.003 (0.05)	-0.003 (0.05)	0.004 (0.06)	0.004 (0.05)	0.037 (0.05)
Hansen over-identification test	—	—	2.07	7.45	2.07	7.45
Effective sample size	50	42	50	42	50	42
R^2	0.36	0.14	0.52	0.69	0.51	0.69

Notes: (1) *, ** and *** indicate regression coefficients significantly above confidence levels of 10%, 5% and 1% respectively.
(2) "—" means that the relevant variable does not exist in the model.
(3) Bracketed values in Model 3 are robust standard deviations.
(4) For reasons of space, the first steps of regression analysis are not shown.

Comparing Models 1 and 2, after accounting for potential estimation bias caused by endogenous variables, the estimated results of the models showed significant differences. Accounting for potential heteroscedasticity and autocorrelation problems (Model 3) also show significant differences in estimated results. The results of the Hansen over-identification test show the model settings to be acceptable, thus Model 3 is accepted as the settings for the analysis.

From Model 3a, it can be seen that the effect of fiscal expenditure ratio on the overall Gini coefficient of the income of regional populations is significantly positive (0.243), showing that increase in the size of expenditure of regional governments also increases the income distribution gap in the regional population. This could be due to the relatively stronger emphasis that regional governments place in promoting economic efficiency and growth, lowering the priority for concerns of distributional justice.[16] Moreover, relative to low income groups, high income groups wield more economic and political influence, such that regional governments are more inclined to consider policy decisions benefitting the interests of high income groups, inevitably compromising those of low income groups wherever there is clash of interests between the two groups, contributing to the widening of the income gap in the regional population.

As to the effect of the structure of expenditure on the general regional population, it can be seen from Model 3b that the regression coefficient for the proportion of economic expenditure is positive and statistically significant, showing that increase in the proportion of economic expenditure significantly widens the income gap. Of course, since regional governments rely on economic expenditure to help achieve rapid economic growth, the goal-directed behavior of its economic expenditure would be more pronounced, further benefiting the interests of high income groups and widening the income distribution gap. In theory, economic expenditure includes expenditure on supporting agriculture, forestry and fisheries, which should help to enhance the income levels of the general rural population; but if the larger timescale is taken into account, then efforts spent in developing agriculture and rural infrastructure may still be considered as grossly inadequate, and that even expenditure behavior for agriculture, forestry and fisheries may be more beneficial to high income groups, the total effects of economic expenditure will be to contribute to the widening of income disparity in the regional population.

Increase in administrative expenditure shows negative effects in helping to reduce the income gap in the general regional population, although the effects are relatively less significant. This is consistent with our theoretical expectations.

For social expenditure, the regression coefficient value is positive but not statistically significant, showing that expenditure on areas such as welfare, education, and health has not of yet demonstrated any positive effects on income distributional justice in the regional population; this is also consistent with findings from previous studies.[17]

As for the controlled variables, it can be seen from Table 8.2 that the effect of size of fiscal revenue of regional governments on the regional population is unclear. Regression coefficient values of fiscal revenue ratio in Models 3a and 3b are negative and positive respectively, and are not statistically significant, showing that regional fiscal revenue policies have yet to perform their role in conditioning the income distribution of residents. Economic development level does not seem favorable for reducing the income gap, indicating that China's position in the Kuznets curve of income inequality may still be on the 'upwards' side.[18] Other factors indicate relative lack of statistical significance in their effects on the income distribution gap.

Effects on the distribution structure of the regional population

In order to examine the effects of size and structure of expenditure of regional governments on the distribution structure of the regional population, HAC-GMM is again used to examine the effects on the income disparity in the urban population, the income disparity in the regional population, and the income disparity between the urban and regional populations. Models 4a and 4b sets the Gini coefficient of income of the urban population as the explained variable, fiscal revenue ratio and economic development level as endogenous variables, and their one-phase lagged values as instrumental variables. Models 5a and 5b sets the Gini coefficient of income of the rural population as the explained variable, economic development level as the endogenous variable, and its one-phase lagged value as instrumental variable. Models 6a and 6b sets the income ratio between urban and rural populations as the explained variable, fiscal revenue ratio, economic development level and physical capital investment ratio as endogenous variables, and their one-phase lagged values as instrumental variables. The respective Hansen test results show that the model settings are generally acceptable.

Table 8.3 Effects of size and structure of expenditure of regional governments on the distribution structure of the regional population

	Gini coefficient of income of urban residents		Gini coefficient of income of rural residents		Ratio between income of urban and rural residents	
	Model 4a	Model 4b	Model 5a	Model 5b	Model 6a	Model 6b
Fiscal expenditure ratio	0.170 (0.17)	—	0.240 (0.10)**	—	-0.064 (0.11)	—
Economic expenditure proportion	—	0.377 (0.12)***	—	0.225 (0.10)**	—	0.096 (0.10)
Administrative expenditure proportion	—	0.031 (0.10)	—	0.177 (0.10)*	—	0.042 (0.10)
Social expenditure proportion	—	0.113 (0.23)	—	0.066 (0.17)	—	-0.002 (0.21)
Fiscal revenue ratio	-0.167 (0.15)	-0.077 (0.11)	0.018 (0.08)	0.054 (0.10)	0.277 (0.09)***	0.277 (0.08)***
Economic development level	0.199 (0.11)*	0.219 (0.11)**	0.040 (0.08)	0.140 (0.10)	0.277 (0.07)***	0.248 (0.09)***
Economic openness level	0.136 (0.06)**	0.133 (0.08)*	-0.082 (0.05)*	-0.070 (0.07)	0.000 (0.03)	-0.016 (0.05)
Physical capital investment ratio	-0.038 (0.13)	0.024 (0.13)	0.108 (0.09)	0.091 (0.10)	-0.043 (0.11)	-0.013 (0.13)
Labor force variables	0.236 (0.23)	0.422 (0.17)**	0.394 (0.24)	0.397 (0.21)*	0.182 (0.16)	0.215 (0.19)

Table 8.3 Effects of size and structure of expenditure of regional governments on the distribution structure of the regional population

(Cont'd)

	Gini coefficient of income of urban residents		Gini coefficient of income of rural residents		Ratio between income of urban and rural residents	
	Model 4a	Model 4b	Model 5a	Model 5b	Model 6a	Model 6b
Urbanization level	-0.043 (0.07)	-0.004 (0.05)	0.025 (0.06)	0.027 (0.06)	-0.098 (0.04)**	-0.072 (0.06)
Hansen over-identification test	6.89	5.52	3.06	8.86	2.98	5.29
Effective sample size	50	42	50	42	54	45
R^2	0.66	0.73	0.28	0.48	0.49	0.50

Notes: (1) *, ** and *** indicate regression coefficients significantly above confidence levels of 10%, 5% and 1% respectively.
(2) "—" means that the relevant variable does not exist in the model. Bracketed values in Model 3 are robust standard deviations.
(3) For reasons of space, the first steps of regression analysis are not shown.

From Table 8.3, it can be seen that effect of the size of the expenditure of regional governments is not significant for the income disparity in the urban population and between the urban and rural population, but it is significant for the income disparity in the rural population. This shows that the negative effects of the size of expenditure of regional governments comes mainly from its effects on the income disparity in the rural population.

Increase in the proportion of economic expenditure significantly increased the income disparity both in the urban population and the rural population, but has no significant effect on the income disparity between the urban and rural populations. This deviates from the findings in past studies,[19] and could merely be due to the limitations in this study (e.g. microdata from 9 provinces is not accurately representative of the nationwide condition, or that past studies had not properly accounted for endogeneity in the explanatory variables.)

Increase in the proportion of administrative expenditure significantly contributes to the widening of the income gap in the rural population, but shows little significant effect on the income gap in the urban population and between the urban and rural populations. Increase in the proportion of social expenditure does not show significant effect on the income gap in the urban population, the rural population and between the urban and rural populations. This is more or less in line with the examination of the effects on the income distribution in the general regional population.

The constraining influence of fiscal decentralization on the effects of size and structure of expenditure of regional governments on income distribution of residents

Having shown, in the above analysis, that the expenditure behavior of China's regional governments has in general negatively impacted the income disparity in the regional population, the next logical step in the inquiry is to find out the reasons causing the expenditure behavior to have such negative impacts on income disparity. An extensive volume of past studies attributes this to the country's fiscal decentralization reform, arguing that it has encouraged regional governments in overzealous pursuits of economic growth, driving goal-oriented expenditure behavior, and neglecting the question of distributional justice. Such a view, however, has not been supplemented with comprehensive analysis, with an obvious shortcoming being the failure to differentiate between the effects caused by the two different processes of fiscal revenue decentralization and fiscal expenditure decentralization. This segment thus uses the interaction term between fiscal decentralization and the size and structure of the expenditure of regional governments to examine the constraining influence that fiscal decentralization has on the effects of size and structure of the expenditure of regional governments on income distribution in the regional population.

The estimated results from HAC-GMM are given in Table 8.4.[20]

Table 8.4 Influence of fiscal decentralization on the effects of size and structure of expenditure of regional governments on income distribution in the regional population

Interaction term	Overall Gini coefficient		Gini coefficient of income of urban residents	
	Expenditure decentralization	Revenue decentralization	Expenditure decentralization	Revenue decentralization
Fiscal decentralization × fiscal expenditure ratio	0.010 (0.02)	0.109 (0.06)*	-0.076 (0.03)***	-0.079 (0.10)
Fiscal decentralization × economic expenditure proportion	-0.007 (0.03)	0.041 (0.08)***	0.022 (0.04)	0.790 (0.15)***
Fiscal decentralization × administrative expenditure proportion	0.002 (0.03)	-0.058 (0.13)	-0.027 (0.04)	-0.168 (0.15)
Fiscal decentralization × social expenditure proportion	0.066 (0.03)**	0.377 (0.13)***	0.104 (0.05)	1.047 (0.20)***

Table 8.4 Influence of fiscal decentralization on the effects of size and structure of expenditure of regional governments on income distribution in the regional population

(Cont'd)

Interaction term	Gini coefficient of income of rural residents		Ratio between income of urban and rural residents	
	Expenditure decentralization	Revenue decentralization	Expenditure decentralization	Revenue decentralization
Fiscal decentralization × fiscal expenditure ratio	0.010 (0.02)	0.109 (0.06)*	0.022 (0.03)	0.107 (0.07)
Fiscal decentralization × economic expenditure proportion	-0.007 (0.03)	0.041 (0.08)***	-0.009 (0.03)	0.380 (0.13)
Fiscal decentralization × administrative expenditure proportion	0.002 (0.03)	-0.058 (0.13)	0.006 (0.03)	-0.112 (0.18)
Fiscal decentralization × social expenditure proportion	0.066 (0.03)**	0.377 (0.13)***	0.057 (0.03)*	0.353 (0.18)*

From Table 8.4, it can be seen that fiscal decentralization exerts, in general, a significant influence on the effects to income distribution of residents from the size and structure of the expenditure of regional governments.

Fiscal expenditure decentralization not only significantly aggravates negative effects that the size of the expenditure of regional governments has on income distribution disparity in the regional population, but also: the negative effects that the proportion of economic expenditure has on income distribution disparity in the general regional population, the income distribution disparity in the urban population, and the income distribution disparity between urban and rural populations; as well as the negative effects that the proportion of social expenditure has on all four income distribution categories.

Granting more autonomy on fiscal revenue to regional governments mitigates the negative influence that size of the expenditure of regional governments has on income distribution in the urban population, and the negative influence that the proportion of economic expenditure has on the income disparity between urban and regional populations; but it also aggravates the negative influence that the proportion of social expenditure has on the income disparity in the general regional population, the income disparity in the rural population, and the income disparity between the urban and regional populations. However, fiscal revenue decentralization shows no significant influence on the knockdown effect to income distribution from the proportion of administrative expenditure.

It can thus be seen that fiscal revenue decentralization can, to a certain extent, correct the goal-directed expenditure behavior of China's regional governments, and mitigate its negative influence on the income distribution disparity in the regional population. Fiscal expenditure decentralization, on the other hand, aggravates the goal-directed expenditure behavior of regional governments. This difference may be attributed mainly to the widespread misplacement of power and financial authority, weakening the constraints on the budgets of regional governments, leading to a significant divergence between overzealous expenditure behavior and constraining mechanisms in regional governments.[21]

Effects of Size and Expenditure of Public Education Expenditure of Regional Governments on Premium of Human Capital

The previous section analysed in general the effects of size and structure of regional governments on the income distribution of residents. It has, however, been pointed out in many existing studies that public education expenditure is an important policy measure in helping to eliminate absolute poverty and promote income distribution justice. Education level has been shown to be a major factor causing wage difference and income disparity.[22] Both the government as well as the general public have thus directed more attention at increasing the efforts spent on public education and optimizing the structure of public education expenditure, in order to better promote income distribution justice.

As mentioned at the beginning of this chapter, regional governments are responsible for a large part of public education work, and this role is set to increase further in prominence in future with the gradual transition of the higher education system into a decentralized mode of teaching. This section aims to provide a comprehensive analysis on the effects that size and structure of public education expenditure of regional governments have on the premium of human capital (i.e. wage difference for different education levels). In addition, considering how regional governments put economic growth as priority in making policy decisions, such that public education policies are formulated based on the effects on economic growth and ultimately influence the effects of public education policies on income distribution, this section will also examine the effects of public education policies of regional governments on economic growth, in the hope of providing possible solutions for public education policies that balance economic growth and income distribution justice.

Currently, studies on public education policies focus on analyzing the mechanism of action for public education policies on economic growth and income distribution, through demonstrating the formation process of human capital, within the endogenous growth theory framework. Some of the studies find that increase in the size of public education expenditure not only contributes to economic growth, but also helps to reduce income disparity.[23] Other studies, however, are uncertain about such effects, arguing instead that it comes down to the internal allocation of public education resources. Lloyd-Ellis points out that allocating more educational resources to higher education will cause a "trickle-down" effect on career choices, but this is also negated by negative effects from the simultaneous decrease in the quality of basic education, leading to an increase in income disparity that does not favor economic growth.[24] Su also finds that the effect of public education resource allocation policies on economic growth and income distribution is correlated with the level of economic development, specifically that in developing countries, allocating more educational resources to basic education helps to reduce income disparity and promote economic growth.[25]

There are also extensive empirical studies on the effects of public education policies on economic growth, but most of these focus on the effects of the size of public education expenditure on economic growth, and differ widely in conclusions. Cullison and Barro and Sala-i-Martin found that expenditure on public education has a significant positive effect on economic growth,[26] but Easterly and Rebelo found, after examing panel data from 28 countries, that the effect of public education expenditure on economic growth is not significant.[27] Devarajan et al. examined panel data from 43 developing countries, concluding that public education expenditure has a significant constraining effect on economic growth;[28] Blankenau et al. used panel data from 23 developed countries and 57 developing countries, finding that public education expenditure has a robust effect in promoting economic growth in developed countries, but has no significant effect on the economic growth in developing countries.[29]

As for studies on the effects of public education policies on income distribution, these have mostly focused on examining the effects of public education policies on wage disparity in developed countries, such as that conducted by Fortin for states in the U.S., and there is a lack of studies conducted for developing countries.[30]

The analysis carried out in this section will examine the mechanism of effect on economic growth and income distribution for both the size and structure of public education expenditure as well as the size of admissions for higher education. The starting point for the analysis on income distribution will be human capital premium (i.e. wage difference based on education level). To clearly demonstrate the mechanism of effect, the analysis model of human capital premium will be divided into the two distinct phases of human capital accumulation, basic and higher education, and two additional factors will be taken into account. One, the mechanism of "championship" competition, which considers the requisite accumulation of human capital accumulation in the basic education phase in relation to the availability and competition for higher education resources. China's higher education resources remain scarce, and its demand far exceeds available resources, which means that access to higher education resources is granted based on examinations of academic ability, resulting in incredible stress during learning in the basic education phase. Two, the complementarity between the different types of labor force given by different education levels and the physical capital that is available. Krusell et al. points out that, due to the difference in levels and structure of knowledge in different educational levels, their value in the production process of economic activity will be significantly influenced by how they complement or compete with physical capital such as machinery automation (capital-skill complementarity effect), and this is a main factor in the formation of human capital premium.[31]

As mentioned, the prominent role played by regional governments in public education is set to grow even further, and so examining the perspective from provincial economics will be useful in revealing the effects of public education policies. The analysis will thus proceed to the perspective from provincial economics, using spatial econometrics and panel data models for empirical examination of the effect of public education policies of regional governments on economic growth and human capital premium.[32] This, though, brings statistical difficulties to the analysis: externalities to regional economic growth brought about by trade and labor movement between provinces, and the effects that economic growth and human capital premium has on the educational demands of residents that thus influence public education policies. To correct the biases to estimation results brought by such endogenous variables, this section will use a dynamic spatial panel model and a two-phased sectional panel data model for system GMM and instrumental variables.

This analysis will thus hopefully provide a comprehensive assessment of the effects of public education policies of China's regional governments, in order to reveal existing problems and future challenges facing policy makers.

Theoretical analysis

Model framework

As mentioned, the analysis model will be divided into the two distinct phases of human capital accumulation, basic and higher education, and will include the "championship" competition mechanism, the higher education resource-scarcity effect and the capital-skill complementarity effect, in order to show comprehensively the formation mechanism of human capital accumulation and human capital premium.[33]

Government

As the scale of "Minban" (private) education in China is relatively small, for the purposes of this analysis, it may be assumed that the government is responsible for all education, including both basic and higher education. Accordingly, public education expenditure is divided into basic education expenditure and higher education expenditure, and further assuming that the government finances public education expenditure through various linear taxes on production, the following may be derived:

$$G_{Bt+1} + G_{Ht+1} = (\theta_{Bt+1} + \theta_{Ht+1})\, G_{t+1} = \tau_t q_t \qquad (8.2)$$

Of which, G_{t+1}, G_{Bt+1}, and G_{Ht+1} are the public education expenditure per capita, public basic education, and public higher education expenditure per captia respectively. θ_{Bt+1} and θ_{Ht+1} are the proportion of public basic education and public higher education expenditure out of the overall public education expenditure respectively, such that θ_{Bt+1} and $\theta_{Ht+1} = 1$. q_t is the production per capita, τ_t is the linear tax rate, and their product is equivalent to the ratio of overall public education expenditure.

Enterprises

Enterprises are defined as fully competitive enterprises, using physical capital per capita (k_t) and human capital (h_t) for production. Economic labor is divided into high-skilled and low-skilled labor, with labor requiring only basic education levels as low-skilled labor, and labor requiring higher education levels as high-skilled labor.[34] The proportions for high-skilled and low-skilled labor out of the overall labor force is Θ_t and $1 - \Theta_t$ respectively, and the mean human capital is $\bar{h}_{Ht}$ and $\bar{h}_{Bt}$ respectively. Θ_t will be dependent on the size of higher education admission in the period $t - 1$. The capital-skill complementarity effect is introduced to demonstrate the difference between the values of high-skilled and low-skilled labor, using the following double function for CES production per capita:[35]

$$q_t = A\left\{\Phi_1[\Phi_2 k_t^{\alpha} + (1-\Phi_2)(\Theta_t \bar{h}_{Ht})^{\alpha}]^{\beta/\alpha} + (1-\Phi_1)[(1-\Theta_t)\bar{h}_{Bt}]^{\beta}\right\}^{1/\beta} \tag{8.3}$$

Of which, A is the technical parameter; $\Phi_1, \Phi_2 \in (0,1)$ are the parameters for shares of production from the two sets of labor and physical capital; $\alpha, \beta \in (-\infty,1)$ are the surrogate parameters, where $\beta > \alpha$ will indicate the existence of the capital-skill complementarity effect. Assuming optimal enterprise behavior, the following conditions are derived:

$$1 + r_t = A\Phi_1\Phi_2\left[\Phi_1\Omega^{\frac{\beta}{\alpha}} + (1-\Phi_1)[(1-\Theta_t)\bar{h}_{Bt}]^{\beta}\right]^{\frac{(1-\beta)}{\beta}} \Omega^{\frac{(\beta-\alpha)}{\alpha}} k_t^{\alpha-1} \tag{8.4}$$

$$W_{Ht} = A\Phi_1(1-\Phi_2)\left[\Phi_1\Omega^{\frac{\beta}{\alpha}} + (1-\Phi_1)[(1-\Theta_t)\bar{h}_{Bt}]^{\beta}\right]^{\frac{(1-\beta)}{\beta}} \Omega^{\frac{(\beta-\alpha)}{\alpha}} (\Theta_t \bar{h}_{Ht})^{\alpha-1} \tag{8.5}$$

$$W_{Bt} = A(1-\Phi_1)\left[\Phi_1\Omega^{\frac{\beta}{\alpha}} + (1-\Phi_1)[(1-\Theta_t)\bar{h}_{Bt}]^{\beta}\right]^{\frac{(1-\beta)}{\beta}} [(1-\Theta_t)\bar{h}_{Bt}]^{\beta-1} \tag{8.6}$$

Of which, $\Omega = [\Phi_2 k_t^{\alpha} + (1-\Phi_2)(\Theta_t h_{Ht})^{\alpha}]$ and are real interest rates; W_{Ht} and W_{Bt} are real efficiency wages for high-skilled and low-skilled labor force respectively. From (8.5) and (8.6), the difference in wage levels for labor forces of different education levels (i.e. human capital premium, ξ_t) can be expressed as:

$$\xi_t = \frac{W_{Ht}\bar{h}_{Ht}}{W_{Bt}\bar{h}_{Bt}} = \frac{\Phi_1(1-\Phi_2)}{(1-\Phi_1)}\left[\Phi_2\left(\frac{k_t}{\Theta_t \bar{h}_{Ht}}\right) + (1-\Phi_2)\right]^{\frac{(\beta-\alpha)}{\beta}} \left(\frac{(1-\Theta_t)}{\Theta_t}\right)^{1-\beta} \left(\frac{\bar{h}_{Ht}}{\bar{h}_{Bt}}\right)^{\beta} \tag{8.7}$$

From (8.7), it can be seen that human capital premium ξ_t is mainly affected by three factors: (1) Effect of relative supply (i.e. the proportion between the two sets of labor force, $(1-\Theta_t)/\Theta_t$). If $\partial\xi_t/\partial\left(\frac{1-\Theta_t}{\Theta_t}\right) > 0$, increase in the proportion of low-skilled labor will increase human capital premium levels; (2) Effect of relative efficiency (i.e. the effects of the proportion between the human capital of the two sets of labor force, $\bar{h}_{Ht}/\bar{h}_{Bt}$). When the elasticity of substitution for the two sets of labor force is larger than 1 (i.e. $\beta > 0$), increase in relative efficiency will increase human capital premium, and if it is smaller than 1, it will decrease human capital premium; (3) the capital-skill complementarity effect, $k_t/\Theta_t\bar{h}_{Ht}$. If $\partial\xi_t/\left(\frac{k_t}{\Theta_t h_{Ht}}\right)\partial > 0$, then increase in capital-skill complementarity will increase human capital premium.

Households

Assuming an N number of households in the economy, with each household comprising of an adult agent (parents) and a youth agent (children). Adult agents participate in inflexible labor force in order to receive income, and are responsible for economic decisions in the families. Youth agents participate in education to accumulate human capital, and have no responsibility for economic decisions. For convenience of analysis, population growth is not considered (i.e. N shall be the population number, or total labor force number, for every phase.) Families are divided into two sets, according to the education level of the adult agent: families where parents are in low-skilled labor force (total number as $(1 - \Theta_t)N$, represented as F_B), and families where parents are in high-skilled labor force (total number as $\Theta_t N$, represented as F_H).

Youth Agents

Assuming all youth agents participate in basic education, the human capital accumulation in this phase will largely be dependant on three factors: the human capital level of parents, h_t^i $(i = F_H, F_B)$; the expenditure by parents on the basic education of children, e_{Bt+1}^i; and the public basic education expenditure per capita, G_{Bt+1}.[36] As we have assumed that all youth agents undergo basic education, G_{Bt+1} will be equivalent to real public education expenditure per capita, measuring the quality of basic education provided. Additionally, considering that China's education resources is, in general, rather scarce, with crowding a common phenomenon across all schools and levels, $N^{1-\phi_B} G_{Bt+1}$ is introduced to account for the crowding effect in basic education, for which $\phi_B \in [0,1]$ is the factor of crowding, measuring the extent of crowding in basic education: $\phi_B = 0$ will mean that every student can receive equal service from the public basic education expenditure, while $\phi_B = 1$ will mean that every student can only enjoy a proportion of the service. Further assuming that human capital accumulation in the basic education phase follows the Cobb-Douglas function with constant size of returns, the following is derived:

$$h_{Bt+1}^i = B(h_t^i)^{\varepsilon}(e_{Bt+1}^i)^{\gamma}(N^{l-\phi B}G_{Bt+1})^{1-\varepsilon-\gamma},\ 0 < \varepsilon,\ \gamma,\ 1 - \varepsilon - \gamma < 1 \qquad (8.8)$$

Of which, h_{Bt+1}^i is the human capital accumulated by the youth agents through basic education; B is the technical parameter; ε, γ and $1 - \varepsilon - \gamma$ are the elasticity of human capital accumulation for h_t^i, e_{Bt+1}^i and G_{Bt+1} respectively.

Not all youth agents may advance to the higher education phase after completing the basic education phase. Scarcity of education resources means that youth agents must undergo admissions examinations, and the size of higher education admissions, Θ_{t+1}, depends mainly on public education policies. In other words, the size of higher education admissions is more due to the exogenous decision of policies, and less a result of the choice of economic agents. This directly triggers an extreme level of competition in basic education, with families of all levels of educations competing to ensure that their children may receive better education opportunities.[37] To demonstrate this, we introduce the "championship" competition model, dividing youth agents from the two sets of families as two groups of competitors, defining π_{t+1}^{i} ($i = F_B, F_H$) as the success probability for youth agents i to succeed in the competition (i.e. the probability for receiving higher education), such that $\Theta_t \pi_{t+1}^{F_H} + (1-\Theta_t)\pi_{t+1}^{F_B} = \Theta_{t+1}$. Additionally, assuming that admission to higher education depends solely on the results of the admissions examinations (in other words, the level of human capital accumulation in the basic education phase), the functions of success for the two groups of youth agents, $\pi_{t+1}^{F_H}$ and $\pi_{t+1}^{F_B}$, may be expressed as:

$$\pi_{t+1}^{F_H} = \frac{h_{Bt+1}^{F_H}\Theta_{t+1}}{\Theta_t h_{Bt+1}^{F_H} + (1-\Theta_t)h_{Bt+1}^{F_B}},\ \pi_{t+1}^{F_B} = \frac{h_{Bt+1}^{F_B}\Theta_{t+1}}{\Theta_t h_{Bt+1}^{F_H} + (1-\Theta_t)h_{Bt+1}^{F_B}} \tag{8.9}$$

From (8.9), it can be seen that increase in the size of higher education admissions Θ_{t+1}will help to increase the overall success probability of youth agents receiving higher education, and that under the conditions of Θ_{t+1}, the success probability for youth agents depends to a large extent on the proportion of the human capital investment input of different families, as well as the human capital level of parents. It can thus be seen that the admissions examinations, in neglecting family background disparity, contains inherent bias, such that the better the family background of the youth agents, the higher the chances of receiving higher education.

For the higher education phase, the human capital accumulation of youth agents are closely related to the education expenditure of parents on their children's higher education, e_{Ht+1}^{i}, and the public higher education expenditure per capita, G_{Ht+1}.[38] $(N^{1-\phi_H} G_{Ht+1})/\Theta_{t+1}^{\phi_H}$ is introduced in order to account for the crowding effect in higher education, with $\phi_H \in [0,1]$ as the crowding factor. In addition, considering that the knowledge accumulation of youth agents in the basic education phase directly affects their education efficiency in the higher education phase, we include the human capital accumulation of youth agents in the basic education phase, h_{Bt+1}^{i}, into the function for human capital accumulation in higher education. Assuming again that human capital accumulation in the higher education phase follows the Cobb-Douglas function with constant size of returns, we derive:

$$h_{Ht+1}^{i} = Z(h_{Bt+1}^{i})\,(e_{Ht+1}^{i})^{\eta}\left(\frac{N^{1-\phi_H} G_{Ht+1}}{\Theta_{t+1}^{\phi_H}}\right)^{1-\upsilon-\eta},\ 0<\upsilon,\ \eta,\ 1-\upsilon-\eta<1 \tag{8.10}$$

Of which, Z is the technical parameter for accumulation of human capital in higher education; υ, η, and $1 - \upsilon - \eta$ are the elasticity for human capital accumulation of h^i_{Bt+1}, e^i_{Ht+1}, and G_{Ht+1} respectively.

Adult Agents

Adult agents participate in inflexible labor force in their working period, with their take-home income given as $y^i_t = (1 - \tau_t)\, w_{it}\, h^i_t$.[39] The function of utility to the household is given as:

$$U(c^i_{it}, c^i_{2t}, h^i_{t+1}) = Ln\,(c^i_{1t}) + \mu_1 Ln\,(c^i_{2t}) + \mu_2 Ln\,(h^i_{t+1}) \tag{8.11}$$

Of which, c^i_{1t} and c^i_{2t} are the consumption expenditure of adult agents in their working phase and retirement phase respectively. $h^i_{t+1} = (1 - \pi^i_{t+1})\, h^i_{Bt+1} + \pi^i_{t+1} + h^i_{Ht+1}$ is the expected human capital level of youth agents, put into the utility function to capture the "altruism spirit" of parents,[40] μ_1 and μ_2 are the elasticity for marginal utilities of c^i_{2t} and h^i_{t+1} respectively. The budget constraints for adult agents in their working phase and retirement phase are given respectively as:

$$c^i_{1t} = y^i_t - (e^i_{Bt+1} + \pi^i_{t+1}\, e^i_{Ht+1}) - s^i_t \tag{8.12}$$

$$c^i_{2t} = (1 + r_{t+1}) s^i_t \tag{8.13}$$

Of which, s^i_t is the household savings. Under the constraints given in (8.12) and (8.13), adult agents choose e^i_{Bt}, e^i_{Ht}, and s^i_t in order to optimize utility, deriving optimal conditions as follows:

$$\frac{1}{c^i_{1t}} = \left[\frac{\mu_2(h^i_{Ht+1} - h^i_{Bt+1})}{(1 - \pi^i_{t+1})h^i_{Bt+1} + \pi^i_{t+1} + h^i_{Ht+1}} - \frac{e^i_{Ht+1}}{c^i_{1t}}\right]\frac{\partial \pi^i_{t+1}}{\partial e^i_{Bt+1}} + \frac{\mu_2 \gamma[(1 - \pi^i_{t+1})h^i_{Bt+1} + \upsilon\pi^i_{t+1} + h^i_{Ht+1}]}{[(1 - \pi^i_{t+1})h^i_{Bt+1} + \pi^i_{t+1} + h^i_{Ht+1}]e^i_{Bt+1}} \tag{8.14}$$

$$\frac{e^i_{Ht+1}}{c^i_{1t}} = \frac{\mu_2 \eta h^i_{Ht+1}}{[(1 - \pi^i_{t+1})h^i_{Bt+1} + \pi^i_{t+1} + h^i_{Ht+1}]} \tag{8.15}$$

$$\frac{c^i_{1t}}{c^i_{2t}} = \frac{1}{\mu_1(1 + r_{t+1})} \tag{8.16}$$

Market Balance

Market balance is given by the series of variables, from individual and enterprise optimal decision behavior and capital market balance conditions, of $\{e^i_{Bt+1}, e^i_{Ht+1}, s^i_t, k_t; w_{Bt}, w_{Ht}, r_t\}$, under conditions of exogenous variables in public education policies

$\{\tau_t, \theta_{Bt+1}, \Theta_{t+1}\}$. Of which, $\{e^i_{Bt+1}, e^i_{Ht+1}, s^i_t\}$ satisfies functions (8.14)–(8.16), $\{w_{Bt}, w_{Ht}, r_t\}$ satisfies (8.4)–(8.6), $\{k_t\}$ satisfies capital market balance conditions:

$$k_{t+1} = \Theta_t s_t^{F_H} + (1 - \Theta_t) s_t^{F_B} \tag{8.17}$$

The economic equilibrium growth rate can then be given as:

$$\Gamma_t = Ln\left(\frac{q_{t+1}}{q_t}\right) = \frac{1}{\beta} Ln\left(\frac{\Theta_1[\Theta_2 k_{t+1}^{\alpha} + (1-\Phi_2)(\Theta_{t+1}\bar{h}_{Ht+1})^{\alpha}]^{\beta/\alpha} + (1-\Phi_1)[(1-\Theta_{t+1})\bar{h}_{Bt+1}]^{\beta}}{\Phi_1[\Phi_2 k_t + (1-\Phi_2)(\Theta_t \bar{h}_{Ht})^{\alpha}]^{\beta/\alpha} + (1-\Phi_1)[(1-\Theta_t)\bar{h}_{Bt}]^{\beta}}\right) \tag{8.18}$$

Of which, $\bar{h}_{Bt+1} = \frac{\Theta_t(1-\pi_{t+1}^{F_H})h_{Bt+1}^{F_H} + (1-\Theta_t)(1-\pi_{t+1}^{F_B})h_{Bt+1}^{F_B}}{(1-\Theta_{t+1})}$ and $\bar{h}_{Ht+1} = \frac{[\Theta_t \pi_{t+1}^{F_H} h_{Ht+1}^{F_H} + (1-\Theta_t)\pi_{t+1}^{F_B} h_{Ht+1}^{F_B}]}{\Theta_{t+1}}$ gives the human capital level per capita of the t+1 generation's basic education and higher education.

Parameters

The theoretical model in this segment is relatively complex, so this segment will attempt to run simple numerical simulations by choosing appropriate model parameters from the sample economy, set as China's economy in the period since the 1990s, in order to demonstrate more directly the mechanism of effect for public education policies changes on economic growth and human capital premium.[41]

The model is constructed as two overlapping phases, and the length of each phase is assumed to be 30 years, i.e. the standard life expectancy is 90 years.[42] For parameter settings of macroeconomics and public education policies in the early stages of the phase, data for China's workforce number and the mean value of capital stock per capita labor force is taken as reference,[43] and the values of N and k_t are set as 70000 and 7646.8 respectively. Human capital is measured with the mean years of received education as measurement, and the valuations of human capital levels are set as 16 for high-skilled labor, $\bar{h}_{Ht}$, and 7.5 for low-skilled labor, $\bar{h}_{Bt}$.[44] With reference to data taken from the period since 1996 for the proportion of tertiary-education labor force out of the total labor force number, the percentage of national fiscal education expenditure out of GDP, and the proportion of national fiscal education expenditure for higher education out of national fiscal education expenditure, valuations for Θ_t, τ_t, and θ_{Bt+1} are set as 0.051, 0.025, and 0.8 respectively.

For the parameter settings of the utility function, discount factor μ_1 is set as 0.41, i.e. annual discount factor is 0.99, consistent with most studies; the "altruism spirit" factor μ_2 is set as 0.271.[45]

For the parameter settings of the production function, for surrogate parameters α and β, current studies give a range of values for the surrogate elasticity of physical capital and high-skilled labor, and the surrogate elasticity of physical capital and low-skilled labor at 0–1.2 and 0.5–3.0 respectively;[46] α and β may thus be set as -0.67 and 0.33 respectively, such that the surrogate elasticity values remain at a moderate level, i.e. 0.6 and 1.5 repectively, in order to clearly examine the effects from the changes in parameters. For shares parameters Φ_1 and Φ_2, valuations are used to allow model results to match with human capital premium and production shares of labor returns in the real-life economy; current studies on the return rates of higher education show that human capital premium levels are estimated to be between 1.1–1.5,[47] so a median valuation of 1.25 is used. For the production shares of labor force returns, the mean returns of employed persons in the urban population give a value of 0.66, although this estimation seems to be clearly high; the national economic accounting data since 1990 gives the proportion of labor returns out of the overall increase value at about 0.5. Thus, we take a value of 0.55, consistent with previous studies.[48] From the human capital premium valuation of 1.25 and labor returns valuation of 0.55, Φ_1 and Φ_2 can be set as 0.4724 and 0.9821 respectively. The technical parameter A will be the size parameter, set as 100, such that the mean annual real interest rate obtained is 0.105.[49]

Finally, there are the parameter settings for the human capital accumulation function. The parameter for human capital accumulation function in the basic education phase, ε, reflects the rate of intergenerational transformation of human capital in the household; present studies give estimated values of 0.2–0.4,[50] and this study will take a median value of 0.3 as benchmark setting. Since public basic education inputs G_{Bt+1} as real expenditure per capita, the elasticity of human capital accumulation of G_{Bt+1}, given as $1-\varepsilon-\gamma$, reflects the effects of basic education quality on human capital accumulation. Early estimation values are between 0.4–0.6, and recent estimation values are between 0.1–0.3.[51] Considering the stronger emphasis on education in China, education is clearly more important, and so $1-\varepsilon-\gamma$ is set as 0.4, such that that the elasticity of human capital accumulation from the household's investment in basic education, γ, is 0.3. For the crowding factor in basic education, ϕ_B, a median value of 0.5 is taken as benchmark value. For the human capital accumulation function in the higher education phase, it may be assumed that the education technology and environment for both higher education and basic education are the same, and robust testing will be performed. Thus, the elasticity of human capital accumulation for public higher education expenditure G_{Ht+1}, given as $1-\upsilon-\eta$, is set as 0.4, and the crowding factor for higher education, ϕ_H, is set as 0.5. Su takes the influence factor of basic education accumulation on higher education, υ, as 0.5, arguing that only human capital exceeding the requisite for higher education will be effective in higher education.[52] This is different from the treatment in this theoretical model, so benchmark value is taken 0.3, meaning that the elasticity of human capital accumulation from the parents' investment in children's higher education, η, is 0.3. For technical parameters of human capital accumulation in the basic education phase B and the higher education phase Z, a value of 1.0 is taken in order to ensure model results are consistent with real-world conditions.

Simulation results

Using the model parameters settings above, numerical simulation is performed in Matlab, and the results are given in Table 8.5.

Table 8.5 Average levels of main economic variables under changes in public education policies

		Benchmark value	τ=0.010	τ=0.050	τ=0.080	τ=0.10	θ_B=0.40	θ_B=0.60	θ_B=0.85
Θ_{t+1} = 0.010	Economic growth rate	6.076	5.172	6.647	7.026	7.191	6.055	6.151	5.987
	Human capital premium	2.110	2.093	2.102	2.094	2.090	5.442	3.501	1.700
	Higher education admission probability	0.983 (1.317)	0.983 (1.316)	0.983 (1.317)	0.983 (1.316)	0.983 (1.316)	0.983 (1.319)	0.983 (1.318)	0.983 (1.316)
Θ_{t+1} = 0.030	Economic growth rate	6.500	5.707	7.002	7.333	7.476	6.362	6.505	6.447
	Human capital premium	1.503	1.492	1.494	1.488	1.484	3.855	2.486	1.211
	Higher education admission probability	2.950 (3.932)	2.950 (3.931)	2.950 (3.931)	2.950 (3.931)	2.950 (3.931)	2.949 (3.947)	2.950 (3.938)	2.950 (3.929)
Θ_{t+1} = 0.051	Economic growth rate	6.635	5.898	7.108	7.418	7.552	6.447	6.608	6.598
	Human capital premium	1.279	1.289	1.272	1.266	1.263	3.272	2.114	1.032
	Higher education admission probability	5.107 (6.647)	5.017 (6.647)	5.017 (6.647)	5.017 (6.647)	5.017 (6.647)	5.015 (6.689)	5.016 (6.664)	5.017 (6.642)

Table 8.5 Average levels of main economic variables under changes in public education policies (Cont'd)

		Benchmark value	τ=0.010	τ=0.050	τ=0.080	τ=0.10	θ_B=0.40	θ_B=0.60	θ_B=0.85
Θ_{t+1} = 0.070	Economic growth rate	6.690	5.973	7.146	7.445	7.574	6.474	6.646	6.662
	Human capital premium	1.165	1.158	1.158	1.153	1.150	2.975	1.924	0.940
	Higher education admission probability	6.889 (9.075)	6.889 (9.077)	6.889 (9.072)	6.889 (9.071)	6.889 (9.071)	6.885 (9.148)	6.887 (9.105)	6.889 (9.066)
Θ_{t+1} = 0.090	Economic growth rate	6.717	6.023	7.161	7.451	7.576	6.481	6.661	6.696
	Human capital premium	1.084	1.078	1.078	1.072	1.070	2.762	1.788	0.876
	Higher education admission probability	8.860 (11.60)	8.860 (11.60)	8.861 (11.59)	8.861 (11.59)	8.861 (11.59)	8.854 (11.71)	8.858 (11.65)	8.861 (11.58)
Θ_{t+1} = 0.11	Economic growth rate	6.727	6.050	7.161	7.445	7.566	6.475	6.662	6.711
	Human capital premium	1.025	1.020	1.019	1.014	1.011	2.607	1.690	0.828
	Higher education admission probability	10.83 (14.10)	10.83 (14.10)	10.83 (14.08)	10.84 (14.08)	10.83 (14.07)	10.82 (14.26)	10.83 (14.16)	10.84 (14.07)

Notes: (1) Parameter values in the benchmark scenario are $\mu_1 = 0.41$, $\mu_2 = 0.271$, $\alpha = -0.67$, $\beta = 0.33$, $\Phi_1 = 0.4724$, $\Phi_2 = 0.9821$, $\varepsilon = \gamma = \upsilon = \eta = 0.3$, $\phi_B = \phi_H = 0.5$, $\tau = 0.026$, $\theta_B = 0.792$, $\Theta_t = 0.051$, $A = 100$, $B = Z = 1.0$

(2) Economic growth rate is the growth rate per annum.

(3) Economic growth rate and Higher education admission probability are given in %.

(4) For the row for higher education admission probability, the value inside the brackets is the value for children from high-skilled labor families, and the value outside the brackets is the value for children from low-skilled labor families.

From Table 8.5, it can be seen that, under benchmark value parameter settings, the economic growth rate is 6.635%, human capital is 1.28, and admission rate for higher education for youth agents from low-skilled labor families is 5.017%, clearly lower than that of high-skilled labor families, which is at 6.646%, revealing the existence of a serious disparity problem in opportunities for higher education admission.

From (8.8) and (8.10), it can be seen that increase in the size of public education expenditure has a double effect on economic growth: on one hand, it helps to raise the quality of basic eduation and higher education, contributing to human capital accumulation and economic growth; on the other hand, by diverting more economic resources from the private sector to the public sector, income for private economic agents decreases, such that investment in children's education also decreases, thus exerting a constraining effect on human capital accumulation and economic growth.

The simulated results in Table 8.5 show that, within a reasonable range, the positive effect of increase in size of public education on economic growth should occupy a dominant position: taking $\Theta_{t+1} = 0.051$ for example, as τ_t increases from 1% to 10%, economic growth rate increases from 5.898% to 7.552%. Increase in the size of public expenditure has a non-linear effect on human capital premium,[53] and this effect is related to the size of higher education admissions: taking $\Theta_{t+1} = 0.010$ as an example, as τ_t increases, human capital premium increased initially before decreasing. Additionally, increase in the size of public education expenditure has no effects on resolving the disparity in higher education opportunities caused by different family backgrounds, with no changes in the probability of higher education admission for children from both high-skilled and low-skilled labor families.

Under certain conditions for the size of public education expenditure, increase in basic education expenditure θ_{Bt+1} means that more resources are moved from higher education to basic education. This has a double effect on economic growth: on one hand, it contributes to an increase in the quality of basic education, promoting human capital accumulation in low-skilled labor, and by extension, contributes to increasing learning efficiency in the higher education phase as well as human capital accumulation in high-skilled labor, and thus contributing to the overall human capital accumulation and economic growth of the country. On the other hand, this also causes a decrease in quality of higher education, creating a constraining effect on human capital accumulation in high-skilled labor and economic growth [see (8.8) and (8.10)].

From Table 5.1, it can be seen that, when θ_{Bt+1} is relatively low, its promoting effects are more significant, but as θ_{Bt+1} increase, its constraining effects gradually increase in strength, until when θ_{Bt+1} passes a threshold, the negative effects will occupy a dominant position, such that the relationship between the proportion of public basic education expenditure and economic growth is revealed as an inverted U-shaped curve. In fact, the simulation results show that the range of values of θ_{Bt+1} is also related to the size of higher education admissions: the higher Θ_{t+1} is, the higher the range of values of θ_{Bt+1}. Thus, the larger the size of higher education admissions, the more economic growth is promoted if basic education investment is also increased. Increase θ_{Bt+1} in also helps in decreasing human capital premium, and may even lead to wage levels of low-skilled labor exceeding that of high-skilled labor, i.e. when human capital premium is lower than 1: when $\Theta_{t+1} = 0.09$ and $\theta_{Bt+1} = 0.85$, human capital premium is 0.85.[54]

It can also be seen from Table 8.5 that increase θ_{Bt+1} in contributes in increasing higher education admission opportunities for children from low-skilled labor families, and to a certain extent lower that for children from high-skilled families, thus contributing to a reduction in disparity in higher education opportunities; but this effect is rather weak, and only presents itself as significant if the size of higher education admissions passes a certain threshold.

From the theoretical model in this segment, it can be seen that increase in the size of higher education admissions Θ_{t+1} contribute to increasing higher education admission opportunities for youth agents in general, as well as the proportion of high-skilled labor, and by extension contribute to economic growth [see (8.9)]. But it can also cause a constraining effect on economic growth, presented mainly in two aspects: one, under the scenario where public higher education expenditure remains unchanged, increase in Θ_{t+1} will lead increase in the crowding effect in higher education, leading to a decrease in higher education quality, obstructing economic growth [see (8.10)]; two, increase in Θ_{t+1} will also weaken to a certain extent the competitive pressure in basic education, constraining the educational investment from families, which ultimately does not favor human capital accumulation and economic growth. Results of the simulation show that when is Θ_{t+1} relatively small, the promoting effect from increasing the size of higher education admission on economic growth is dominant, but as Θ_{t+1} continue to increase, the constraining effect will be gradually more significant, until when Θ_{t+1} passes a threshold point, increase in higher education admissions will not be favorable to economic growth, i.e. the relationship between Θ_{t+1} and economic growth is also revealed as an inverted U-shaped curve.

Further more, it can be seen that the size of the range of values for Θ_{t+1} is related to τ_t: the larger τ_t, the smaller the range of values, i.e. when the size of public education expenditure is relatively small, increase in higher education admissions will promote economic growth, contributing to increase in supply of high-skilled labor, and under the condition that τ_t remains constant, the quality of higher education will decrease; these two effects together will cause human capital premium levels to decrease. Additionally, although increase in the size of higher education admissions contributes to increase in opportunities for youth agents in higher education admissions, children from high-skilled labor families benefit relatively more, such that the disparity in higher education opportunities will increase: using the benchmark scenario as example, as Θ_{t+1} increases by 1%, it causes an increase in higher education admissions opportunity by 1.226% for children from high-skilled labor families, and 0.986% for children from low-skilled labor families.

The above analysis shows that public education policies has a relatively significant effect on human capital premium: increase in the proportion of basic education expenditure and size of higher education admissions both help to decrease human capital premium, but the mechanism of effect on economic growth is relatively complex. In fact, robust analysis shows that the effect of changes in public education on economic growth is also related to the crowding effect in education as well as education technology (human capital accumulation technology and human capital accumulation efficiency from public education expenditure).[55] Thus, it is not difficult to understand why conclusions from past empirical studies do not reach a consensus. It is therefore necessary to conduct a comprehensive assessment from an empirical perspective on the effects of China's public education policies, in order to give a clear analysis on the existing problems and future challenges facing public education policy making in China.

Empirical analysis

This segment aims to show the effects of China's public education policies on economic growth and especially human capital premium, using real life data from China as basis, and also perform empirical tests on major conclusions from the theoretical analysis given in this section, using spatial econometrics and panel data models.

Effects of size and structure of regional education expenditure on economic growth

Model framework

As mentioned previously, regional governments play an extremely vital role in the development of China's education system. Thus, this segment sets provincial economics as the subject of examination, in order to examine clearly the effects of regional education expenditure on economic growth.[56] Again, this brings statistical difficulties to the analysis: spatial endogenous variables such as externalities to regional economic growth brought about by trade and labor movement between provinces;[57] dynamic endogenous variables such as the dynamic process of economic growth, which is dependant on and affected by changes in current and past factors;[58] and existing endogenous problems in the explanatory variable such as constraining effects from economic development levels on the size and structure of regional public education expenditure. All these cause significant biases and inconsistencies to estimated results. To account for this problem, the following dynamic spatial panel data model is used:

$$Gy_t = \sum_{i=1}^{M} \phi_j Gy_{t-i} + \rho WGy_t + \alpha X_t + \beta Z_t + \eta + \mu_t \tag{8.19}$$

Of which, Gy_t is the GDP growth rate per capita for the provinces, Gy_{t-i} is the lagged term of the GDP growth rate per capita, and M is the largest lagged order. WGy_t is the spatially lagged term of the production growth rate per capita, and the parameter ρ reflects the effect of interaction between provinces on economic growth. W is the spatial neighboring weights matrix, X_t is the endogenous explanatory variables, Z_t is the exogenous explanatory variables, η is the individual effects, and μ_t is the time effects.

The spatial neighboring weights matrix W is set apriori, taking into consideration two kinds of spatial weights matrices: one, geographical neighboring spatial weight matrix, based on whether two provinces share a border. If provinces i and j share a border, the value of spatial weight W_{ij} is set as 1; otherwise it is set as 0. Two: population movement spatial weight matrix, based on the size of interprovincial population movement, constructed as $W_{ij} = PM_{ij}$, where W_{ij} is the spatial weight matrix and PM_{ij} is the population movement between provinces i and j.[59]

The explanatory variables X_t and Z_t include the core explanatory variable in this segment, the variable of regional education policies (inclusive of the size and structure of regional education expenditure, and the size of higher education admissions). Public education expenditure in China includes national fiscal education expenditure and budgetary education expenditure, but since there is a lack of multi-provincial data for national fiscal education expenditure across different education levels, budgetary education expenditure as a proportion of GDP will be used to measure the size of public education expenditure. For the structure of public education expenditure, the proportion of budgetary basic education expenditure, budgetary vocational education expenditure, and budgetary higher education expenditure are taken into consideration.[60]

Additionally, there are important control variables taken into consideration: one, the investment ratio of physical capital (i.e. the ratio between physical capital investment and GDP), examining the effects of physical capital accumulation; two, labor force variables, represented by the likelihood ratio between provincial labor force and total provincial population, examining the effects of the performance of the labor market; three, fiscal revenue ratio (i.e. the ratio between fiscal revenue and production), examining the effect of provincial economic burden; four, economic openness level, measured as the ratio between provincial import and export volume and production; five, economic development level, measured as actual GDP per capita, examining potentially existing convergent effects of provincial economic growth; and six, fiscal revenue decentralization, measured as {provincial fiscal revenue (expenditure) per capita / [provincial fiscal revenue (expenditure) + national fiscal revenue (expenditure) per capita]}, examining the effects of fiscal revenue policies of regional governments.

Estimation results

As mentioned, the endogenous variables will bring biases and inconsistencies to the dynamic spatial panel data model given in (8.19) if ordinary panel data and spatial measurements are used to obtain estimated results. Thus, system GMM as proposed by Arellano and Bover, and Blundell and Bond, is used instead to obtain the estimated results.[61] For the geographical neighboring spatial weights matrix model, comparing results from the Arellano-Bond residual autocorrelation test for estimation results of different lagged orders, the largest lagged order containing the endogenous variables is determined to be 2. Also, given that existing studies have not reached a consensus regarding the nature of the variables of the size and structure of regional education expenditure and the control variables, different scenarios will be considered: Model 1a sets these variables as exogenous variables; Model 1b sets them as endogenous variables; Model 1c sets the variables of the size and structure of regional education expenditure, physical capital investment rate, and variables in labor as endogenous variables, and other control variables as exogenous variables. The estimated results are given in Table 8.6.

Table 8.6 Estimated results of system GMM for the dynamic spatial panel data model of the size and structure of regional education expenditure and the effects on economic growth

Model	Geographical neighboring spatial weight matrix				Population movement spatial weight matrix	
Explanatory variable	Model 1a	Model 1b	Model 1c	Model 1d	Model 2a	Model 2b
Constant term	-0.243 (0.14)*	-0.388 (0.18)**	-0.226 (0.12)*	-0.374 (0.23)*	-0.207 (0.11)*	-0.356 (0.23)
L1.GDP growth rate per capita	0.177 (0.17)	0.197 (0.19)	0.169 (0.18)	0.289 (0.17)*	0.133 (0.26)	0.289 (0.22)
L2.GDP growth rate per capita	0.250 (0.16)	0.234 (0.17)	0.241 (0.16)	—	0.343 (0.28)	—

Table 8.6 Estimated results of system GMM for the dynamic spatial panel data model of the size and structure of regional education expenditure and the effects on economic growth (Cont'd)

Model	Geographical neighboring spatial weight matrix				Population movement spatial weight matrix	
Explanatory variable	Model 1a	Model 1b	Model 1c	Model 1d	Model 2a	Model 2b
GDP growth rate per capita spatially lagged term	0.001 (0.10)	-0.050 (0.10)	0.011 (0.09)	0.013 (0.14)	-0.546 (0.36)	-0.394 (0.31)
Public education expenditure ratio	0.554 (0.61)	0.876 (0.63)	0.402 (0.49)	-0.466 (0.59)	0.394 (0.64)	-0.528 (0.67)
Basic education expenditure proportion	0.232 (0.12)**	0.320 (0.14)**	0.213 (0.11)**	0.307 (0.18)*	0.226 (0.12)*	0.328 (0.19)*
Vocational education expenditure proportion	-0.174 (0.15)	-0.038 (0.16)	-0.155 (0.14)	0.009 (0.09)	-0.181 (0.19)	0.005 (0.11)
Higher education expenditure proportion	0.129 (0.07)*	0.196 (0.09)**	0.111 (0.06)*	0.093 (0.06)	0.119 (0.06)*	0.093 (0.07)
Size of higher education	-0.142 (1.22)	-0.463 (1.22)	0.097 (1.07)	1.060 (0.97)	0.125 (1.19)	1.576 (1.17)
Production per capita (taking natural logarithms)	0.019 (0.01)**	0.028 (0.01)**	0.018 (0.01)**	0.022 (0.01)*	0.022 (0.01)**	0.024 (0.02)
Physical capital investment ratio	0.025 (0.04)	0.029 (0.04)	0.027 (0.04)	-0.015 (0.05)	0.027 (0.04)	-0.018 (0.05)
Variables in labor	-0.092 (0.06)*	-0.094 (0.05)*	-0.085 (0.05)*	-0.042 (0.04)	-0.095 (0.07)	-0.040 (0.05)
Economic openness level	0.001 (0.00)	0.002 (0.00)	0.001 (0.00)	0.002 (0.01)	0.001 (0.00)	-0.001 (0.01)
Fiscal revenue ratio	-0.211 (0.20)	-0.128 (0.21)	-0.151 (0.18)	0.045 (0.23)	-0.240 (0.23)	-0.087 (0.26)
Fiscal revenue decentralization	-0.007 (0.0 3)	-0.018 (0.04)	-0.018 (0.03)	-0.122 (0.07)	-0.016 (0.04)	-0.116 (0.08)
Fiscal expenditure decentralization	0.058 (0.07)	0.046 (0.08)	0.063 (0.08)	0.203 (0.14)	0.063 (0.07)	0.209 (0.14)
Arellano-Bond AR(1) test	-2.02**	-1.88*	-2.09**	-2.19**	-2.04**	-1.72*
Arellano-Bond AR(2) test	-0.31	-0.15	-0.35	-0.46	-0.94	-1.02
Hansen over-identification test	22.95	19.42	24.05	16.65	23.15	17.95
DHansen GMM instrumental variables effectiveness test	0.00	0.16	-0.00	0.00	0.00	0.00

Table 8.6 Estimated results of system GMM for the dynamic spatial panel data model of the size and structure of regional education expenditure and the effects on economic growth (Cont'd)

Model	Geographical neighboring spatial weight matrix				Population movement spatial weight matrix	
Explanatory variable	Model 1a	Model 1b	Model 1c	Model 1d	Model 2a	Model 2b
DHansen IV instrumental variables effectiveness test	3.93	—	2.77	0.42	4.11	2.66
Effective sample size	290	290	290	253	290	253
Wald value	608.2***	326.1***	594.4***	483.2***	572.0***	289.9***

Notes: (1) Difference-in-Hansen GMM tests for effectiveness of endogenous variables and predetermined variables, IV tests for effectiveness of exogenous variables.
(2) L1 and L2 are first-order and second-order lagged operators respectively.
(3) *, ** and *** indicate regression coefficients significantly above confidence levels of 10%, 5% and 1% respectively.
(4) Values in brackets are robust standard deviations.

The Arellano-Bond AR(1) and (2) tests show that residual series of Models 1a, 1b, and 1c have significant first-order autocorrelation but not 2nd order autocorrelation, so the model settings are acceptable. The results of the Hansen test for effectiveness of the overall instrumental variable, and the results of the Difference-in-Hansen test for collective effectiveness of GMM class and IV class instrumental variables, also show that the construction of instrumental variables in the model is generally effective. However, it should be noted that the number of instrumental variables are high relative to the sample size, potentially causing high losses of degrees of freedom and to a certain extent weakening the results of the Hansen test. As Bond points out, endogenous problems will cause the OLS estimation of one-phase lagged variables to bias upwards, and SSW estimation to bias downwards, meaning that the real values of the one-phase lagged parameters of the endogenous variables should be between the OLS and SSW estimates.[62] Taking this into consideration, it may be seen that the estimated results from Models 1a and 1b are relatively less satisfactory, meaning that not all explanatory variables should be seen strictly as exogenous or endogenous variables.[63]

Likewise, for the population movement spatial weight matrix model, the largest lagged order for production growth rate per capita is 2, and Model 2a (public policy variables, physical capital investment ratio and variables in labor set as endogenous variables, all other control variables set as exogenous variables) gives relatively acceptable estimated results. Additionally, there are still a number of senior high schools directly run from the Central Committee rather than regional governments, with their students having relatively higher inter-regional mobility, contributing to bias in estimated results. As there is a lack of data on funding, student numbers and enrollment/graduation movements for these schools, provinces and cities with relatively high concentrations of centrally-run senior high schools are altogether eliminated from the sample data (Beijing, with 33; Shanghai, 9; Jiangsu, 10; Hubei, 8; Sichuan, 6; Shaanxi, 6), in order to account for the biases to estimated results. In this case, we take the largest lagged order for GDP growth rate per capita as 1, with Models 1d and 2b (size of public education expenditure, proportion of basic education expenditure and proportion of higher education expenditure set as endogenous variables, all other explanatory variables as exogenous variables) giving relatively acceptable estimated results.

From the estimated results of Models 1c and 2a, after accounting for biases in estimated results from endogenous variables, the regression coefficients for public education expenditure ratio and proportion of vocational education expenditure are positive and negative respectively, but not statistically significant; the regression coefficients for proportion of basic education expenditure and proportion of higher education expenditure are both positive and statistically significant. Additionally, after accounting for the biases in estimated results caused by centrally-run senior high schools, the estimated results show significant changes: the regression coefficients for public education expenditure ratio and proportion of vocational education expenditure are now negative and positive respectively, but still not statistically significant; the positive effect of proportion of higher education expenditure is greatly weakened and is no longer statistically significant, while the positive effect of proportion of basic education expenditure is greatly increased and remain statistically significant (see Models 1d and 2b). This means that regional public education policies has yet to realize its potential in promoting regional economic growth, perhaps due to insufficient investment size or unreasonable investment structure in education: continued marginalizaton of vocational education and excessive attention on higher education has, to different extents, limited the effects of public education policies.[64] In fact, at the current stage, tilting the support more towards basic education better contributes to promoting regional economic growth in China. While in recent years higher education admissions policies has been a topic of contention, this study shows that increasing the size of higher education admissions has a positive but not significant effect on regional economic growth.

Effects of size and structure of education expenditure of regional governments on human capital premium

In examining the effect of public education policies on human capital premium, the first challenge faced is the estimation of human capital premium. Based on the theoretical analysis in this segment, we define human capital premium as the wage ratio between labor force with tertiary education background and labor force with only senior high school education background. Thus, the estimation of human capital premium requires large and comprehensive samples of multi-provincial microdata related to labor wage, education background etc. Again, the CHNS database is able to provide us with a sizeable amount of data. The estimation of human capital premium can be given by the following wage-determining function:

$$Ln(W_{it}) = \mu E_{it} + \eta U_{it} + \varepsilon_{it} \tag{8.20}$$

Of which, W_{it} is the wage level of laborer i, E_{it} is the dummy variable for education level of the laborer, U_{it} is the control variables, including dummy variables for the laborer's age, sex, nature and size of work unit, etc. ε_{it} is the error term.

Fig. 8.3 Human capital premium for nine provinces for 1997, 2000, 2004 and 2006 (Epanechnikov kernel)

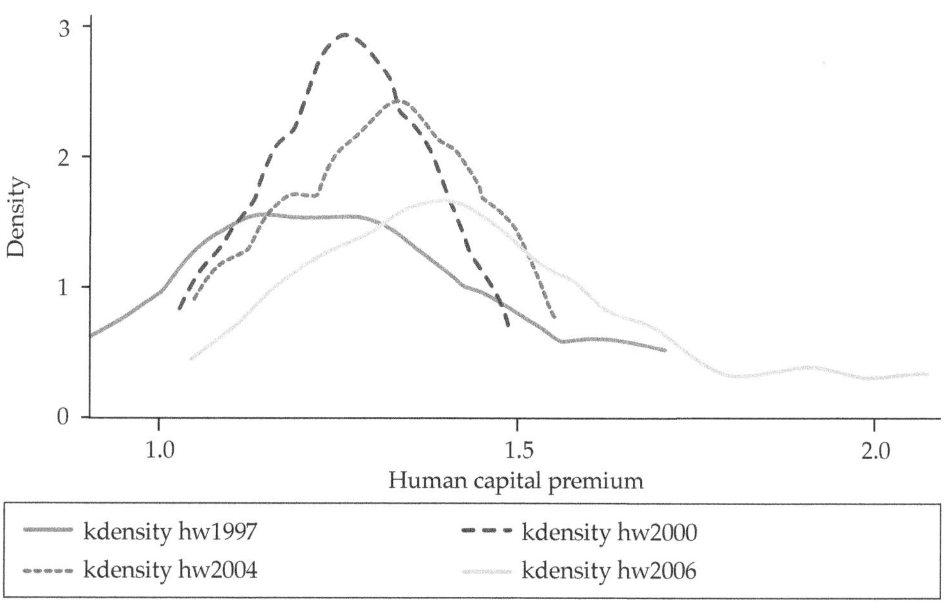

It can be seen from Figure 8.3 that since 2000, the human capital premium in China has steadily increased, and the disparity between regions has also continually increased, shown in the continued shift to the right for the peaks of the density curves in 2000, 2004, and 2006.[65]

As previously mentioned in the theoretical analysis, relative supply and efficiency between high-skilled and low-skilled labor force is a main factor affecting human capital premium, and they are in turn affected mainly by the size and structure of regional government expenditure. Thus, the size of higher education admission and the size and structure of public education expenditure are used to examine the effects of relative supply and efficiency between the two sets of labor forces on human capital premium. The other main factor affecting human capital premium is the capital-skill complementarity effect, for which, owing to the lack of concrete data on high-skilled labor, physical capital investment ratio and variables in labor are used to estimate the effects of the capital-skill complementarity effect and labor market performance on human capital premium. Additionally, considering that labor forces with different education backgrounds may receive different benefits from economic growth, actual GDP per capita is also introduced in the explained variable. From the results of Moran's I and LM spatial autocorrelation tests, it may be seen that there is no significant spatial autocorrelation in the human capital premium within the sample period; thus, the panel data model is as follows:

$$\xi_{it} = \alpha Ln(X_{it}) + \beta Ln(Z_{it}) + \eta_i + \mu_t + \varepsilon_{it} \tag{8.21}$$

Of which, $\xi_{it} = Ln(w_{Hit}/w_{Bit})$ is the natural logarithm for human capital premium, η_i is the individual effect, μ_t is the temporal effect, and ε_{it} is the error term. X_{it} is the variable for regional education policies, and Z_{it} is the control variables (which includes physical capital investment ratio, variables in labor, and actual GDP per capita).

In evaluating (8.21), there are also endogenous problems in regional education policy variables that needs to be considered: human capital premium directly affects expectations on education returns, which in turn affects the demands in different phases of education, eventually affecting the variables in public education policies. Since the effect of human capital premium on vocational education is likely to be very small, the proportion of expenditure for vocational education is set as exogenous variable, while the ratio of public education expenditure, proportion of basic education expenditure, proportion of higher education expenditure, and size of higher education admissions are set as endogenous variables.[66] The endogenous variables will be accounted for using instrumental variables: proportion of population aged 14, population density, proportion of population of minority races, fiscal revenue, and expenditure decentralization. While the mechanisms of effect for population factors are different from that for fiscal factors,[67] they all do not directly affect human capital premium levels, and the results of the corresponding Hansen and Sargan over-identification tests also show that the choices of the instrumental variables are acceptable.

Using these instrumental variables, IV-2SLS is first used to obtain estimated results of (8.21). Additionally, considering that human capital premium in the current analysis is obtained using estimates from microdata, and that feedback of wage rigidity and human capital premium is a lengthy process, there are potential heteroscedasticity and autocorrelation problems in the sample data, and so two-step GMM estimations for effective heteroscedasticity and autocorrelation are also given. For convenience of comparison, the estimated results for fixed effects model are also given. The estimated results for these three models are given in Table 8.7.

Table 8.7 Estimated results for the effects of size and structure of regional education expenditure on human capital premium

Model / Explanatory variable	Model 1 (Fixed effects)	Model 2 (IV-2SLS)	Model 3 (Two-step GMM)				
			Human capital premium (8.21)	First-stage regression results			
				Public education expenditure ratio	Proportion of basic education expenditure	Proportion of higher education expenditure	Size of higher education
Constant term	-7.476 (5.54)	—	—	—	—	—	—
Public education expenditure ratio	-0.104 (0.49)	2.295 (1.73)	2.500 (1.21)**	—	—	—	—
Proportion of basic education expenditure	-0.363 (0.092)	-2.861 (2.72)	-3.186 (2.36)	—	—	—	—
Proportion of vocational education expenditure	0.104 (0.36)	1.062 (0.83)	1.039 (0.69)	-0.424 (0.15)***	0.102 (0.05)*	0.130 (0.16)	-0.219 (0.19)
Proportion of higher education expenditure	-0.526 (0.42)	0.563 (1.20)	0.676 (0.91)	—	—	—	—
Size of higher education	-0.235 (0.23)	-0.688 (0.54)	-0.777 (0.42)*	—	—	—	—
Production per capita	0.659 (0.51)	1.862 (1.17)	1.961 (1.08)**	0.009 (0.24)	0.159 (0.10)	-0.192 (0.15)	2.217 (0.30)***
Physical capital investment ratio	0.024 (0.35)	0.040 (0.49)	-0.012 (0.42)	-0.075 (0.20)	0.046 (0.12)	-0.086 (0.14)	-0.454 (0.33)
Variables in labor	-0.227 (0.62)	-1.712 (1.38)	-1.848 (1.12)*	0.499 (0.25)*	-0.231 (0.17)	-0.279 (0.27)	-0.850 (0.48)*

Table 8.7 Estimated results for the effects of size and structure of regional education expenditure on human capital premium (Cont'd)

Model / Explanatory variable	Model 1 (Fixed effects)	Model 2 (IV-2SLS)	Model 3 (Two-step GMM)				
			Human capital premium (8.21)	First-stage regression results			
				Public education expenditure ratio	Proportion of basic education expenditure	Proportion of higher education expenditure	Size of higher education
Population density	—	—	—	0.200 (0.98)	0.078 (0.61)	2.010 (0.53)***	0.995 (1.46)
Proportion of population of minority races	—	—	—	-0.305 (0.34)	-0.055 (0.20)	0.211 (0.29)	0.061 (0.58)
Proportion of population aged 14 and below	—	—	—	0.039 (0.36)	0.234 (0.17)	-0.047 (0.23)	0.949 (0.55)*
Fiscal expenditure decentralization	—	—	—	-0.150 (0.21)	0.394 (0.21)*	1.044 (0.26)***	-1.515 (0.29)***
Fiscal revenue decentralization	—	—	—	-0.386 (0.36)	-0.208 (0.21)	0.165 (0.29)	-1.107 (0.43)**
Hansen over-identification test	—	0.311	0.442	—	—	—	—
Effective sample size	35	35	35	35	35	35	35
R^2	0.261	0.504	0.765	0.904	0.610	0.754	0.986

Notes: (1) For Model 2, Sargan test is used as the effectiveness test for instrumental variables.
(2) *, ** and *** indicate regression coefficients significantly above confidence levels of 10%, 5% and 1% respectively.
(3) Values in brackets are standard deviations.
(4) "—" means that the respective variable does not exist in the regression formula.
(5) For reasons of space, first-step regression analysis for Model 2 is not shown.

From Model 2, it can be seen that, after accounting for endogeneity, the regression results are in general consistent with the conclusions from the theoretical analysis in this section. The regression coefficients are negative for proportion of basic education expenditure and size of higher education admission size are both negative, and positive for the proportion of higher education expenditure, proportion of vocational education expenditure, and public education expenditure ratio. None of these are statistically significant.

After using GMM to account for biases to estimations from heteroscedasticity and autocorrelation, the regression coefficients for public education expenditure ratio and size of higher education admissions greatly increase in significance, meaning that increase in investment into public education will further increase labor wage disparity, and increase in size of admissions for higher education contributes to decrease in human capital premium. Additionally, increase in the level of employment for the labor force also contributes to decrease in human capital premium, and increase in economic development level further increases labor wage disparity. Increase in physical capital investment has a negative but not significant effect on human capital premium levels.

The above conclusion has important significance for the future direction of China's public education policies. In increasing the investment input in public education, policy makers need to pay special attention to the optimization of the structure of public expenditure. It can be seen that investment of the limited educational resources in China should be tilted in favor of basic education, which not only helps to better realize long-term economic growth, but also contributes to reducing labor wage disparity and, by extension, income distribution disparity.

Additionally, higher education admissions policies need to be managed cautiously. Increase in the size of higher education admissions contributes to alleviating the problem of social stratification in higher education admission opportunities, reducing labor wage disparity, and better realizing income distribution justice. At the same time, rushing to increase the size of higher education admissions on an unrealistic scale should be avoided, in order to prevent the quality of higher education from slipping. Instead, there should be an increase in the effort to optimize infrastructure and supportive measures, and explore better structures in higher education admissions, so as to increase the higher education admissions rate for students from low-income, low-skilled labor and rural families, in order to effectively tackle the problem of disparity in higher education opportunities.

A final point to note: in order to better emphasize the effects of the scarcity of higher education resources, this section has largely ignored the effects of human capital premium on the human capital investment behavior in microeconomical agents. It is expected that, if the situation in higher education opportunites significantly improves, this mechanism of effect will gradually increase in importance; in which case, a more detailed study on the effects of endogenous variables such as human capital premium, and exogenous variables such as higher education policies on the human capital investment behavior in microeconomical agents, over the different development stages of higher education, shall make a valuable contribution to existing research.

Optimization of Size and Structure of Regional Governments for Promoting Income Distribution Justice

Currently, China's regional governments are tasked with large numbers of income redistribution projects, occupying an important role in the income distribution policy system. It is therefore of vital significance to explore effective ways to encourage regional governments to increase their attention on social and livelihood issues, as well as income redistribution projects, in order to better realize the optimization of the size and structure of regional governments.

The analysis in the above two sections show that, from the perspective of income distribution, the current size and structure of regional governments in China has not been beneficial in promoting income distribution justice, and it may have even contributed to the worsening of the income distribution disparity situation. The problems that need to be addressed can mainly be seen from the following three issues:

1. The size of provincial government expenditure has increased the income distribution disparity among residents, as seen in the significantly positive effect it has on the Gini coefficient of income of the regional population. This may be attributed to the flawed structure of the provincial government expenditure, where the bulk of fiscal resources are spent on economic and administrative expenditure, such that the proportion of social expenditure, which is closely tied to income distribution projects, is relatively small in comparison;
2. In comparison to the urban population, increase in the size of expenditure and proportion of administrative expenditure for provincial governments has a much more significant and negative impact on income disparity in the rural population, and while increase in the proportion of social expenditure contributes to reducing the income disparity between the urban and rural populations, it has a relatively limited impact on income disparity within the urban population and the rural population. This indicates that regional governments have been seriously neglecting the income distribution situation in the rural population;
3. The size of public education expenditure, as it currently stands, is unfavorable for reducing the labor wage disparity, demonstrating the flawed size and structure of the public education expenditure of regional governments. This can be attributed mainly to a significant lack of investment input in public education, especially basic education, and the neglect of the development of

vocational education in favor of excessive attention on the development of higher education.

It is therefore prudent for the government of China to take effective measures in actively guiding regional governments to increase attention on social and livelihood issues, adjusting the structure of fiscal expenditure, in order to achieve optimization of size and structure of regional governments beneficial to income distribution justice. Some of the areas that should be emphasized are:

- Active adjustment of structure of fiscal expenditure to increase the input in expenditure for projects closely related to social and livelihood issues, such as education, health, and social security, so as to effectively constrain excessive inflation in economic and administrative expenditure.
- Taking effective measures to optimize the structure of expenditure of regional governments, with special attention on vulnerable groups in the rural population, in order to effectively tackle the problem of income disparity, especially in the rural population.
- Taking effective measures to guide regional governments in increasing the input on public education, especially basic education, while increasing the size of higher education admissions with caution and moderation, in order to alleviate the serious problem of social stratification resulting from the obtainability of higher education opportunities and reduce labor wage disparity. Care must be taken to avoid unrealistic expansion of the size of higher education admissions, and it must be ensured that relevant infrastructure and measures must be put in place to avoid decrease in the quality of higher education. At the same time, there should be more exploration on building better structures for higher education admissions, so as to increase the higher education admissions rate for students from low-income, low-skilled labor and rural families, in order to effectively tackle the problem of disparity in higher education opportunities.

Finally, it must be noted that, as pointed out by Wang et al. and Qiao et al.,[68] the main reason for the emphasis of regional governments on fiscal expenditure that favors economic growth but not income distribution justice lies with a combination of fiscal decentralization and a cadre evaluation system which uses GDP as a core criterion of judgment, leading to a perversion of policies as a casualty of cadre competition. Thus, the key in truly realizing optimization of size and structure of regional governments that promotes income distribution justice lies in actively promoting fiscal management system reform, properly managing fiscal decentralization, instituting better structures in the cadre evaluation system, perfecting the constraining mechanisms for regional governments, so as to promote fundamental transformations in the policy directions of regional governments.

Summary

This chapter began by using census microdata obtained from CHNS to examine the effects of size and structure of China's provincial governments on the income disparity among residents, thereafter using spatial econometrics and panel data models to examine the effects of size and structure of education expenditure of regional governments on human capital premium. Finally, there was a brief exploration into potential measures in optimization of size and structure of regional governments that would promote income distribution justice.

The analysis in this chapter has shown the following:

- During the 1990s, the income distribution situation in the provincial population was generally stable, but the situation since the 2000s has been one of continued rapid deterioration, with the deterioration of income distribution situation most significant in the urban population;
- Increase in the size of expenditure of regional governments significantly increased income disparity in the provincial population, mainly due to its unfavorable impact on income distribution in the rural population. Increase in the proportion of economic expenditure significantly increased the income distribution disparity in the general provincial population, as well as in the rural population and urban population, but has no significant impact on income disparity between the urban and rural populations. Increase in the proportion of administrative expenditure increased the income disparity in the rural population, but did not have significant impact on the income disparity in the general provincial population and the urban population, nor on the income disparity between urban and rural populations. The proportion of social expenditure has no significant general or structural effect on income distribution in the general provincial population;
- Fiscal decentralization has a significant and assymetrical impact on the effect of size and structure of expenditure of regional governments on income distribution among residents. In general, fiscal expenditure decentralization increased the unfavorable impact of size and structure of expenditure of regional governments on income disparity in the general provincial population. Granting more autonomy in fiscal revenue powers contributes to constraining both the negative impact of the size of fiscal expenditure of regional governments on income disparity in the urban population, as well as the proportion of economic expenditure on income disparity between the urban and rural populations; at the same time, it increases the unfavorable impact of the proportion of social expenditure on income distribution among residents;

- Public education policies affect the human capital investment behavior of families with different education backgrounds, as well as the relative supply and efficiency of high-skilled and low-skilled labor, thus impacting economic growth and human capital premium. The impact of public education policies on economic growth are uncertain: the size of public education expenditure, the proportion of basic education expenditure, and the size of higher education admissions have an inverted U-shaped relationship with economic growth; increase in the size of the proportion of basic education and the size of higher education admissions contributes to a decrease in human capital premium levels and a reduction in labor wage disparity; in general, public education policies do not contribute to reducing the disparity in higher education opportunities, and increase in the size of higher education admissions will further aggravate the disparity situation;
- The formulation and implementation of education policies of regional governments has been lacking in an organically balanced combination of economic growth targets and income distribution, such that the policies have not demonstrated any promoting effect on regional economic growth, and have also been unfavorable for reducing labor wage disparity. Allocating more educational resources to basic education contributes to promoting regional economic growth, as well as favoring reduction in labor wage disparity, although the effect of the latter is not significant. The effect of vocational education expenditure and higher education expenditure policies on regional economic growth and human capital levels are, in general, unclear. Increase in admissions for higher education contributes to decrease in human capital premium levels, but has no significant effect in promoting regional economic growth.

The above summary shows that, from the perspective of income distribution, the fiscal expenditure behavior and, by extension, the size and structure of China's regional governments contain significant flaws. China's government should therefore look to actively improve the financial system in regional governments as well as the cadre evaluation system, thus guiding regional governments to increase the focus on social and livelihood issues, increase the input in public education, health and social security expenditure, in order to better promote income distribution justice.

9

Chapter

Optimization of the Size and Structure of Regional Governments from the Perspective of Social Welfare

Chapters 6 to 8 examined the optimization of size and structure of China's regional governments from the perspectives of economic growth, economic stability, and income distribution respectively. This chapter now takes into consideration the crucial point in this exercise: that the ultimate goal in the development of the optimal size and structure of government is to ensure that economic progress is well-coordinated with social developments. Thus, the purpose of this chapter is to explore for proposals which ensure that promotion of social welfare is taken care of in the optimization of the size and structure of regional governments.

As demonstrated in the analyses in the previous chapters, reforms in organizational structure, especially institutional reforms in the financial system, have been the main driving force behind the progressive development of the size and structure of regional governments. Any discussion of optimization of size and structure of regional governments without taking into account the fiscal relationships in the multi-tier government structure and the structure of regional governance found in China is meaningless; thus, a reasonable degree of fiscal decentralization and organizational structure in the multi-tier government organization is the key to optimization in the size and structure of regional governments.

This chapter will therefore integrate fiscal decentralization, government organizational structure and optimization of size and structure of regional governments into a unified framework of analysis. First, a theoretical model of an optimal size of regional government is constructed to find the optimal size for maximized social welfare, as well as the effects and mechanisms of action of fiscal decentralization and government organizational structure. Second, theoretical models of an optimal structure of regional government are constructed, under the frameworks of a single-tier and a multi-tier government, in order to find the optimal structure for maximized social welfare, as well as the effects of fiscal decentralization, central transfer payments, and taxation policies. Finally, the results are summarized to come up with proposals for optimization in the size and structure of regional governments, fiscal decentralization, and government organizational structures.

Optimal Size of Regional Government for Maximized Social Welfare

This section constructs a theoretical model for the optimal size of regional government, under the conditions of incomplete information, in order to find the optimal size of regional government for maximized social welfare, as well as the effects of fiscal decentralization and government organizational structure.

The constructed model follows closely the optimal territorial decentralization model in Gilbert and Picard.[1] That model, however, assumes only a hierarchy of two, as well as benevolent local (regional) governments that implement socially optimal policies for residents. The model constructed here, on the other hand, takes into consideration the multi-tier government organizational structure and the rent-seeking behavior of regional governments in the real-world situation in China. Under this multi-tier government structure, central transfer payments often have to be processed through secondary-level regional governments before being redistributed to grassroots-level regional governments; when the secondary-level regional governments have different policy objectives from the central government, it leads to deviations from the central transfer payment policies, causing additional negative effects from common pool channels to the expenditure behavior of regional governments.[2] Clearly, this type of distribution policy deviation and its negative effects are dependent on the number of levels in the organizational structure and the degree of fiscal decentralization in regional governments at the grassroots level. Thus, in addition to the spillover effects and mechanism of production costs information emphasized in Gilbert and Picard, the mechanism of common pool is also introduced, in order to better reveal the critical factors for the optimal size of regional governments. In particular, a multi-tier government structure is taken into consideration, i.e. a central government and $n - 1$ levels of regional governments, where each secondary-level government administers an m number of jurisdictions, such that the entire country has m^{n-1} grassroots-level regional governments.

Basic framework

Suppose that the utility function for residents administered by grassroots-level regional governments is $U_n^c(Q_n, \alpha_n)$, of which Q_n is the volume of regional public goods, and $\alpha_n > 0$ is the preferential parameter. For simplicity's sake, a quadratic multi-term utility function $U_n^c(Q_n, \alpha_n) = \frac{1}{2}Q_n^2 + \alpha_n Q_n$ is used. Taxes paid by residents, τ_n, includes regional taxes τ_n^l and central taxes τ_n^c, i.e. $\tau_n = \tau_n^l + \tau_n^c$. It is assumed that the taxes paid are distortionary, leading to unnecessary losses of $\lambda\tau_n$, where $\lambda > 0$ shows the degree of distortion. Taking into account distortion in taxes paid, then, the total cost for residents is $(1 + \lambda)\tau_n$. Thus, the consumer surplus is $S_n = U_n^c(Q_n, \alpha_n) - (1 + \lambda)\tau_n$.

Regional governments assign public goods to local enterprises for production, and the marginal production cost for enterprises is θ_n. Additionally, in order to obtain production contracts, enterprises have to pay rent to regional governments, with η_n being marginal rental cost. Thus, the total cost for enterprises is $C_n = (\theta_n, \eta_n) Q_n$. Enterprises sell the public goods produced to regional governments, with revenue equivalent to regional government expenditure G_n. Thus, the profit for enterprises is $\Pi_n = G_n - (\theta_n + \eta_n)Q_n$.

Regional governments use local tax revenues τ_n^l and central transfer payments ξ_n for expenditure capital G_n, of which the funding for $\bar{\xi}_n$ comes from central tax revenues. Net central transfer payment is $\xi_n = \bar{\xi}_n - \tau_n^c$, and is also linearly dependent on the volume of regional public goods (i.e. $\xi_n = \gamma_n Q_n$).

Under a multi-tier government structure, central transfer payments are often not directly administered to grassroots-level regional governments, but redistributed through secondary-level regional governments which often have different policy objectives from the central government, and this gives secondary-level regional governments plenty of room to reassign the destination of the central transfer payments. Assuming that the actual central transfer payments received by the regional government is $[1 - \phi(n)]\bar{\xi}_n$, where $\phi(n)$ is the loss function — an increasing function of government level n, i.e. $\phi(n) > 0$. $\phi(n)$ thus measures the degree of deviation in distribution policy at different government levels. The function for the budget constraints of the regional government is thus:

$$G_n = \tau_n^l + [1 - \phi(n)]\bar{\xi}_n = [1 - (1 - \mu_n)\phi(n)]\tau_n + [1 - \phi(n)]\gamma_n Q_n \tag{9.1}$$

Of which, $\mu_n = \tau_n^l / \tau_n$ measures the degree of tax decentralization of the regional government.

The traditional view in public economics assumes a benevolent government which pursues socially optimized policies, while public choice theorists consider governments as primarily concerned with optimal self-interests.[3] In the real-world economy, the objectives of governments are more complex, often seeking to balance between upholding public interests and pursuing self-interests. The function for the objectives of regional governments may thus be supposed as follows:

$$U_n^l = (1 - \omega_n)\eta_n Q_n + \omega_n W_n \tag{9.2}$$

Of which, $\eta_n Q_n$ is the total rental revenue, $W_n = S_n + \Pi_n$ is the function for district welfare. $\omega_n \in [0,1]$ is the weighting parameter, demonstrating the nature of regional government: $\omega_n = 0$ means that the regional government is only concerned with maximizing self-interests, and $\omega_n = 1$ means that it is only concerned with maximizing public interests.[4]

Suppose that the central government is concerned with maximizing social welfare $\hat{W}$.[5] Social welfare $\hat{W}$ is not equivalent to district welfare W_n, mainly due to two reasons: one, the existence of localized spillover effects in regional public goods, which causes the evaluation of district residents for public goods to deviate (i.e. preference parameter for district residents α_n is not the same as that for general society α), with $\alpha - \alpha_n$ measuring the spillover effects of regional public goods; two, the existence of external costs in financing regional public goods production, i.e. net central transfer payments to the regional government are funded by central tax revenues collected from other districts, such that costs are practically transferred to residents of other districts. Thus, social welfare may be derived as:

$$\hat{W} = W_n + (\alpha - \alpha_n)Q_n - (1 + \lambda)\xi_n \tag{9.3}$$

Finally, there is the incomplete information problem, arising out of the imbalance between production costs of public goods and information on preferences of residents. Suppose that enterprises have complete understanding of marginal costs θ_n. Neither the central government nor regional governments have complete knowledge of this information, but regional governments do have a definite advantage on this information. Thus, it may be assumed that the central government only has the probability distribution of θ_n, while regional governments have access to a signal σ_n for θ_n. If $\theta_n \in [\frac{k}{h}, \frac{k+1}{h}]$, then it may be assumed that $\sigma_n = \frac{k}{h}$, $k \in \{0, 1, \ldots, h-1\}$ where h measures the degree of accuracy of the signal σ_n: the larger the value of h, the more accurate σ_n is to the true information θ_n. District area and, by extension, the number of regional governments m^{n-1} is clearly a major factor affecting the accuracy of σ_n: the higher m^{n-1}, the better the potential for regional governments to accurately know the actual production costs for enterprises. Thus, it is assumed that $h = \varphi(m^{n-1})$, and also that $\varphi'(m^{n-1}) > 0$, i.e. h is an increasing function.

The parameter α_n is assumed to be a random variable, and its probability distribution to be common knowledge. Regional governments may gain knowledge of actual preferences of residents by surveying their volume of usage and evaluation of public goods. Thus, regional governments may be able to observe the random variable α_n, but the central government is unable to gain knowledge of actual information on α_n, and thus it is also unable to accurately know the scale of the spillover effects $(\alpha - \alpha_n)$. Additionally, considering that the larger the district size, the higher the potential to produce economies of scale, it is also assumed that expected spillover effects $E(\alpha - \alpha_n)$ is a non-decreasing function of m^{n-1}, i.e. increase in the number of regional governments will tend to increase the spillover effects.

Optimal size of regional government

For the production of public goods, regional governments and enterprises form a type of contract relationship between them. Thus, under the conditions of incomplete information, the problem that regional governments face is to design an optimal incentive mechanism that encourages enterprises to provide actual information on costs, so as to determine optimal volume of public goods and size of government. A mechanism is defined as $\{Q_n(\theta_n), G(\theta_n)\}$, that is, it must satisfy both incentive compatibility and individual rational constraints.

Assuming that $\pi(\theta_n, \tilde{\theta}_n) = G(\tilde{\theta}_n) - (\theta_n + \eta_n) Q_n(\tilde{\theta}_n)$ is the profit that enterprises gain in misstating θ_n as $\tilde{\theta}_n$, and that $\Pi_n(\theta_n) = \pi(\theta_n, \theta_n)$ is the profit gained for enterprises in providing actual costs information. Enterprises choose $\tilde{\theta}_n$ in order to maximize profits $\pi(\theta_n, \tilde{\theta}_n)$, giving the first-order optimality condition as $G(\tilde{\theta}_n) - (\theta_n + \eta_n)Q_n(\tilde{\theta}_n) = 0$. An incentive mechanism will demand that $\pi(\theta_n, \theta_n) \geq \pi(\theta_n, \tilde{\theta}_n), \forall \theta_n, \tilde{\theta}_n \in [\sigma_n, \sigma_n + 1/(\varphi(m^{n-1}))]$, such that the optimal decision for enterprises is to provide actual information on marginal costs (i.e. $\tilde{\theta}_n^* = \theta_n$), and so $G(\theta_n) - (\theta_n + \eta_n) Q_n(\theta_n) = 0$. Thus, there is:

$$\begin{aligned}\Pi_n(\theta_n) &= -\int_{\theta_n}^{\sigma_n+1/\varphi(m^{n-1})} [G(y) - (y + \eta_n)Q_n(y) - Q_n(y)]dy + \Pi_n \\ &= \int_{\theta_n}^{\sigma_n+1/\varphi(m^{n-1})} Q_n(y)dy + \Pi_n\end{aligned} \tag{9.4}$$

Of which, $\Pi_n^* = \Pi_n(\sigma_n + 1/\varphi(m^{n-1}))$ is the marginal conditions.[6]

From (9.1), $\tau_n = \frac{1}{[1-(1-\mu_n)\phi(n)]}(\Pi_n + \{\theta_n + \eta_n - [1-\phi(n)]\gamma_n\}Q_n)$. Substituting this into the district welfare function W_n, taking mathematic expectation $E_{\theta_n}(\cdot \mid \sigma_n, \alpha_n)$, and further substituting in (9.4), the expected district welfare function satisfying incentive compatibility and restraints may be derived as:

$$E_{\theta_n}(W_n \mid \sigma_n, \alpha_n) = \varphi(m^{n-1})\int_{\sigma_n}^{\sigma_n+1/\varphi(m^{n-1})}[-\tfrac{1}{2}Q_n(\theta_n)^2 + \Phi_n(\theta_n)Q_n(\theta_n)]d\theta_n - (\beta_n - 1)\Pi_n^* \tag{9.5}$$

Of which, $\Phi_n(\theta_n) = \alpha_n - \beta_n\{\theta_n + \eta_n - [1-\phi(n)]\gamma_n\} - (\beta_n - 1)(\theta_n - \sigma_n)$, and $\beta_n = (1+\lambda)/[1-(1-\mu_n)\phi(n)]$ measures the negative effects from the different distribution policy directions at different government levels.

Regional governments pursue maximization of (9.2) under individual rational constraints, giving:

$$Max\ E_{\theta_n}(U_n^l \mid \sigma_n, \alpha_n) = E_{\theta_n}((1-\omega_n)\eta_n Q_n(\theta_n) \mid \sigma_n, \alpha_n) + E_{\theta_n}(\omega_n W_n \mid \alpha_n, \alpha_n) \tag{9.6}$$

Solving for the above optimization problems, the following second-order optimality conditions may be derived:

$$Q_n^*(\theta_n \mid \sigma_n, \alpha_n) = \alpha_n - \beta_n\{\theta_n - [1-\phi(n)]\gamma_n\} - (\beta_n - 1)(\theta_n - \sigma_n) \tag{9.7}$$

$$\omega_n^* = 1/(1+\beta_n) \tag{9.8}$$

$$\eta_n^*(\theta_n \mid \sigma_n, \alpha_n) = [\alpha_n - \beta_n\{\theta_n - [1 - \phi(n)]\gamma_n\} - (\beta_n - 1)(\theta_n - \sigma_n)]/2(1 + \beta_n) \quad (9.9)$$

(9.7) shows that, since production costs may be transferred to residents of other districts through common pool channels, regional governments may be encouraged to increase an additional volume $\beta_n[1 - \phi(n)]\gamma_n$ of public goods, causing deviations in the optimal regional public goods volume. The negative effects from the different distribution policy directions at different levels of regional governments causes regional governments to increase focus on self-interests, such that even if the actual amount of common pool resources (i.e. net central transfer payments) are reduced, the common pool effect is still strengthened. Additionally, incomplete information causes the optimal regional public goods to decrease in volume, with a degree of reduction of $(\beta_n - 1)(\theta_n - \sigma_n)$. This may be attributed to the information rent incurred in getting enterprises to provide actual costs information, which requires additional funding through distortionary tax, and this causes additional loss in efficiency; differences in distribution policy at different levels of government also strengthens this type of distortion.[7]

It may further be seen from (9.7) and (9.8) that tax revenue decentralization helps to reduce the negative impact of differences in distribution policy, and thus helps to increase the accountability of regional governments ($\partial\omega^* / \partial\mu_n > 0$), thereby also helping to reduce distortionary effects related to production costs, information rent, and common pool resources. The effects of the first two factors are more significant, so tax revenue decentralization has a direct and positive effect on optimal volume of regional public goods provided. Tax revenue decentralization causes reduction in central transfer payments, leading to an indirect and negative effect on optimal volume of regional public goods provided, so its effects here is unclear. On the other hand, increase in the levels of government n will increase the differences in distribution policy, weakening the accountability of regional governments ($\partial\omega^* / \partial n < 0$), leading to increased distortion in production costs, information rent and common pool resources, thus causing a direct and negative effect on the volume of regional public goods provided. The effects of increasing the levels of government n on central transfer payments policy is unclear, so its effects on the volume of regional public goods provided is also unclear.

Under the conditions of incomplete information, the central government would choose the strength of transfer payments that maximizes expected social welfare. For the function of expected social welfare, taking the mathematical expectations from both sides of (9.3), $E_{\theta_n}(\cdot \mid \sigma_n, \alpha_n, \alpha)$, and substituting in (9.5), (9.8), and (9.9), along with the consideration that $\Pi_n^* = 0$, it may be derived as:

$$E_{\theta_n}(\hat{W} \mid \sigma_n, \alpha_n, \alpha) = \varphi(m^{n-1}) \int_{\sigma_n}^{\sigma_n + 1/\varphi(m^{n-1})} \{\frac{Q_n^2}{2(1+\beta_n)} + [\alpha - \alpha_n - (1+\lambda)\gamma_n]Q_n\} d\theta_n$$
$$= \frac{1}{6(1+\beta_n)}(3\beta_n^2\sigma_n^2 + 3\beta_n\psi_n\sigma_n + \psi_n^2) \qquad (9.10)$$
$$+ \frac{1}{2}[\frac{\beta_n\tilde{\alpha}_n}{(1+\beta_n)} - \alpha + \beta_n\mu_n\phi(n)\gamma_n](2\beta_n\sigma_n + \psi_n) - \frac{(2\beta_n+1)\tilde{\alpha}_n^2}{2(1+\beta_n)} + [\alpha - \beta_n\mu_n\phi(n)\gamma_n]\tilde{\alpha}_n$$

Of which, $\upsilon = (2\beta_n - 1)\theta_n - (\beta_n - 1)\sigma_n$, $\tilde{\alpha}_n = \alpha_n + \beta_n[1 - \phi(n)]\gamma_n$, and $\psi_n = (2\beta_n - 1)/\varphi(m^{n-1})$. Taking into consideration that σ_n has a uniform distribution of $\{0, 1/h, \ldots, (h-1)/h\}$ and is uncorrelated to α, then $E\hat{W} = E_{\alpha,\alpha_n}\left\{\frac{1}{h}\sum_{k=0}^{h-1} E_{\theta_n}(\hat{W} \mid \frac{k}{h}, \alpha_n, \alpha)\right\}$. Substituting in (9.10), the function for expected social welfare may be derived as:

$$E\hat{W} = E_{\alpha,\alpha_n}\left\{\tilde{\alpha}_n, \alpha - \frac{(2\beta_n+1)}{2(1+\beta_n)}\tilde{\alpha}_n^2 - \beta_n\mu_n\phi(n)\gamma_n\tilde{\alpha}_n\right\}$$
$$+ \frac{[\beta_n\varphi(m^{n-1}) + \beta_n - 1]}{2\varphi(m^{n-1})} E_{\alpha,\alpha_n}\left[\frac{\beta_n\tilde{\alpha}_n}{(1+\beta_n)} - \alpha + \beta_n\mu_n\phi(n)\gamma_n\right] \qquad (9.11)$$
$$+ \frac{\beta_n^2}{6(1+\beta_n)} + \frac{\beta_n(\beta_n - 1)}{4(1+\beta_n)\varphi(m^{n-1})} + \frac{(3\beta_n^2 - 5\beta_n + 2)}{12(1+\beta_n)\varphi(m^{n-1})^2}$$

Also, since $\partial E\hat{W}/\partial\gamma_n = 0$, the optimal central fiscal transfer payment may be derived as:

$$\gamma_n^* = \frac{(1+\beta_n)}{\beta_n\Theta_n}\left[E(\alpha - \alpha_n) - \frac{\beta_n}{1+\beta_n} + \frac{\mu_n\phi(n)}{1-\phi(n)}E(\alpha_n)\right]$$
$$+ \frac{[\beta_n\varphi(m^{n-1}) + \beta_n - 1][\beta_n(1-\phi(n)) + (1+\beta_n)\mu_n\phi(n)]}{2\beta_n\varphi(m^{n-1})[1-\phi(n)]\Theta_n} \qquad (9.12)$$

Of which, $\Theta_n = (2\beta_n + 1)(1 - \phi(n)) + 2(1+\beta_n)\mu_n\phi(n)$. Optimally, the profits gained by enterprises in providing costs information is zero ($\Pi_n^* = 0$), and so the optimal size of regional government may be derived as:

$$G_n^* = (\theta_n + \eta_n^*)Q_n^*(\theta_n \mid \sigma_n, \alpha_n) = \theta_n Q_n^*(\theta_n \mid \sigma_n, \alpha_n) + \frac{Q_n^*(\theta_n \mid \sigma_n, \alpha_n)^2}{2(1+\beta_n)} \qquad (9.13)$$

Substituting in (9.9), and also substituting (9.12) into (9.13), and taking into consideration expected spillover effects $E(\alpha - \alpha_n)$ as a function of m^{n-1}, it may further be derived that:

$$G_n^* = G_n\{\lambda, \theta_n, \mu_n, n, Q_n^*[\lambda, \alpha_n, \theta_n, \mu_n, n, \gamma_n^*(\lambda, \alpha_n, \mu_n, n, m)]\} \qquad (9.14)$$

From (9.12) and (9.14), it may be seen that the optimal size of regional governments not only depends on particular regional factors such as the preferences of residents α_n, production costs of public goods θ_n, degree of tax revenue distortion λ etc., but also the degree of fiscal decentralization μ_n, as well as the government organizational structure m (including levels of government and number of districts): if $\theta_n - \sigma_n = dz / \varphi(m^{n-1})$, then it can be derived from (9.14) that,

$$\frac{\partial G_n^*}{\partial m} = [\theta_n + \frac{Q_n^*}{1+\beta_n}]\{\beta_n[1-\phi(n)]\frac{\partial \gamma_n^*}{\partial m} + \frac{dz(\beta_n - 1)(n-1)\, m^{n-2}\varphi'(m^{n-1})}{\varphi(m^{n-1})^2}\} = X_1 \frac{\partial E(\alpha - \alpha_n)}{\partial n} + X_2 \varphi'(m^{n-1}),$$

of which $X_1 > 0$, and dz measures the performance of regional governments in collecting costs information.

It may thus be seen that the number of districts m affects the optimal size regional governments through two main mechanisms, spillover effects and the mechanism of costs information. Increase in m will increase spillover effects, such that an increase in central transfer payments is needed for correction, and so this has a positive effect on the optimal size of regional governments. On the other hand, increase in m will also increase the accuracy of costs information, helping to reduce information rent, leading to a reduction in central transfer payments and optimal size of regional governments [see (9.12)]; however, since decrease in information rent will also lead to increase in optimal volume of regional public goods provided and, by extension, the optimal size of regional governments [see (9.7)], the effects of costs information are on the whole unclear. If the performance of regional governments in collecting costs information is relatively poor (value of dz being relatively high), then the effects of m on costs information and, by extension, the overall effects of optimal size of regional governments will tend to be positive ($X_2 > 0$,).

For the levels of government n, it may be derived from (9.14) that

$$\frac{\partial G_n^*}{\partial n} = (\theta_n + \frac{Q_n^*}{1+\beta_n})\{\beta_n[1-\phi(n)]\frac{\partial \gamma_n^*}{\partial n} + \frac{(\beta_n - 1)m^{n-1}\,\mathrm{In}(m)dz}{\varphi(m^{n-1})^2}\} - \Omega_n\phi'(n) = \Delta_1 \partial E(\alpha - \alpha_n)/\partial n + \Delta_2\varphi'(m^{n-1}) + \Delta_3\phi'(n),$$

of which $\Omega_n = \frac{\beta_n^2}{1+\lambda}\{[\theta_n + \frac{Q_n^*}{1+\beta_n}][(1-\mu_n)(2\theta_n - \sigma_n) + \mu_n\gamma_n] + \frac{(1-\mu_n)Q_n^2}{2(1+\beta_n)^2}\} > 0$, $\Delta_1 > 0$,

$\Delta_3 = \Delta_{31} E(\alpha - \alpha_n) + \Delta_{32} E(\alpha_n) + \Delta_{33}/\varphi(m^{n-1}) - \Omega_n$, $\Delta_{31} < 0$, $\Delta_{32} < 0$, and $\Delta_{33} > 0$.

Similar to the effects of number of districts m, then, when the performance of regional governments in collecting costs information is relatively poor (value of dz being relatively high), then the effects of levels of government on optimal size of regional governments through spillover effects and the mechanism of costs information will be positive ($\Delta_2 > 0$); as previously mentioned, however, differences in distribution policy will have negative effects on common pool resources. The effects of n on optimal regional government expenditure is thus complex, and so the theoretical effects of n on optimal size of regional government remains unclear.

For tax revenue decentralization μ_n, it may be derived from (9.14) that

$$\frac{\partial G_n}{\partial \mu_n} = -[(\theta_n + \frac{Q_n^*}{1+\beta_n})\{2\theta_n - \sigma_n - [1-\phi(n)]\gamma_n\} + \frac{(Q_n^8)^2}{2(1+\beta_n)^2}]\frac{\partial \beta_n}{\partial \mu_n} + \beta_n(\theta_n + \frac{Q_n^*}{1+\beta_n})[1-\phi(n)]\frac{\partial \gamma_n}{\partial \mu_n},$$

of which $\partial\beta_n / \partial\mu_n < 0$ and $\partial\gamma_n / \partial\mu_n < 0$. It can thus be seen that, on the one hand, tax revenue decentralization has a negative effect on the optimal strength of central transfer payments and, by extension, the optimal expenditure of regional governments; on the other hand, it also helps to reduce the distortionary effects of differences in distribution policy, strengthening the accountability of regional governments, which leads to a positive effect on the optimal volume of regional public goods provided and the optimal size of regional governments. Thus, the overall effect of tax revenue decentralization on optimal regional government expenditure is also unclear.

The above analysis shows that optimization of the size of regional governments is a rather complex problem. Not only must it be taken into account factors of public service demands such as preferences of regional residents, supply-side factors such as production costs of regional public services, and distortionary local and central taxes; special consideration also has to be given to objectives of regional governments, as well as environmental factors in the relevant institution such as fiscal decentralization, central transfer payments system, and government organizational structures (especially the mechanisms of incentives and restraints, given by the levels and numbers of governments, and the impact on the behavior of regional government.)

Optimal Structure of Regional Government for Maximized Social Welfare: Single-tier Government Framework

Having dealt with the problem of optimal size of regional government structure for maximized social welfare, this section will explore for the optimal structure under the assumption of a single-tier government framework.

Public investment in physical capital such as infrastructure is an important item in the expenditure of regional governments, making a crucial contribution to economic growth and the elevation of social welfare levels.[8] As endogenous economic growth theories gain increasing popularity, there is also increasing awareness of the importance of public investment into human capital, such as public education and healthcare, in promoting coordinated economic and social development.[9]

In the real-world economy, however, due to limitations in fiscal resources and rigidity of administrative expenses, regional governments often have to look for trade-offs between public investments in physical capital and human capital. In China, this phenomenon is especially prominent: extensive studies show that under fiscal and promotional incentives, regional governments tend to focus more on infrastructure expenditure, and less on education and healthcare, and this leads to a series of serious socioeconomic problems.[10]

This section, then, does not seek to answer all aspects of the problems involved in an optimal government structure, but to focus on the optimal arrangements for public investments in physical capital and human capital. Using Agénor's two-capital endogenous growth model as reference,[11] a two-capital endogenous growth model for optimal allocation of public investment under a fiscal decentralization framework is constructed,[12] examining the two problems of the structure of public capital investment and capital development expenditure decentralization (i.e. the division of investment authority between central and regional governments) under a unified framework of analysis, in order to examine closely the effects of fiscal decentralization on the optimal structure of regional governments.[13]

Model framework

Consider a closed economy with a perfectly competitive market, and assume that private economic agents are both producers and consumers, rational, and have infinite lifespans. Assume also that there are two production departments in the economy, a physical capital production department and a human capital production department (education and healthcare). Private economic agents must receive education and healthcare services and accumulate human capital, in order to obtain a certain level of production skill, before participating in physical production. There are two levels of government (central and regional), with each level of government investing in public capital to provide public infrastructure, education and healthcare services for physical production and human capital accumulation of private economic agents.

Government

Assuming that the government works on a "balanced budget" principle, and uses linear tax revenues to fund public investment g (including investment in physical capital and human capital), then:[14]

$$g = g_k + g_h = g_{ck} + g_{ch} + g_{lk} + g_{lh} = \tau y \tag{9.15}$$

Of which, g_k and g_h are the per capita public investment in physical capital (including central investment g_{ck} and regional investment g_{lk}) and human capital (including central investment g_{ch} and regional investment g_{lh}) respectively, τ is the linear tax rate, and y is the production per capita. Let the proportion of public investment in physical capital out of total public capital investment be υ, then:

$$g_k = g_{ck} + g_{lk} = \upsilon\tau y,\ g_h = g_{ch} + g_{lh} = (1 - \upsilon)\tau y \tag{9.16}$$

Clearly, the size of υ decides the structure of public capital investment. Also let the proportions of per capita central investment in physical capital and human capital, as well as per capita regional investment in physical capital and human capital, be θ_{ck}, θ_{ch}, θ_{lk}, and θ_{lh}, i.e.:

$$\theta_{ck} = g_{ck}/g,\ \theta_{ch} = g_{ch}/g,\ \theta_{lk} = g_{lk}/g,\ \theta_{lh} = g_{lh}/g \tag{9.17}$$

From (9.16) and (9.17), it may be seen that $\upsilon = \theta_{ck} + \theta_{lk}$, $1 - \upsilon = \theta_{ch} + \theta_{lh}$. The degree of decentralization for expenditure on physical capital d_k and the degree of decentralization for expenditure on human capital d_h may further be derived as:[15]

$$d_k = g_{lk}/g_k = \theta_{lk}/\upsilon,\ d_h = g_{lh}/g_h = \theta_{lh}/(1 - \upsilon) \tag{9.18}$$

Private economic agents: Physical capital accumulation

Assume that the physical capital production department uses private physical capital per capita k, private human capital per capita h, per capita central public investment in physical capital g_{ck} and per capita regional investment in physical capital g_{lk} for production, and follows the Cobb-Douglas production function with constant size of returns per capita. Substituting (9.17) into the production function, there is:

$$y = Ak^{\alpha}k^{\beta}g_{ck}^{\gamma}g_{lk}^{1-\alpha-\beta-\gamma} = A\theta_{ck}^{\gamma}\theta_{lk}^{1-\alpha-\beta-\gamma}k(h/k)^{\beta}(g/k)^{1-\alpha-\beta} \tag{9.19}$$

Of which, α, β, γ, and $(1 - \alpha - \beta - \gamma) \in (0,1)$, are the production elasticity for physical capital per capita, human capital per capita, central and regional investment in physical capital per capita respectively. A is the technical parameter, assumed to be constant for simplicity's sake. The output of the physical capital production department consists of three parts: consumption per capita c, physical capital accumulation per capita and tax revenue per capita (τy). Thus, there is:

$$\dot{k} = (1 - \tau)\,Ak^{\alpha}h^{\beta}g_{ck}^{\gamma}g_{lk}^{1-\alpha-\beta-\gamma} - c = (1 - \tau)A\theta_{ck}^{\gamma}\theta_{lk}^{1-\alpha-\beta-\gamma}(h/k)^{\beta}(g/k)^{1-\alpha-\beta}k - c \tag{9.20}$$

Private economic agents: Dynamic growth in consumption

Under the constraints of (9.20), private economic agents choose c for maximizing utility of discounted cash flow. Using a utility function for fixed intertemporal substitution elasticity, there is:

$$\underset{c}{Max}U = \int_0^{\infty} e^{-pt} \frac{[c(t)^{1-\sigma} - 1]}{1-\sigma} dt \tag{9.21}$$

Of which, $\rho > 0$ is the rate of discount, $\sigma > 0$ is the elasticity of marginal utility of consumption, σ^{-1} is the intertemporal substitution elasticity of consumption. Solving for the problem using the Hamiltonian system, the first order optimality conditions may be obtained as:

$$c^{-\sigma} = \lambda \tag{9.22}$$

$$\dot{\lambda} = \rho\lambda - \lambda A\alpha(1-\tau)\theta_{ck}^{\gamma}\theta_{lk}^{1-\alpha-\beta-\gamma}(h/k)^{\beta}(g/k)^{1-\alpha-\beta} \tag{9.23}$$

Of which, λ is the Hamilton multiplier, i.e. the shadow price (marginal utility of physical capital per capita k. (9.22) means that under optimal conditions, marginal utility of consumption $c^{-\sigma}$ is equivalent to the marginal utility of physical capital accumulation, λ. (9.23) is an Euler equation.

The transversality condition and initial value condition are given by:

$$\lim_{t\to\infty} \lambda k e^{-pt} = 0,\ k(0) = h(0) = 0 \tag{9.24}$$

The transversality condition means that, given sufficient time, if $\lambda > 0$, then private economic agents will consume all physical capital in order to increase utility; if $k \neq 0$, then it must be the case that $\lambda > 0$, that is, the consumption of physical capital cannot increase the utility of private economic agents. From (9.22) and (9.23), the function for dynamic growth of consumption per capita may be derived as:

$$\frac{\dot{c}}{c} = \frac{1}{\sigma}[A\alpha(1-\tau)\theta_{ck}^{\gamma}\theta_{lk}^{1-\alpha-\beta-\gamma}(h/k)^{\beta}(g/k)^{1-\alpha-\beta} - \rho] \tag{9.25}$$

Private entities: Human capital accumulation

Lucas assumes that private economic agents use non-leisure time for human capital accumulation (training, learning-by-doing, healthcare), and so human capital accumulation depend on the desires of economic agents to participate in human capital accumulation activities.[16] This, however, does not take into consideration that education, especially basic education, as well as certain healthcare services are compulsory; China, for instance, passed the compulsory education law in 1986. Under these conditions, human capital accumulation is, to a certain extent, compulsory. Agénor, on the other hand, assumes that private economic agents must receive education and healthcare services for human capital accumulation before they can participate in physical production, and separates the process of human capital formation into two phases, i.e. in the first phase, government investment and teachers produce public education services, and government investment and relevant vocational technicians produce public healthcare services, and in the second phase, the services are provided to youths for human capital accumulation; he further assumes that these two phases follows the Cobb-Douglas production function with constant size of returns, in order to better demonstrate the human capital formation process in developing countries.[17]

This segment thus follows the assumptions made by Agénor, and also introduces central and regional public investment in human capital into the human capital formation process of economic agents, in order to find out which type of public investment is more important to human capital accumulation for the general society. Assuming that there is no depreciation of human capital, the function for human capital production per capita is as follows:

$$\dot{h} = B(g_{ch}^{\omega} g_{lh}^{\eta} g^{1-\omega-\eta})^{\varepsilon}(\phi h)^{1-\varepsilon},\ 0 < \omega,\ \eta,\ (\omega+\eta),\ \varepsilon < 1 \tag{9.26}$$

Of which, $\omega\varepsilon$ and $\eta\varepsilon$ are the human capital accumulation elasticity for per capita central and regional public investment in human capital g_{ch} and g_{lh} respectively. B is the technical parameter, assumed to be constant. h is the human capital investment of education and healthcare departments (teachers and doctors), ϕh is the number of youths receiving education and healthcare services, $\phi > 0$ is the ratio of investment to youths (teachers : students or doctors : students), with the implicit assumption that governments regulate the quality of education and healthcare services through ensuring a stable ratio. Substituting (9.17) into (9.26), the function for human capital production per capita may be given as:

$$\frac{\dot{h}}{h} = B\phi^{1-\varepsilon}\theta_{ch}^{\omega\varepsilon}\theta_{lh}^{\eta\varepsilon}(g/k)^{(\omega+\eta)\varepsilon}(h/k)^{-(\omega+\eta)\varepsilon} \tag{9.27}$$

Balanced growth equilibrium analysis

Using (9.15) and (9.19) to obtain g/k, then substituting in (9.25) and (9.27), and further considering $\upsilon = \theta_{ck} + \theta_{lk}$, $1 - \upsilon = \theta_{ch} + \theta_{lh}$, there is:

$$\frac{\dot{c}}{c} = \frac{1}{\sigma}[\Theta\alpha(\upsilon - \theta_{lk})^{\gamma/(\alpha+\beta)}\theta_{lk}^{(1-\alpha-\beta-\gamma)/(\alpha+\beta)}(h/k)^{\beta/(\alpha+\beta)} - \rho] \tag{9.28}$$

$$\frac{\dot{h}}{h} = \Psi(1 - \upsilon - \theta_{lh})^{\omega\varepsilon} \theta_{lh}^{\eta\varepsilon} (\upsilon - \theta_{lk})^{\gamma\chi} \theta_{lk}^{(1-\alpha-\beta-\gamma)\chi} (h/k)^{-\alpha\chi} \tag{9.29}$$

Of which, $\Theta = A^{1/(\alpha+\beta)}(1 - \tau)\tau^{(1-\alpha-\beta)/(\alpha+\beta)}$, $\Psi = B\phi^{1-\varepsilon}(A\tau)^{\chi}$, and $\chi = (\omega + \eta)\varepsilon/(\alpha + \beta)$. Let $z = c/k$ be the ratio of consumption to physical capital, and $m = h/k$ be the ratio of human capital to physical capital. From (9.20), (9.28), and (9.29), it may be derived that:

$$\frac{\dot{z}}{z} = \frac{1}{\sigma}[\Theta(\alpha - \sigma)(\upsilon - \theta_{lk})^{\gamma/(\alpha+\beta)} \theta_{lk}^{(1-\alpha-\beta-\gamma)/(\alpha+\beta)} m^{\beta/(\alpha+\beta)} - \rho] + z \tag{9.30}$$

$$\begin{aligned}\frac{\dot{m}}{m} &= \Psi(1 - \upsilon - \theta_{lh})^{\omega\varepsilon} \theta_{lh}^{\eta\varepsilon} (\upsilon - \theta_{lk})^{\gamma\chi} \theta_{lk}^{(1-\alpha-\beta-\gamma)\chi} m^{-\alpha\chi} \\ &\quad - \Theta(\upsilon - \theta_{lk})^{\gamma/(\alpha+\beta)} \theta_{lk}^{(1-\alpha-\beta-\gamma)/(\alpha+\beta)} m^{\beta/(\alpha+\beta)} + z\end{aligned} \tag{9.31}$$

The non-linear differential equations given by (9.30) and (9.31) demonstrate the dynamic equilibrium of the economy, setting (z^*, m^*) as the point of equilibrium.[18] Let $z = 0$ and $m = 0$, then from (9.18), (9.30), and (9.31), it may be derived that:

$$z^* = \frac{1}{\sigma}[\rho - \Theta(\alpha - \sigma)(1 - d_k)^{\gamma/(\alpha+\beta)} d_k^{(1-\alpha-\beta-\gamma)/(\alpha+\beta)} \upsilon^{(1-\alpha-\beta)/(\alpha+\beta)} (m^*)^{\beta/(\alpha+\beta)}] \tag{9.32}$$

$$Q(m^*, d_k, d_h, \upsilon) = 0 \tag{9.33}$$

Of which, $Q(m^*, d_k, d_h, \upsilon) = \Psi(1 - d_h)^{\omega\varepsilon} d_h^{\eta\varepsilon} (1 - d_k)^{\gamma\chi} d_k^{(1-\alpha-\beta-\gamma)\chi} (1 - \upsilon)^{(\omega+\eta)\varepsilon} \upsilon^{(1-\alpha-\beta)\chi} (m^*)^{-\alpha\chi}$

$$+ \frac{1}{\sigma}\left[\rho - \Theta\alpha(1 - d_k)^{\frac{\gamma}{(\alpha+\beta)}} d_k^{\frac{(1-\alpha-\beta-\gamma)}{(\alpha+\beta)}} \upsilon^{\frac{(1-\alpha-\beta)}{(\alpha+\beta)}} (m^*)^{\frac{\beta}{(\alpha+\beta)}}\right]$$

(9.30)–(9.33), as well as the transversality condition and initial value condition given by (9.24), demonstrates the balanced-growth path of the economy, for which consumption per capita, human capital per capita, and physical capital per capita have an equivalent and constant growth rate of ξ, which is also the growth rate for production per capita, i.e. $\xi = \dot{c}/c = \dot{h}/h = \dot{k}/k = \dot{y}/y$.[19] From (9.18), (9.28), and (9.29), the following theorem may be derived:

Theorem 1: In a closed economy, the balanced growth rate of the economy is:

$$\xi = \frac{1}{\sigma}[\Theta\alpha(1 - d_k)^{\gamma/(\alpha+\beta)} d_k^{(1-\alpha-\beta-\gamma)/(\alpha+\beta)} \upsilon^{(1-\alpha-\beta)/(\alpha+\beta)} (m^*)^{\beta/(\alpha+\beta)} - \rho] \tag{9.34}$$

which may also be expressed as:

$$\xi = \Psi(1-d_h)^{\omega\varepsilon} d_h^{\eta\varepsilon}(1-d_k)^{\gamma\chi} d_k^{(1-\alpha-\beta-\gamma)\chi}(1-\upsilon)^{(\omega+\eta)\varepsilon}\upsilon^{(1-\alpha-\beta)\chi}(m^*)^{-\alpha\chi} \tag{9.35}$$

Of which, m^*, υ, d_k, and d_h satisfies (9.33).

Thus, theorem 1 shows that if all other parameters remain fixed, then the determining factors in long-term economic growth are the degree of decentralization in capital development expenditure and the compositional structure of public capital investment.

Comparative statics analysis

In order to understand more clearly the optimal degree of decentralization of capital development expenditure and the optimal proportion of public investment in physical capital, comparative statics analysis is used to examine their effects on balanced growth rates and equilibrium ratio of human to physical capital, and thus determine their optimal levels.

From (9.33) and (9.34), a second theorem may be derived:[20]

Theorem 2: (1) If and only if $d_h \le \eta/(\omega+\eta)$, then, $\partial m^*/\partial d_h \ge 0$ and $\partial\xi/\partial d_h \ge 0$. (2) If and only if $d_k \ge (1-\alpha-\beta-\gamma)/(1-\alpha-\beta)$, then $\partial m^*/\partial d_k \ge 0$; if and only if $\mu_{m^*/d_k} \ge [\gamma d_k/(1-d_k)-(1-\alpha-\beta-\gamma)]/\beta$ then $\partial\xi/\partial d_k \ge 0$. (3) $\partial m^*/\partial v \ge 0$; if and only if $-\mu_{m^*/\upsilon} \le (1-\alpha-\beta)/\beta$, then $\partial\xi/\partial\upsilon \ge 0$.[21]

Theorem 2 thus demonstrates the following:

1. The effect of decentralization in expenditure for human capital development on the human capital to physical capital equilibrium ratio and balanced economic growth is unclear, although the condition of effect are the same for both, i.e. only if the degree of decentralization in expenditure for human capital development drops below a certain threshold will it cause a positive effect on the human capital to physical capital equilibrium ratio and balanced economic growth;
2. The effect of decentralization in expenditure for physical capital development on the human capital to physical capital equilibrium ratio and balanced economic growth is also unclear, and the conditions of effect are different for both, but the effect on balanced economic growth is dependent on the effect on the human capital to physical capital equilibrium ratio, i.e. only if its positive effect ($\partial m^*/\partial d_k > 0$) is sufficiently large or its negative effect ($\partial m^*/\partial d_k < 0$) is negligible (that is, when the degree of decentralization in physical capital development expenditure drops below a certain threshold) will decentralization in expenditure for physical capital development promote balanced economic growth;

3. Increase in public investment in physical capital does not favor increase in the human capital to physical capital equilibrium ratio, and its effects on balanced economic growth depends on its effects on the human capital to physical capital equilibrium ratio, i.e. only if its negative effect on the human capital to physical capital equilibrium ratio is negligible (that is, when the proportion of public investment in physical capital drops below a certain threshold) will the increase in public investment in physical capital promote long-term economic growth.

The effects of decentralization in capital development expenditure and the proportion of public investment in physical capital on long-term economic growth are unclear because it has a double effect on long-term economic growth: on the one hand, in affecting the human capital to physical capital equilibrium ratio, it indirectly affects long-term economic growth, and the nature of this effect depends on both the effect on the human capital to physical capital equilibrium ratio and also the effect of the human capital to physical capital equilibrium ratio on long-term economic growth [see (9.34) and (9.35)]; on the other hand, assuming that all other factors remain fixed, increase in the degree of decentralization in capital development expenditure and the proportion of public investment in physical capital means that the proportion of central out of total public capital investment and proportion of public investment in human capital out of total public investment will both decrease, causing a totally opposite effect on the mechanism of long-term economic growth.

Thus, only if decentralization in capital development expenditure and proportion of public investment in physical capital are both below a certain threshold will their positive effects on economic growth exceed their negative effects and promote long-term economic growth, but as they gradually increase in degree and proportion, their positive marginal effects gradually decrease and negative marginal effects gradually increase, until the threshold is exceeded and positive marginal effects are smaller than negative marginal effects, and constrain balanced economic growth. It may thus be seen that the degree of decentralization in capital development expenditure and the proportion of public investment in physical capital, and balanced economic growth leading to social welfare, exhibit an inverted U-shaped relationship, such that there is an optimal value for maximized social welfare. A third theorem may thus be derived as follows:

Theorem 3: The relationship between the degree of decentralization in capital development expenditure and the proportion of public investment in physical capital, and balanced economic growth leading to social welfare, is exhibited in an inverted U-shaped curve. Thus, the functions for the optimal degrees and proportions for maximized social welfare may be derived as $d_k^* = (1 - \alpha - \beta - \gamma)/$

$(1-\alpha-\beta)$ for decentralization in physical capital development expenditure, $d_h^* = \eta/(\omega+\eta)$ for decentralization in human capital development expenditure, and $\upsilon^* = (1-\alpha-\beta)/(1-\alpha)$ for proportion of public investment in physical capital.[22]

Theorem 3 shows that the optimal degree of decentralization in physical capital development expenditure is equivalent to the ratio of output elasticity of regional public investment in physical capital $(1-\alpha-\beta-\gamma)$ and total output elasticity of central and regional public investment in physical capital (γ and $1-\alpha-\beta-\gamma$); the optimal degree of decentralization in human capital development expenditure is equivalent to the ratio of elasticity of regional public investment in human capital accumulation ($\eta\varepsilon$) and elasticity of central and regional public investment in human capital accumulation ($\omega\varepsilon$ and $\eta\varepsilon$). This means that the larger the regional output elasticity of public capital investment and elasticity of human capital accumulation, and the smaller the central output elasticity of public capital investment and elasticity of human capital accumulation, then the higher will be the degree of decentralization in capital development expenditure, and so the higher possibility for decentralization in capital development expenditure to promote social welfare. The optimal proportion of public investment in physical capital is equivalent to the ratio of total output elasticity of central and regional public investment in physical capital $(1-\alpha-\beta)$, and the total of output elasticity of central and regional public investment in physical capital and the output elasticity of human capital β. The larger the output elasticity of central and regional public investment in physical capital, and the smaller the output elasticity for human capital, then the larger the optimal proportion of public investment in physical capital, and only then will increase in the proportion of public investment in physical capital lead to a higher possibility of promoting social welfare.

Likewise, the optimal ratio of public investment in physical capital to that of human capital may be derived as $\upsilon^*/(1-\upsilon^*) = (1-\alpha-\beta)/\beta$, i.e. the ratio of the total output elasticity of central and regional public investment in physical capital to the output elasticity of human capital. This is consistent with the result obtained by Agénor in that the optimal ratio of public investment in physical capital to human capital is equivalent to the ratio of the output elasticity of public investment in physical capital to the output elasticity of human capital, without considering for a fiscal decentralization framework.[23] Agénor further points out that when human capital can completely and rapidly depreciate, then the optimal ratio of public investment in physical capital to human capital will be equivalent to the ratio of the output elasticity of physical capital to the output elasticity of public investment in human capital.[24] In addition, the optimal tax rate $\tau^* = 1 - \alpha$ may be readily obtained, that is, the total of output elasticity of human capital and the per capita central and regional public investment in physical capital; this is also consistent with the optimal tax rate obtained by Barro.[25]

Thus, this section has managed to obtain the model for obtaining the optimal degree of decentralization in capital development expenditure and the structure of regional public capital investment, which is crucial to realizing the optimal structure of regional governments. The fact is, it can be roughly determined from actual data that the optimal degree of decentralization in physical capital development expenditure is about 0.463, which means that the marginal productivity of central public investment in physical capital is slightly higher than that of the regional (see Theorem 3).[26] This may be attributed to that China's fiscal decentralization is in its nature a system of appointment by the central government, and that there are still large obstacles to population mobility, and so the mechanisms of the so-called "vote with hands" and "vote with feet" do not really come into play,[27] such that regional governments often fail to take as priority the preferences of local residents, leading to a relatively low efficiency in regional public investment in physical capital. It may also be due to the fact that there is a wide disparity in the level of development across different regions, such that the external costs of economic infrastructure are relatively higher, and so allows central public investment in physical capital to better demonstrate its effectiveness. At the moment, decentralization in physical capital development expenditure is clearly higher than what would be optimal; the central government should thus moderate the degree of decentralization by considering taking on more responsibility in public investment in physical capital.

The optimal proportion of public investment in physical capital is 0.587; judging from past experience, then, the marginal productivity of human capital is relatively low (see Theorem 3). This may be attributed to the fact that China is still in the early stages of industrialization, and its economic and social infrastructure is still very weak, and so the external environment favorable for human capital to fulfill its potential is still lacking.[28] As the country's continues its economic growth and the infrastructure gradually improves, the effect of human capital is expected to gradually increase, and the optimal proportion of public investment in physical capital will also decrease. As of now, however, public investment in physical capital is still clearly insufficient, with the proportion of investment far lower than the optimal level, meaning that for the foreseeable future, China's government still cannot afford to neglect public investment in physical capital.

Optimal Structure of Regional Government for Maximized Social Welfare: Multi-tier Government Framework

The previous section examined the optimal structure of regional governments under a single-tier government framework. The obvious limitation is that a single-tier government framework is unable to comprehensively reveal the effects of the interactive behavior between the central and regional governments, as well as the intergovernmental fiscal relationships and the institutional arrangements, on the optimal structure of regional governments for China's unique organizational structure. This section thus further examines for the optimal structure of regional governments and the optimal arrangements in the decentralized institution for maximized social welfare, under a multi-tier government framework.

Gordon used a static model to examine the role played by federal transfer payments on correcting the externalities of regional public goods and its effects on regional government behavior, and then explored the optimal policies for intergovernmental transfer payments and local tax revenue.[29] Persson and Tabellini used a static model to examine risk sharing and redistribution policies for regional governments in a federal system.[30] Gong and Zou used a dynamic growth model with multi-tier governments to examine for optimal central transfer payment policies and central and regional tax revenues, but the model used was a one-sector growth model, and so it is rather limited for examining the optimal structure of regional governments.[31]

This section will thus follow closely the work of Gong and Zou, constructing a two-capital endogenous growth model for physical and human capital production, introducing central and regional public capital investment; this would help to analyze comprehensively the determining factors in the optimal regional government structure as well as the effects of fiscal decentralization and central fiscal transfer payments.

Model framework

Based on the two-capital endogenous economic growth theory, a dynamic Stackelberg game theory model containing private economic agents, regional governments and the central government working under a multi-tier government framework is constructed, examining under a unified framework of analysis the optimal structure of regional government, the optimal central and regional tax policies, the optimal degree of fiscal decentralization, and the optimal central fiscal transfer payment policies.

Suppose that there is a central government and an N number of regional governments in the economy, with each regional district containing a representative private economic agent. The Stackelberg game theory model is used to demonstrate the tactical interactions between private economic agent, regional government and central government, and it is assumed that for the tactical interactions between private economic agents and regional governments, the regional government is the leader and the private economic agent the follower, while for that between central and regional governments, the central government is the leader and the regional government the follower.

Also suppose that there are two production departments in the economy, the physical capital production department and the human capital (education and healthcare) production department. Private economic agents must receive education and compulsory healthcare services to accumulate a certain level of human capital before they can participate in physical capital production. The share of time spent on physical capital production for private economic agents is u, and the share of time spent on human capital accumulation is $1 - u$.[32] The central and regional governments use public capital investment g_f and g_s^i ($i = 1, \cdots, N$) respectively to provide infrastructure, public education and healthcare services for the physical capital production and human capital accumulation for private economic agents. α_f and α_s^i are the central proportion of public investment in physical capital and the regional proportion of public investment in physical capital respectively, and $1 - \alpha_f$ and $1 - \alpha_s^i$ are the central proportion of public investment in human capital and the regional proportion of public investment in human capital respectively.

Assume that the central and regional governments all follow a "balanced budget" principle, and fund their own public expenditure autonomously under the tax sharing system. Funding for the central government is obtained through central tax revenues, i.e. income tax revenues (with a tax rate of τ_y), and the funding for regional governments is obtained through regional tax revenues, i.e. consumption tax revenues (with a tax rate of τ_c^i), as well as central fiscal transfer payments.[33] Let t^i be the percentage of central fiscal transfer payments, i.e. the ratio of central fiscal transfer payments to the autonomous fiscal revenue of regional governments. The functions of budget constraints for central and regional governments are thus:

$$g_f + \sum_{i=1}^{N} t^i(\tau_c^i c^i) = \sum_{i=1}^{N} \tau_y y^i \tag{9.36}$$

$$g_s^i = \tau_c^i c^i + t^i \tau_c^i c^i \tag{9.37}$$

Assuming that the physical capital production department uses private physical capital k^i, private human capital uh^i, central public investment in physical capital

$\alpha_f g_f$, and regional public investment in physical capital for production $\alpha_s^i g_s^i$, and follows the Cobb-Douglas function of production, there is:[34]

$$y^i = A(k^i)^{\theta_1}(uh^i)^{\theta_2}(\alpha_f g_f)^{\theta_3}(\alpha_s^i g_s^i)^{\theta_4} h^{\theta_5}, \theta_1 + \theta_2 + \theta_3 + \theta_4 = 1 \qquad (9.38)$$

Of which, $\theta_i\,(i = 1, 2, 3, 4)$ are the output elasticity for private physical capital, private human capital, central public investment in physical capital, and regional public investment in physical capital respectively. h is the human capital per capita, showing the external effects of human capital, and θ_5 measures the magnitude of the external effects. A is the technical parameter.

Consider that physical capital output has four main aspects, consumption c^i, private physical capital accumulation, tax revenue, and capital depreciation, then the function for private physical capital accumulation may be given as:

$$k^i = (1 - \tau_y)A(k^i)^{\theta_1}(uh^i)^{\theta_2}(\alpha_f g_f)^{\theta_3}(\alpha_s^i g_s^i)^{\theta_4} h^{\theta_5} - (1 - \tau_c^i)c^i - \delta k^i \qquad (9.39)$$

Of which, δ is the rate of depreciation of private physical capital.

Assume that the human capital production department uses human capital $(1 - u)h^i$, central public investment in human capital $(1 - \alpha_f)g_f$, and regional public investment in human capital $(1 - \alpha_s^i)g_s^i$ for production, and also follows the Cobb-Douglas function of production with constant returns. Assuming that there is no human capital depreciation, the function for human capital accumulation may be given as:

$$h^i = B[(1 - u)h^i]^{\omega_1}[(1 - \alpha_f)g_f]^{\omega_2}[(1 - \alpha_s^i)g_s^i]^{\omega_3}, \omega_1 + \omega_2 + \omega_3 = 1 \qquad (9.40)$$

Of which, $\omega_1\ (i = 1, 2, 3)$ are the human capital accumulation elasticity for human capital, central public investment in human capital, and regional public investment in human capital respectively. B is the technical parameter.

Private economic agents

Under given conditions of initial states of regional government policy $k^i(0) = k_0^i$ and $h^i(0) = h_0^i$, and the constraints of (9.39) and (9.40), private economic agents choose c^i, k^i, and h^i to achieve maximum lifetime utility. Using a utility function for fixed intertemporal substitution elasticity, there is:

$$\underset{c^i,k^i,h^i,}{Max U} = \int_0^\infty e^{-pt} \frac{[(c^i)^{1-\alpha} - 1]}{1-\sigma} dt \qquad (9.41)$$

Of which, $\rho > 0$ is the rate of discount, $\sigma > 0$ is the marginal utility elasticity, and its inverse σ^{-1} is the intertemporal substitution elasticity of consumption. Solving with the Hamiltonian system, the first-order optimal condition may be given as:

$$c^{i-\sigma} = \lambda_1^i (1 + \tau_c^i) \tag{9.42}$$

with the Euler equations being:

$$\dot{\lambda}_1^i = \rho\lambda_1^i - \lambda_1^i (1 - \tau_y) A\theta_1 u^{\theta_2} k^{i\theta_1 - 1} h^{i\theta_2} (\alpha_f g_f)^{\theta_3} (\alpha_s g_s)^{\theta_4} h^{\theta_5} + \lambda_1{}^i\delta \tag{9.43}$$

$$\begin{aligned}\dot{\lambda}_2^i = {} & \rho\lambda_2^i - \lambda_1^i (1 - \tau_y) A\theta_2 u^{\theta_2} k^{i\theta_1} h^{i\theta_2} (\alpha_f g_f)^{\theta_3} (\alpha_s^i g_s^i)^{\theta_4} h^{\theta_5} \\ & - \lambda_2^i \omega_1 B(1 - u)^{\omega_1} h^{i\omega_1 - 1} [(1 - \alpha_f) g_f]^{\omega_2} [(1 - \alpha_s^i) g_s^i]^{\omega_3}\end{aligned} \tag{9.44}$$

and the transversality condition is:

$$\lim_{t \to 0} \lambda_1^i k^i e^{-\rho t} = 0\,;\ \lim_{t \to 0} \lambda_2^i h^i e^{-\rho t} = 0 \tag{9.45}$$

Of which, λ_1^i and λ_2^i are the Hamiltonian multipliers, i.e. the shadow prices of private physical capital k^i and private human capital h^i, reflecting the increase in marginal utility from the increases in k^i and h^i. The transversality condition (9.45) means that, given sufficient time, if $\lambda_1^i > 0$ (or $\lambda_2^i > 0$), then private economic agents will consume all physical capital (or human capital) to increase utility; if $h^i \neq 0$ (or $h^i \neq 0$), then there will be $\lambda_1^i > 0$ (or $\lambda_2^i > 0$), i.e. consumption of physical capital (or human capital) cannot increase the utility of private economic agents. When the economy reaches the balanced-growth equilibrium, then $h = h^i$, and consumption, private physical capital, and private human capital all moves at the same growth rate.[35] Let ϕ^i be the regional economic balanced-growth rate, then $\frac{\dot{k}^i}{k^i} = \frac{\dot{c}^i}{c^i} = \frac{\dot{h}^i}{h^i} = \frac{\dot{y}^i}{y^i} = \phi^i$. From (9.42), there is $\frac{\dot{\lambda}_1^i}{\lambda_1^i} = \sigma\phi^i$, and substituting into (9.43), there is:

$$\sigma\phi^i + \rho + \delta = (1 - \tau_y)\, A\theta_1 k^{i\theta_1 - 1} u^{\theta_2} h^{i\theta_2} (\alpha_f g_f)^{\theta_3} (\alpha_s^i g_s^i)^{\theta_4} h^{i\theta_5} \tag{9.46}$$

From (9.39), (9.40), and (9.46), the optimal decision for private economic agents may be given as:

$$h^i = \left(\frac{B}{\phi^i}\right)^{\frac{1}{1-\omega_1}} (1 - u)^{\frac{\omega_1}{1-\omega_1}} (1 - \alpha_f)^{\frac{\omega_2}{1-\omega_1}} (1 - \alpha_s^i)^{\frac{\omega_3}{1-\omega_1}} g_f^{\frac{\omega_2}{1-\omega_1}} g_s^{i\,\frac{\omega_3}{1-\omega_1}} \tag{9.47}$$

$$k^i = M\left[\frac{\theta_1(1-\tau_y)}{\rho+\delta+\sigma\phi^i}\right]^{\frac{1}{1-\theta_1}} \alpha_f^{\frac{\theta_3}{1-\theta_1}} \alpha_s^{i\frac{\theta_4}{1-\theta_1}} (1-\alpha_f)^{\frac{\omega_2(\theta_2+\theta_5)}{(1-\omega_1)(1-\theta_1)}} (1-\alpha_s^i)^{\frac{\omega_3(\theta_2+\theta_5)}{(1-\omega_1)(1-\theta_1)}} g_f^{\frac{\theta_3(1-\omega_1)+\omega_2(\theta_2+\theta_5)}{(1-\omega_1)(1-\theta_1)}} g_s^{i\frac{\theta_4(1-\omega_1)+\omega_3(\theta_2+\theta_5)}{(1-\omega_1)(1-\theta_1)}} \quad (9.48)$$

$$c^i = \frac{[(\rho+\delta+\sigma\phi^i)-\theta_1(\delta+\phi^i)]k^i}{\theta_1(1-\tau_c^i)} \quad (9.49)$$

$$y^i = \frac{[\rho+\delta+\sigma\phi^i]k^i}{\theta_1(1-\tau_y)} \quad (9.50)$$

Of which, $M = \left[A\left(\frac{B}{\phi^i}\right)^{\frac{\theta_2+\theta_5}{1-\omega_1}} u^{\theta_2}(1-u)^{\frac{\omega_1(\theta_2+\theta_5)}{1-\omega_1}}\right]^{\frac{1}{1-\theta_1}}$.

Regional governments

Under the given conditions of central government policy and the optimal decisions of private economic bodies given in (9.47)–(9.50), and the constraints of (9.37), regional governments choose the proportion of regional public investment in physical capital α_s^i and consumption tax rate τ_c^i, in order to maximize utility for private economic bodies under the balanced-growth path:

$$\underset{\alpha_s^i,\tau_c^i}{Max} U = \frac{[(c^i)^{1-\sigma}-1]}{1-\sigma} \quad (9.51)$$

Solving for this gives the following first-order conditions:

$$\frac{(1-\omega_1)[c^i(\cdot)]^{1-\sigma}}{[(1-\omega_1)(1-\theta_1-\theta_4)-\omega_3(\theta_2+\theta_5)]}\left[\frac{\theta_4}{\alpha_s^i}-\frac{\omega_3(\theta_2+\theta_5)}{(1-\omega_1)(1-\alpha_s^i)}\right]=0 \quad (9.52)$$

$$\frac{(1-\omega_1)[c^i(\cdot)]^{1-\sigma}}{[(1-\omega_1)(1-\theta_1-\theta_4)-\omega_3(\theta_2+\theta_5)]}\left[\frac{1-\theta_1}{1+\tau_c^i}-\frac{\theta_4(1-\omega_1)+\omega_3(\theta_2+\theta_5)}{(1-\omega_1)\tau_c^i}\right]=0 \quad (9.53)$$

The optimal proportion of regional public investment in physical capital α_s^{i*} and the optimal consumption tax rate τ_c^{i*} may thus be respectively given as:

$$\alpha_s^{i*} = \frac{(1-\omega_1)\theta_4}{(1-\omega_1)\theta_4+\omega_3(\theta_2+\theta_5)} \quad (9.54)$$

$$\tau_c^{i*} = \frac{\theta_4(1-\omega_1)+\omega_3(\theta_2+\theta_5)}{(1-\omega_1)(1-\theta_1-\theta_4)-\omega_3(\theta_2+\theta_5)} \quad (9.55)$$

From (9.54) and (9.55), it may be seen that the optimal proportion of regional public investment in physical capital α_s^{i*} and the optimal consumption tax rate τ_c^{i*}

is entirely the same across different regions. Of which, the optimal proportion of regional public investment in physical capital α_s^{i*} is mainly dependent on the output elasticity of regional public investment in physical capital θ_4, total human capital accumulation elasticity of central and regional public investment in human capital $1 - \omega_1$, and the output elasticity of regional public investment in human capital $\omega_3\,(\theta_2+\theta_5)$.

It can thus be seen that, under a decentralized system with a multi-tier government structure, the optimal structure of regional governments is not only related to the efficiencies of the various types of expenditure of regional governments, but also dependent to a large extent on the efficiency of the expenditure of the central government. In fact, it will be seen from the following analysis that the optimal structure of regional governments is dependent to a certain extent on the degree of fiscal expenditure decentralization and the structure of the central government.

From (9.54), the ratio of optimal regional public investment in physical capital to that of human capital may be given as $\frac{\tau_c^{i*}}{(1-\alpha_s^{i*})} = \frac{(1-\omega_1)\theta_4}{\omega_3(\theta_3+\theta_5)}$. This differs from the results given by Agénor and the previous section (under a single-tier government framework),[36] which demonstrates the limitations for analysis under a single-tier government framework with respect to the unique organizational structure in the real-life situation of China. On the other hand, as an important type of tax for regional governments, the optimal consumption tax rate not only depends on the factors mentioned above, but also the total output elasticity of human capital and regional public physical capital $(1 - \theta_1 - \theta_4)$. This is consistent with the results obtained by Gong and Zou for a one-sector growth model framework,[37] while the model in this section allows a relatively clearer examination of the effects of human capital accumulation on the optimal consumption tax rate.

Central government

Under the given conditions of the optimal decisions of private economic bodies in (9.47)–(9.50) and the optimal policies of regional governments given in (9.54) and (9.55), as well as the constraints given in (9.36), the central government chooses the proportion of central public investment in physical capital α_f, central fiscal transfer payment ratio t^i, and income tax rate τ_y, in order to maximize total utility of private economic agents across all regions under a balanced-growth path:

$$\underset{\alpha_t, t^i, \tau_y}{Max} \sum_{i=1}^{N} \frac{\chi^i[(c^i)^{1-\sigma}-1]}{1-\sigma} \tag{9.56}$$

Of which, χ^i is a weight for the various regions, measuring the different levels of attention from the central government on the different regions, satisfying $\sum_{i=1}^{N}\chi^i = 1$. Solving for this gives the following functions:

$$\frac{\chi^i (1-t^i)^{-\sigma\tau_c^{i*}}}{\Phi^\sigma[\tau_c^{i*}(\frac{\tau_y}{1-\tau_y}\Theta - \Omega t^i) - \Omega(1-t^i)]} = \frac{\Delta\sum\chi^j\Phi^{1-\sigma}(1+t^j)^{\tau_c^{j*}(1-\sigma)}}{\tau_c^{j*}\sum\Phi(1+t^j)^{\tau_c^{j*}}[\frac{\tau_y}{1-\tau_y}\Theta - \Omega t^j]} \tag{9.57}$$

$$(1-\tau_y)\sum\Phi\,(\frac{\tau_y}{1-\tau_y}\Theta - \Omega t^i)(1+t^i)^{\tau_c^{i*}} = \theta_5\Delta\sum\Phi\Theta(1+t^i)^{\tau_c^{i*}} \tag{9.58}$$

$$\alpha_f^* = \frac{(1-\omega_1)\theta_3}{(1-\omega_1)\theta_3 + \omega_2(\theta_2+\theta_5)} \tag{9.59}$$

Of which, $\Phi = [\rho+\delta+\sigma\phi^j]^{-\frac{(1-\omega_1)}{(1-\theta_1-\theta_4)(1-\omega_1)-\omega_3(\theta_2+\theta_5)}}[(\rho+\delta+\sigma\phi^j)-\theta_1(\delta+\phi^j)]^{\frac{(1-\omega_1)(1-\theta_1)}{(1-\theta_1-\theta_4)(1-\omega_1)-\omega_3(\theta_2+\theta_5)}}$, $\Theta = \frac{(\rho+\delta+\sigma\phi^j)}{[(\rho+\delta+\sigma\phi^j)-\theta_1(\delta+\phi^j)]}$, $\Omega = \frac{[\theta_4(1-\omega_1)+\omega_3(\theta_2+\theta_5)]}{(1-\omega_1)(1-\theta_1)}$, and $\Delta = \frac{(1-\omega_1)\theta_3+\omega_2(\theta_2+\theta_5)}{(1-\omega_1)\theta_5}$.

Together, (9.57) and (9.58) decides the optimal central fiscal transfer payment ratio t^{i*} and optimal income tax rate τ_y^* for maximized social welfare. Across all regions, the right hand side of (9.57) is entirely the same, and so the disparity in the optimal central fiscal transfer payment ratio t^{i*} for maximized social welfare across different regions may be entirely attributed to the different levels of attention from the central government on the different regions (i.e. regional weight χ^i), as well as the different balanced-growth rates ϕ^i across the various regions. This is a reflection of how the distribution policy of the central fiscal transfer payments is drawn up according to the central government's main policy intention of fiscal transfer payments, that is, to achieve coordinated growth across the various regions.

The above analysis gives the optimal central government policy for maximized social welfare. For comparison, the optimal central government policy for maximized growth will also be given. From (9.36), (9.37), (9.47)–(9.50), (9.54), (9.55), (9.57), and (9.59), the following implicit function for economic balanced-growth rate ϕ may be given as:

$$\Psi(\phi^i) = c^{i*} - \Gamma(1-\tau_y^*)^{-\frac{1}{\theta_5}}(1+t^i)^{\tau_c^*}\left\{\sum\Phi\left(\frac{\tau_y^*}{1-\tau_y^*}\Theta - \Omega t^i\right)(1+t^i)^{\tau_c^*}\right\}^{-\Delta} = 0 \tag{9.60}$$

Of which, c^{i*} in $\Gamma = M^{-\frac{1-\theta_1}{\theta_5}}\Phi\theta_1^{-\frac{\omega_1}{\theta_5}}\alpha_s^{*\frac{-\theta_4}{\theta_5}}\alpha_s^{*\frac{-\theta_3}{\theta_5}}[(1-\alpha_s^*)^{\omega_3}(1-\alpha_f^*)^{\omega_2}]^{\frac{-(\theta_2+\theta_5)}{(1-\omega_1)\theta_5}}\tau_c^{*-\frac{\theta_4(1-\omega_1)+\omega_3(\theta_2+\theta_5)}{(1-\omega_1)\theta_5}}(1-\tau_c^*)^{\frac{(1-\omega_1)(1-\theta_1-\theta_3)\omega_2(\theta_2+\theta_5)}{(1-\omega_1)\theta_5}}$ is given from (9.47)–(9.50), α_s^* and τ_c^* are given from (9.54) and (9.55) respectively, and τ_y^* and α_f^* are given from (9.57) and (9.59) respectively.

From (9.60), it can be seen that the economic balanced-growth rate is entirely dependent on structural parameters of the model, such as the discount rate and central fiscal transfer payment policy. From the derivative of the implicit function and that $\frac{\partial \phi}{\partial t^i} = 0$, the optimal central fiscal transfer payment ratio for maximized growth $\hat{t}^i$ may be given. Due to the complexity of the model, however, in order to obtain a simplified and relatively intuitive result, it may be assumed that the regional weight χ^i is the same for this instance, so as to obtain the optimal central fiscal transfer payment ratio for maximized growth $\hat{t}^i$ as:

$$\hat{t}^i = -1 + \frac{(\Delta - 1)\theta_5 \tau_c^{i*}(\Theta - \Omega)}{(1 - \theta_5 \Delta)\,\Omega - (\Delta - 1)\theta_5 \tau_c^{i*} \Omega} \tag{9.61}$$

From (9.61), it may be seen that the optimal central fiscal transfer payment ratio for maximized growth is not only dependent on the output elasticity of various investment factors and human capital accumulation elasticity, but also the preference parameters of private economic bodies, physical capital depreciation rate, optimal regional consumption tax rate, and regional economic growth rate ϕ^i. In fact, when the effects that are brought about by differences in region is neglected, it may be given from (9.57) and (9.60) that $t^{i*} = -1 + \frac{(\Delta-1)\theta_5 \tau_c^{i*}(\Theta-\Omega)}{(1-\theta_5 \Delta)\,\Omega - (\Delta-1)\theta_5 \tau_c^{i*} \Omega}$, that is, the optimal central fiscal transfer payment ratio t^{i*} for maximized social welfare and the optimal central fiscal transfer payment ratio for maximized growthare entirely the same, i.e. achieving a size of central fiscal transfer payment for maximized growth will necessarily achieve maximized social welfare.

Additionally, replacing Ω and Δ in (9.61) with α_s^{i*} and α_f^*, there is $\hat{i}^i = -1 + \frac{(\theta_3 - \theta_5 \alpha_f^*)\tau_c^*[(1 - \theta_1)\alpha_s^* \Theta - \theta_4]}{[\theta_4 (\alpha_f^* - \theta_3) - \theta_4 (\theta_3 - \theta_2 \alpha_f^*)\tau_c^*]}$. It can thus be seen that in determining the optimal size of central fiscal transfer payment and the optimal income tax rate, the central government is also affected by variables in regional government policies such as consumption tax rates and regional public capital investment. In other words, if the central fiscal transfer policy is already given, then the optimal structure of regional governments and the optimal consumption tax rates will be dependent on the policy of the central government.

(9.61) may also be re-expressed to give:

$$\hat{t}^i = -1 + \frac{Dec_g^i}{Dec_r^i} \tag{9.62}$$

Of which, $Dec_g^i = \frac{g_s^i}{g_s^i + g_f / N}$ is the degree of fiscal expenditure decentralization, and $Dec_r^i = \frac{\tau_c^i c^i}{\tau_c^i c^i + \tau_y y^i}$ is the degree of fiscal revenue decentralization. (9.62) shows that the optimal size of central fiscal transfer payments for maximized growth depends on the degree of fiscal decentralization, and it may further be known from $\frac{\partial \hat{t}^i}{\partial Dec_g^i} > 0$ and $\frac{\partial \hat{t}^i}{\partial Dec_r^i} < 0$ that, the higher the degree of fiscal expenditure decentralization and the lower the degree of fiscal revenue decentralization, then the larger the size of the optimal central fiscal transfer payments. This result is very intuitive: the higher the degree of fiscal expenditure decentralization, the more the responsibilities of expenditure for regional governments, such that under a certain arrangement of responsibilities of revenue between the central and regional governments, this will definitely lead to vertical fiscal imbalance in regional governments, and in this scenario the optimal policy for the central government is to increase the strength of transfer payments to regional governments to ensure that regional governments are able to fulfill their expenditure responsibilities. Also, the lower the degree of fiscal revenue decentralization, the less the fiscal resources managed by regional governments, such that under a certain arrangement of responsibilities of revenue between the central and regional governments, this will also lead to vertical fiscal imbalance in regional governments, and in this scenario the optimal policy for the central government is also to increase the strength of transfer payments to regional governments.[38] Additionally, (9.61) and (9.62) also means that the theoretical effects of central fiscal transfer payments on long-term economic growth is uncertain: when the central fiscal transfer payments are smaller than the optimal size, increase in transfer payments is favorable for long-term economic growth; when the transfer payments are larger than the optimal size, then increase in transfer payments is unfavorable for long-term economic growth.

From (9.36), (9.37), (9.47)–(9.50), (9.54), and (9.59), the optimal degree of decentralization in physical capital development expenditure (i.e. the ratio of central to regional public investment in physical capital) and the optimal degree of decentralization in human capital development expenditure (i.e. the ratio of central to regional public investment in human capital) may be respectively given as $\frac{\alpha_s^* \bar{g}_s^*}{\alpha_f^* \bar{g}_f^*} = \frac{\theta_4}{\theta_3}$ and $\frac{(1-\alpha_s^*)\bar{g}_s^*}{(1-\alpha_f^*)\bar{g}_f^*} = \frac{\omega_3}{\omega_2}$, of which $\bar{g}_s^*$ and $\bar{g}_f^*$ are the optimal regional and central public capital investment per capita respectively. This is consistent with the results obtained in the previous section.

The above analysis shows that, under a multi-tier government framework, the optimal decisions for the structure of regional government and tax policies has to be considered within the entire fiscally decentralized institution, taking into account not only the particular features of the region, but also the behavior of the central government, as well as the degree of fiscal decentralization and the relevant institutional arrangements.

Optimization of the Size and Structure of Regional Governments for the Promotion of Social Welfare

From the theoretical analysis in the previous three sections, it may be seen that a rationally deliberated intergovernmental fiscal relationship with relevant institutional arrangements, along with an efficient and comprehensive regional governance structure, are the keys to optimizing the size and structure of regional governments. To achieve this and promote the long-term sustainable growth of the economy and society of the country, the central government should thus look into working on the following three areas:

Rigorous planning and execution of institutional reforms in financial and administrative management

The size and structure of regional governments is, fundamentally speaking, dependent on the goals, motives, and modes of behavior of regional governments, which is in turn dependent on intergovernmental fiscal relationships with their relevant institutional arrangements, and the mechanisms of incentives and restraints formed from the regional governance structure. The critical point to achieving a rational arrangement in the intergovernmental fiscal relationships and an efficient and comprehensive regional governance structure is in whether institutional reforms in fiscal and administrative management can achieve compatibility in goals and incentives. For a long time, China's government did not possess comprehensive knowledge on this crucial matter, and in attempting to promote regional government efficiency and administrative roles for optimizing the size and structure of regional governments, did not look to consider an organic integration and long-term planning of institutional reforms in fiscal and administrative management. Many existing reform measures exhibit signs of being 'band-aid' fixes, leading to the conundrum of reforms increasing the complexity of the problems instead of being the solutions, and further aggravating the distortionary behavior of regional governments.

Since the tax sharing reforms of 1994, many deep-seated conflicts within the country's fiscal management have appeared, leading to distortionary behavior in regional governments and give rise to the numerous socioeconomic problems present in China today. Also around the mid-1990s, there has been a gradual introduction of administration system reforms aimed at streamlining the administration structure, but the execution of these reforms have been slow and unimpressive in achieving any regulation of regional government behavior. Within the present Five-Year Plan period (2011 to 2015), then, China's government must ensure its own awareness of the mutual interactions between the financial and administration systems and their effects on the behavior of regional governments, and accordingly plan for their reforms under a unified framework of consideration. In designing a much-needed set of comprehensive reforms for the financial and administration system that is compatible with goals and incentives, it should consider contemporary fiscal decentralization and governance theories, along with particular features in the country's unique political and economic system, in studying the patterns of development of the size and structure of regional governments, such that the new set of reforms can truly achieve optimal coordination in fiscal and administrative decentralization, and fundamentally correct the distortionary behavior of regional governments.

Institution of reforms to streamline and flatten the administration system

Currently, regional administration in China operates on five tiers of governments *de facto*. Excessive levels of governments increases the costs of implementing policies, hampering the efficient execution of central policies and the strategic development of the country; at the same time, it also causes distortionary effects of the mechanisms of incentives and restraints and the behavior of regional governments: one, excessive levels of administration, together with overemphasis of growth results in the mechanism of political evaluation, furthers aggravates the existing problems in the sub-provincial financial and administration system, leading to inflated expenditure and misplacement of authorities; two, excessive levels of administration with relatively few administration districts means that the area of administration for the regional government is overly large, increasing the difficulty of obtaining information, such that the regional government is unable to effectively obtain knowledge of the preferences of residents in the region and the relevant costs of public services, and so hampers the efforts to optimize administration efficiency and allocation of regional public services; three, excessive levels of administration not only weakens greatly the administrative autonomy of grassroots-level governments, limiting their ability to develop the local economy according to local conditions, but also aggravates deviations in fiscal transfer payments, putting grassroots-level governments at a significantly disadvantaged position in allocation of fiscal resources, such that they are unable to effectively fulfill their responsibilities in managing the local economy and society. The excess in administration levels thus have a huge negative impact on coordinated economic and social development, and it does not favor the political stability of the country.

The government should also take careful consideration of particular features of the political system as well as regional geospatial features in assessing the principles of adjustment for the optimization of the structure of government organization, and actively explore for the optimal mode of administrative decentralization. In particular, it needs to take a serious review of the successes and shortfalls in recent reform exercises for the merger of villages into townships and the direct administration of provinces on prefectures. This will help to avoid reforms causing conflicts in the administration and financial systems and the subsequent distortion in the behavior of regional governments.

China's government should thus make a serious push for a flattening of the administrative organization, implementing a four-tier government structure, with the provincial-level government directly responsible for the administrative jurisdiction of the prefecture-level government, while promoting the administrative rank of prefecture-level governments (from division-level to bureau-level), so as to achieve a correct arrangement between the powers and responsibilities of the prefecture-level governments. On this basis, it should look to suitably increase the number of provincial and prefectural administrative units, in order to increase the administrative capabilities of regional governments and their competence in obtaining local information and providing relevant public services.

Organized decentralization and reform in the financial management system, particularly on the sub-provincial level

Contemporary theories of fiscal decentralization point out that misarranged administrative and fiscal authorities weakens the effects of incentives and restraints of fiscal decentralization on regional governments, leading to expansion in the size and distortion in the structure of regional governments. In the actual economy, however, not many countries can achieve a perfect arrangement of fiscal powers and administrative authority.

The fiscal contracting system implemented in the country in the 1980s put regional governments in the dominant fiscal position, with the central government needing to rely on contradirectional transfer payments, i.e. regional governments turning over revenue to the central government. The tax sharing reforms of 1994 completely abolished this untenable mode of decentralization, but it also takes decentralization towards a different and dangerous direction of extremity, where the current structure of centralized fiscal powers and decentralized administrative authority leads to huge distortions in the behavior of regional governments: one, the lack of reliable fiscal protection encourages regional governments to pursue extrabudgetary and irregular sources of revenue, such as land transaction fees, hidden debts and bank loans, weakening the budget constraints and rapidly expanding the size of expenditure of regional governments; two, grassroots-level governments across the country, in particular those in the central and western regions, are running into rather serious financial difficulties, not only jeopardizing the country's political and social stability, but also causing public services such as basic education and healthcare to stagnate at low levels; three, the central government is increasingly reliant on fiscal transfer payments to fix the problems arising out of the current fiscal decentralization structure, but there is a lack of proper design of a comprehensive system for doing so, leading to fragmentation and short-termism in the transfer payments, and not only is this unfavorable for the formation of stable and sustainable mechanisms of incentives and restraints, it also leads to the increasing reliance of regional governments on fiscal transfer payments, bringing in various kinds of ethical risk problems associated with the transfer payments and causing huge wastage of fiscal resources.

Within this current Five-Year Plan period, then, the government needs to actively explore for the optimal structure and degree of fiscal decentralization between the central and regional governments. In particular, in the process of flattening the administration system, it should look into granting more fiscal powers to regional and especially prefectural-level governments (e.g. sharing of important taxes such as value-added tax between central, provincial, and prefectural governments), determining a reasonable level of the sharing of resources, in order to ensure that prefectural-level governments have access to a stable source of fiscal resources, from which they can fulfill their various administrative responsibilities. On the other hand, the terms of expenditure that regional and especially prefectural-level governments are responsible for should be reduced accordingly with the proper arrangement between fiscal powers and administrative authority. The usage of the fiscal transfer payment system as the go-to for fixing problems arising out of misarranged decentralization also needs to be abandoned, in order to optimize the mechanisms of incentives and restraints and fundamentally correct the behavior of regional governments.

Summary

This chapter first constructed a theoretical model for the optimal size of regional governments to find the optimal size of regional governments for maximized social welfare, as well as the effects and mechanisms of fiscal decentralization and the organizational structure of the government; second, theoretical models for the optimal structure of regional governments were constructed under a single-tier and a multi-tier government framework respectively, examining the optimal structure of regional governments for maximized social welfare, as well as the effects of fiscal decentralization, central transfer payments, and central and regional tax policies; finally, proposals were suggested for revamping the size and structure of regional governments, fiscal decentralization, and the organizational structure of the government, in order to promote increased social welfare levels and coordinated economic and social development of the country.

The analysis in this chapter has shown the following:

- The optimal size of regional governments for maximized social welfare depends on factors of the institutional environment, such as the preferences of local residents, the production costs of public services, the degree of distortion in taxation, fiscal decentralization, and the organizational structure of the government, of which, the spillover effects, information costs and common pool mechanism brought about by fiscal decentralization and government organization structure are the critical factors in determining the optimal size of regional governments;
- Under a single-tier government framework, the expenditure structure of regional governments for both maximized social welfare and maximized growth are entirely the same, dependent on the degree of decentralization for expenditure, the structure of expenditure of the central government, and the efficiencies of the various types of expenditure of regional governments;
- Under a multi-tier government framework, the expenditure structure of regional governments for maximized social welfare and maximized growth are significantly different: expenditure structure of regional governments for maximized social welfare is not only dependent on the degree of decentralization for expenditure, the structure of expenditure of the central government, and the efficiencies of the various types of expenditure of regional governments, but also the central and regional taxation policies, as well as the disparity in the level of attention paid by the central government to the welfare levels for different regions and the respective differences in fiscal transfer payment policies.

The analysis in this chapter shows that the key to optimization for the size and structure of regional governments lie in optimizing the intergovernmental fiscal relationships as well as the relevant institutional arrangements and the organizational structure of the government. The government should therefore look to consider the optimization of the size and structure of regional governments together with institutional reforms in the financial and administration systems under a unified framework for thorough and systematic planning and coordinated execution, in order to achieve optimal decentralization and the mechanisms of incentives and restraints for regional governments, and so fundamentally correct the behavior of regional governments.

1

Annex

Analysis of the Dynamic Factors Affecting the Economic Cycles of China's Provinces

Introduction

In the second half of 2003, China's economy experienced extremely rapid growth and showed signs of overheating, especially in the investment sector. Thus, at the start of 2004, China's government implemented a series of macroeconomic regulation measures aimed at cooling investment overheating, while there is increasing academic interest in studying the reasons for the rise of investment overheating, focusing mainly on issues such as monetary policies, fiscal policies, international capital movement, and so on.[1]

If one were to consider the history of development of the actual economy of China since the Chinese Economic Reform, however, it may be seen that the behavior of regional governments is often a major factor in causing investment and economic overheating. Out of consideration for local economic and political interests, regional governments often offer investment perks such as tax rebates and preferential land policies to attract private and overseas investors, even if these perks represent deviations from national regulations; the case of Jiangsu Tieben Steel, exposed in 2004, is a classic example. During periods of macroeconomic recession, the self-interested behavior of regional governments is actually favorable for economic recovery; but when the economy has recovered, such behavior can lead to investment overheating, initially in the local economy and then the national economy.[2] It is thus of both theoretical and practical importance to examine the role of the regional and provincial economy behind the macroeconomic fluctuations in the country.

This paper uses provincial macroeconomic data (output, investment, and consumption) as basis for Gibbs sampling estimations in a multi-dynamic-factor model of the provincial economic cycles in China, in order to examine the dynamic features in the macroeconomic fluctuations across different regions and provinces of the country, as well as the effects of the dynamic factors on the dynamics of the provincial economy. First, the multi-dynamic-factor model is constructed and the estimation calculations performed; next, the estimation results will be used as basis for examining changing and continuing features in the dynamic factors; variance decomposition will then be used to analyze the roles played by the various dynamic factors in contributing to the fluctuations in the provincial economy; finally, regression analysis is used to examine the relationships between the dynamic factors and the features of the provincial economy.

Multi-dynamic-factor Model Construction

Model framework

Dynamic factor models have been a popular choice as econometrics models for economic cycles since the pioneering work of Stock and Watson.[3] There are mainly two types of dynamic factor models for economic cycles: one, non-linear regime-switching factor models, such as the multi-variable dynamic Markov-switching model proposed in Diebold and Rudebusch, which have the advantage of being able to integrate the two major features of economic cycles, co-movement, and nonlinearity of variables, but are one-factor models;[4] two, multi-dynamic-factor models, which are in principle linear models, but capable of examining multiple dynamic factors, and have thus been applied in many studies on co-movements in a multi-agent economy.[5]

Since multi-dynamic-factor models are convenient for examining co-movements in a multi-agent economy and can help avoid estimation difficulties brought by nonlinearity, a multi-dynamic-factor model is used in this paper as the basis for constructing an econometrics model of the country's provincial economic cycles. This paper uses the 29 provinces of the country, classified into Eastern, Central and Western regions, as the objects of sampling.[6] For each province, three major macroeconomic variables of output (O), investment (I), and consumption (C) are taken into consideration, shown in the standardized form of $y_{i,t}$ ($i = 1, 2, \cdots, 29 \times 3$). Assume that $y_{i,t}$ is mainly affected by three types of factors: national dynamic factor fac^N, measuring the co-movements among all regional and provincial macroeconomic variables in the country; regional dynamic factors fac^R, measuring the co-movements among all provincial macroeconomic variables in the region; provincial dynamic factors fac^P, measuring the co-movements among all macroeconomic variables in the province. Thus, $y_{i,t}$ may be expressed as:

$$y_{i,t} = a_i + b_i^N fac_t^N + b_i^R fac_{r,t}^R + b_i^P fac_{p,t}^P + \varepsilon_{i,t},\ r = 1,2,3;\ p = 1, \cdots, 29 \quad \text{(A1.1)}$$

Of which, b_i^N, b_i^R and b_i^P are the coefficients for the national, regional and provincial dynamic factors respectively, showing the strength of the effects of each dynamic factor on $y_{i,t}$. $\varepsilon_{i,t}$ is the error term, which may be considered as unexplained or idiosyncratic factors. Assuming that $\varepsilon_{i,t}$ satisfies $E\varepsilon_{i,t}\varepsilon_{j,t-s} = 0$ (when $i \neq j$), follows a normal distribution, but with potential serial correlation, it may be supposed that it follows an autoregressive model of order Q:

$$\varepsilon_{i,t} = \phi_{i,1}\varepsilon_{i,t-1} + \phi_{i,2}\varepsilon_{i,t-2} + \cdots + \phi_{i,Q}\varepsilon_{i,t-Q} + u_{i,t} \quad \text{(A1.2)}$$

Of which, $\phi_{i,j}$ $(j = 1, 2, \cdots, Q)$ is the autoregressive coefficient, $u_{i,t}$ is the error term satisfying:

$$Eu_{i,t}u_{j,t-s} = \begin{cases} \sigma_i^2\ i = j,\ s = 0 \\ 0,\ \text{Others} \end{cases} \tag{A1.3}$$

Likewise, it may be assumed that the changes in the national, regional and provincial dynamic factors follow an autoregressive model of order M:

$$fac_{k,t} = \varphi_{k,1} fac_{k,t-1} + \varphi_{k,2} fac_{k,t-2} + \cdots + \varphi_{k,M} fac_{k,t-M} + v_{k,t} \tag{A1.4}$$

Of which, $\varphi_{k,j}$ (j = 1, 2, ⋯ , M) is the autoregressive coefficient, $v_{k,t}$ is the error term satisfying:

$$Ev_{k,t}v_{k,t} = \sigma_k^2;\ Ev_{k,t}v_{i,t-s} = 0, \forall k, i, s \tag{A1.5}$$

Data

This paper uses annual data for a sampling period 1978 to 2003, obtained from the provincial Statistical Yearbooks as well as the *Collection of Historical Statistical Data of Provinces, Autonomous Regions and Directly-Administered Municipalities of the People's Republic of China, 1949–1989*. Data for output, investment, and consumption are all considered as nominal values, so as to avoid deviations in estimating actual investment, and also to allow for the consideration of price factors for a better simulation of the actual economic operations.[7]

Natural logarithms are taken for the economic variables and processed using first difference and mean subtraction, in order to ensure that economic variables remain in stationary sequence, and also that the model will only consider growth rates, eliminating the effects of economy size on estimation results.

Estimation method

There are mainly two types of estimation methods in a multi-dynamic-factor model: one is maximum likelihood estimation, using EM algorithms and LQE to perform variance decomposition of forecast errors and obtain the maximum likelihood estimation for the model;[8] the other is Gibbs sampling, a type of the Markov Chain Monte Carlo (MCMC) simulation technique, which uses the conditional distribution of random variables to obtain large quantities of continuous samples, such that when the sample size is sufficiently large, the joint distribution of the obtained samples will converge into the actual joint distribution of the random variables, and the model samples are then obtained based on the actual joint distribution of these random variables.

For the multi-dynamic-factor model in this paper, there are a total of 609 parameters and 33 dynamic factor sequences, and such complex data processing cannot be done using EM algorithms. Gibbs sampling is thus chosen as the estimation method for the multi-dynamic-factor model, performed in Gauss 6.0. The estimation process consists of four key steps: first, the posterior distribution of the model parameters are obtained by sampling based on all the dynamic factors; second, the posterior distribution of the national dynamic factor is obtained by sampling based on the model parameters and the provincial and regional dynamic factors; third, the posterior distribution of the particular regional dynamic factors are obtained by sampling based on the national dynamic factors and all the provincial dynamic factors of the particular region; fourth, the posterior distribution of all the provincial dynamic factors of the particular region is obtained by sampling the national and the particular regional dynamic factors; and so finishing a complete MCMC process.

There are some issues in the estimation process that needs additional consideration. The first is the problem of identification: a multi-dynamic-factor model cannot identify on its own the sign and scale of each dynamic factor and its coefficient. For identification of sign, following the method used by Kose et al.,[9] the coefficient of the national dynamic factor for the output function of Shanghai is set as positive for identifying the national dynamic factor, the coefficients of the provincial dynamic factor for the output functions of the provinces are set as positive for identifying the provincial dynamic factors, and the coefficients of the regional dynamic factors for the output function of the representative province in each region are set as positive for identifying the regional dynamic factors. For identification of scale, following the method used by Stock and Watson,[10] the innovation variance σ_k^2 in the autoregression function of all the dynamic factors are set as constants.

The second is the determination of the autoregression order of the dynamic factors. After performing comparative studies, the autoregression order of the functions (A1.2) and (A1.4) is taken as Q = M = 3.

The third is the prior distribution settings. A normal distribution N(0,1) is used as the prior distribution for the dynamic factor coefficients, and a normal distribution of N(0, Σ) is used as the prior distribution for the autocorrelation coefficients in (A1.2) and (A1.4), of which $\Sigma = \begin{bmatrix} 1 & 1 & 1 \\ 0 & 0.5 & 0 \\ 0 & 0 & 0.25 \end{bmatrix}$. This will ensure that there is no serial correlation in growth as well as the stability of the lagged terms in examining the growth rates of the economic variables. For the prior distribution of the innovation variance in (A1.1), following the method used by Otrok and Whiteman,[11] an inverted Gamma (6, 0.001) distribution is used.

The fourth is the Markov chain convergence problem. To overcome this, different initial values and sampling sizes are attempted, using only that for which the estimation results are the same. Here, it was determined as 11000 samples (discarding the first 1000 results).[12]

Analysis of Dynamic Factors

The estimation results from the model are represented in Figures A1.1–1.4. Figure A1.1 shows the changes in the median value of the posterior distribution of the national dynamic factor for 1979 to 2003, with the broken lines giving the first and second tercile values.

Fig. A1.1 Changes in national dynamic factor, 1979–2003

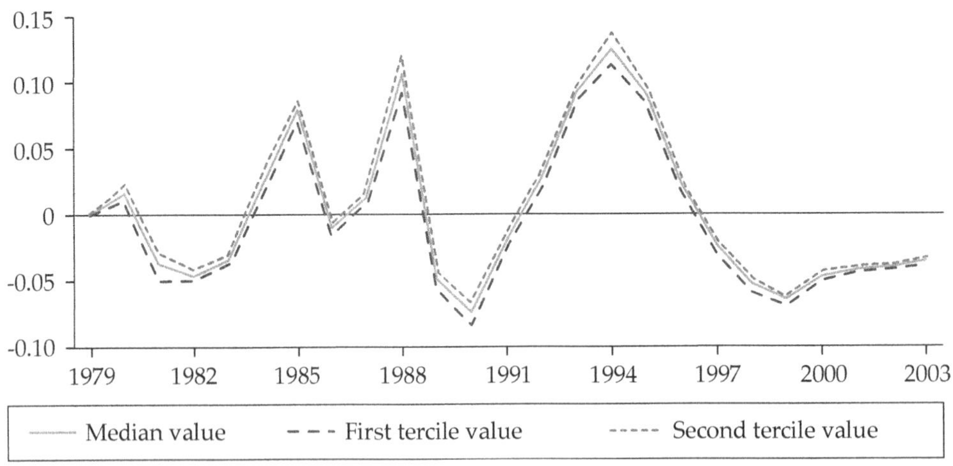

From Figure A1.1, it can be seen that the lines for the first and second tercile values are very close to the line for the median value, showing that the estimation for the national dynamic factor is accurate. The changes in the national dynamic factor is a good reflection of the state of the national macroeconomics for 1979 to 2003: in the three periods of economic boom (1985, 1988, and 1994), the national dynamic factors are situated at relatively high points, and in the periods of economic recession (1981, 1990, and 1999), the national dynamic factors are situated at relatively low points; the figure, however, does not demonstrate the overheating in 2003.

Figure A1.2 shows the changes in the median values of the posterior distribution of the regional dynamic factors for 1979 to 2003.

Fig. A1.2 Changes in regional dynamic factors, 1979–2003

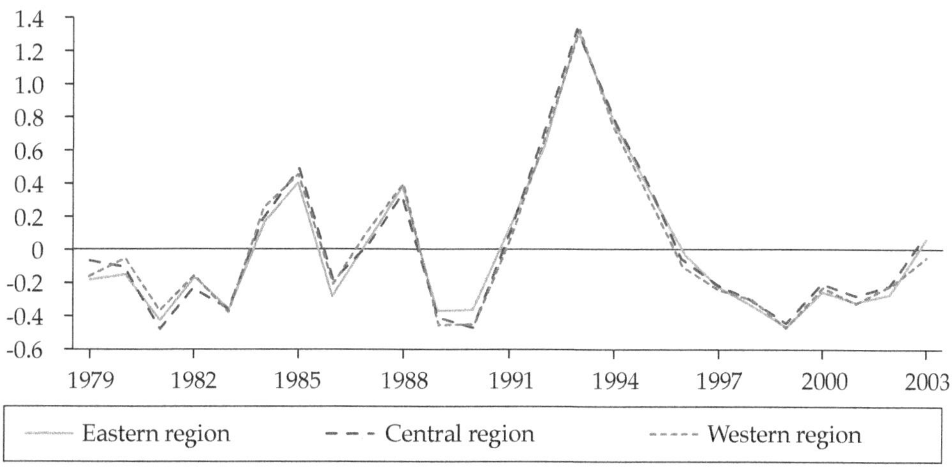

From Figure A1.2, it can be seen that the changes in the regional dynamic factors are consistent with each other, and are well-synchronized with the changes in the national dynamic factor. In addition, the figure demonstrates that the economy in the Eastern and Central regions exhibit relatively higher overheating compared to the economy in the Western region in 2003.

Figure A1.3 is the histogram of the autocorrelation coefficients of the provincial dynamic factors.

Fig. A1.3 Autocorrelation of provincial dynamic factors

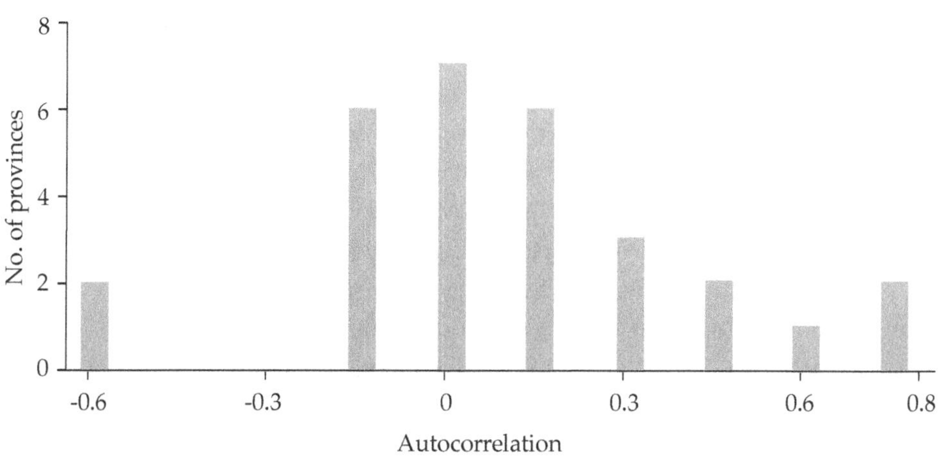

The first-order autocorrelation coefficients for the national and regional (Eastern, Central and Western) dynamic factors are 0.539, 0.615, 0.599, and 0.589 respectively, showing that the changes in national and regional dynamic factors have very strong sustainability. On the other hand, Figure A1.3 shows that close to 40% of provincial dynamic factors have autocorrelation coefficients with negative value (the lowest being -0.587 for Ningxia), meaning that the changes in the provincial dynamic factors have a certain degree of reversibility. Even though more than 60% of provincial dynamic factors have autocorrelation coefficients with positive value (the highest being 0.773 for Shanghai), the sustainability of the changes in provincial dynamic factors are far less than the national and regional dynamic factors. The results show that national and regional dynamic factors capture mainly the changes in the provincial economy that have a stronger sustainability (lower frequency), whereas changes of higher frequency are exhibited in the provincial dynamic factors.

To further examine how the various dynamic factors and provincial economic output growth affect each other, four representative provinces (Shanghai, Hainan, Henan and Guizhou) are chosen as the objects of study.[13] Figure A1.4 gives the changes in the national and regional dynamic factors as well as the changes in the provincial dynamic factors and output growth (after mean subtraction).

Figure A1.4(a) gives the changes in national dynamic factors, regional (Eastern) dynamic factors, provincial (Shanghai) dynamic factors (median values), and output growth rate (Shanghai) for Shanghai for 1979 to 2003. In order to enable commensurability of these variables, the dynamic factors are multiplied by their respective coefficients in the output growth function for Shanghai [the same process is repeated for Figures A1.4(b)–(d)], such that the sum of the dynamic factors and the idiosyncratic factors in the output growth function for Shanghai is equal to the output growth rate for Shanghai.

The changes in the provincial dynamic factors for Shanghai exhibit an overall upwards trend within the sampling period. This is very different from the changes in the national and regional (Eastern) dynamic factors (the correlation coefficients for provincial dynamic factors of Shanghai and national and regional (Eastern) dynamic factors are -0.203 and 0.002 respectively). On the other hand, the national and regional (Eastern) dynamic factors are good representations of the changes in the output growth for Shanghai (the correlation coefficients of output growth for Shanghai and the national and regional (Eastern) dynamic factors are 0.762 and 0.911 respectively). The results show that economic fluctuations in Shanghai is a major contributor to the economic fluctuations in the Eastern region as well as the entire country.

Fig A1.4(a) Changes in dynamic factors for Shanghai

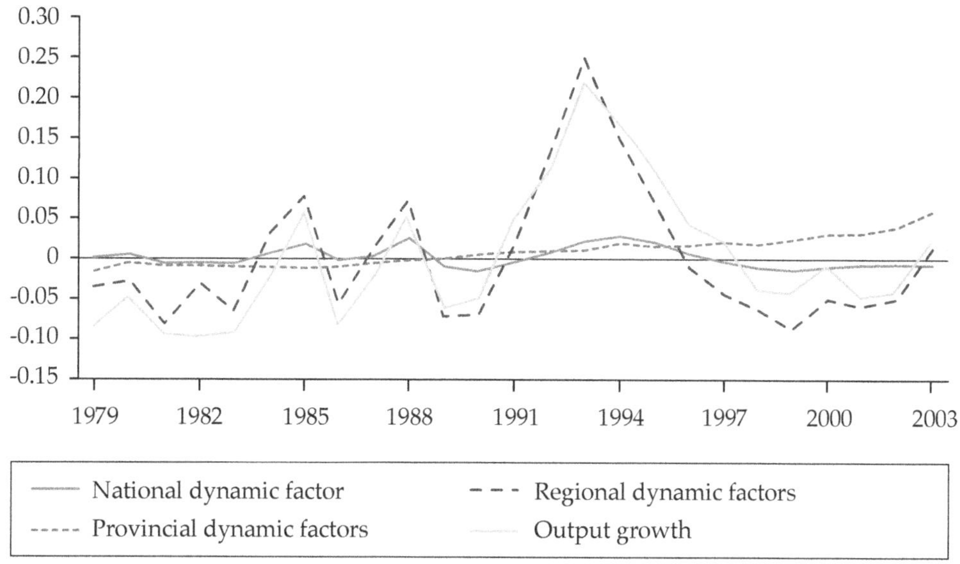

Figure A1.4(b) gives the changes in national dynamic factors, regional (Eastern) dynamic factors, provincial (Hainan) dynamic factors (median values), and output growth rate (Hainan) for Hainan for 1979 to 2003.

Fig A1.4(b) Changes in dynamic factors for Hainan

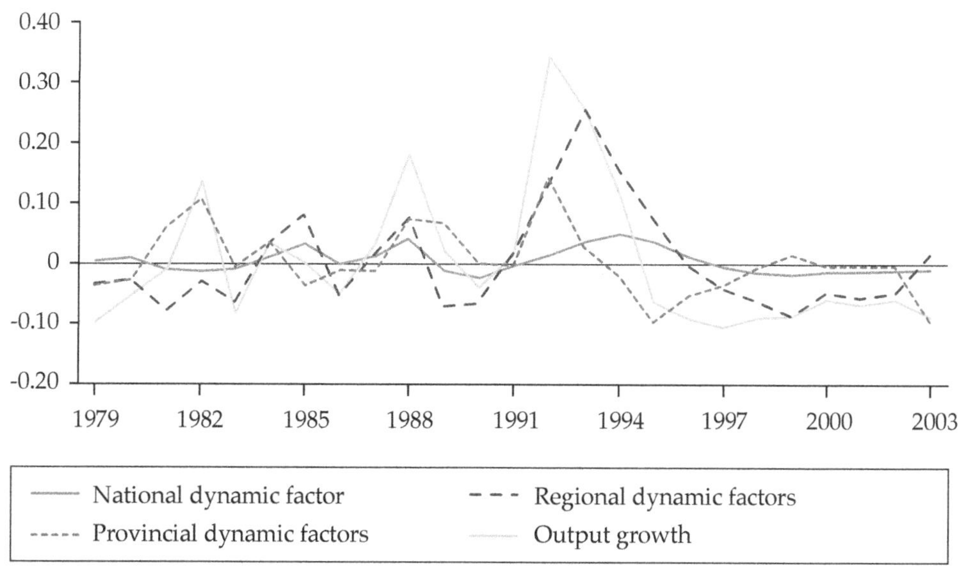

In contrast to the results for Shanghai, the provincial dynamic factors for Hainan are a good representation of the changes in output growth for the province (the correlation coefficient is 0.712), while the national and regional dynamic factors are only able to show the economic boom in 1988 and the recession in 1990, with poor synchronization at other significant periods. This shows that the economy of Hainan exhibits relatively high autonomy.

Figure A1.4(c) gives the changes in national dynamic factors, regional (Central) dynamic factors, provincial (Central) dynamic factors (median values) and output growth rate (Henan) for Henan in 1979 to 2003.

Fig A1.4(c) Changes in dynamic factors for Henan

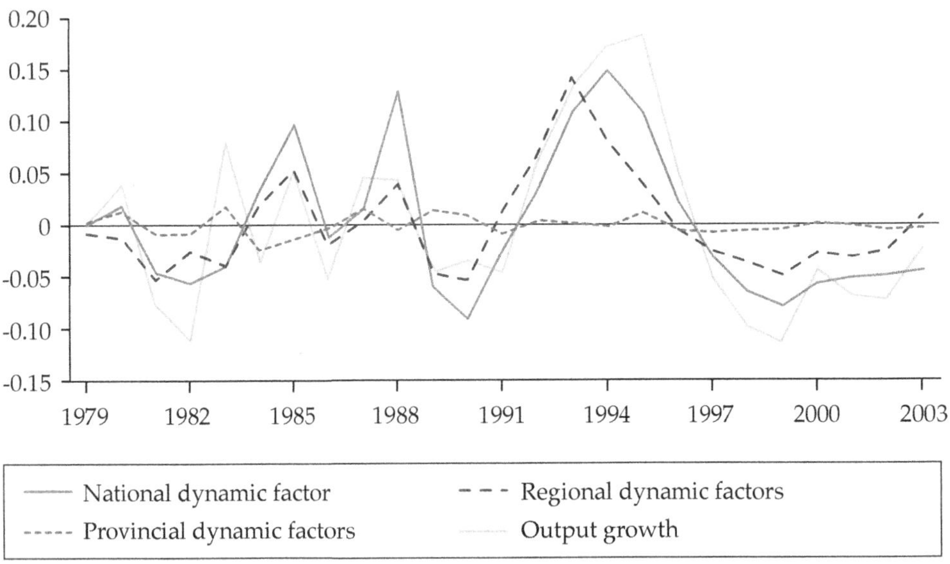

The national and regional dynamic factors and the output growth for Henan are well synchronized. The changes in the provincial dynamic factors are also in sync with the fluctuations in output growth, but the effects are much less significant. This shows that the economy of Henan is very much affected by fluctuations in the national and regional economy.

Figure A1.4(d) gives the changes in national dynamic factors, regional (Western) dynamic factors, provincial (Western) dynamic factors (median values), and output growth rate (Guizhou) for Guizhou in 1979 to 2003.

Within the sampling period, the provincial dynamic factors of Guizhou are a good representation for the changes in output growth rate of the province (the correlation coefficient is 0.68). Starting from the mid-1980s, the national dynamic factor and the output growth rate of Guizhou has been relatively synchronized,

Fig A1.4(d) Changes in dynamic factors for Guizhou

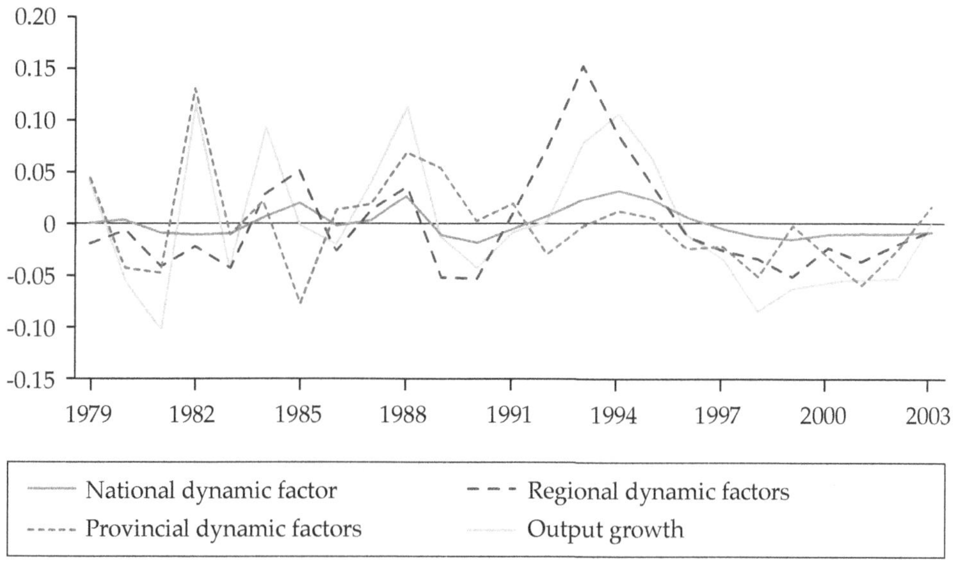

showing that the economy of Guizhou exhibited high levels of autonomy before the mid-1980s, and thereafter show signs of integration into the national economy.

The analysis in this section shows that the provincial economy in China is affected to different extents by national, regional, and local shock factors: for example, at certain periods of time, some provincial economies exhibit higher levels of autonomy (i.e. stronger shocks from provincial idiosyncratic factors), while being more affected by national and regional shock factors at other periods of time.

Variance Decomposition Analysis

To examine the relative importance of national, regional and provincial dynamic factors on the provincial economic cycles, orthogonal decomposition is performed on the growth variance of output, investment and consumption of the provincial economy, according to national, regional, and provincial dynamic factors as well as idiosyncratic factors:

$$Var(y_{i,t}) = (b_i^N)^2\, Var(fac_t^N) + (b_i^R)^2\, Var(fac_{r,t}^R) + (b_i^P)^2\, Var(fac_{p,t}^P) + Var(e_{i,t}) \qquad \text{(A1.6)}$$

Of which, $Var(y_{i,t})$ and $Var(fac)$ are the variances of $y_{i,t}$ and the various dynamic factors, measuring the fluctuation in $y_{i,t}$ and the dynamic factors respectively. From

(A1.6), the relative contribution of each dynamic factor to the variance of $y_{i,t}$ may be obtained. For instance, the relative contribution of the national dynamic factor may be given as:

$$\frac{(b_i^N)^2\ Var(fac_t^N)}{Var(y_{i,t})} \tag{A1.7}$$

Tables A1.1 to 1.3 give the variance decomposition for the growth of output, investment and consumption of the provinces in the Eastern, Central, and Western regions respectively and the median province of the respective region, while Table A1.4 shows the variance decomposition for the median province of the entire country. For each table, the median values, first tercile values, and second tercile values of the posterior distribution of the variance decomposition are given.

Table A1.1 Variance decomposition of the Eastern provinces (%)

		National dynamic factors			Regional dynamic factors			Provincial dynamic factors			Idiosyncratic factors		
		1/3Q	Med	2/3Q	1/3Q	Med	2/3Q	1/3Q	Med	2/3Q	1/3Q	Med	2/3Q
	O	43.1	45.9	46.6	17.8	19.3	20.6	2.1	3.2	4.6	29.8	31.6	33.2
Beijing	I	19.5	21.6	24.1	31.8	33.0	34.2	33.3	35.6	36.8	7.6	9.8	11.3
	C	65.8	68.4	70.7	5.1	6.0	7.5	4.2	5.9	7.3	17.5	19.8	21.1
	O	45.3	48.7	50.1	30.9	33.6	35.4	2.5	3.8	5.1	11.8	13.9	15.2
Tianjin	I	1.2	2.5	4.3	42.1	44.7	46.5	15.6	16.4	18.7	34.9	36.4	37.7
	C	70.8	73.2	75.7	1.0	2.1	3.9	4.1	5.9	7.6	16.8	18.8	20.4
	O	50.9	52.4	51.8	22.6	24.2	25.1	8.3	10.8	12.1	10.1	12.6	14.2
Hebei	I	15.1	17.0	19.4	49.2	52.7	54.1	20.1	21.7	23.4	6.3	8.5	9.9
	C	55.9	58.1	61.5	0.1	0.4	0.6	17.8	19.2	21.8	20.1	22.3	25.4
	O	30.8	33.3	34.8	36.7	38.9	41.1	8.2	9.7	10.6	16.5	18.2	21.1
Liaoning	I	7.1	8.2	10.1	13.1	14.9	16.4	32.9	34.7	36.4	39.5	42.2	44.8
	C	81.3	84.8	87.6	0.2	0.5	0.9	2.1	2.9	3.5	9.8	11.8	13.6
	O	31.3	33.8	35.2	48.1	51.6	54.0	10.4	11.6	13.0	2.1	3.0	4.7
Shanghai	I	42.3	44.5	46.2	30.8	32.3	34.5	7.8	9.0	10.1	13.1	14.3	15.8
	C	59.0	61.0	63.8	8.3	10.2	11.2	12.6	14.0	16.0	13.0	14.8	16.0
	O	45.6	48.2	50.3	38.6	40.3	43.5	4.1	4.9	5.3	5.2	6.6	7.9
Jiangsu	I	0.9	1.6	2.1	16.6	18.1	21.0	32.1	33.8	35.9	43.2	46.5	48.3
	C	70.2	74.8	78.5	15.8	17.8	19.3	0.7	1.1	1.6	5.2	6.4	7.8

Table A1.1 Variance decomposition of the Eastern provinces (%) (Cont'd)

		National dynamic factors			Regional dynamic factors			Provincial dynamic factors			Idiosyncratic factors		
		1/3Q	Med	2/3Q	1/3Q	Med	2/3Q	1/3Q	Med	2/3Q	1/3Q	Med	2/3Q
Zhejiang	O	49.3	52.9	56.0	29.5	31.7	33.5	3.2	4.7	6.0	9.3	10.7	12.5
	I	15.6	17.1	18.9	64.5	67.5	70.3	8.9	10.5	12.1	3.3	4.9	5.6
	C	75.0	78.3	82.0	10.0	11.3	12.0	3.8	4.6	5.7	4.3	5.8	7.1
Fujian	O	61.9	65.5	68.2	18.6	20.1	22.0	4.3	5.6	6.8	7.3	8.9	11.0
	I	1.3	2.1	3.6	55.1	58.7	61.6	1.2	1.9	3.1	15.9	18.7	20.8
	C	79.6	83.8	88.0	4.0	5.2	6.9	0.1	0.3	0.6	8.7	10.6	12.0
Shandong	O	48.3	50.9	53.1	14.1	15.8	18.0	0.01	0.03	0.13	30.8	33.3	35.6
	I	2.0	3.2	4.9	36.3	38.6	40.5	44.9	47.6	49.8	9.2	10.6	12.0
	C	73.5	76.1	80.0	11.9	13.7	14.9	0.2	0.4	0.8	8.6	9.9	11.0
Guangdong	O	48.6	51.1	53.9	28.3	29.7	31.5	10.0	11.3	13.0	6.1	7.9	9.6
	I	0.3	0.5	1.0	31.2	33.5	35.6	25.7	27.7	29.6	36.5	38.3	40.1
	C	64.0	66.0	68.2	14.1	15.2	16.7	9.8	11.4	12.6	6.2	7.4	8.4
Hainan	O	11.3	12.0	13.2	37.1	39.4	41.3	30.5	32.0	34.1	14.9	16.6	18.0
	I	0.6	0.9	1.1	48.2	51.1	54.0	17.8	19.0	20.8	27.5	29.1	31.1
	C	38.0	40.6	43.1	18.1	19.5	21.3	27.0	28.9	30.6	9.2	10.9	12.0
Median	O	45.6	48.7	50.3	29.5	31.7	33.5	4.3	5.6	6.8	10.1	12.6	14.2
	I	7.1	8.2	10.1	36.3	38.6	40.5	20.1	21.7	23.4	15.9	18.7	20.8
	C	70.8	73.2	75.7	8.3	10.2	11.2	4.1	5.9	7.6	9.2	10.9	12.0

It can be seen from Table A1.1 that the fluctuations in the growth of output and consumption in the Eastern provinces may to a large extent be attributed to the national dynamic factor: for the median province, the national dynamic factor accounts for 48.7% of the fluctuations in output growth and 73.2% of the fluctuations in consumption growth, meaning that the correlation of the fluctuations in consumption growth is far higher than that of the output growth.[14] On the other hand, for the fluctuations in investment growth, the effects of the national dynamic factor is relatively small, while that of the regional and provincial dynamic factors are much more significant: for the median province, regional, and provincial dynamic factors account for 38.6% and 21.5% of the fluctuations in investment growth respectively.

The effects of the national dynamic factor on individual provinces vary greatly: a low 12% contribution to fluctuations in output growth for Hainan but a high

65.5% contribution for Fujian; a low 0.5% contribution to fluctuations in investment growth for Guangdong but a high 44.5% contribution for Shanghai.

Table A1.2 Variance decomposition of the Central provinces (%)

		National dynamic factors			Regional dynamic factors			Provincial dynamic factors			Idiosyncratic factors		
		1/3Q	Med	2/3Q	1/3Q	Med	2/3Q	1/3Q	Med	2/3Q	1/3Q	Med	2/3Q
	O	11.2	13.5	15.1	6.9	8.2	9.0	27.6	29.5	31.2	46.2	48.7	51.1
Shanxi	I	1.6	2.3	3.0	22.8	24.0	25.5	8.0	9.1	10.8	60.2	63.8	66.6
	C	66.9	70.5	74.0	2.1	3.2	4.4	1.3	2.2	3.4	21.8	24.2	26.5
	O	36.8	38.4	41.2	10.9	12.6	14.1	4.2	5.8	7.5	40.5	43.3	45.8
Jilin	I	2.1	2.8	3.6	55.2	57.7	59.8	0.3	0.4	0.7	37.6	39.1	41.1
	C	66.8	69.4	72.8	12.0	13.3	14.9	5.1	6.7	9.2	9.2	10.6	11.6
	O	52.0	54.6	57.5	6.5	7.9	8.6	4.3	5.7	6.6	30.0	31.8	32.4
Heilongjiang	I	11.8	13.3	14.8	17.3	18.8	20.0	0.3	0.5	0.8	65.2	67.4	69.8
	C	75.0	77.9	81.1	0.1	0.3	0.4	0.004	0.01	0.02	20.0	21.9	23.1
	O	60.0	63.5	66.2	7.8	8.6	9.8	0.9	1.3	1.8	25.0	26.6	28.4
Anhui	I	5.0	5.9	6.6	44.2	46.9	49.0	9.9	11.0	12.3	34.8	36.2	38.0
	C	80.3	84.6	87.8	1.4	1.8	2.3	1.5	1.7	2.1	11.0	12.0	13.3
	O	48.1	51.1	54.0	10.9	12.1	13.5	0.8	1.2	1.7	34.3	35.6	37.0
Jiangxi	I	3.0	3.4	4.1	38.9	41.2	44.0	16.6	17.5	19.2	36.3	38.0	40.4
	C	82.0	86.1	88.9	2.5	4.0	6.0	0.2	0.3	0.5	8.2	9.6	11.0
	O	55.8	58.3	61.6	9.0	9.7	10.9	1.3	1.8	2.1	28.7	30.2	33.1
Henan	I	26.8	28.8	30.5	30.4	31.7	33.0	13.3	14.2	15.8	22.9	25.3	27.0
	C	77.3	79.8	83.4	3.6	4.6	5.4	8.8	9.8	10.6	5.0	5.9	6.6
	O	49.3	51.6	54.0	8.8	9.9	11.7	1.5	1.9	2.3	33.8	36.6	34.6
Hubei	I	15.3	17.3	20.3	39.0	40.4	42.4	32.6	34.5	36.1	7.0	7.8	8.8
	C	78.2	80.2	83.6	3.6	5.3	6.0	4.3	5.3	5.9	7.9	9.3	10.1
	O	56.8	59.0	62.0	9.6	10.5	11.7	0.3	0.4	0.5	28.8	30.1	33.0
Hunan	I	8.6	9.7	11.0	28.0	30.8	32.2	20.0	21.7	23.1	35.2	37.7	39.9
	C	70.6	73.6	77.1	0.04	0.06	0.1	5.4	6.4	7.1	18.0	19.9	21.6
	O	50.7	53.1	55.8	8.9	9.8	11.3	1.4	1.9	2.2	31.9	33.7	34.8
Median	I	6.8	7.8	8.8	34.7	36.1	37.7	11.6	12.6	14.1	35.8	37.9	40.2
	C	76.2	78.8	82.3	2.3	3.6	4.9	2.9	3.8	4.7	10.1	11.3	12.5

As shown in Table A1.2, the effects of the national dynamic factor on the fluctuations in growth of output and consumption for the Central provinces is greater than that for the Eastern provinces, with the idiosyncratic factors contributing significantly to the fluctuations in investment growth: for the median province, the national dynamic factor accounts for 53.1% of the fluctuations in output growth and 78.8% of the fluctuations in consumption growth, while idiosyncratic factors account for 37.9% of the fluctuations in investment growth.

In particular, the case of Shanxi province is rather unique: the fluctuations in output growth for Shanxi is more affected by provincial dynamic factors and idiosyncratic factors, with the national dynamic factors only contributing 13.5%, while idiosyncratic factors also contribute a significantly high 63.8% on the fluctuations in investment growth.

Table A1.3 Variance decomposition of the Western provinces (%)

		National dynamic factors			Regional dynamic factors			Provincial dynamic factors			Idiosyncratic factors		
		1/3Q	Med	2/3Q	1/3Q	Med	2/3Q	1/3Q	Med	2/3Q	1/3Q	Med	2/3Q
Inner Mongolia	O	37.2	39.3	42.0	27.6	30.0	32.1	4.7	5.4	6.3	23.8	25.3	26.8
	I	1.4	1.7	2.3	50.7	53.8	56.2	16.1	17.2	19.0	25.6	27.3	29.1
	C	36.5	38.8	41.1	25.6	27.1	29.0	16.9	18.3	20.1	14.2	15.8	17.5
Guangxi	O	50.2	53.1	56.7	9.8	11.1	12.8	8.9	9.9	11.0	23.7	25.9	28.0
	I	3.2	3.8	4.6	49.2	52.2	54.9	0.3	0.4	0.6	41.1	43.5	46.0
	C	67.6	71.5	74.7	18.9	20.7	22.1	0.04	0.1	0.2	6.9	7.7	8.8
Sichuan	O	54.0	56.7	59.2	11.0	12.4	13.8	7.0	7.9	8.6	21.8	23.0	24.4
	I	4.4	5.5	6.4	70.2	73.5	76.3	9.2	10.5	12.0	9.2	10.5	11.3
	C	85.5	88.5	91.2	4.3	5.1	6.0	0.01	0.02	0.04	5.6	6.4	7.1
Guizhou	O	29.5	31.8	33.0	12.3	13.6	15.1	28.3	30.6	33.0	22.7	24.1	25.2
	I	5.9	6.8	8.5	42.7	45.6	47.9	17.6	19.0	21.4	26.8	28.6	31.0
	C	45.5	48.2	50.3	15.9	17.7	19.2	0.4	0.5	0.7	27.1	29.1	31.5
Yunnan	O	38.0	40.4	43.1	1.6	2.4	3.4	4.9	5.4	7.5	49.8	51.9	54.0
	I	5.7	6.7	8.2	60.3	63.9	67.2	13.5	15.8	17.9	11.7	13.6	15.2
	C	43.8	46.5	49.3	22.1	24.8	26.7	3.0	3.7	4.6	23.1	25.0	27.0
Shaanxi	O	36.7	39.5	41.8	14.0	15.3	17.1	9.2	10.4	11.8	32.5	34.8	36.3
	I	4.7	5.2	6.3	45.3	47.2	50.1	33.8	35.9	37.9	10.0	11.7	13.4
	C	70.1	73.9	77.8	6.0	6.6	7.5	0.2	0.3	0.6	17.0	19.2	21.0
Gansu	O	29.2	31.7	34.4	4.0	4.8	6.1	53.6	56.9	60.1	5.6	6.6	7.5
	I	16.0	18.6	20.8	33.5	36.2	38.7	2.8	3.4	4.3	39.2	41.9	44.9
	C	61.3	64.7	68.2	8.7	9.8	10.5	0.04	0.06	0.1	23.4	25.4	27.6

Table A1.3 Variance decomposition of the Western provinces (%) (Cont'd)

		National dynamic factors			Regional dynamic factors			Provincial dynamic factors			Idiosyncratic factors		
		1/3Q	Med	2/3Q	1/3Q	Med	2/3Q	1/3Q	Med	2/3Q	1/3Q	Med	2/3Q
	O	33.2	36.0	39.0	20.7	23.5	26.0	0.6	0.9	1.5	36.8	39.6	42.4
Qinghai	I	0.5	0.7	1.4	23.5	25.5	28.1	6.0	6.9	7.8	63.8	67.0	70.1
	C	54.9	59.6	64.0	2.8	3.3	3.9	0.6	0. 8	1.2	34.0	36.3	38.4
	O	63.5	67.1	70.1	8.7	10.3	11.5	15.1	17.1	19.4	4.8	5.5	6.6
Ningxia	I	2.5	3.4	4.4	50.0	52.5	55.5	0.03	0.06	0.1	41.3	44.1	46.9
	C	75.6	79.7	83.5	4.4	5.6	7.0	0.02	0.04	0.09	12.6	14.7	16.0
	O	32.1	34.5	36.9	8.9	10.2	11.6	17.8	19.8	22.1	33.1	35.6	37.2
Gansu	I	2.1	3.0	4.3	45.0	47.4	50.5	0.4	0.6	1.1	45.6	49.0	52.3
	C	59.0	62.1	65.8	0.1	0.2	0.6	6.8	7.7	8.8	27.7	29.9	32.5
	O	37.0	39.4	41.9	10.4	11.8	13.3	9.1	10.2	11.4	23.8	25.6	27.4
Median	I	3.8	4.5	5.5	47.3	49.8	52.7	7.6	8.7	9.9	33.0	35.3	38.0
	C	60.2	63.4	67.0	7.4	8.2	9.0	0.3	0.5	0.7	20.1	22.1	24.0

From Table A1.3, it can be seen that the effects of the national dynamic factors on the fluctuations in the growth of output and consumption in the Western provinces are relatively weaker compared to that for the Eastern and Central provinces but are still significant: for the median province, the national dynamic factor accounts for 39.4% of the fluctuations in output growth and 63.4% of the fluctuations in consumption growth. The regional dynamic factors also contribute a significant 49.8% to the fluctuations in investment growth.

Table A1.4 Variance decomposition of the median province of the whole country(%)

		National dynamic factors			Regional dynamic factors			Provincial dynamic factors			Idiosyncratic factors		
		1/3Q	Med	2/3Q	1/3Q	Med	2/3Q	1/3Q	Med	2/3Q	1/3Q	Med	2/3Q
	O	45.6	48.7	50.3	12.3	13.6	15.1	4.7	5.7	7.5	23.8	25.9	28.0
Median	I	4.4	5.2	6.3	42.1	44.7	46.5	13.5	15.8	17.9	34.8	36.2	37.7
	C	70.1	73.2	75.7	4.4	5.6	7.0	2.1	3.7	4.8	12.6	14.7	16.0

Despite the various dynamic factors having varying extents of effects on different economic variables in different regions and different provinces, the above analysis demonstrates the following general patterns:

1. The national economic cycle has a significant impact on the provincial economic cycles. As Table A1.4 shows, the national dynamic factor accounts for around 49% of the fluctuations in output growth and 73% of the fluctuations in consumption growth. This is further validated by Figure A1.5, which shows that the contribution of the national dynamic factor on the fluctuations in the growth of provincial output and consumption are concentrated in the 30%–70% range and the 60%–90% range respectively.

Fig A1.5(a) Contribution of the national dynamic factor on provincial output growth

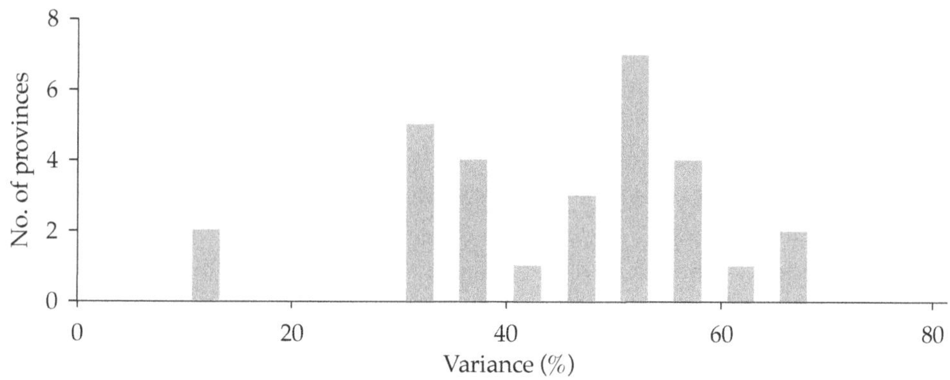

Fig A1.5(b) Contribution of the national dynamic factor on provincial consumption growth

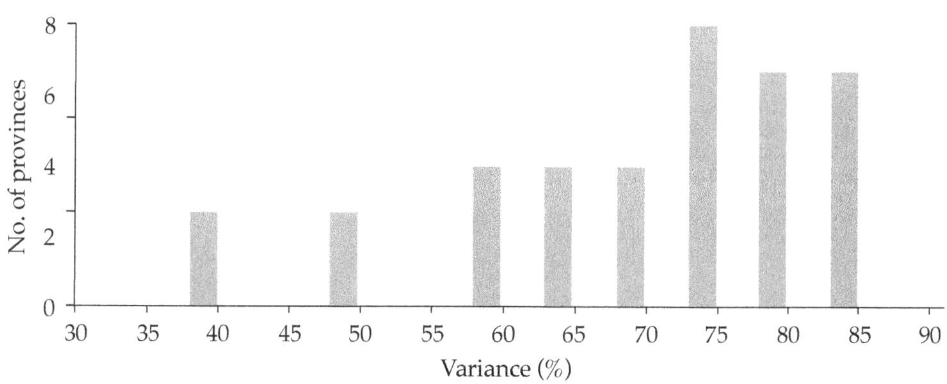

On the other hand, there are also significant variations in the effects of the national dynamic factor on the fluctuations in the provincial economies. Generally speaking, the impact of the national dynamic factor is significantly larger on the fluctuations in the developed provinces compared to that for the underdeveloped provinces: for the median province of the entire country, the national dynamic factor accounts for 48.7%, 5.2%, and 73.2 % of the fluctuations in the growth of output, investment, and consumption (see Table 1.4), significantly higher than that for the Western provinces. This also means that the economic shocks from developed provinces have a greater impact on the fluctuations in the national economy;

2. The regional dynamic factors and idiosyncratic factors have a significant impact on provincial economic cycles, in particular the fluctuations in investment growth, for which their contributions are 44.7% and 36.2% respectively, far greater than that from national and provincial dynamic factors (see Table A1.4). Generally speaking, the regional dynamic factors and the idiosyncratic factors have a higher impact on the fluctuations in investment growth for underdeveloped provinces, with regional dynamic factors contributing to 38.6%, 36.1%, and 49.8% of the fluctuations in investment growth for the median Eastern, Central, and Western provinces respectively, and that for the idiosyncratic factors at 18.7%, 37.9%, and 35.3% respectively;
3. The effects of provincial dynamic factors on the provincial economic cycles are, on the whole, relatively small, with their contributions to the fluctuations in the growth of provincial output, investment, and consumption at 5.7%, 15.8%, and 3.7% respectively. Figure A1.6 further validates this: the contribution of provincial dynamic factors on fluctuations in the growth of output is mainly concentrated in the 10% range. Overall, the effect of provincial dynamic factors on the fluctuations in growth of output is more significant in the underdeveloped provinces compared to the developed provinces, while they have a larger impact on the fluctuations in investment growth for the developed provinces.

Fig. A1.6 Contribution of the provincial dynamic factors on the growth of output

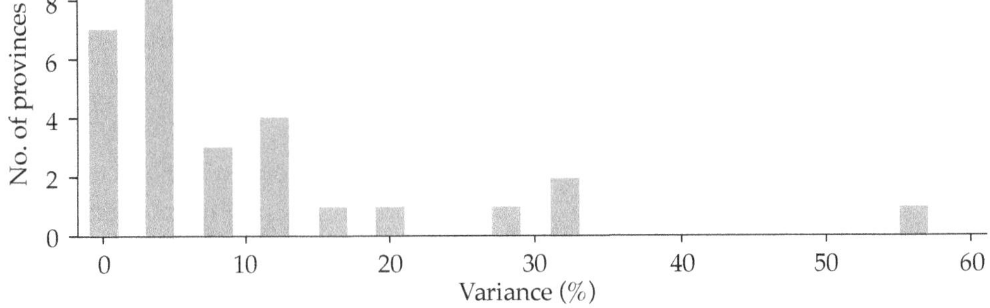

Relationship Between Dynamic Factors and Features in the Economy

To examine the relative importance of the various dynamic factors to the important features in the provincial economic cycles mentioned in the previous section, regression analysis is used to demonstrate the relationships between the features in the provincial economy and the variance decomposition of the dynamic factors.

Four main types of variables of the features in the economy are taken into consideration: relative per capita provincial output level (PcY), i.e. the ratio of per capita provincial output to per capita output of Shanghai, used to measure the relative income levels in the various provinces; percentage of provincial government expenditure (G), i.e. the ratio of government expenditure to output, used to measure the size of provincial governments; ratio of the provincial industrial value-added (Ind), i.e. the ratio of industrial value-added to output, used to measure the level of industrialization of the various provinces; output growth standard deviation of the various provinces (Yvol), used to measure the fluctuations in the growth of output in the various provinces. Table A1.5 gives the average values of these four variables for the provinces in the period 1979 to 2003.

Table A1.5 Variables of the features in the economy for the provinces in 1979–2003

Province	PcY	G	Ind	Yvol	Province	PcY	G	Ind	Yvol
Beijing	0.5497	0.1414	0.4369	0.0618	Jiangxi	0.1143	0.1255	0.2815	0.0693
Tianjin	0.4548	0.1331	0.5389	0.0760	Henan	0.1092	0.1004	0.3686	0.0837
Hebei	0.1536	0.0977	0.4201	0.0846	Hubei	0.1543	0.1034	0.3852	0.0814
Liaoning	0.2631	0.1101	0.5034	0.0719	Hunan	0.1087	0.1083	0.3180	0.0750
Shanghai	1	0.1054	0.5849	0.0846	Inner Mongolia	0.1401	0.2018	0.3160	0.0705
Jiangsu	0.2513	0.0728	0.4574	0.0975	Guangxi	0.0818	0.1502	0.2798	0.0920
Zhejiang	0.2271	0.0818	0.4314	0.0975	Sichuan	0.1122	0.1026	0.3289	0.0733
Fujian	0.1653	0.1217	0.3364	0.1103	Guizhou	0.0708	0.1951	0.3804	0.0643
Shandong	0.1676	0.0792	0.4119	0.0750	Yunnan	0.0926	0.2159	0.3321	0.0782
Guangdong	0.2351	0.1055	0.3847	0.0903	Shaanxi	0.1190	0.1503	0.3595	0.0640
Hainan	0.1852	0.1281	0.1464	0.1190	Gansu	0.1249	0.1162	0.3915	0.0687
Shanxi	0.1378	0.1458	0.457	0.0823	Qinghai	0.1299	0.2778	0.3028	0.0683
Jilin	0.1639	0.1531	0.3915	0.0797	Ningxia	0.1333	0.2685	0.3430	0.0677
Heilongjiang	0.1899	0.1223	0.4964	0.0706	Xinjiang	0.1431	0.2041	0.2899	0.0739
Anhui	0.1117	0.1031	0.3476	0.0982					

To examine the correlation between the variables in the economic features and the variances in the dynamic factors, regression analysis is performed using the four variables as above as the explanatory variable, and the contributions from the national, regional, and provincial dynamic factors as well as the idiosyncratic factors to the growth variance in provincial output, investment, and consumption as the explained variable. Tables A1.6 to 1.8 gives the regression results for the variance decomposition of the growth of output, investment, and consumption respectively.[15]

Table A1.6 Regression results for the variables of economic features and the variance decomposition of the output growth

Variable	National dynamic factor			Regional dynamic factors			Provincial dynamic factors			Idiosyncratic factors		
	$R^2 = 0.906$			$R^2 = 0.862$			$R^2 = 0.438$			$R^2 = 0.782$		
	Coefficient	t value	P	Coefficient	t value	P	Coefficient	t value	P	Coefficient	t value	P
PcY	-0.29	-1.61	0.12	0.47	4.08	0.00	-0.05	-0.29	0.78	-0.327	-1.97	0.06
G	0.14	0.33	0.75	-0.15	-0.54	0.60	0.37	0.92	0.37	0.98	2.47	0.02
Ind	0.71	2.45	0.02	-0.15	-0.82	0.42	0.02	0.09	0.93	0.42	1.60	0.12
Yvol	2.76	2.33	0.03	2.18	2.91	0.01	0.70	0.65	0.52	0.20	0.18	0.86

It can be seen from Table A1.6 that the industrial value added and the output growth standard deviation have a significant and positive effect on the fluctuations in the provincial output growth (the effect coefficients are 0.71 and 2.76 respectively), meaning that the higher the level of industrialization in the province, the higher the fluctuations in the output growth, and the more significant the contribution of the national dynamic factor on the fluctuations in the output growth. Generally speaking, developed provinces have higher levels of industrialization, along with higher fluctuations in output growth (see Table A1.5), and so the contribution of the national dynamic factor to the fluctuations in the output growth for developed provinces are more significant; this is consistent with the results obtained in the previous section.

There is no significant effect from the provincial relative income levels and size of governments on the contribution of the national dynamic factors. As for the effects of the regional dynamic factors on the fluctuations in provincial output growth, the output growth standard deviation and the relative per capita output level all exhibit significant and positive effects, while the effects of industrial value-added and percentage of government expenditure are not significant. This means that the relative importance of the regional dynamic factors is dependent on the fluctuations of the output growth, as well as the relative income level, and has little inherent relation with the level of industrialization and the size of government.

There seems to be no inherent relationship between the relative importance of the provincial dynamic factors and the variables of economic features. In the regression coefficient for the contribution of idiosyncratic factors, the regression coefficient for relative per capita output and percentage of government expenditure is negative and positive respectively, and both exhibit statistical significance. This shows that the effects of the idiosyncratic factors on the output dynamics are stronger for underdeveloped provinces with relatively large sizes of government.

Table A1.7 Regression results for the variables of economic features and the variance decomposition of the investment growth

Variable	National dynamic factor			Regional dynamic factors			Provincial dynamic factors			Idiosyncratic factors		
	$R^2 = 0.693$			$R^2 = 0.895$			$R^2 = 0.438$			$R^2 = 0.775$		
	Coefficient	t value	P	Coefficient	t value	P	Coefficient	t value	P	Coefficient	t value	P
PcY	0.28	2.68	0.01	-0.10	-0.54	0.600	-0.08	-0.47	0.64	-0.30	-1.37	0.18
G	-0.31	-1.24	0.23	0.89	2.02	0.050	-0.46	-1.14	0.26	1.22	2.36	0.03
Ind	0.13	0.80	0.43	-0.11	-0.38	0.700	0.49	1.82	0.08	0.49	1.43	0.17
Yvol	0.39	0.57	0.57	4.51	3.77	0.001	0.68	0.62	0.54	0.26	0.19	0.85

Table A1.7 demonstrates the inherent relation between the relative importance of the fluctuations in the provincial investment growth and the features of the provincial economy: the national dynamic factor makes a stronger contribution to the fluctuations in the investment growth of the developed provinces; the regional dynamic factors make a stronger contribution to the fluctuations in the investment growth of provinces with larger government sizes and higher fluctuations in output growth; the relative importance of the provincial dynamic factors to fluctuations in investment growth are only positively correlated to the level of industrialization of the province; and the idiosyncratic factors make a stronger contribution to the fluctuations in the investment growth of provinces with larger government sizes and higher levels of industrialization.

Table A1.8 shows the correlation between the provincial economic features and the relative contributions of the dynamic factors on the fluctuations of the consumption growth: for the developed provinces, the fluctuations in consumption growth exhibits stronger autonomy, demonstrated in the negative correlation between the contribution of the national dynamic factor and the relative per

Table A1.8 Regression results for the variables of economic features and the variance decomposition of the consumption growth

Variable	National dynamic factor			Regional dynamic factors			Provincial dynamic factors			Idiosyncratic factors		
	$R^2 = 0.968$			$R^2 = 0.626$			$R^2 = 0.592$			$R^2 = 0.874$		
	Coefficient	t value	P	Coefficient	t value	P	Coefficient	t value	P	Coefficient	t value	P
PcY	-0.40	-2.32	0.03	0.05	0.51	0.62	0.19	2.49	0.02	-0.04	-0.46	0.65
G	-0.03	-0.07	0.95	0.29	1.25	0.22	0.06	0.31	0.76	1.02	5.32	0.00
Ind	1.27	4.64	0.00	-0.19	-1.27	0.22	-0.32	-2.62	0.02	0.25	1.95	0.06
Yvol	3.68	3.28	0.00	1.39	2.21	0.04	1.62	3.24	0.00	-0.85	-1.65	0.11

capita output level, while the contributions of the provincial dynamic factors are positively correlated to the relative per capita output level; for provinces with larger government sizes, the contributions of the regional dynamic factors and the idiosyncratic factors on the consumption dynamics are stronger; the effects of level of industrialization and fluctuations in output growth are more extensive: other than the regional dynamic factors, the contribution to consumption growth fluctuations of all dynamic factors have a closely positive correlation with the level of industrialization, and other than the idiosyncratic factors, the fluctuations in output growth have a large and positive effect on the relative importance of all dynamic factors.

Summary

Using Gibbs sampling for estimation in the multi-dynamic-factor model of China's provincial economic cycles, this paper examined the fluctuations in the national, regional and provincial dynamic factors affecting the provincial economic cycles, and then used variance decomposition to analyze the effects of the various dynamic factors on the fluctuations in the provincial macroeconomy. Finally, the paper examined the correlation between the provincial economic features and the strength of the effects of the dynamic factors. The paper managed to find the following conclusions:

- The national economic cycle has an important impact on the provincial economic cycles. Fluctuations in the provincial economy, in particular the dynamics of output and consumption, are to a large extent dependent on the national dynamic factor, although the effects vary for different provinces: overall, the national dynamic factor has a more significant impact on the economy of developed provinces. Conversely, economic shocks from developed provinces have a more significant impact on fluctuations in the national economy as well;

- The investment dynamics of the provincial economy, on the other hand, exhibit more autonomy and idiosyncrasy from the national economy. This can be seen from that the contributions of regional dynamic factors, idiosyncratic factors and provincial dynamic factors to fluctuations in investment growth are significantly higher than the national dynamic factor. Generally speaking, the investment dynamics in underdeveloped provinces are more affected by idiosyncratic factors and regional dynamic factors, while that for developed provinces are more affected by provincial dynamic factors;
- Economic features such as relative income levels, size of government, level of industrialization, and fluctuations in output growth all affect to a certain extent the modes of the provincial economic cycles. For provinces with higher fluctuations in output growth and higher levels of industrialization, fluctuations in the economy is more affected by national and regional dynamic factors; while for provinces with larger sizes of government, the fluctuations in the economy is more affected by idiosyncratic factors.

Clearly, it is not enough to simply consider the problem of fluctuations in China's macroeconomy on a national perspective, but also on deeper levels of examination in the regional and provincial economies. Likewise, the country's macroeconomic stabilization policies should also take into consideration the dynamics of the economy of different regions and provinces, in particular the features in the investment dynamics, in order to truly resolve the problem of investment and economic overheating. In practice, this means that, since economic shocks from developed provinces have a more significant impact on the fluctuations in the national economy, the focus of macroeconomic stabilization policies should be on the developed provinces. Additionally, considering that the behavior of regional governments play a major role in triggering investment overheating, it is not enough to rely on economic policies; moderation through administrative measures is also needed, in order to truly achieve a continuously stable operation of the country's macroeconomy.

This annex is published under the same title in* Management World *(11), 2005. Only the numbering of the sections is changed for purposes of standardization in this book.

2

Annex

The Effects of Intergovernmental Arrangement of Fiscal Responsibilities on Regional Economic Growth

Introduction

When the Chinese Economic Reform started in 1978, reforms in the country's financial and tax systems were introduced to resolve the government-enterprise relationship, i.e. the questions of responsibility, authority and interests between the government and (state-run) enterprises. With the maturation of the market economy, the tax-sharing system reform was introduced in 1994, aimed at resolving the intergovernmental relationship, i.e. the questions of responsibility, authority, and interests between the central and the various levels of regional governments. While the government-enterprise relationship is more or less established today, the intergovernmental relationship remains in question. In particular, the conflict arising out of misarrangements and imbalance in the administrative roles of the various levels of government (fiscal expenditure responsibilities) and the relevant financial backing (fiscal revenue responsibilities) is especially prominent. Resolving this conflict is thus arguably the key in a much-needed reform of the country's financial and taxation system today.

There is a lack of academic consensus on the effects of reform in the financial and taxation system on economic growth. One view holds that reforms centering on decentralization of power and interests have helped to strengthen the role played by regional governments in the vertical structure of government, encouraging regional governments to keep pace with the progress of marketization, and so promoting economic growth.[1] Another view holds that excessive and unreasonable decentralization has caused the efficiency of resource allocation to dip, and along with a vertical administration structure, overemphasis on GDP in the mechanism of political promotion, and the shortcomings of relevant mechanisms of constraints, has strengthened protectionism and predation in the tactical behavior of regional governments over regional competition, thus hindering economic growth.[2] Clearly, a fair assessment on the effects of reform in the financial and taxation system on economic growth will depend on giving a full account of the mechanisms of incentives and restraints arising out of the intergovernmental arrangements of fiscal responsibilities resulting from decentralization reforms, and their effects on the behavior of regional governments. On this basis, this paper will proceed to examine the problems existing in the current structure of intergovernmental arrangements of fiscal responsibilities and determine a rational relationship for responsibilities, authority, and interests between the central and regional governments, so as to promote optimization in the role played by regional governments, which will hopefully encourage better regional economic development.

The main features of this paper are as follows:

- Existing studies mainly focus on the intergovernmental arrangement of fiscal responsibilities (i.e. degree of fiscal decentralization). In the real-world economy, however, there is more attention on the specific arrangements of responsibilities for individual terms of expenditure (e.g. public education, public healthcare and infrastructure) between the central and regional governments (i.e. optimization of the structure of fiscal decentralization). Thus, in examining the effects of intergovernmental arrangements of fiscal responsibilities on economic growth, this paper will take extra consideration for the effects of specific arrangements of responsibilities for individual terms of expenditure on regional economic growth;
- In analyzing the effects of intergovernmental arrangements of fiscal responsibilities on regional economic growth, existing studies often examine only a single aspect of fiscal responsibility arrangement. This paper aims to examine the intergovernmental arrangements of fiscal responsibilities under a unified framework of empirical analysis, in order to better demonstrate the interactive effects of the fiscal responsibility arrangements;
- To account for potential deviations in estimation, this paper will employ a progressive method, first using a fixed-effects panel model to resolve the heterogeneity problem in different regions, and then use a dynamic-effects panel model and system GMM to correct potential endogeneity problems. Finally, a threshold panel model is used to examine non-linear effects of intergovernmental arrangements of fiscal responsibility and the main factors behind these effects.

Historical Overview of Intergovernmental Arrangements of Fiscal Responsibilities

Since the implementation of the Chinese Economic Reform in 1978, there have been two major reforms in China's financial system. The first is the fiscal contracting system reforms in the mid-1980s, which allowed regional governments to administer surplus in tax revenues; and the second is the tax sharing reforms in 1994, which centralized the powers of fiscal revenue. Accompanying these two major reforms are significant changes in the intergovernmental arrangements of fiscal responsibilities. Figure A2.1 gives the density graphs of the fiscal responsibility arrangements of the 29 provinces of the country for the years 1978, 1985, 1993, and 2005.[3]

Fig. A2.1(a) Kernel density graph of intergovernmental arrangement in fiscal expenditure responsibilities (Epanechnikov kernel)

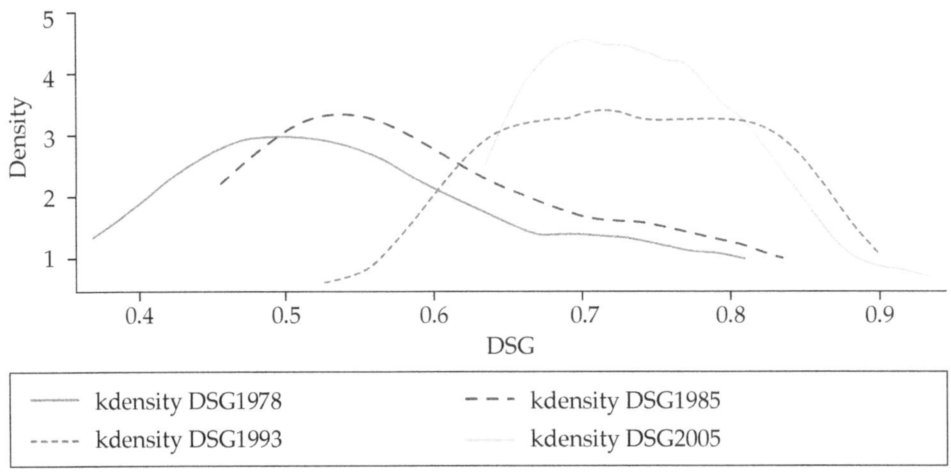

It can be seen from Figure A2.1(a) that between 1978 to 1993, the density curves continuously shifted to the right, with the most significant shift being between 1985 to 1993, showing that the amount of expenditure responsibilities assumed by regional governments in this period is relatively high. The density curve for 2005 shifted to the left of that for 1993 with an increase in height, showing that since the 1994 tax sharing reforms, there has been a reverse in the trend of administrative decentralization.

Fig. A2.1(b) Kernel density graph of intergovernmental arrangement in fiscal revenue responsibilities (Epanechnikov kernel)

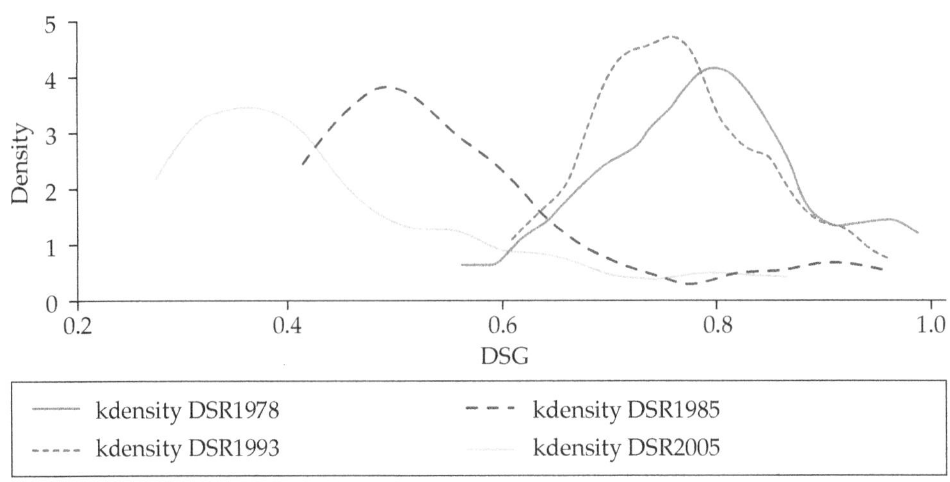

In contrast, Figure A2.1(b) shows that between 1978 to 1985, the intergovernmental arrangements for revenue responsibilities exhibit a strong trend of centralization, with a clear reversal happening after 1985 (when regional governments were placed in a dominating position in revenue administration), and then moving back to a very strong trend of centralization again after 1994. It can thus be seen that with the exception of the period 1985 to 1993, the intergovernmental arrangements of fiscal responsibilities are in a clear state of misarrangement, with the correlation coefficient within the entire sample period being a mere 0.272.

In order to better understand the administrative roles of the central and regional governments, the arrangements of responsibility for different terms of expenditure are examined. Fiscal expenditure are classified as three types (economic, social and administrative), with infrastructure expenditure, education, science, culture, and healthcare expenditure, and administration expenditure used to representatively measure the changing trends in these three types of fiscal expenditure.[4]

Fig. A2.2(a) Kernel density graph of intergovernmental arrangement in economic expenditure responsibilities (Epanechnikov kernel)

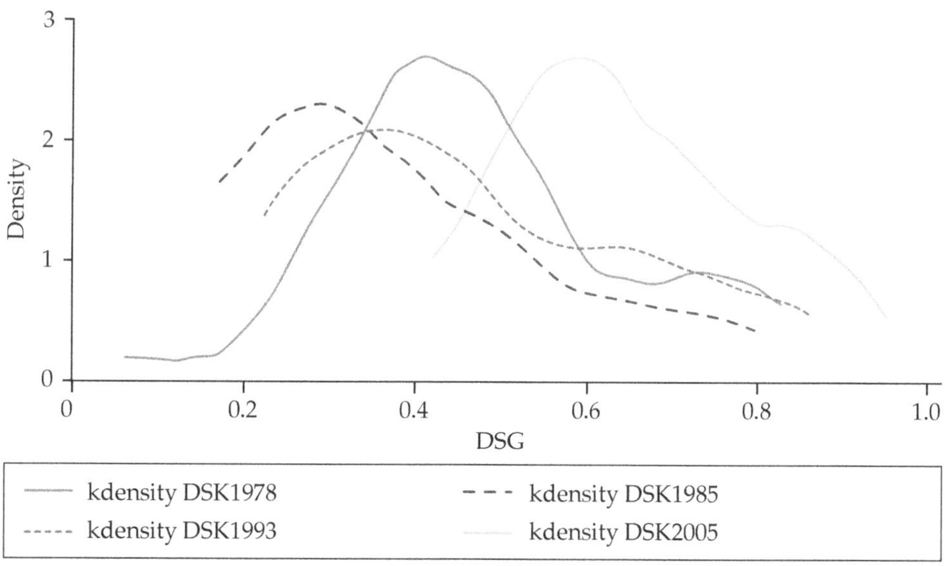

Figure A2.2(a) shows that the arrangement of responsibilities for economic expenditure exhibits a trend of centralization between 1978 to 1985, and a reversal thereafter as regional governments assume an increasing amount of infrastructure responsibilities, most prominently exhibited after the 1994 tax sharing reforms. Figure A2.2(b) shows that the arrangement of responsibilities for social expenditure is on the overall consistent with the changing trends for that

Fig. A2.2(b) Kernel density graph of intergovernmental arrangement in social expenditure responsibilities (Epanechnikov kernel)

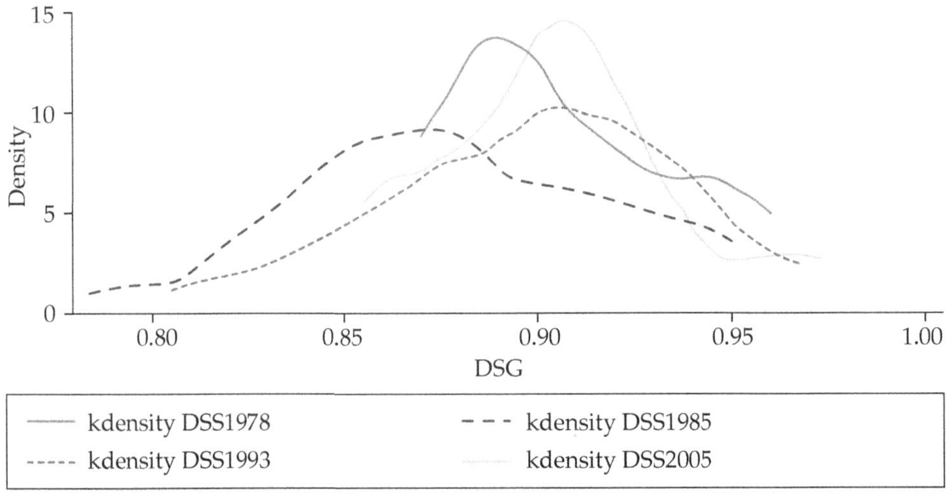

Fig. A2.2(c) Kernel density graph of intergovernmental arrangement in administrative expenditure responsibilities (Epanechnikov kernel)

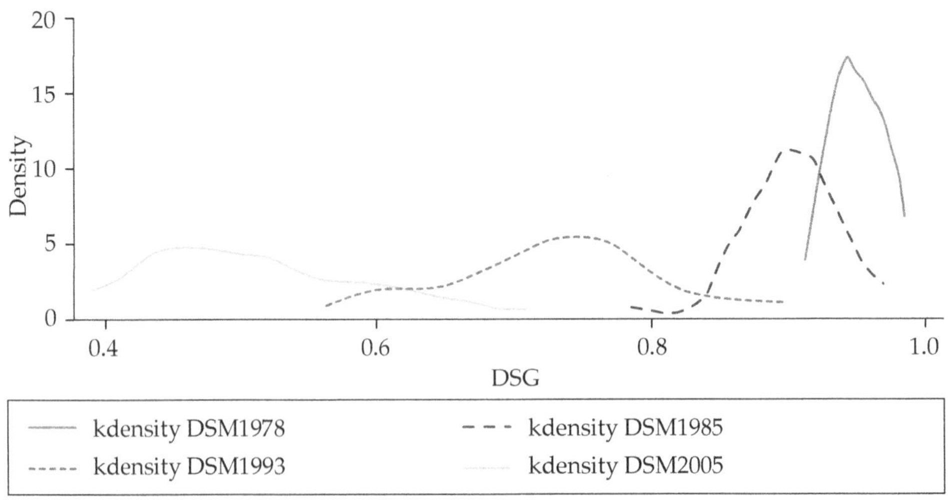

of economic expenditure. The pace of decentralization after the 1994 tax sharing reforms is not as prominent, although regional governments still assumes around 90% of responsibilities for social expenditure. Figure A2.2(c) shows that the arrangement of responsibilities for administrative expenditure exhibits a clear and continuous trend of centralization, and is especially prominent after the 1994 tax sharing reforms.

Table A2.1 Summary of changing trends in intergovernmental responsibility in fiscal arrangement (1978–2005)

Period / Responsibility	1978–1985	1986–1993	1994–2005
Overall expenditure	Decentralize	Strong decentralize	Weak centralize
- Economic expenditure	Centralize	Weak decentralize	Strong decentralize
- Social expenditure	Centralize	Decentralize	Weak decentralize
- Administrative expenditure	Weak centralize	Centralize	Strong centralize
Overall revenue	Strong centralize	Strong decentralize	Strong centralize

As Table A2.1 shows, the intergovernmental arrangements of fiscal responsibilities, as well as that for the various terms of expenditure, all exhibit different features of developmental change. The following sections will look to address how these changing trends affect the behavior of regional governments and regional economic growth, and the extent of these effects.

Effects of Intergovernmental Arrangements of Fiscal Responsibilities on Economic Growth: Fixed-effects Estimation

Given China's vast expanse of territory, the geographical environment, resource availability and local customs vary greatly across different provinces. These factors, while being difficult to measure accurately, affect to different extents regional economic growth. To correct the deviations brought about by these heterogeneity problems, this section will use a fixed-effects panel model for estimating the effects of intergovernmental arrangements in fiscal responsibilities on regional economic growth.

Model framework

Using as basis data from the 29 provinces of the country for the period 1978 to 2005, the following panel data model is constructed:

$$Gy_{it} = \alpha X_{it} + \beta Ds_{it} + \gamma DsD94_{it} + \eta DsDE_{it} + \mu_i + \lambda_t + \varepsilon_{it} \quad (A2.1)$$

Of which, Gy_{it} is the actual output growth rate per capita for province i in the period t, and X_{it} is a group of control variables. Ds_{it} is the core explanatory variable — the variables in intergovernmental arrangements in fiscal responsibilities, of which for expenditure, the arrangements in total expenditure as well as economic, social and administrative expenditure are considered, and for revenue, only the arrangements in total revenue is considered.[5] $DsD94_{it}$ is the temporal dummy variables for intergovernmental arrangements in fiscal responsibilities, i.e. Ds_{it} before 1994 is multiplied by 0, and that after 1994 is multiplied by 1, in order to capture the effects of the 1994 tax sharing system reforms. $DsDE_{it}$ is the regional dummy variables for intergovernmental arrangements in fiscal responsibilities, i.e. Ds_{it} for Eastern provinces is multiplied by 1, and that for the other provinces is multiplied by 0, in order to capture the different effects of intergovernmental arrangements in fiscal responsibilities on the Eastern and other regions. μ_i is the individual effect, λ_t is the temporal effect, and ε_{it} is the random error term.

For X_{it}, the variables considered are: (1) ratio of physical capital investment, i.e. physical capital investment as a percentage of GDP; (2) human capital investment levels, measured using the ratio of total students enrolled in middle and higher education to the labor force, and a moving average over five years is taken to reflect the long-term effects of human capital investment on economic growth;[6] (3) variables in labor force, used to capture the performance of the labor market, including the effects of employment rate, changes in the labor force participation rate, and interregional labor force mobility on economic growth. Due to the lack of provincial data for unemployment rate and labor force participation rate, the ratio of labor force to total population number is used as an approximate substitute; (4) economic development level, measured using the actual output per capita (taking natural logarithms of the moving average over five years), in order to capture potential economic convergence effects;[7] (5) level of economic openness, measured using the percentage of total volume of import and export out of GDP; (6) provincial economic responsibilities, measured using the percentage of fiscal revenue out of GDP.

Estimation results

In operating the fixed-effects panel model (A2.1), the inclusion and exclusion of the variables in intergovernmental arrangements in revenue responsibilities were both considered.[8] As the sampling period spans a relatively long period of time, potential serial correlation problems were also taken into consideration; in fact, the LBI statistics for the function of the effects of the arrangements of responsibilities in the overall expenditure and the terms of expenditure are 1.46 and 1.55 respectively, indicating a certain extent of serial correlation problems in these two function, and so AR(1) correction was performed.[9] The results are given in Table A2.2.

Table A2.2 Fixed-effects estimation results for intergovernmental arrangements in fiscal responsibilities

		Fixed-effects model for the arrangements of responsibilities					
		Overall expenditure			Terms of expenditure		
Explanatory variable		Model 1a	Model 1b	Model 1c [AR(1) correction]	Model 2a	Model 2b	Model 2c [AR(1) correction]
Constant term		0.214 (0.070)***	0.340 (0.080)***	0.023 (0.070)	0.076 (0.130)	0.097 (0.140)	-0.458 (0.110)***
Economic development level		-0.097 (0.050)**	-0.166 (0.050)***	0.049 (0.060)	0.028 (0.060)	0.028 (0.060)	0.244 (0.080)***
Rate of physical capital investment		0.167 (0.020)***	0.154 (0.020)***	0.165 (0.030)***	0.097 (0.030)***	0.096 (0.030)***	0.091 (0.030)***
Human capital investment level		-0.023 (0.070)	-0.011 (0.070)	-0.146 (0.090)	-0.075 (0.070)	-0.079 (0.07)	-0.159 (0.100)*
Variables in labor		0.101 (0.060)*	0.082 (0.060)	0.142 (0.070)**	0.056 (0.060)	0.051 (0.060)	0.075 (0.070)
Level of economic openness		0.043 (0.010)	0.058 (0.020)***	0.055 (0.020)***	0.041 (0.010)***	0.045 (0.020)***	0.027 (0.020)
Ratio of fiscal revenue		-0.015 (0.040)	-0.028 (0.050)	-0.256 (0.060)***	-0.126 (0.040)	-0.097 (0.050)*	-0.315 (0.070)***
Arrangements of responsibilities	Revenue	—	-0.019 (0.030)	0.024 (0.040)	—	-0.040 (0.030)	-0.020 (0.040)
	Overall expenditure	-0.056 (0.040)	-0.020 (0.050)	-0.168 (0.050)***	—	—	—
	Economic expenditure	—	—	—	0.096 (0.030)***	0.099 (0.030)***	0.039 (0.040)
	Social expenditure	—	—	—	-0.148 (0.050)***	-0.136 (0.050)***	-0.068 (0.040)
	Administrative expenditure	—	—	—	0.139 (0.040)***	0.134 (0.040)***	0.254 (0.050)***
Temporal dummy variables in arrangement of re ponsibilities	Revenue	—	-0.105 (0.040)**	-0.076 (0.050)	—	-0.013 (0.050)	-0.034 (0.050)
	Overall expenditure	0.009 (0.010)	0.082 (0.030)**	0.028 (0.040)	—	—	—
	Economic expenditure	—	—	—	-0.042 (0.020)*	-0.036 (0.030)	-0.005 (0.030)
	Social expenditure	—	—	—	0.099 (0.030)***	0.073 (0.050)	0.128 (0.060)**
	Administrative expenditure	—	—	—	-0.098 (0.040)**	-0.069 (0.050)	-0.165 (0.060)***

Table A2.2 Fixed-effects estimation results for intergovernmental arrangements in fiscal responsibilities (Cont'd)

Explanatory variable		Fixed-effects model for the arrangements of responsibilities					
		Overall expenditure			Terms of expenditure		
		Model 1a	Model 1b	Model 1c [AR(1) correction]	Model 2a	Model 2b	Model 2c [AR(1) correction]
Regional dummy variables in arrangement of responsibilities	Revenue	—	-0.010 (0.030)	0.012 (0.040)	—	0.007 (0.040)	0.016 (0.040)
	Overall expenditure	-0.023 (0.040)	-0.002 (0.040)	-0.050 (0.050)	—	—	—
	Economic expenditure	—	—	—	-0.040 (0.030)	-0.033 (0.040)	-0.044 (0.040)
	Social expenditure	—	—	—	-0.280 (0.100)***	-0.286 (0.100)***	-0.225 (0.090)**
	Administrative expenditure	—	—	—	0.034 (0.030)	0.021 (0.030)	0.055 (0.040)
Breusch-Pagan test		2.720*	2.970*	2.970*	3.260*	3.270*	3.270*
Hausman test		34.620***	32.850***	32.850***	51.450***	31.000***	31.000***
LBI test (ρ)		—	—	1.460 (0.286)	—	—	1.550 (0.277)
Effective sample size		812	812	783	812	812	783
F value		9.440***	9.170***	9.180***	10.700***	9.000***	9.100***

Notes: (1) ρ is the first-order autoregressive coefficient of the residual term.
(2) All other bracketed values are standard deviations.
(3) *, ** and *** indicate regression coefficients significantly above confidence levels of 10%, 5% and 1% respectively.

It can be seen from the estimation results of Models 1a and 1b that after introducing the variable in intergovernmental arrangements of revenue responsibilities, the regression coefficients and statistical significance of the overall expenditure responsibility arrangement and its respective temporal and regional dummy variables both exhibit significant change, meaning that solely considering a single aspect of fiscal responsibilities arrangements can lead to deviations in estimation.

Further correcting for serial correlation problems in Model 1c, the estimation results also show significant changes, meaning that the intergovernmental arrangements of revenue responsibilities has a rather long-lasting effect on regional economic growth.

The estimation results from Model 1c shows that the overall expenditure responsibility arrangement has a significant constraining effect on regional economic growth, meaning that the intergovernmental arrangements in overall expenditure responsibility has not been reasonable, with regional governments assuming excessive expenditure responsibilities. The situation varies, however, in examining individual regions: the arrangements for the Eastern provinces are more reasonable relative to the entire country, shown by the negative but relatively small and statistically insignificant regression coefficient for the regional dummy variable in the overall expenditure responsibility arrangement.

After the 1994 tax sharing system reforms, there is a clear improvement in the overall situation, shown by the positive regression coefficient for the temporal variable in the overall expenditure responsibility arrangement. The effect of revenue responsibility arrangement on regional economic growth is, on the other hand, rather unclear, shown by the positive and negative regression coefficients with no statistical significance for the variables in revenue responsibility arrangement in Models 1c and 2c respectively.

For the arrangements of responsibilities for the various terms of expenditure, it can be seen from Model 2c that the arrangements for economic and administrative expenditure responsibilities has helped in regional economic growth, with the administrative term having greater promoting effect and excellent statistical significance. The arrangement for social expenditure responsibilities is not favorable to regional economic growth but its regression coefficient is not statistically significant. This means that the arrangements in economic and administrative expenditure responsibilities have been reasonable, but regional governments have assumed excessive responsibilities in social expenditure.

Again, the situation varies for different individual regions. The economic, administrative but especially social expenditure responsibilities arrangements in the Eastern provinces are less reasonable relative to the entire country, shown by the negative regression coefficient for the regional dummy variables in the economic and social expenditure terms, and that for social expenditure is statistically significant, while that for administrative expenditure is positive but not statistically significant. Since the implementation of the tax sharing reforms in 1994, the pace of decentralization in economic expenditure and centralization in administrative expenditure is clearly faster, and is unfavorable to regional economic growth; while moderate centralization in social expenditure has led to a more reasonable arrangement in responsibilities, which favors regional economic growth.

Effects of Intergovernmental Arrangements of Fiscal Responsibilities on Economic Growth: Dynamic-effects Estimation

While the fixed-effects model in the previous section largely resolves the problems of heterogeneity for different provinces, it also treats all explanatory variables as strictly exogenous variables. Actual economic growth is, however, a dynamic process, dependent on both present on past factors. This means that there is a potential endogenous problem arising from the dynamic data structure in the fixed-effects model, leading to deviations and inconsistencies in the estimation of parameters.[10] AR(1) correction in the temporal sequences also cannot fundamentally resolve this issue.[11] Thus, this section will use a dynamic-effects panel model and system GMM to further examine the effects of intergovernmental arrangements in fiscal responsibilities on regional economic growth.

Model framework

The dynamic-effects panel model is constructed as follows:

$$Gy_{it} = \sum_{j=1}^{M} \alpha_j Gy_{it-j} + \beta Z_{it} + \gamma W_{it} + \mu_i + \lambda_t + \varepsilon_{it} \qquad \text{(A2.2)}$$

Of which, Gy_{it-j} is the lagged term for output growth rate per capita, and M is the largest order of the lagged term. Z_{it} is the exogenous explanatory variable (satisfying $\forall t$, $E(Z_{it}\varepsilon_{it}) = 0$), W_{it} includes the predetermined explanatory variable (satisfying $s < t$, $E(Z_{it}\varepsilon_{it}) \neq 0$ and $s \geq t$, $E(Z_{it}\varepsilon_{is}) = 0$) and the endogenous explanatory variable (satisfying $E(Z_{it}\varepsilon_{it}) \neq 0, \forall t$). μ_i is the individual effect, and ε_{it} is the random error term, satisfying $E(\mu_i) = E(\varepsilon_{it}) = 0$, $E(\mu_i\varepsilon_{it}) = 0$, $E(\varepsilon_{it}\varepsilon_{is}) = 0$ ($\forall i, t, s, t \neq s$) and $E(\mu_i D.\varepsilon_{is}) = 0$.

The presence of endogenous problems in the model will cause the estimations of the OLS regression to deviate upwards, and the mean-subtracted SSW estimations to deviate downwards.[12] Holtz-Eakin et al. and Arellano and Bond devised the method of difference GMM to resolve this problem, using first difference transformation to purge individual effects, and first difference lagged terms of predetermined and endogenous explanatory variables as instrumental variables to perform GMM.[13] A clear shortcoming of difference GMM, however, is that if the predetermined and endogenous explanatory variables have significant unit roots, then the instrumental variables constructed on the basis of these first difference lagged term variables will have serious problems with weak instrumental variables and limited sample deviation.[14] To resolve this problem, Arellano and Bover, and Blundell and Bond proposed the method of system GMM, introducing an initial level set function to construct a function system, and setting level variables as the instrumental variables of first difference lagged terms, thus resolving the problem of weak instrumental variables and increase estimation efficiency.[15]

Estimation results

In performing estimation for the model, IPS unit root test for panel data was first used to examine the serial features in the various variables.[16] The results, given in Table A2.3, shows that it is not possible to reject the assumption of setting the variables in labor, economic openness, and variables in arrangements of responsibilities in total expenditure and administrative expenditure as I(1) series. This further shows that system GMM should be used for estimation of the dynamic panel data model in A2.2, in order to avoid the problem of weak instrumental variables in difference GMM.

Table A2.3 IPS unit root test results for the main economic variables

Variable	Labor force	Economic openness	Total expenditure responsibility arrangement	Revenue responsibility arrangement	Administrative expenditure responsibility arrangement
$\bar{t}$ statistic	-0.94	0.2	-1.59	-1.77	-1.14
(P value)	(0.99)	(1.0)	(0.23)	(0.04)	(0.97)

Additionally, the largest lagged order of the output growth rate per capita and the nature of the explanatory variable — the variable in intergovernmental arrangements in fiscal responsibilities, Ds_{it}. Comparing the results of the Arellano-Bond second-order residual autocorrelation tests for estimation results in different lagged orders, the largest lagged order of the output growth rate per capita is determined to be 2. The exact nature of Ds_{it} is unclear: if it is assumed that in managing the division of administrative authority and fiscal power, the central government has certain specific goals unrelated to regional economic growth, then Ds_{it} may be seen as strictly an exogenous variable; otherwise, it has to be set as either an endogenous or a predetermined variable. Since existing studies do not give a clear conclusion for this, both possibilities are considered: in Models 3a and 4a, all explanatory variables are set as exogenous variables; in Models 3b and 4b, variables in intergovernmental arrangements in fiscal responsibilities, economic development level, physical capital investment ratio, human capital investment level, variables in labor, level of economic openness, and fiscal revenue ratio are set as predetermined variables; and in Models 3c and 4c, the above variables are set as endogenous variables. The temporal and regional dummy variables in intergovernmental arrangements in fiscal responsibilities are consistently set as strictly exogenous variables. The estimation and test results are given in Table A2.4.

Table A2.4 System GMM estimation results for dynamic effects panel model of intergovernmental arrangements in fiscal responsibilities

Explanatory variable	Total expenditure responsibility arrangement			Revenue terms responsibility arrangement		
	Model 3a	Model 3b	Model 3b	Model 4a	Model 4b	Model 4c
Constant term	-0.162 (0.040)***	-0.213 (0.040)***	-0.215 (0.040)***	-0.172 (0.070)***	-0.186 (0.060)***	-0.185 (0.060)***
L1.Output growth rate per capita	0.035 (0.040)	-0.049 (0.050)	-0.048 (0.050)	0.035 (0.040)	-0.064 (0.050)	-0.064 (0.050)
L2.Output growth rate per capita	-0.238 (0.040)***	-0.330 (0.030)***	-0.329 (0.030)***	-0.207 (0.040)***	-0.323 (0.030)***	-0.323 (0.030)***
Economic development level	6.926 (0.570)***	9.238 (0.480)***	9.219 (0.480)***	6.117 (0.640)***	9.161 (0.570)***	9.164 (0.570)***
L1.Economic development level	-6.805 (0.570)***	-9.117 (0.480)***	-9.096 (0.480)***	-5.958 (0.630)***	-9.037 (0.570)***	-9.040 (0.570)***
Physical capital investment ratio	0.466 (0.040)***	0.349 (0.030)***	0.348 (0.030)***	0.458 (0.040)***	0.323 (0.030)***	0.323 (0.030)***
L1.Physical capital investment ratio	-0.445 (0.050)***	-0.289 (0.030)***	-0.289 (0.030)***	-0.464 (0.050)***	-0.294 (0.030)***	-0.294 (0.030)***
Human capital investment level	-0.389 (0.340)	-0.388 (0.210)*	-0.393 (0.210)*	-0.261 (0.400)	-0.316 (0.240)	-0.314 (0.240)
L1.Human capital investment level	0.341 (0.330)	0.394 (0.190)**	0.399 (0.190)***	0.169 (0.380)	0.315 (0.220)	0.314 (0.220)
Variables in labor	0.049 (0.040)	0.053 (0.030)*	0.051 (0.030)	0.088 (0.040)**	0.065 (0.030)**	0.066 (0.030)**
L1.Variables in labor	-0.087 (0.040)**	-0.056 (0.040)	-0.054 (0.040)	-0.116 (0.050)***	-0.053 (0.040)	-0.055 (0.040)
Economic openness level	0.034 (0.020)*	0.051 (0.020)***	0.050 (0.020)***	0.024 (0.020)	0.046 (0.020)**	0.046 (0.020)***
L1.Economic openness level	-0.017 (0.020)	-0.034 (0.020)*	-0.033 (0.020)*	-0.002 (0.030)	-0.030 (0.020)	-0.030 (0.020)
Fiscal revenue ratio	-0.672 (0.160)***	-0.427 (0.080)***	-0.443 (0.090)***	-0.742 (0.190)***	-0.465 (0.090)***	-0.468 (0.090)***

Table A2.4 System GMM estimation results for dynamic effects panel model of intergovernmental arrangements in fiscal responsibilities

(Cont'd)

Explanatory variable		Total expenditure responsibility arrangement			Revenue terms responsibility arrangement		
		Model 3a	Model 3b	Model 3b	Model 4a	Model 4b	Model 4c
L1.Fiscal revenue ratio		0.541 (0.150)***	0.303 (0.070)***	0.317 (0.080)***	0.595 (0.180)***	0.322 (0.080)***	0.325 (0.070)***
Arrangements of responsibilites	Revenue	-0.002 (0.030)	0.017 (0.020)	0.016 (0.020)	-0.016 (0.030)	-0.014 (0.020)	-0.014 (0.020)
	Overall expenditure	-0.031 (0.020)*	-0.047 (0.020)***	-0.047 (0.020)***	—	—	—
	Economic expenditure	—	—	—	0.008 (0.020)	0.016 (0.020)	0.017 (0.020)
	Social expenditure	—	—	—	-0.117 (0.030)***	-0.080 (0.020)***	-0.080 (0.020)***
	Administrative expenditure	—	—	—	0.061 (0.030)***	0.036 (0.030)	0.036 (0.030)
Temporal dummy variables in arrangement of responsibilities	Revenue	0.014 (0.030)	-0.016 (0.020)	-0.014 (0.030)	0.047 (0.040)	0.018 (0.030)	0.019 (0.030)
	Overall expenditure	-0.013 (0.030)	0.008 (0.020)	0.006 (0.020)	—	—	—
	Economic expenditure	—	—	—	-0.005 (0.020)	-0.015 (0.020)	-0.015 (0.020)
	Social expenditure	—	—	—	0.025 (0.040)	0.024 (0.030)	0.023 (0.030)
	Administrative expenditure	—	—	—	-0.069 (0.040)	-0.043 (0.040)	-0.043 (0.040)
Regional dummy variables in arrangement of responsibilities	Revenue	0.018 (0.020)	0.012 (0.020)	0.013 (0.020)	-0.006 (0.020)	0.010 (0.020)	0.010 (0.020)
	Overall expenditure	-0.016 (0.020)	-0.012 (0.010)	-0.013 (0.020)	—	—	—
	Economic expenditure	—	—	—	-0.025 (0.020)	-0.008 (0.020)	-0.008 (0.020)
	Social expenditure	—	—	—	-0.013 (0.010)	-0.017 (0.010)	-0.017 (0.010)
	Administrative expenditure	—	—	—	0.034 (0.020)*	0.018 (0.020)	0.018 (0.060)

Table A2.4 System GMM estimation results for dynamic effects panel model of intergovernmental arrangements in fiscal responsibilities

(Cont'd)

Explanatory variable	Total expenditure responsibility arrangement			Revenue terms responsibility arrangement		
	Model 3a	Model 3b	Model 3b	Model 4a	Model 4b	Model 4c
Arellano-Bond AR(1) test	-4.210***	-3.850***	-3.870***	-3.810***	-3.770***	-3.770***
Arellano-Bond AR(2) test	0.210	1.160	1.150	0.070	1.010	1.000
Hansen overidentification test	10.120	61.150	33.400	5.230	11.300	11.230
Diff-in-Hansen GMM instruments effectiveness test	0.000	0.000	-0.000	0.000	0.000	-0.000
Diff-in-Hansen IV instruments effectiveness test	6.680	38.900***	4.500	4.390	-0.670	-1.440
Effective sample size	754	754	754	754	754	754
Wald value	2519.7***	4251.5***	4863.3***	6715.6***	10705.2***	10817.8***

Notes: (1) L1 and L2 are the first and second-order lagged operators respectively.
(2) Difference-in-Hansen GMM tests for the effectiveness of GMM-style instruments (endogenous variables and predetermined variables).
(3) Difference-in-Hansen IV tests for the effectiveness of IV-style instruments (exogenous variables).
(4) Bracketed values are standard deviations.
(5) *, ** and *** indicate regression coefficients significantly above confidence levels of 10%, 5% and 1% respectively.

The Arellano-Bond AR(1) and AR(2) tests show that there is significant first-order serial autocorrelation in the residuals of the models but not second-order serial autocorrelation, showing that the model settings are in general acceptable. The Hansen, GMM, and IV tests also show that, with the exception of the IV-style instruments in Model 3b, the structure of the instruments in the various models are in general effective.

It should be noted, though, that the number of instruments constructed is high relative to the sampling size, causing a relatively large loss in the degree of freedom and weakening to a certain extent the results of the Hansen test; however, as previously mentioned, endogenous problems will cause OLS estimations to deviate upwards and SSW estimations to deviate downwards, meaning that the actual values of the parameters in the model should lie between the OLS and SSW estimations.[17] It may thus be seen that the estimation results for Models 3a and 4a are in general relatively poor, meaning that not all explanatory variables should be taken as strictly exogenous variables.[18]

It may be seen from Models 3c, 4b, and 4c that the estimation results for the effects of intergovernmental arrangements in fiscal responsibilities on regional economic growth are rather robust, and even though there are clear differences compared to the estimation results from the fixed-effects model in the previous section, the conclusions reached are in general consistent:

- Total expenditure responsibility arrangement has a significant constraining effect on regional economic growth, although for the Eastern region, the constraining effect is relatively weaker with no statistical significance, while the effect after the 1994 tax sharing reforms has been favorable to regional economic growth but also with no statistical significance;
- Revenue responsibility arrangement has an unclear effect on regional economic growth and has no statistical significance, and the intertemporal and interregional differences are not significant either;
- Economic and administrative expenditure responsibilities arrangements have a promoting effect on regional economic growth but there is no statistical significance, while the social expenditure responsibility arrangement has a significant constraining effect on regional economic growth. These effects also have significant intertemporal and interregional differences: for the Eastern region, economic and social arrangements have a constraining effect on regional economic growth and administrative arrangement has a promoting effect, although none of these has statistical significance; since the 1994 tax sharing system reform, economic and administrative arrangements have a constraining effect on regional economic growth, while the social arrangement has a promoting effect, although again, none of these has statistical significance.

Effects of Intergovernmental Arrangements of Fiscal Responsibilities on Economic Growth: Threshold-Effects Estimation

The analysis in the previous section shows that there are significant intertemporal and interregional differences in the effects of intergovernmental arrangements in fiscal responsibilities on regional economic growth. This means that the relationship between intergovernmental arrangements in fiscal responsibilities and regional economic growth is very likely not a simple linear relationship.[19] Thus, this section will use a threshold-effects panel model as proposed by Hansen to examine the threshold effects of the effects of intergovernmental arrangements in fiscal responsibilities on regional economic growth and the factors behind these effects.[20]

Model framework

Consider the following single-threshold panel data model:

$$Gy_{it} = \alpha X_{it} + \beta_1 Ds_{it}\, I(Thre_{it} \leq \gamma) + \beta_2 Ds_{it}\, I(Thre_{it} > \gamma) + \mu_i + \lambda_t + \varepsilon_{it} \qquad \text{(A2.3)}$$

Of which, X_{it} includes the one and two phase lagged terms of output growth rate per capita, as well as the current and one phase lagged terms of economic development level, physical capital investment ratio, human capital investment level, variables in labor, level of economic openness, and fiscal revenue ratio, so as to capture the features in the dynamic data structure. $I(\cdot)$ is the index function, $Thre_{it}$ is the threshold variable, for which output per capita (natural logarithms) and variables in revenue responsibilities arrangements are considered, in order to capture the effects of economic development level and division of fiscal powers respectively. Additionally, the variables in total expenditure responsibility and for the various terms of expenditure are considered as threshold variables, in order to measure the interactive effects between them. γ is the threshold.

This single-threshold panel model may further be expanded into the following double-threshold panel model:

$$\begin{aligned} Gy_{it} = {} & \alpha X_{it} + \beta_1 Ds_{it}\, I(Thre_{it} \leq \gamma_1) + \beta_2 Ds_{it}\, I(\gamma_1 < Thre_{it} \leq \gamma_2) \\ & + \beta_3 Ds_{it}\, I(Thre_{it} > \gamma_1) + \mu_i + \lambda_t + \varepsilon_{it} \end{aligned} \qquad \text{(A2.4)}$$

Of which, γ_1 and γ_2 are the two thresholds.[21]

Estimation results

In performing estimation for (A2.3) and (A2.4), a likelihood-ratio test is first performed on the various threshold variables to test for the presence of threshold effects and the number of thresholds present. The results are given in Table A2.5.

It can be seen from Table A2.5 that when the variables in revenue responsibility, economic and administrative expenditure responsibilities are set as threshold variables, there are no significant threshold effects from the intergovernmental arrangements of fiscal responsibilities on regional economic growth. The following will therefore briefly analyze the effects of intergovernmental arrangements of fiscal responsibilities on regional economic growth when economic development level, total expenditure and administrative expenditure responsibilities are set as threshold variables.

Table A2.5 Threshold-effects tests and estimation results for intergovernmental arrangements in fiscal responsibilities

Core explanatory variable		Threshold variable	Economic development level	Arrangements in responsibilities				
				Revenue	Total expenditure	Economic expenditure	Social expenditure	Administrative expenditure
Arrangements in responsibilities	Revenue	Initial assumption 1	9.580	8.370	12.430	11.790	16.270***	8.870
		Initial assumption 2	—	—	—	—	5.330	—
		Threshold	—	—	—	—	0.920 (0.920 1.030)	—
		β_1	—	—	—	—	0.006 (0.020)	—
		β_2	—	—	—	—	-0.022 (0.020)	—
	Total expenditure	Initial assumption 1	18.150***	6.780	13.330*	9.880	14.750**	9.520
		Initial assumption 2	14.200*	—	4.930	—	3.940	—
		Initial assumption 3	13.600	—	—	—	—	—
		Threshold 1	6.280 (6.180 6.390)	—	0.770 (0.750 0.840)	—	0.92 (0.916 1.03)	—
		Threshold 2	7.140 (5.660 7.270)	—	—	—	—	—
		β_1	-0.094 (0.040)**	—	-0.129 (0.040)***	—	-0.106 (0.040)***	—
		β_2	-0.139 (0.040)***	—	-0.151 (0.040)***	—	-0.128 (0.040)***	—
		β_3	-0.165 (0.040)***	—	—	—	—	—
	Economic expenditure	Initial assumption 1	24.600**	10.880	11.680	12.530	10.150	9.470
		Initial assumption 2	11.200	—	—	—	—	—
		Threshold	6.330 (6.180 6.430)	—	—	—	—	—
		β_1	0.051 (0.020)**	—	—	—	—	—
		β_2	-0.011 (0.020)	—	—	—	—	—

Table A2.5 Threshold-effects tests and estimation results for intergovernmental arrangements in fiscal responsibilities (Cont'd)

Threshold variable / Core explanatory variable			Economic development level	Arrangements in responsibilities				
				Revenue	Total expenditure	Economic expenditure	Social expenditure	Administrative expenditure
Arrangements in responsibilities	Social expenditure	Initial assumption 1	21.700**	7.680	13.600	10.140	10.950	19.950
		Initial assumption 2	11.030	—	—	—	—	—
		Threshold	6.280 (6.200 6.370)	—	—	—	—	—
		β_1	-0.057 (0.040)	—	—	—	—	—
		β_2	-0.082 (0.040)**	—	—	—	—	—
	Administrative expenditure	Initial assumption 1	22.700*	9.640	19.820*	12.100	15.700*	19.150
		Initial assumption 2	11.840	—	12.860	—	3.850	—
		Threshold	6.280 (6.200 6.390)	—	0.770 (0.750 0.780)	—	0.920 (0.916 1.030)	—
		β_1	0.022 (0.030)	—	0.046 (0.030)	—	0.051 (0.030)*	—
		β_2	-0.006 (0.030)	—	0.018 (0.030)	—	0.028 (0.030)	—

Notes: (1) Values for Initial assumptions 1 and 2 are likelihood ratio statistics. Initial assumption 1 is the absence of threshold effects, Initial assumption 2 is the absence of two thresholds, and Initial assumption 3 is the absence of three thresholds. If Initial assumption 1 is rejected, then Initial assumption 2 needs to be tested using the estimation results of the double threshold panel model, and so on, and the significance of likelihood ratio (P value) is obtained after 100 bootstrap instances.

(2) Bracketed values in the threshold value row give the 95% confidence interval.

(3) If there is only one threshold, β_1 is the regression coefficient for being below the threshold, and β_2 is the regression coefficient for exceeding the threshold; if there are two thresholds, β_1 is the regression coefficient for being below Threshold 1, β_2 is the regression coefficient for being between Thresholds 1 and 2, and β_3 is the regression coefficient for exceeding Threshold 2.

(4) *, ** and *** indicate regression coefficients significantly above confidence levels of 10%, 5% and 1% respectively.

(5) For reasons of space, the estimation results of the other explanatory variables are not shown.

When the economic development level is set as the threshold variable, total expenditure responsibility arrangement has a significant double threshold and constraining effect on regional economic growth, and this effect is strengthened with increase in economic development level, shown in that the two thresholds of 6.28 and 7.14 have regression coefficients of -0.094, -0.139, and -0.165, with good statistical significance. The arrangements of responsibilities for the various terms of expenditure also has significant single threshold effects, of which for the economic and administrative terms, their effects on regional economic growth changes from promoting to constraining once a certain level of economic development is reached, and for the social term, the constraining effect on economic growth is increased in prominence with increase in economic development level. In general, the thresholds for economic, social, and expenditure responsibilities arrangements are 6.33, 6.28, and 6.28 respectively, with corresponding regression coefficients of 0.051 and -0.011, -0.057 and -0.082, 0.022 and -0.006, with relatively poor statistical significance.

When the variable in total expenditure responsibilities arrangements is set as the threshold variable, only the total expenditure and administrative expenditure responsibilities arrangements showed significant threshold effects on regional economic growth, with the threshold being 0.77 for both. Total expenditure responsibilities arrangements has a significant constraining effect on regional economic growth, with increasing strength as the degree of decentralization in total expenditure increases, shown by its regression coefficients of -0.129 and -0.151, with excellent statistical significance. Administrative expenditure responsibility arrangement is favorable to regional economic growth, but this effect significantly weakens as the as the degree of decentralization in total expenditure increases, shown by its regression coefficients of 0.046 and 0.018, although not having statistical significance.

When the variable in social expenditure responsibility arrangement is set as the threshold variable, revenue responsibilities, total expenditure responsibilities, and administrative expenditure responsibility all have significant threshold effects with a threshold of 0.92. From their regression coefficients (0.006 and -0.022, -0.106 and -0.128, 0.051 and 0.028 respectively) and their statistical significance, it can be seen that the effects of revenue responsibilities arrangements are unclear; that the total expenditure responsibilities have a significant constraining effect on regional economic growth, with the effect significantly increasing in strength as the degree of decentralization in social expenditure increases; and that administrative expenditure responsibility arrangement is favorable for regional economic growth, but the effect weakens in strength and significance as the degree of decentralization in social expenditure increases.

Summary

This paper used fixed-effects, dynamic-effects, and threshold-effects panel models to examine the effects of intergovernmental arrangements of fiscal responsibilities, with special focus on examining the effects of different terms of expenditure, on regional economic growth, revealing the problems present in China's financial and tax system over the major reforms since 1978, and the direction that future reforms should take.

The findings in this paper show that the intergovernmental arrangements of fiscal responsibilities still have much room for improvement. Regional governments assume excessive responsibilities in total expenditure and social expenditure, negatively impacting regional economic growth. The effects of revenue responsibilities arrangements are unclear, while economic and administrative expenditure responsibilities have relatively reasonable arrangements which promote regional economic growth. These effects all show significant non-linearity, and are mainly related to the regional economic development level, total expenditure and especially social expenditure responsibilities arrangements: when the regional economic development and degree of decentralization in total and social expenditures exceed a certain threshold, moderate centralization will help to optimize fiscal responsibilities arrangements, hence promoting regional economic growth. Additionally, since the implementation of the tax sharing system reforms in 1994, the situation of poor arrangements of responsibilities in total and social expenditures has significantly improved, but the pace of centralization in economic and administrative expenditure has been rather rapid, which is unfavorable to regional economic growth. The findings are summarized in Table A2.6.

Three policy recommendations may be given from the findings in this paper:

1. In the process of reforming the financial and tax systems and reordering fiscal relationships, the central government should consider carefully the state of economic development in different regions, and accordingly determine the appropriate arrangements of fiscal responsibilities between the central and regional governments;
2. From the perspective of favorability to regional economic growth, revenue responsibilities arrangements are of little consequence, that is, whether regional governments or the central government assume more revenue responsibilities (proportion of revenue) is unimportant; the crucial point lies with the arrangements in expenditure responsibilities;[22]
3. Most importantly, the particular features in different terms of public expenditure must be taken into account when dividing the responsibilities of the various terms of expenditure. In particular, regional governments

Table A2.6 Summary of the effects of intergovernmental arrangements of fiscal responsibilities on regional economic growth

Model	Fixed-effects panel model		Dynamic-effects panel model		Threshold-effects panel model
Responsibility arrangement	1978–2005	Post-1994	1978–2005	Post-1994	1978–2005
Overall expenditure	Unfavorable***	Favorable	Unfavorable***	Favorable	Unfavorable***
Economic expenditure	Favorable	Unfavorable	Favorable	Unfavorable	Favorable** → Unfavorable
Social expenditure	Unfavorable	Favorable**	Unfavorable***	Favorable	Unfavorable → Unfavorable**
Administrative expenditure	Favorable***	Unfavorable***	Favorable	Unfavorable	Favorable → Unfavorable, Favorable → Favorable, Favorable* → Favorable
Revenue	Unclear	Unfavorable	Unclear	Unclear	Unclear

Notes: (1) → indicates the change in the effects of intergovernmental arrangement in fiscal responsibilities on regional economic growth when the threshold variable exceeds the threshold, of which economic and social expenditure responsibilities are given by the results in setting economic development level as the threshold variable, and administrative expenditure responsibility is given by the results in setting economic development level, total expenditure and social expenditure responsibilities as the threshold variables.

(2) *, ** and *** indicate regression coefficients significantly above confidence levels of 10%, 5% and 1% respectively.

should be assigned more administrative expenditure responsibilities, while effective measures should be taken to change the current situation where economic expenditures such as infrastructure, and social expenditures such as education, sciences, and healthcare are overly reliant on regional governments, so as to optimize the allocation of roles at different levels of government.

Finally, it should be noted that this paper approached the problem of intergovernmental arrangements in fiscal responsibilities from the perspective of their effects on regional economic growth, and that additional studies on the problem based on the effects on income distribution will be a necessary topic of research in the future. Also, for this paper, the determining factors in the examination of threshold effects from intergovernmental arrangements in fiscal responsibilities on regional economic growth stopped at the economic level, and a closer examination of the constraining effects of the country's administrative system will also make a valuable study.

This annex is published under the same title in **Economic Research Journal** *(6), 2008. Only the numbering of the sections is changed for purposes of standardization in this book.*

Notes

Chapter 6

1. Oates, "An Essay on Fiscal Federalism."
2. McKinnon and Nechyba, "Competition in Federal Systems: The Role of Political and Financial Constraints"; Strumpf and Oberholzer-Gee, "Endogenous Institutions and Policy Decentralization: Local Liquor Control from 1934–1970"; Zhang and Zou, "Fiscal Decentralization, Public Spending and Economic Growth in China"; Oates, "An Essay on Fiscal Federalism"; Rhode and Strumpf, "Assessing the Importance of Tiebout Sorting: Local Heterogeneity from 1850 to 1990"; Zhang and Gong, "Interregional Disparity, Factor Mobility, and Fiscal Decentralization"; Qiao et al., "Fiscal Decentralization and Compulsory Primary Education in China"; Jia et al., "Capital Expenditure Decentralization, Public Capital Investment Composition and Economic Growth."
3. Gramlich, "A Policymaker's Guide to Fiscal Decentralization"; Bayoumi and McDonald, "On the Optimality of Consumption across Canadian Provinces"; Crucini, "On International and National Dimensions of Risk Sharing"; Hess and Shin, "Intranational Business Cycles in the United States"; Bahl, *Financing State and Local Government in the 1980's.*
4. Feldstein and Wrobel, "Can State Taxes Redistribute Income?"
5. Stigler, "The Tenable Range of Function of Local Governments."
6. Pauly, "Income Redistribution as a Local Public Good."
7. Devarajan et al., "The Composition of Public Expenditure and Economic Growth"; Miller and Russek, "Fiscal Structures and Economic Growth: International Evidence"; Brown et al., "State and Local Policy, Factor Markets, and Regional Growth"; Schaltegger and Torgler, "Growth Effects of Public Expenditure on the State and Local Level: Evidence from a Sample of Rich Governments."
8. Aschauer, "Is Public Expenditure Productive?"; Aschauer, "Why Is Infrastructure Important?"; Barro and Sala-i-Martin, "Public Finance in Models of Economic Growth"; Easterly and Rebelo, "Fiscal policy and Economic Growth: An Empirical Investigation"; Agell et al., "Growth and the Public Sector: A Critical Review Essay"; Agell et al., "Growth and the Public Sector: A Replay"; Sturm, "Determinants of Public Capital Spending in Less-Developed Countries"; Blankenau et al., "Public Education Expenditures, Taxation and Growth: Linking Data to Theory."
9. Zhuang and Zou, "Does Public Expenditure Boost Economic Growth? An Analysis of China's Experience."
10. Zhang and Duan, "Positive Analysis on Local Fiscal Expenditure Structures and Local Economic Growth in China."
11. Liao and Yu, "Structure of the Public Expenditure of Regional Governments and Economic Growth: Empirical Analysis of the Panel Data of Provinces in China."
12. Jia et al., "Capital Expenditure Decentralization, Public Capital Investment Composition and Economic Growth."
13. Brennan and Buchanan, *The Power to Tax.*
14. Wilson, "A Theory of Interregional Tax Competition"; Zodrow and Mieszkowski, "Pigou, Tiebout, Property Taxation, and the Underprovision of Local Public Goods."

15. Qian and Weingast, "Federalism as a Commitment to Preserving Market Incentives"; Qian and Roland, "Federalism and the Soft Budget Constraint."
16. Zhou, "The Incentive and Cooperation of Government Officials in the Political Tournaments: An Interpretation of the Prolonged Local Protectionism and Duplicative Investments in China"; Zhou, "Governing China's Local Officials: An Analysis of Promotion Tournament Model."
17. Zhou, "Local Government Competition and Economic Growth."
18. Qiao et al., "Fiscal Decentralization and Compulsory Primary Education in China."
19. Guo and Jia, "Behavior of Regional Governments, Impulsive Investment, and Macroeconomic Stability."
20. Mankiw et al., "A Contribution to the Empirics of Economic Growth."
21. Lin and Liu, "Fiscal Decentralization and Economic Growth in China."
22. Anselin, *Spatial Econometrics: Methods and Models*; Anselin and Bera, "Spatial Dependence in Linear Regression Models with an Application to Spatial Econometrics."
23. Anselin, *Spatial Econometrics: Methods and Models*; LeSage, "The Theory and Practice of Spatial Econometrics."
24. To test for the robustness of the results, it was also attempted to set directly the one-phase lagged terms of the variables in provincial fiscal expenditure as the explained variable, omitting fiscal revenue ratio from the model, and including other budgetary expenditure into the function for economic growth effects of expenditure projects for regression analysis, but there was in general no significant differences in the results obtained. Additionally, it was also attempted to breakdown predictive values of fiscal expenditure into predictive values of neighboring spatially lagged terms (for measuring the direct interactive effects of regional policies) and that of other factors for regression analysis, and there was also no significant changes in the results obtained.
25. For 1986 to 1993, actual provincial budgetary expenditure per capita hovered at around the considerably low level of CNY127.0.
26. Arrow and Kurz, *Public Investment, the Rate of Return, and Optimal Fiscal Policy*; Barro, "Government Spending in A Simple Model of Endogenous Growth"; Lucas, "On the Mechanics of Economic Development"; Turnovsky and Fisher, "The Composition of Government Expenditure and its Consequences for Macroeconomic Performance"; Lou, "Public Investment Policy in Long-Run Economic Growth: General Congestion Public Infrastructure in Long-run Growth Model"; Economic Growth Frontier Subject Team, "The Supply Effects of Fiscal Policy and Economic Development"; Glomm and Ravikumar, "Opting Out of Publicly Provided Services: A Majority Voting Result"; van Zon and Muysken, "Health and Endogenous Growth"; Creedy and Gemmell, "The Optimal Composition of Government Expenditure"; Viaene and Zilcha, "Education Technology, Human Capital Distribution and Growth"; Blankenau and Simpson, "Public Education Expenditures and Growth"; Liao, "Research on Regional Imbalance of Government Educational Expenditures"; Rioja and Glomm, "Populist Budgets and Long-Run Growth"; Agénor, "Infrastructure, Public Education and Growth with Congestion Costs"; Guo and Jia, "The Effects of Government Public Capital Investment on Long-Run Economic Growth."
27. Arellano and Bond, "Some Tests of Specification for Panel Data: Monte Carlo Evidence and an Application to Employment Equations"; Blundell and Bond, "Initial Conditions and Moment Restrictions in Dynamic Panel Data Models"; Bond, "Dynamic Panel Data Models: A Guide to Micro Data Methods and Practice."

28. Due to a lack of detailed provincial data, the effects of the structure of central public capital investment and central tax burdens such as income tax on regional economic growth are not taken into consideration.
29. Im et al., "Testing for Unit Roots in Heterogeneous Panels."
30. On the endogenous problems arising from the dynamic structure of data, Holtz-Eakin et al. and Arellano and Bond proposed the difference GMM method for estimation, which is a good solution to the problem (Holtz-Eakin et al., "Estimating Vector Autoregressions with Panel Data"; Arellano and Bond, "Some Tests of Specification for Panel Data: Monte Carlo Evidence and an Application to Employment Equations"). However, difference GMM also has a significant flaw, in that if predetermined and endogenous variables have significant unit root features, then the instrumental variables constructed on the basis of these first-order lagged term variables will have serious problems with weak instrumental variables and limited sample bias (Arellano and Bover, "Some Tests of Specification for Panel Data: Monte Carlo Evidence and an Application to Employment Equations"; Blundell and Bond, "Initial Conditions and Moment Restrictions in Dynamic Panel Data Models"; Bond, "Dynamic Panel Data Models: A Guide to Micro Data Methods and Practice"). Thus, Arellano and Bover, and Blundell and Bond proposed system GMM to resolve the problems of weak instrumental variables, thus increasing the efficiency of estimations. For detailed comparative analysis about the application of difference GMM and system GMM on dynamic panel data model estimations, see Bond, "Dynamic Panel Data Models: A Guide to Micro Data Methods and Practice"; Roodman, "How to Do Xtabond2: An Introduction to 'Difference' and 'System' GMM in Stata"; and Guo and Jia, "The Transfer Payments from the Central Government and the Provision of Regional Public Services."
31. Bond, "Dynamic Panel Data Models: A Guide to Micro Data Methods and Practice"; Roodman, "How to Do Xtabond2: An Introduction to 'Difference' and 'System' GMM in Stata."
32. Using OLS and SSW estimations, the one-phase lagged coefficients of the effects of per capita production growth rate in Model (6.2) is calculated to be 0.436 and 0.289 respectively.
33. Based on the levels of fiscal decentralization in 2006, research by Guo et al. gives the maximized optimal central fiscal transfer payment ratio as 67.8% (Guo et al., "The Transfer Payments from the Central Government and Regional Economic Growth"). The actual central fiscal transfer payment ratio in 2006 is 74%.
34. In 2006, the extrabudgetary revenue of China's regional governments is more than CNY594 billion, or 25% of budgetary revenue of regional governments, and further exhibits autonomy in revenue and expenditure.
35. County-level fiscal revenue total refers to the sum of local fiscal revenue and transfer payments, minus the balance from the previous year. Fund revenue was considered extrabudgetary revenue before 1996; after the 1996 manifesto from the State Council on strengthening the management of extrabudgetary funds, 13 of the larger government funds were transferred to budgetary management. Since fund revenues are currently classified as a single item, this section also takes into account fund revenue. From 1999, records on fiscal fund revenue is kept in *Financial Statistics of Cities and Counties*.
36. In estimating for county-level economic growth effects, both one-step system GMM and Windmeijer's limited sample correction two-step system GMM were used, and there was no significant differences in the results obtained. For reasons of space, the estimation results of two-step system GMM are not shown.

37. Devarajan et al., "The Composition of Public Expenditure and Economic Growth"; Tanzi and Zee, "Fiscal Policy and Long-Run Growth"; Tanzi and Schuknecht, *Public Spending in the 20th Century*; Fölster and Henrekson, "Growth Effects of Government Expenditure and Taxation in Rich Countries"; Zou and Gong, "Public Expenditures, Taxes, Federal Transfer, and Endogenous Growth"; Zou and Gong, "Optimal Tax Rate, Government Transfer Payments, and Economic Growth"; Jia et al., "Capital Expenditure Decentralization, Public Capital Investment Composition and Economic Growth."
38. For more information on the inadequacies present in the arrangement of responsibilities for intergovernmental fiscal expenditure, and their effects on economic growth, see Annex 2.

Chapter 7

1. Guo and Jia, "Analysis of the Dynamic Factors Affecting the Economic Cycle of Provinces in China"; Guo and Jia, "Behavior of Regional Governments, Impulsive Investment, and Macroeconomic Stability."
2. Musgrave, *The Theory of Public Finance*.
3. Guo and Jia, "Behavior of Regional Governments, Impulsive Investment, and Macroeconomic Stability."
4. Fang and Zhang, "Expansionary Fiscal Spending among Chinese Local Governments: Observations and Explanations."
5. Li and Shen, "Effects of Regional Governments' Behavior on China's Economic Fluctuations."
6. Brandt and Zhu, "Redistribution in a Decentralized Economy: Growth and Inflation in China under Reform"; Brandt and Zhu, "Soft Budget Constraints and Inflation Cycles: A Positive Model of the Macro-Dynamics in China during Transition"; Bennett and Dixon, "Monetary Policy and Credit in China: A Theoretical Analysis"; Feltenstein and Iwata, "Decentralization and Macroeconomic Performance in China: Regional Autonomy Has Its Costs."
7. Zhao and Zhou, "Research on the Relationship between Fiscal Expenditure and Inflation Based on Provincial Panel Data."
8. Prud'homme, "The Dangers of Decentralization"; Treisman, "Decentralization and Inflation: Commitment, Collective Action, or Continuity."
9. In recent years, academic interest in the relationship and asynchrony between the regional and national economic cycles has been increasing. See for example Hess and Shin, "Intranational Business Cycles in the United States"; Crucini, "On International and National Dimensions of Risk Sharing"; and Guo and Jia, "Analysis of the Dynamic Factors Affecting the Economic Cycle of Provinces in China."
10. Samuelson, "The Pure Theory of Public Expenditure."
11. Prud'homme, "The Dangers of Decentralization"; Treisman, "Decentralization and Inflation: Commitment, Collective Action, or Continuity."
12. Riker, *Federalism: Origin, Operation, Significance*.
13. Wibbels, "Federalism and the Politics of Macroeconomic Policy and Performance."
14. In fact, as pointed out by Guo and Jia, regional governments have a tendency to find covert means to pursue regional self-interests and avoid central supervision and regulations, such as allowing irregularities in land and tax breaks policies for the sake of driving rapid economic growth (Guo and Jia, "Behavior of Regional Governments, Impulsive Investment, and Macroeconomic Stability").

15. Here, only the most representative province in each of the 3 regions are used for demonstration purposes, and there will be more comprehensive analysis provided in the next section. Actual data is used to demonstrate the dynamic relationships among provincial fiscal expenditure, provincial GDP and national GDP, taking natural logarithms and processed with first difference and mean subtraction. See Guo and Jia, "Analysis of the Dynamic Factors Affecting the Economic Cycle of Provinces in China", for a previous examination of the asynchrony between the provincial and national economic cycles.
16. Exactly how regional governments look for the optimal balancing point in maximizing regional self-interest and protecting national interests will make for very interesting research, but it is out of the scope of this study.
17. Guo et al., "Capital Expenditure Decentralization, Public Capital Investment Composition and Economic Growth."
18. Fang and Zhang, "Expansionary Fiscal Spending among Chinese Local Governments: Observations and Explanations"; Zhao and Zhou, "Research on the Relationship between Fiscal Expenditure and Inflation Based on Provincial Panel Data."
19. Ibid.
20. Guo et al., "Capital Expenditure Decentralization, Public Capital Investment Composition and Economic Growth."
21. The mean value of vertical fiscal imbalance level for 1978–2009 is 16.7%, and it is even higher for 1994–2009 at 44.5%.
22. Vertical fiscal imbalance refers to the situation where the provincial fiscal revenue is seriously insufficient to satisfy the demands of budgetary expenditure, and heavily rely on the fiscal transfer payments from the central government.
23. Rodden and Wibbels, "Beyond the Fiction of Federalism: Macroeconomic Management in Multitiered Systems"; Rodden et al., *Fiscal Decentralization and The Challenge of Hard Budget Constraints.*
24. The common-pool problem refers to the situation where fiscal costs spill over to residents belonging to other districts, through common-pool avenues such as intergovernment transfer payments. The central assistance problem refers to the situation where regional governments have extreme expectations that the central government will and must undertake their expenditure behavior.
25. Zhou, "Governing China's Local Officials: An Analysis of Promotion Tournament Model."
26. On the 12th National Congress of the Communist Party of China in 1982, the four directions of reform for the cadre body — to revolutionize the cadre system and to promote younger, knowledgeable and professionally competent cadres into leadership positions — were official incorporated into the party constitution. Also in 1982, the central committee also issued a manifesto concerning the establishment of a cadre retirement system, and in 1990, the manifesto concerning the exchange system for cadres in party and state department leadership was also issued. For more details on the history of the reforms in the human resource system for China's cadre institution since the Chinese Economic Reform, see Ji, "Contribution of Deng Xiaoping to the changes of the Cadres System in the New China."
27. See Zhang and Gao "Term of Office, Communications and Exchange, and Economic Growth: Experience of Provincial Governments"; and Wang and Xu, "Origin, Whereabouts, and Office Term of Regional Government Officials, and Economic Growth: Evidence from the Provincial Secretaries of China for a

detailed examination", for the effects of term of office, interregional exchange, replacement of officials etc. on economic growth.

28. Ji, "Contribution of Deng Xiaoping to the Changes of the Cadres System in the New China."
29. Gu, "Four Aspects of the Failings of Cadres Exchange."
30. Zhang and Gao, "Term of Office, Communications and Exchange, and Economic Growth: Experience of Provincial Governments."
31. Kose et al., "International Business Cycles: World, Region, and Country-Specific Factors"; Owyang et al., "State and the Business Cycle"; Guo and Jia, "Analysis of the Dynamic Factors Affecting the Economic Cycle of Provinces in China."
32. For details on multi-dynamic-factor models, see Guo and Jia, "Analysis of the Dynamic Factors Affecting the Economic Cycle of Provinces in China." For reasons of data, Tibet is left out while Chongqing is considered together as part of Sichuan province.
33. Currently, there are three main methods of estimation for multi-dynamic-factor models: maximum likelihood estimation, extended principal component analysis, and Bayesian Markov Chain Monte Carlo simulation. Due to the relatively high number of parameters, the first two methods may be incapable of ensuring consistency in estimation methods, while Bayesian estimation is relatively capable of resolving this problem.
34. For reasons of space, Table 7.1 only gives the mean values of the various loading coefficients, and the corresponding median values and upper and lower quartile values are omitted. As the focus is on the national and provincial periodic features of provincial fiscal expenditure, the estimation results for the loading coefficients of provincial fiscal expenditure and periodic fluctuations in regional economies are also omitted.
35. Guo and Jia, "Analysis of the Dynamic Factors Affecting the Economic Cycle of Provinces in China."
36. Currently, measurement of fiscal decentralization is performed mainly through either total volume or per capita as indicators. Here, per capita is used, i.e. {provincial fiscal revenue (expenditure) per capita / [provincial fiscal revenue (expenditure) per capita + central fiscal revenue (expenditure) per capita]} is used to measure fiscal revenue (expenditure) decentralization. At this point, only the regression coefficients for fiscal revenue decentralization on national periodic features in the expenditure behavior of regional governments show relatively significant changes: the regression coefficients in Models 1a–1c are negative and significant in value, meaning that fiscal revenue decentralization helps to strengthen national countercyclical features in the expenditure behavior of regional governments, which is in fact very much in consistent with theoretical expectations (see Proposition 2). Still, taking into consideration that using per capita as indicator gives good regulation over the effects of the population factor on fiscal resources distribution between central and regional authorities (Qiao, *The Trade-Off between Growth and Equity*; Guo and Jia, "The Transfer Payments from the Central Government and the Provision of Regional Public Services"), per capita is still used as the main method for obtaining estimation results.

    The construction of the dummy variables in tertiary education levels is as follows: if the provincial committee secretary has tertiary level education, a value of 1 is taken; otherwise, a value of 0 is taken. The construction of the dummy variables in central appointment history is as follows: if the provincial committee secretary has a history of central appointment, a value of 1 is taken; otherwise, a value of 0 is taken. In addition, for changes in officials, if the change occurred in the first half of the year, the official taking over is set as the examined target; otherwise, the incumbent official remains the examined target. Zhang and Gao argue that term of office has a non-linear effect on economic growth (Zhang and Gao, "Term of Office, Communications and Exchange, and Economic Growth: Experience of Provincial Governments"), hence, it was also attempted to use the squared terms of term of office to measure non-linear effects, but subsequent analysis shows that non-linear effects of term of office on periodic expenditure behavior in regional governments are not significant.

37. Baicker, "The Spillover Effects of State Spending"; Zhao and Zhou, "Research on the Relationship between Fiscal Expenditure and Inflation Based on Provincial Panel Data."
38. LeSage and Pace, *Introduction to Spatial Economics.*
39. As the province of Hainan was only established in 1988, Hainan is omitted from the sub-sample period of 1979 to 1993.
40. Economic, social and administrative expenditure are measured with infrastructure expenditure, education, health, culture and sciences expenditure, and administration and management expenditure respectively (see Guo and Jia, "The Transfer Payments from the Central Government and the Provision of Regional Public Services"). Since fiscal classification reforms were implemented in 2007, the sample period is set as 1979 to 2006 in order to ensure commensurability. For reasons of space, specific estimation results for loading coefficients of the various expenditures and periodic fluctuations in provincial and national economies and the effects of fiscal decentralization and governance are omitted.
41. There is a lack of consistency within both the two sub-sample periods between the effect of fiscal decentralization on the periodic features in the various expenditure types and in the overall expenditure. This might be attributed to differences between the effects of vertical fiscal imbalance and central transfer payments on the various types of expenditure in regional governments. More in-depth analysis on this problem awaits further research.

Chapter 8

1. Li and Ding, "Trends of the Yield of Education of Urban China in the Long Run"; Li and Hackman, "Choice Deviation, Comparative advantage, and the Heterogeneous Return on Education: An Empirical Analysis of the Microeconomic Data of China"; Fortin, "Higher-Education Policies and the College Wage Premium: Cross-State Evidence from the 1990s."
2. Lu and Chen, "Urbanization, Urban-Biased Economic Policies, and Urban-Rural Inequality"; Wan et al., "Globalization and Regional Income Gap: Evidence in China"; Wang and Fan, "Income Inequality in China and Its Influential Factors"; Chen et al., "Changes of the Income Gap of the Urban Labor Force in China and the Reasons Behind It: 1990–2005"; Li, "A Survey on China's Inequality."
3. Martin, "Public Policies, Regional Inequalities and Growth"; Volscho, "Unions, Government Employment, and the Political Economy of Income Distribution in Metropolitan Areas."
4. Liu and Nie, "The Effect of Indirect Tax Incidence on Income Distribution"; Tao and Liu, "China's Urban-Rural Income Gap, Regional Government Expenditure, and Financial Autonomy."
5. For the period 2000 to 2009, the average value of the proportion of regional fiscal expenditure out of national fiscal expenditure is 73.14%.

6. Extensive research show that income disparity in the urban population and in the rural population is significantly higher than income disparity between urban and rural populations, and that income disparity between urban and rural populations is significantly less important in the overall income disparity in the population (see World Bank, "Sharing Rising Incomes-Disparities in China"; and Li, "A Survey on China's Inequality").
7. Lu and Chen, "Urbanization, Urban-Biased Economic Policies, and Urban-Rural Inequality."
8. Li and Shen, "Effects of Regional Governments' Behavior on China's Economic Fluctuations."
9. Tao and Liu, "China's Urban-Rural Income Gap, Regional Government Expenditure, and Financial Autonomy."
10. The CHNS database does not have census data for Liaoning province in 1997, and Heilongjiang province in 1989, 1991, and 1993. It must also be noted that CHNS only takes data from four counties for each province, and so leaves concerns regarding the representativeness of the data; however, considering that the choice of the counties sampled are usually made specifically for purposes of reference, such concerns may not be significantly important. Similarly, the 9 provinces sampled in the CHNS database may be considered as representative enough for purposes of reference, and able to reflect to a large extent the basics of the provincial economy situation in China.
11. Whitehouse, "Measures of Inequality in Stata."
12. The estimated results of Gini coefficients for income of regional residents in China, and its developing trend, is very similar to the conclusions reached by other researchers who used other sources of census data such as Zhao ("The Problem of Income and Asset Distribution in China") and Li ("A Survey on China's Inequality").
13. Data for other variables are obtained mainly from past publications of *China Statistical Yearbook, Finance Yearbook of China*, Statistical Yearbooks from relevant provinces, and the *China Economic Information Network Database*.
14. Jia and Guo, "The Effects of Intergovernmental Assignments of Public Revenue and Expenditure Responsibility on the Regional Economic Growth."
15. The results of the Difference-in-Hansen tests show that the assumption of the above variables as endogenous variables may not be rejected. Since income distribution may also affect the size and structure of the expenditure of regional governments, it was also attempted to set size of fiscal expenditure, as well as the proportions of economic, administrative and social expenditure as endogenous variables, and it was also considered to set physical capital investment ratio, variables in labor and economic openness as endogenous levels; but results from corresponding Difference-in-Hansen tests show that the model settings were not acceptable.
16. Wang et al., "On China's Development Model: The Costs and Benefits of China's Decentralization Approach to Transition."
17. Li and Shen, "Competition among Jurisdictions, Strategical Fiscal Policies, and Regional Characteristics of FDI's Growth Achievements."
18. Wang and Fan, "Income Inequality in China and Its Influential Factors."
19. Lu and Chen, "Urbanization , Urban-Biased Economic Policies, and Urban-Rural Inequality."

20. Fiscal revenue decentralization is measured by {provincial fiscal revenue (expenditure) per capita / [provincial fiscal revenue (expenditure) per capita + national fiscal revenue (expenditure) per capita]} (see Jia and Guo, "The Effects of Intergovernmental Assignments of Public Revenue and Expenditure Responsibility on the Regional Economic Growth"). Since there are a large number of functions involved, detailed estimation results for the various scenarios are omitted for reasons of space.
21. Jia and Guo, "The Effects of Intergovernmental Assignments of Public Revenue and Expenditure Responsibility on the Regional Economic Growth."
22. Li and Ding, "Trends of the Yield of Education of Urban China in the Long Run"; Li and Hackman, "Choice Deviation, Comparative advantage, and the Heterogeneous Return on Education: An Empirical Analysis of the Microeconomic Data of China"; Fortin, "Higher-Education Policies and the College Wage Premium: Cross-State Evidence from the 1990s."
23. For example, Glomm and Ravikumar ("Public versus Private Investment in Human Capital: Endogenous Growth and Income Inequality") and Viaene and Zilcha ("Human Capital Formation, Income Inequality and Growth"; and "Education Technology, Human Capital Distribution and Growth") consider the effects of investment in private education on human capital accumulation and argue that increase in the size of public education expenditure contributes to economic growth.
24. Lloyd-Ellis, "Public Education, Occupational Choice, and the Growth-Inequality Relationship."
25. Su, "The Allocation of Public Funds in a Hierarchical Educational System."
26. Cullison, "Public Investment and Economic Growth"; Barro and Sala-i-Martin, *Economic Growth*.
27. Easterly and Rebelo, "Fiscal policy and Economic Growth: An Empirical Investigation."
28. Devarajan et al., "The Composition of Public Expenditure and Economic Growth."
29. Blankenau et al., "Public Education Expenditures, Taxation and Growth: Linking Data to Theory."
30. Fortin, "Higher-Education Policies and the College Wage Premium: Cross-State Evidence from the 1990s."
31. Krusell et al., "Capital-Skill Complementarity and Inequality: A Macroeconomic Analysis."
32. At the moment, studies conducted on China's public education policy is still focused on the effects of public education expenditure on economic growth, as well as imbalance in distribution for different regions (see Liao, "Dynamic Analysis of Imbalance in Government Education Expenditure in Different Regions"; Liao, "Structure of Human and Physical Capital and Government Education Investment in China"; Guo and Jia, "The Effects of Government Public Capital Investment on Long-Run Economic Growth"; and Guo, Jia and Liu, "Capitalist Fiscal Decentralization, Formation of Public Capital Investment and Economic Growth"), and there is a lack of more comprehensive research.
33. For reasons of simplicity, vocational education is left out for the theoretical analysis in this section; but the empirical analysis has detailed examination on the effects of changes in the proportion of public vocational education expenditure.
34. Krusell et al., "Capital-Skill Complementarity and Inequality: A Macroeconomic Analysis."
35. For a detailed exposition on the capital-skill complementarity effect and the relevant production function settings, see Krusell et al., "Capital-Skill Complementarity and Inequality: A Macroeconomic Analysis".
36. This segment leaves out the problem of individuals who are of age but unable to receive basic education, as well as students forced to leave school without graduating. This, however, is unlikely to significantly affect the conclusions in this segment. Restuccia and Urrutia points out that human capital of parents

have an important effect on learning in their children's basic education phase (see Restuccia and Urrutia, "Intergenerational Persistence of Earnings: The Role of Early and College Education.")

37. Existing research normally assumes that youth bodies make their decision on undergoing higher education based on the returns rate of education, with the goal of maximizing income within the entire life cycle. Under the conditions of scarcity of educational resources, however, the exogenously determined size of higher education admissions are often lower than the results of the choices of the economic body. The notorious difficulty in the examinations for higher education examinations has meant that many excellent students are refused admission into tertiary institutions, resulting directly in the extreme competition in the basic education phase.
38. Considering that human capital of parents are more important mainly during the children's basic education phase, this segment does not directly consider the effects of human capital of parents on the children's higher education phase; but it is acknowledged that human capital of parents will indirectly affect the human capital accumulation during the children's higher education phase through their effects on human capital accumulation during the basic education phase.
39. Here, it is implicitly assumed that the tax rate for labor income and the tax rate inclusive of investment returns are the same, denoted by τ_t.
40. Viaene and Zilcha, "Education Technology, Human Capital Distribution and Growth."
41. Prior to the 1990s, allocation of labor resources and labor wages were under planned control, and thus income had little correlation with education background. Thereafter, the situation changed significantly as market economy reforms gradually took effect, with education background becoming an important factor affecting labor wage and, by extension, income distribution disparity (see Li and Ding, "Trends of the Yield of Education of Urban China in the Long Run"). Thus, the period after the 1990s is taken as the sample period. Data is obtained mainly from past publications of China Statistical Yearbook, Statistical Yearbooks from relevant provinces, China Educational Finance Statistical Yearbook, and the China Labour Statistical Yearbook.
42. De la Croix and Michel, *A Theory of Economic Growth: Dynamics and Policy in Overlapping Generations.*
43. Data for capital stock is taken from Guo and Jia, "Estimating Potential Output and the Output Gap in China".
44. The maximum period of study for primary and secondary education are set as 6 years each, and that for higher education set as 4 years. Taking data from 1996 to 2005 for the proportions for labor forces of different education background, estimates of average maximum periods of study for high-skilled and low-skilled labor forces are obtained. It was also attempted to directly set the value for human capital for low-skilled labor as 12, but there was no significant change in the simulated results obtained.
45. Guo et al., "Chinese Traditional Cultural Beliefs, Human Capital Accumulation, and Family Pension Protection Mechanism."
46. Krusell et al., "Capital-Skill Complementarity and Inequality: A Macroeconomic Analysis."
47. Li and Ding, "Trends of the Yield of Education of Urban China in the Long Run"; Luo, "Return to Education and Its Distribution in Urban China"; Wang et al., "The Differences of Rate of Return to Schooling in Urban China and an Explanation."

48. This is consistent with the result in Yang et al., "Human Capital Formation and its Effects on Economic Growth", which used a two-department endogenous growth model to obtain production share value of human capital as 0.57.
49. From (8.3), (8.5), and (8.6), the shares in labor return can be derived as: $[\Phi_1(1-\Phi_2)][\Phi_2 k_t^{\alpha} + (1-\Phi_2)(\Theta_t \bar{h}_{Ht})^{\alpha}]^{\frac{(\beta-\alpha)}{\alpha}}(\Theta_t \bar{h}_{Ht})^{\alpha} + (1-\Phi_1)[(1-\Theta_t)\bar{h}_{Bt}]^{\beta}] / [\Phi_1[\Phi_2 k_t^{\alpha} + (1-\Phi_2)(\Theta_t \bar{h}_{Ht})^{\alpha}]^{\beta/\alpha} + (1-\Phi_1)[(1-\Theta_t)\bar{h}_{Bt}]^{\beta}] = 0.55$. Together with $\xi_t = 1.25$, Φ_1 and Φ_2 may also be obtained.
50. Restucca and Urrutia, "Intergenerational Persistence of Earnings: The Role of Early and College Education"; De la Croix and Michel, *A Theory of Economic Growth: Dynamics and Policy in Overlapping Generations.*
51. Card and Krueger, "School Resources and Students Outcomes: An Overview of the Literature and New Evidence from North and South Carolina"; Restucca and Urrutia, "Intergenerational Persistence of Earnings: The Role of Early and College Education"; Blankenau et al., "Public Education Expenditures, Taxation and Growth: Linking Data to Theory."
52. Su, "The Allocation of Public Funds in a Hierarchical Educational System."
53. Numerical simulation shows that, once the public education expenditure ratio exceeds a certain threshold (27% using benchmark settings), the negative impact of increase in the size of public education expenditure on economic growth will move into a dominant position.
54. In theory, when human capital premium is less than 1, the rational economic body will, upon completion of basic education, not choose to continue with higher education, such that human capital premium level will be maintained at above 1, assuming a balanced economy. For the numerical simulation in this analysis, the human capital value is set as less than 1, so as to better reveal the impact of public education policy on human capital premium in the real-world situation. Furthermore, the rational economic body does not only consider the rate of education returns in deciding whether to continue with higher education.
55. Since there is some arbitrariness in the selection of certain model parameters in this segment, robust tests were performed on the mentioned parameters. While the test results returned some significant differences, the conclusions obtained are generally consistent. The test results are omitted for reasons of space.
56. The empirical analysis in this segment uses data from 29 provinces for the period 1995 to 2006. For reasons of data, Tibet is left out while Chongqing is considered together as part of Sichuan province.
57. Anselin and Brea, "Spatial Dependence in Linear Regression Models with an Application to Spatial Econometrics."
58. Bond, "Dynamic Panel Data Models: A Guide to Micro Data Methods and Practice."
59. There is a lack of comprehensive data on interprovincial labor force and population movement. For the construction of the population movement spatial weight matrix model, data for interprovincial movement of population for 1985 to 1990 and 1995 to 2000 was used, obtained from the Fourth National Population Census of the People's Republic of China (1990) and the Fifth National Population Census of the People's Republic of China (2000).
60. Although using the proportion of number of students admitted to higher education out of the overall population of eligible age for higher education would be a better measure of size of higher education admissions, there is a lack of relevant data on the population of eligible age for higher education. Other

measures attempted include using the proportion of number of students admitted to higher education out of the overall population number, and out of the number of graduates from senior high school, and no significantly different conclusions were obtained.

61. Arellano and Bover, "Another Look at the Instrumental Variable Estimation of Error-Components Models"; Blundell and Bond, "Initial Conditions and Moment Restrictions in Dynamic Panel Data Models." The Moran's I and LM tests both show the existence of spatial autocorrelation in the function for production growth per capita. Kukenova and Monteiro compared several estimation methods for dynamic spatial panel data models, concluding that system GMM is the optimal method (Kukenova and Monteiro, "Spatial Dynamic Panel Model and System GMM: A Monte Carlo Investigation").
62. Bond, "Dynamic Panel Data Models: A Guide to Micro Data Methods and Practice."
63. The OLS and SSW estimated values for the one-phase lagged parameters of production growth per capita are 0.171 and -0.024 respectively. As the sample size used is relatively small, system GMM is used to avoid potential small sample bias, and two instrumental variable collections were constructed: one, GMM-class instrumental variables, including instrumental variables for the 1st order differential function (i.e. lagged terms of predetermined and endogenous explanatory variables) and instrumental variables for the level function (i.e. first differenced lagged terms of predetermined and endogenous explanatory variables); and two, IV-class instrumental variables, including instrumental variables for exogenous explanatory variables. It was also attempted to use the Collapse technique in system GMM to reduce the number of GMM-class instrumental variables to mitigate the problem of loss of degrees of freedom from the relatively large number of instrumental variables, Windmeijer's finite sample correction to perform two-step system GMM estimations, and to change the settings of the natures of the explanatory variables, but the results obtained were not satisfactory.
64. For the sample period, the mean provincial values of size of public education expenditure, proportion of higher education expenditure, proportion of vocational education expenditure, and proportion of basic education expenditure, is 2.54%, 19.9%, 8.92%, and 62.2% respectively, while the real mean higher education expenditure is 6.4 times that of basic education.
65. Robust OLS was used to derive the wage-determining functions for the various regions in various years, and from there obtain the relevant human capital premium levels, which were very similar to that obtained by other researchers, such as Li and Ding ("Trends of the Yield of Education of Urban China in the Long Run"), using other forms of census data. It should be admitted that there is a lack of census data for Liaoning province in 1997, such that the human capital premium sample size is 35; the relatively small sample size may have a negative impact of the precision of the empirical analysis, but since the sample period spans a relatively long period of time (1997 to 2006), it may still be considered capable of measuring the gradual transformation of human capital premium. It is hoped that future research will provide more comprehensive microdata which will greatly enhance the depth of analysis for the effects of public education policy on human capital premium.
66. In the regression analysis below, Difference-in-Hansen test was performed on the endogeneity of variables in public education policy, and the results show that the settings are acceptable.
67. Qiao et al., "Fiscal Decentralization and Compulsory Primary Education in China."

68. Wang et al., "On China's Development Model: The Costs and Benefits of China's Decentralization Approach to Transition"; Qiao et al., "Fiscal Decentralization and Compulsory Primary Education in China."

Chapter 9

1. Gilbert and Picard, "Incentives and Optimal Size of Local Jurisdictions."
2. For example, under the current intergovernment transfer payment system in China, even though most of the central transfer payments have been pre-allocated down to county-level regional governments, they are still distributed first to the provincial-level, and sometimes even to prefecture city-level governments before being administered to grassroots-level regional governments, leaving much room for the provincial-level and prefecture city-level governments to alter the size and usage of the transfer package. For more details on China's fiscal transfer payment system, see Xie, "Thirty Years of Financial Reform in China."
3. Buchanan and Musgrave, *Public Finance and Public Choice: Two Contrasting Visions of the State.*
4. The point may further be understood as this: regional governments are comprised of officials of different natures, that is, there are officials who pursue maximum self-interests and those who pursue maximum public interests. Thus, ω_n may be seen as the proportion of officials in the regional government pursuing maximum public interests. In the scenario where there is a lack of effective supervision from the central government, the regional government leader chooses the necessary proportion ω_n of officials to achieve a balance of political power favorable for obtaining maximum support across all types of officials.
5. No account is taken for any self-interested behavior from the central government, but this will not substantially affect the conclusions.
6. Conversely, if (9.4) is true, then the conditions for incentive compatibility and constraints are true, i.e. (9.4) is true is a necessary and sufficient condition for the mechanism $\{Q_n(\theta_n), G(\theta_n)\}$.
7. Without considering differences in distribution policy, the results for the optimal volume of regional public goods obtained in this segment are the same as that for Gilbert and Picard, who worked under the assumption of an absolutely benevolent government pursuing maximized public interests (see Gilbert and Picard, "Incentives and Optimal Size of Local Jurisdictions"). This means that self-interested behavior from regional governments do not directly affect the optimal volume of regional public goods provided, but there will be additional government expenses for compensating enterprises incurring losses from the rent-seeking behavior of regional governments, leading to loss in efficiency.
8. Arrow and Kurz, *Public Investment, the Rate of Return, and Optimal Fiscal Policy*; Barro, "Government Spending in a Simple Model of Endogenous Growth"; Turnovsky and Fisher, "The Composition of Government Expenditure and its Consequences for Macroeconomic Performance"; Lou, "Public Investment Policy in Long-Run Economic Growth: General Congestion Public Infrastructure in Long-run Growth Model"; Economic Growth Frontier Subject Team, "The Supply Effects of Fiscal Policy and Economic Development"; Guo and Jia, "The Effects of Government Public Capital Investment on Long-Run Economic Growth."
9. Glomm and Ravikumar, "Opting Out of Publicly Provided Services: A Majority Voting Result"; van Zon and Muysken, "Health and Endogenous Growth"; Creedy and Gemmell, "Publicly Financed Education

in an Endogenous Growth Model"; Viaene and Zilcha, "Human Capital Formation, Income Inequality and Growth"; Blankenau and Simpson, "Public Education Expenditures and Growth"; Liao, "Structure of China's Human and Physical Capital and the Government's Input into Education"; Guo and Jia, "The Effects of Government Public Capital Investment on Long-Run Economic Growth."

10. Qiao et al., "Fiscal Decentralization and Compulsory Primary Education in China"; Zhang, "Fiscal Decentralization and Political Centralization in China: Implications for Regional Inequality"; OECD, *Challenges for China's Public Spending: Toward Greater Effectiveness and Equity*; Wang et al., "On China's Development Model: The Costs and Benefits of China's Decentralization Approach to Transition."
11. Agénor, "Infrastructure, Public Education and Growth with Congestion Costs."
12. Two-sector endogenous growth models are excellent for demonstrating the role of human capital accumulation in economic growth, which makes it a popular framework of analysis for researchers looking at a wide variety of economic growth issues since its introduction in the groundbreaking research of Lucas ("On the Mechanics of Economic Development").
13. In recent years, there has been extensive studies on optimal fiscal decentralization and the effects on China's socioeconomic development (see for example Zhang and Zou, "Fiscal Decentralization, Public Spending and Economic Growth in China"; Lin and Liu, "Fiscal Decentralization and Economic Growth in China"; Zhu, "Reform of Decentralization, Financial Incentives, and Reform of Public Companies"; and Zhang and Gong, "Interregional Disparity, Factor Mobility, and Fiscal Decentralization"), but the main focus of these research is on the overall degree of fiscal decentralization; while in actual economic life, the concern is mainly on the effects of different types of fiscal decentralization, especially capital development expenditure decentralization — for instance, whether public education and healthcare should be considered the responsibility of the central or regional government.
14. For reasons of simplification and emphasis on the problem of analysis, this section does not take into consideration consumption expenditure of governments. It would be quite reasonable to assume that governments direct part of tax revenue for funding public capital investment, but this will simply require an addition of a constant coefficient, and so omitting this from consideration does not have any significant effects on the results in this section.
15. Currently, there are two main methods of measuring fiscal decentralization: the first and more popular one, through the proportion of regional fiscal revenue out of total fiscal revenue; the second, through the marginal increase in autonomous revenue (see Zhang and Gong, "Interregional Disparity, Factor Mobility, and Fiscal Decentralization"). The main focus of this section is on examining the intergovernment division of administrative authority in public capital investment, so the first method is used — accordingly, the degree of capital development expenditure decentralization is measured as the proportion of regional public capital investment out of total public capital investment.
16. Lucas, "On the Mechanics of Economic Development."
17. Agénor, "Infrastructure, Public Education and Growth with Congestion Costs."
18. Linearizing the differential systems given in (9.30) and (9.31) around the point of equilibrium, there is $\begin{bmatrix} \dot{z} \\ \dot{m} \end{bmatrix} = \begin{bmatrix} a_{11} & a_{12} \\ a_{21} & a_{22} \end{bmatrix} \begin{bmatrix} z - z^* \\ m - m^* \end{bmatrix}$. From $\Delta = a_{11}a_{22} - a_{12}a_{21} = -\alpha\chi\Psi\theta_{ch}^{\omega\varepsilon}\theta_{lh}^{\eta\varepsilon}\theta_{ck}^{\gamma\chi}\theta_{lk}^{(1-\alpha-\beta-\gamma)\chi}(m^*)^{-\alpha\chi}z^* - [\beta\alpha\Theta(\upsilon - \theta_{lk})^{\gamma/(\alpha+\beta)}\theta_{lk}^{(1-\alpha-\beta-\gamma)/(\alpha+\beta)}(m^*)^{\beta/(\alpha+\beta)}z^*]/(\alpha+\beta)\sigma < 0$, it can be known that the

Jacobian matrix for the partial derivatives in the linear dynamic system is negative, i.e. the point of equilibrium is a stable saddle point.

19. From (9.19), it can be seen that the production function at equilibrium is an AK model production function, so for the balanced-growth path, the growth rates of per capita consumption, per capita human capital and per capita physical capita are same and constant. It may further be known from (9.18) that $\dot{y}/y = (\alpha/(\alpha+\beta))(\dot{k}/k) + (\beta/(\alpha+\beta))(\dot{h}/h)$, thus there is $\dot{y}/y = \dot{k}/k$.
20. For reasons of space, this section has omitted analysis of the effects of capital development expenditure decentralization and proportion of public investment in physical capital on the equilibrium ratio between consumption and physical capital. In reality, when the marginal utility elasticity of consumption exceeds the output elasticity of physical capital, the conditions of effect of capital development expenditure decentralization and proportion of public investment in physical capital on the equilibrium ratio between consumption and physical capital are entirely equivalent to their conditions of effect on balanced economic growth; while if the marginal utility elasticity of consumption does not exceed the output elasticity of physical capital, the conditions of effect are the opposite. The reason for this is simple: as the balanced economic growth rate increases, then the ratio of stable state output to capital will increase correspondingly, and where marginal utility elasticity of consumption is larger than the output elasticity of physical capital, the marginal utility from consumption to private economic agents will exceed the utility from physical capital accumulation, and so private economic agents will choose higher consumption, leading to an increase in the equilibrium ratio between consumption and physical capital.
21. Deriving d_h, d_k, and υ from (9.33) and (9.34) can establish Theorem 2, of which $\mu_{m^*/d_k} = (\partial m^* / \partial d_k)(d_k/m^*)$ and $\mu_{m^*/\upsilon} = (\partial m^* / \partial \upsilon)(\upsilon/m^*) < 0$ are the m^* elasticities for d_k and υ. In establishing the conditions of effect of d_k and υ on m^*, it only has to be noted that from (9.34), (9.35) and $\rho > 0$ that $\alpha\Theta(1-d_k)^{\gamma/(\alpha+\beta)} d_k^{(1-\alpha-\beta-\gamma)/(\alpha+\beta)} \upsilon^{(1-\alpha-\beta)/(\alpha+\beta)} (m^*)^{\beta/(\alpha+\beta)} / \sigma > \Psi(1-d_h)^{\omega\varepsilon} d_h^{\eta\varepsilon} (1-d_k)^{\gamma\chi} d_k^{(1-\alpha-\beta-\gamma)\chi} (1-\upsilon)^{(\omega+\eta)\varepsilon} \upsilon^{(1-\alpha-\beta)\chi} (m^*)^{-\alpha\chi}$.
22. Deriving d_h, d_k, and υ from (9.34) and (9.35), taking derivative as 0, can establish Theorem 3, which shows that the optimal proportion of public capital investment for both maximized social welfare and growth are entirely equivalent.
23. Agénor, "Infrastructure, Public Education and Growth with Congestion Costs."
24. Ibid.
25. Barro, "Government Spending in a Simple Model of Endogenous Growth."
26. Using actual data to fit into the quadratic function for decentralization in capital development expenditure and proportion of public investment in physical capital, and long-term economic growth, helps to test for Theorems 2 and 3 (the theoretical analysis here shows that the structural composition of public capital investment for maximized growth and for maximized social welfare are the same), thus giving the optimal degree of decentralization in capital development expenditure and the optimal proportion of public investment in physical capital. Guo and Jia used fiscal investments (i.e. the budgetary portions of the fixed capital investment in the whole society) to measure public investment in physical capital (Guo and Jia, "The Effects of Government Public Capital Investment on Long-Run Economic Growth"), and the Economic Growth Frontier Subject Team used fiscal infrastructure expenditure to measure public investment in physical capital (Economic Growth Frontier Subject Team, "The Supply Effects of Fiscal Policy and Economic Development"). Due to the lack of provincial fiscal investment data, in order to

retain consistency for the analysis, this section also uses fiscal infrastructure expenditure to measure public investment in physical capital. Yang et al. points out that human capital includes health capital and education capital (Yang et al., "Human Capital Formation and its Effects on Economic Growth"), but since the theoretical model in this section mainly demonstrates private economic agents as accumulating human capital through education, and further considering limitations in data, this section will follow the standard methodology in using educational index to measure human capital, and accordingly use fiscal education expenditure to measure public investment in human capital. However, since there is only provincial fiscal education expenditure data for 1995 to 2003, and the sample size will be even more limited if lagged effects are taken into consideration, it is not possible to examine if decentralization in human capital development expenditure and growth rate of per capita output exhibits an inverted U-shaped relationship. For the proportion of public investment in physical expenditure, lagged terms of 1–5 were attempted, and the fitting results all exhibit an inverted U-shaped curve, with the best result being a lagged term of 3. For more details on this analysis, see Jia et al., "Capital Expenditure Decentralization, Public Capital Investment Composition and Economic Growth."

27. Qiao et al., "Fiscal Decentralization and Compulsory Primary Education in China."
28. Extensive studies show that the relative importance of physical capital and human capital accumulation on economic growth is related to the stage of economic development: in the early stages of industrialization, due to the relative lack of physical capital constraining the role that human capital can play, physical capital accumulation becomes the main driving force behind economic growth; when the industrialization process is basically complete, the relative abundance of physical capital allows for better integration between human capital and physical capital and a more important role for human capital, such that human capital becomes the main driving force behind economic growth (see Abramovitz and David, "American Macroeconomic Growth in the Era of Knowledge-Based Progress: The Long-Run Perspective"; and Goldin and Katz, "The Legacy of U.S. Educational Leadership: Notes on Distribution and Economic Growth in the 20th Century"). This point receives additional verification in the real-life situation in China: in recent years, there has been large-scale admissions conducted for higher education, but due to the relative lag in economic development, there is a relative lack of suitable employment opportunities for many tertiary graduates, and so the effect of human capital accumulation on promoting long-term economic growth and social welfare is extremely limited.
29. Gordon, "An Optimal Taxation Approach to Fiscal Federalism."
30. Persson and Tabellini, "Federal Fiscal Constitutions: Risk Sharing and Moral Hazard"; Persson and Tabellini, "Federal Fiscal Constitutions: Risk Sharing and Redistribution."
31. Gong and Zou, "Optimal Taxation and Intergovernmental Transfer in a Dynamic Model with Multiple Levels of Government."
32. It should be noted that the assumption made in this section regarding the formation of human capital follows the methodology of Agénor, who assumed that the share of time that private economic agents spend on human capital accumulation is determined exogenously (Agénor, "Infrastructure, Public Education and Growth with Congestion Costs"). This is different from the assumptions made by Lucas, who assumed that private economic agents choose the time spent on human capital accumulation based on maximized utility (Lucas, "On the Mechanics of Economic Development"); this fails to consider that human capital

accumulation may often be compulsory in nature: one, basic education is for most countries compulsory, with certain healthcare services also being free and compulsory (e.g. China passed the compulsory education law in 1986); two, education and healthcare resources is in many countries very limited, unable to satisfy the general demands of education and healthcare, and this means that admissions to higher education is dependent on tough entry examinations and exogenous conditions in admission sizes, and that higher quality of healthcare services also exhibit significant exogenous constraints. All these means that in China, the share of time that private economic agents spend on human capital accumulation is more exogenously determined and less the result of autonomous decisions. Of course, the problem of dropouts still exists, especially in agrarian regions of the country, and so the ideal assumption is to suppose that the share of time for human capital accumulation is a combination of exogenous and endogenous factors; however, considering that exogenous factors is the more dominant set of factors, and out of consideration for the viability of the model, this section assumes that the share of time for human capital accumulation is exogenously determined. A more comprehensive study covering both exogenous and endogenous factors and their effects on the share of time for human capital accumulation will make a valuable contribution to existing research.

33. It should be noted that in this section, consumption tax refers to its usage in the broad sense, i.e. taxation on all consumption activities, rather than the narrow use of the term for taxation on particular commodities in the actual economy.
34. Taking into consideration that central government expenditure has relatively larger externalities on regional economies, it is the total central public investment in physical capital and the total central public investment in human capital that are considered in the production functions for physical capital and human capital.
35. When the economy reaches equilibrium, the production function in this segment is essentially an AK model [see (9.38)]; thus, the rate of growth for consumption, private physical capital and private human capital are the same, i.e. the economy reaches a balanced-growth equilibrium.
36. Agénor, "Infrastructure, Public Education and Growth with Congestion Costs."
37. Gong and Zou, "Optimal Taxation and Intergovernmental Transfer in a Dynamic Model with Multiple Levels of Government."
38. Additionally, in the real-world situation in China, there exists a significant disparity in the degree of fiscal decentralization across different regions (e.g. for 2006, the fiscal revenue and expenditure decentralization levels for Shanxi province is 0.53 and 0.78 respectively, while that for Jiangxi province is 0.31 and 0.68 respectively (see Guo and Jia, "The Transfer Payments from the Central Government and the Provision of Regional Public Services," for more details on provincial fiscal decentralization levels). Thus, it may be seen from (9.63) that, from the perspective of efficiency (i.e. maximized growth), the optimal size of central transfer payments should vary for individual provinces, and from (9.60), it may further be known that the optimal long-term economic growth rate will be different.

Annex 1

1. Liu, "Why is the Economic Fluctuation in China so High?"; Economic Growth Frontier Subject Team, "The Supply Effects of Fiscal Policy and Economic Development"; Economic Growth Frontier Subject Team, "International Capital Flows, Economic Distortions, and Macroeconomic Stability: The Trend Analysis of Current Economic Growth."

2. Guo and Jia proposed a hypothesis for the behavior of regional governments in an unstable macroeconomy, examining in detail the mechanisms of effect of the behavior of regional governments on macroeconomic stability (Guo and Jia, "Behavior of Regional Governments, Impulsive Investment, and Macroeconomic Stability.")
3. Stock and Watson, "New Indexes of Coincident and Leading Economic Indicators"; Stock and Watson, "A Probability Model of the Coincident Economic Indicators"; Stock and Watson, "A Procedure for Predicting Recession with Leading Indicators: Econometric Issues and Recent Experience."
4. Diebold and Rudebusch, "Measuring Business Cycles: A Modern Perspective."
5. See for example Norrbin and Schlaggenhauf, "The Role of International Factors in the Business Cycle: A Multi-Country Study"; Gregory et al., "Measuring World Business Cycles"; and Kose et al., "International Business Cycles: World, Region, and Country-Specific Factors."
6. For the purposes of this paper, provinces, directly-administered municipalities and autonomous regions are all considered as provinces. Excluding Hong Kong, Macau, and Taiwan, there are 31 provinces in the country, and for reasons of data, Chongqing is considered as part of Sichuan province while Tibet is excluded from consideration. The rest of the 29 provinces are classified into three regions: for the Eastern region, Beijing, Tianjin, Hebei, Liaoning, Shanghai, Jiangsu, Zhejiang, Fujian, Shandong, Guangdong, and Hainan; for the Central region, Shanxi, Jilin, Heilongjiang, Anhui, Jiangxi, Henan, Hubei, and Henan; for the Western region, Inner Mongolia, Sichuan, Guangxi, Guizhou, Yunnan, Shaanxi, Gansu, Qinghai, Ningxia, and Xinjiang. Also, investment as used in this paper refers to fixed capital investments in the whole society, and due to a lack of comprehensive provincial consumption data, consumption refers to the total retail volume of consumer goods in the whole society.
7. Here, actual investment is obtained from dividing nominal investment by the price index of fixed capital investment.
8. For more details on using EM algorithms and LQE for estimation in a multi-dynamic-factor mode, see Stock and Watson, "New Indexes of Coincident and Leading Economic Indicators"; Stock and Watson, "A Procedure for Predicting Recession with Leading Indicators: Econometric Issues and Recent Experience"; and Gregory et al., "Measuring World Business Cycles."
9. Kose et al., "International Business Cycles: World, Region, and Country-Specific Factors."
10. Stock and Watson, "New Indexes of Coincident and Leading Economic Indicators"; Stock and Watson, "A Procedure for Predicting Recession with Leading Indicators: Econometric Issues and Recent Experience."
11. Otrok and Whiteman, "Bayesian Leading Indicators: Measuring and Predicting Economic Conditions in Iowa."
12. For more details on the process of using Gibbs sampling for estimation in a multi-dynamic-factor model, see Otrok and Whitman, "Bayesian Leading Indicators: Measuring and Predicting Economic Conditions in Iowa"; and Kose et al., "International Business Cycles: World, Region, and Country-Specific Factors." To ensure robustness in the estimation results, different sampling sequences, prior distribution, initial values and sampling sizes were attempted.
13. For reasons of space, the complete analysis for all provinces for the correlation between provincial dynamic factors and the change in growth rate is not given. Generally speaking, the situations of the various provinces may be classified into four main types, and these four provinces are chosen for their representativeness.

14. Standard theories on actual economic cycles point out that the correlation between the fluctuations in consumption of different economic agents is far higher than that for the fluctuations in output (see for example Backus et al., "International Business Cycles: Theory vs. Evidence"). However, extensive empirical studies on international economic cycles have produced totally opposite conclusions; this is also known as the "quantity anomaly". The exact reasons for the existence of the "quantity anomaly" is uncertain: research by Bayoumi and Mcdonald ("On the Optimality of Consumption across Canadian Provinces"), Bayoumi and Klein("A Provincial View of Capital Mobility") and Crucini ("On International and National Dimensions of Risk Sharing") on the provincial economic cycles in Canada are consistent with the results in this paper, while research by Hess and Shin("Intranational Business Cycles in the United States") and van Wincoop ("Regional Risksharing") on the economic cycles of U.S. states and prefectures of Japan show that "quantity anomaly" does exist.
15. In performing the regression analysis for the contributions of the dynamic factors to provincial economic growth fluctuations and the variables of the economic features, it was also attempted to use other explanatory variables such as the total-factor growth rate, the rate of technical progression, the rate of efficiency change, the degree of openness the regional population etc. The results obtained show that these variables are not important to the regression analysis.

Annex 2

1. Qian and Roland, "Federalism and the Soft Budget Constraint"; Jin et al., "Regional Decentralization and Fiscal Incentives: Federalism, Chinese Style"; Lin and Liu, "Fiscal Decentralization and Economic Growth in China;" Zhu, "Reform of Decentralization, Financial Incentives, and Reform of Public Companies"; Zhang and Gong, "Interregional Disparity, Factor Mobility, and Fiscal Decentralization."
2. Zhang and Zou, "Fiscal Decentralization, Public Spending and Economic Growth in China"; Zhou, "Local Government Competition and Economic Growth"; Zhou, "The Incentive and Cooperation of Government Officials in the Political Tournaments: An Interpretation of the Prolonged Local Protectionism and Duplicative Investments in China"; Zhou, "Governing China's Local Officials: An Analysis of Promotion Tournament Model"; Guo and Jia, "Behavior of Regional Governments, Impulsive Investment, and Macroeconomic Stability"; Jia et al., "Capital Expenditure Decentralization, Public Capital Investment Composition and Economic Growth." Also see Wang et al., "The Differences of Rate of Return to Schooling in Urban China and An Explanation", for a detailed description on the pros and cons from the reforms in decentralization, as well as the challenges faced in future reform plans.
3. For the purposes of this paper, provinces, directly-administered municipalities, and autonomous regions are all considered as provinces. Also, for reasons of data, Chongqing is considered as part of Sichuan province while Tibet is excluded from consideration. Provinces classified as Eastern region are Beijing, Tianjin, Hebei, Liaoning, Shanghai, Jiangsu, Zhejiang, Fujian, Shandong, Guangdong, and Hainan. This paper uses [total provincial fiscal expenditure per capita / (total provincial fiscal expenditure per capita + total central fiscal expenditure per capita)] to measure the overall arrangements in expenditure responsibilities, [total provincial fiscal revenue per capita / (total provincial fiscal revenue per capita + total central fiscal revenue per capita)] to measure the overall arrangements in revenue responsibilities, and similar equations for infrastructure, education, science, culture and healthcare, and administration

to measure the arrangements in responsibilities of production, social and administrative expenditure (see Zhang and Zou, "Fiscal Decentralization, Public Spending and Economic Growth in China"; Zhang and Gong, "Interregional Disparity, Factor Mobility, and Fiscal Decentralization"; and Jia et al., "Capital Expenditure Decentralization, Public Capital Investment Composition and Economic Growth"). Data is obtained from past publications of the *China Statistical Yearbook* and the statistical yearbooks from the various provinces.

4. Guo and Zhao, *Public Economics*; Jia et al., "Capital Expenditure Decentralization, Public Capital Investment Composition and Economic Growth."
5. The two major tax system reforms — the 1984 industrial-commercial tax system reforms and the 1994 tax sharing system reforms — both involve the abolishment and establishment of various tax types, meaning that tax revenue data across different historical periods are largely incommensurable. Revenue from fees are affected by this incommensurability problem, and for other types of revenues such as revenue from (state-owned) enterprises, there is a lack of comprehensive provincial data. Thus, this paper does not examine the effects of arrangements of responsibilities for the various types of terms of revenue.
6. Mankiw et al., "A Contribution to the Empirics of Economic Growth"; de la Fuente, "Convergence Equations and Income Dynamics: The Source of OECD Convergence, 1970-1995."
7. Lin and Liu, "Fiscal Decentralization and Economic Growth in China."
8. The Lagrange multipliers of the Breusch-Pagan test and the results of the Hausman tests also show that fixed-effects panel data model is the correct choice here. Of course, it may be argued that the choice between a fixed-effects or a random-effects model depends more on the purpose of research: a fixed-effects model is usually for resolving the problem agent heterogeneity, while a random-effects model mainly uses variance analysis to differentiate the different extents of changes between SSW and SSB, and neither are usually employed to test for settings (see Gao and Yao, "Effects of Health Shocks on the Income of Rural Households"). It was also attempted to use a random-effects model, and the estimation results are generally consistent with those obtained from the fixed-effects model. Additionally, it may be seen that the intercept variables of the estimations for the Western provinces are generally negative, meaning that the economic growth situation in the Western region is relatively poor.
9. Baltagi and Wu, "Unequally Spaced Panel Data Regressions with AR(1) Disturbance."
10. Arellano and Bond, "Some Tests of Specification for Panel Data: Monte Carlo Evidence and an Application to Employment Equations"; Arellano and Bover, "Another Look at the Instrumental Variable Estimation of Error-Components Models"; Blundell and Bond, "Initial Conditions and Moment Restrictions in Dynamic Panel Data Models"; Bond, "Dynamic Panel Data Models: A Guide to Micro Data Methods and Practice."
11. Gao and Yao, "Effects of Health Shocks on the Income of Rural Households."
12. Bond, "Dynamic Panel Data Models: A Guide to Micro Data Methods and Practice"; Roodman, "How to Do Xtabond2: An Introduction to 'Difference' and 'System' GMM in Stata."
13. Holtz-Eakin, "Estimating Vector Autoregressions with Panel Data"; Arellano and Bond, "Some Tests of Specification for Panel Data: Monte Carlo Evidence and an Application to Employment Equations."
14. Arellano and Bover, "Another Look at the Instrumental Variable Estimation of Error-Components Models"; Blundell and Bond, "Initial Conditions and Moment Restrictions in Dynamic Panel Data Models"; Bond, "Dynamic Panel Data Models: A Guide to Micro Data Methods and Practice."

15. Arellano and Bover, "Another Look at the Instrumental Variable Estimation of Error-Components Models"; Blundell and Bond, "Initial Conditions and Moment Restrictions in Dynamic Panel Data Models." For detailed comparative analysis on using OLS estimation, SSW estimation, difference GMM and system GMM for dynamic panel data models, see Bond, "Dynamic Panel Data Models: A Guide to Micro Data Methods and Practice"; and Roodman, "How to Do Xtabond2: An Introduction to 'Difference' and 'System' GMM in Stata."
16. Im et al., "Testing for Unit Roots in Heterogeneous Panels."
17. Bond, "Dynamic Panel Data Models: A Guide to Micro Data Methods and Practice"; Roodman, "How to Do Xtabond2: An Introduction to 'Difference' and 'System' GMM in Stata."
18. For reasons of space, the OLS and SSW estimation results of the model are not shown. As the sample size is relatively small, system GMM estimation is used to avoid small sample bias, and two groups of instruments are constructed: GMM-style instruments, which includes the instrumental variables in the first differenced function [i.e. the lagged terms of the predetermined and endogenous explanatory variables, $Z_{it\text{–}S}$ $(t = 3, \cdots, T;\ 2 \leq s \leq t - 1)$] and the instrumental variables in the level function [i.e. the first differenced lagged terms of the predetermined and endogenous explanatory variables, $\Delta Z_{it\text{–}1}$ $(t = 3, \cdots, T)$] (see Arellano and Bond, "Some Tests of Specification for Panel Data: Monte Carlo Evidence and an Application to Employment Equations"; and Blundell and Bond, "Initial Conditions and Moment Restrictions in Dynamic Panel Data Models"); IV-style instruments, which includes the instrumental variables constructed on the basis of exogenous explanatory variables. Since the Sargan overidentification test is inconsistent, the Hansen test and Difference-in-Hansen test is preferred for testing the effectiveness of the instruments. Additionally, it was attempted to use the Collapse technique to reduce the number of GMM-style instruments in order to overcome the problem of relatively high loss in degree of freedom, and two-stop system GMM with Windmeijer limited sample correction for estimation, but the results obtained were not satisfactory. For more details on estimation in dynamic panel data model, see Roodman, "How to Do Xtabond2: An Introduction to 'Difference' and 'System' GMM in Stata."
19. Zhang and Zou and Jia et al. point out that in theory, the optimal level for maximized economic growth exists for both fiscal decentralization and decentralization in capital development expenditure, i.e. the relationship between the two is non-linear (Zhang and Zou, "Fiscal Decentralization, Public Spending and Economic Growth in China"; Jia et al., "Capital Expenditure Decentralization, Public Capital Investment Composition and Economic Growth").
20. Hansen, "Threshold Effects in Non-Dynamic Panels: Estimation, Testing and Inference."
21. For more details on the tests and estimation process for threshold panel data models, see Hansen, "Threshold Effects in Non-Dynamic Panels: Estimation, Testing and Inference."
22. The policy meaning of this point disagrees with the majority's view that "in the current revenue arrangements, the proportion of revenue for regional governments is relatively low, and thus autonomy in revenue for regional governments should be increased." In fact, even under the trend of centralization in fiscal revenue over the past few years, the proportion of local fiscal revenues for regional governments far exceeds that of most countries: a whopping 147% higher than that for unitary states, and 48% higher than the average levels in federal countries (see Guo and Zhao, *Public Economics*, 355). In which case, it may be said that the degree of fiscal decentralization in China is actually very high!

Bibliography

Chinese sources:

Bai Zhongen 白重恩, Du Yinjuan 杜穎鵑, Tao Zhigang 陶志剛, and Tong Yueting 仝月婷. "Difang baohu zhuyi ji chanye diqu jizhongdu de jueding yinsu he biandong qushi" 地方保護主義及產業地區集中度的決定因素和變動趨勢 (Local Protectionism and Industrial Concentration in China: Overall Trend and Important Factors). *Jingji yanjiu* 經濟研究 (Economic Research Journal), 4 (2004).

Bo Guili 薄貴利. "Lun youhua zhengfu zuzhi jiegou" 論優化政府組織結構 (Optimization of the Administrative Organizational Structure in China). *Zhongguo xingzheng guanli* 中國行政管理 (Chinese Public Administration), 5 (2007).

Chen Binkai 陳斌開, Yang Yishan 楊依山, and Xu Wei 許偉. "Zhongguo chengzhen jumin laodong shouru chaju yanbian ji qi yuanyin: 1990–2005" 中國城鎮居民勞動收入差距演變及其原因: 1990 - 2005 (Changes of the Income Gap of the Urban Labor Force in China and the Reasons Behind It: 1990–2005). *Jingji yanjiu* 經濟研究 (Economic Research Journal), 12 (2009).

Chen Kang 陳抗, Arye L. Hillman, and Gu Qingyang 顧清揚. "Caizheng jiquan yu difang zhengfu xingwei bianhua: Cong huanzhuzhishou dao juequzhishou" 財政集權與地方政府行為變化: 從援助之手到攫取之手 (Fiscal Re-Centralization and Behavioral Change of Local Governments: From the Helping Hand to the Grabbing Hand). *Jingjixue (Jikan)* 經濟學 (季刊) (China Economic Quarterly), 2(1) (2002).

Ding Congming 丁從明, and Cheng Zhongchang 陳仲常. "Caizheng fenquan yu jingji zhouqi bodong yanjiu: Jiyu AS-AD de Shijiao" 財政分權與經濟週期波動研究：基於AS-AD的視角 (Study of Fiscal Decentralization and Economic Fluctuation: From the Perspective of AS-AD). *Jingji yanjiu* 經濟研究 (Economic Research Journal), 11 (2009).

Fang Hongsheng 方紅生, and Zhang Jun 張軍. "Zhongguo difang zhengfu kuangzhang pianxiang de caizheng xingwei" 中國地方政府擴張偏向的財政行為: 觀察與解釋 (Expansionary Fiscal Spending among Chinese Local Governments: Observations and Explanations). *Jingjixue (Jikan)* 經濟學 (季刊) (China Economic Quarterly), 8(3) (2009).

Fu Yong 傅勇, and Zhang Yan 張晏. "Zhongguoshi fenquan yu caizheng zhichu jiegou pianxiang: Wei zengzhang er jingzheng de daijia" 中國式分權與財政支出結構偏向：為增長而競爭的代價 (Chinese-Style Fiscal Decentralization and the Bias in the Fiscal Expenditure Structure: The Costs of the Competition for Growth). *Guanli shijie* 管理世界 (Management World), 1 (2007).

Gao Mengtao 高夢滔, and Yao Yang 姚洋. "Jiankang fengxian chongji dui nonghu shouru de yingxiang" 健康風險衝擊對農戶收入的影響 (Effects of Health Shocks on the Income of Rural Households). *Jingji yanjiu* 經濟研究 (Economic Research Journal), 12 (2005).

Gong Feng 龔鋒, and Lu Hongyou 盧洪友. "Gonggong zhichu jiegou、pianhaopipei yu caizheng fenquan" 公共支出結構、偏好匹配與財政分權 (Public Expenditure, Preference-Matching, and Fiscal Decentralization). *Guanli shijie* 管理世界 (Management World), 1 (2009).

Gu Wanyong 顧萬勇. "Jingti ganbu jiaoliu de sige wuqu" 警惕幹部交流的四個誤區 (Four Aspects of the Failings of Cadres Exchange). *Zuzhi renshixue yanjiu* 組織人事學研究 (Organization and Personnel Management Studies), 5 (2006).

Guo Qingwang 郭慶旺. *Shuishou zhichu jianlun* 稅收支出簡論 (Brief Discussions on Tax Expenditures). Dalian: Dongbei University of Finance and Economics Press, 1990.

Guo Qingwang 郭慶旺, and Jia Junxue 賈俊雪. "Caizheng fenquan、zhengfu zuzhi jiegou yu difang zhengfu zhizhu guimo" 財政分權、政府組織結構與地方政府支出規模 (Fiscal Decentralization, Government Organizational Structure, and the Size of Regional Government Expenditure). *Jingji yanjiu* 經濟研究 (Economic Research Journal), 11 (2010).

———. "Difang zhengfu jian celüe hudong xingwei、caizheng zhichu jingzheng yu diqu jingji zengzhang" 地方政府間策略互動行為、財政支出競爭與地區經濟增長 (Strategic Interactions among Regional Governments, Fiscal Expenditure Competition, and Regional Economic Growth). *Guanli shijie* 管理世界 (Management World), 10 (2009).

———. "Difang zhengfu xingwei, touzi chongdong yu hongguan jingji wending" 地方政府行為、投資衝動與宏觀經濟穩定 (Behavior of Regional Governments, Impulsive Investment, and Macroeconomic Stability). *Guanli shijie* 管理世界 (Management World), 5 (2006).

———. "Gonggong jiaoyu zhengce、jingji zengzhang yu renli ziben yijia" 公共教育政策、經濟增長與人力資本溢價 (Public Education Policies, Economic Growth, and Human Capital Premium). *Jingji yanjiu* 經濟研究 (Economic Research Journal), 10 (2009).

———. "Wenjian caizheng zhengce de feiKaiensi xiaoying ji qi kechixuxing" 穩健財政政策的非凱恩斯效應及其可持續性 (Non-Keynesian Effects in Stable Fiscal Policy and Its Sustainability). *Zhongguo shehui kexue* 中國社會科學 (Social Sciences in China), 5 (2006).

———. "Zhengfu gonggong ziben touzi de changqi jingji zengzhang xiaoying" 政府公共資本投資的長期經濟增長效應 (The Effects of Government Public Capital Investment on Long-Run Economic Growth). *Jingji yanjiu* 經濟研究 (Economic Research Journal), 7 (2006).

———. "Zhongguo qianzai changchu yu quekou de gusuan" 中國潛在產出與產出缺口的估算 (Estimating Potential Output and the Output Gap in China). *Jingji yanjiu* 經濟研究 (Economic Research Journal), 5 (2004).

———. "Zhongguo shengfen jingji zhouqi de dongtai yinsu fenxi" 中國省份經濟週期的動態因素分析 (Analysis of the Dynamic Factors Affecting the Economic Cycle of Provinces in China). *Guanli shijie* 管理世界 (Management World), 11 (2005).

———. "Zhongyang caizheng zhuanyi zhifu yu difang gonggong fuwu tigong" 中央財政轉移支付與地方公共服務提供 (The Transfer Payments from the Central Government and the Provision of Regional Public Services). *Shijie jingji* 世界經濟 (The Journal of World Economy), 9 (2008).

Guo Qingwang 郭慶旺, Jia Junxue 賈俊雪, and Gao Li 高立. "Zhongyang caizheng zhuanyi zhifu yu diqu jingji zengzhang" 中央財政轉移支付與地區經濟增長 (The Transfer Payments from the Central Government and Regional Economic Growth). *Shijie jingji* 世界經濟 (The Journal of World Economy), 12 (2009).

Guo Qingwang 郭慶旺, Jia Junxue 賈俊雪, and Liu Xiaolu 劉曉路 "Zibenxing zhichu fenquan、gonggong ziben touzi goucheng yu jingji zengzhang" 資本性支出分權、公共資本投資構成與經濟增長 (Capitalist Fiscal Decentralization, Formation of Public Capital Investment and Economic Growth). *Jingji yanjiu* 經濟研究 (Economic Research Journal), 12 (2006).

Guo Qingwang 郭慶旺, Jia Junxue 賈俊雪, and Zhao Zhiyun 趙志耘. "Zhongguo chuantong wenhua xinnian、renli ziben jilei yu jiating yanglao baozhang jizhi" 中國傳統文化信念、人力資本積累與家庭養老保障機制 (Chinese Traditional Cultural Beliefs, Human Capital Accumulation, and Family Pension Protection Mechanism). *Jingji yanjiu* 經濟研究 (Economic Research Journal), 8 (2007).

Guo Qingwang 郭慶旺, and Zhao Zhiyun 趙志耘. *Gonggong jingji xue* 公共經濟學 (Public Economics). Higher Education Press, 2006.

Guo Qingwang 郭慶旺, Zhao Zhiyun 趙志耘, and Jia Junxue 賈俊雪. "Zhongguo shengfen jingji de quanyaosu shengchanlü fenxi" 中國省份經濟的全要素生產率分析 (Economic Analysis of the Total Factor Productivity of Provinces in China). *Shijie jingji* 世界經濟 (The Journal of World Economy), 5 (2005).

Guo Xuxin 郭旭新. "Jingji zhuanxing zhong de caizheng fenquanhua yu jingji wending" 經濟轉型中的財政分權化與經濟穩定 (Fiscal Decentralization and Economic Stability in Economic Transition). *Jingji shehui tizhi bijiao* 經濟社會體制比較 (Comparative Economic & Social Systems), 2 (2007).

Hu Jiayong 胡家勇. "Gonggong wupin gonggei fenxi" 公共物品供給分析 (Analysis of the Demand for and Supply of Public Goods). *Zhongnan caijing daxue xuebao* 中南財經大學學報 (Journal of Zhongnan University of Economics and Law), 2 (1996).

Hu Shudong 胡書東. *Jingji fazhan zhong de zhongyang yu difang guanxi: Zhongguo caizheng zhidu bianqian yanjiu* 經濟發展中的中央與地方關係: 中國財政制度變遷研究 (Relationships between the Central Government and Regional Governments: Study of the Changes in the Financial System of China). Shanghai: Shanghai Joint Publishing Company, Shanghai People's Publishing House, 2001.

Wong, Christine 黃佩華, and Deepak Bhattasali 迪派克. *Zhongguo: Guojia fazhan yu difang caizheng* 中國: 國家發展與地方財政 (China: National Development and Sub-national Finance). Translated by Wu Suping 吳素萍, Wang Guijuan王桂娟 et al. Beijing: CITIC Press, 2003.

Ji Liping 姬麗萍. "Deng Xiaoping dui xinshiqi ganbu renshi zhidu gaige de gongxian" 鄧小平對新時期幹部人事制度改革的貢獻 (Contribution of Deng Xiaoping to the Changes of the Cadres System in the New China). *Nanfang conglun* 南方論叢 (Southern Forum), 3 (2004).

Jia Junxue 賈俊雪, and Guo Qingwang 郭慶旺. "Zhengfu jian caizheng shouzhi zeren anpai de diqu jingji zengzhang xiaoying" 政府間財政收支責任安排的地區經濟增長效應 (The Effects of Intergovernmental Assignments of Public Revenue and Expenditure Responsibility on the Regional Economic Growth). *Jingji yanjiu* 經濟研究 (Economic Research Journal), 6 (2008).

Jia Junxue 賈俊雪, Guo Qingwang 郭慶旺, and Gao Li 高立. "Zhongyang caizheng zhuanyi zhifu、jili xiaoying yu diqu jian caizheng zhichu jingzheng" 中央財政轉移支付、激勵效應與地區間財政支出競爭 (Transfer Payments from the Central Government, Incentive Mechanism, and Regional Expenditure Competition). *Caimao jingji* 財貿經濟 (Finance & Trade Economics), 11 (2010).

Jia Junxue 賈俊雪, Guo Qingwang 郭慶旺, and Liu Xiaolu 劉曉路. "Zibenxing zhichu fenquan、gonggong ziben touzi goucheng yu jingji zengzhang" 資本性支出分權、公共資本投資構成與經濟增長 (Capital Expenditure Decentralization, Public Capital Investment Composition and Economic Growth). *Jingji yanjiu* 經濟研究 (Economic Research Journal), 12 (2006).

Jia Junxue 賈俊雪, Guo Qingwang 郭慶旺, and Ning Jing 寧靜. "Caizheng fenquan、zhengfu zhili jiegou he xianji difang zhengfu caizheng jiekun" 財政分權、政府治理結構和縣級地方政府財政解困 (Fiscal Decentralization,

Government Governance Structure, and Solving the Financial Problems of County-Level Governments). *Guanli shijie* 管理世界 (Management World), 1 (2011).

Jia Junxue 賈俊雪, Guo Qingwang 郭慶旺, and Zhao Xujie 趙旭傑. "Difang zhengfu zhichu xingwei de zhouqixing tezheng ji qi zhidu genyuan" 地方政府支出行為的週期性特徵及其制度根源 (Periodic Features of the Expenditure of Regional Government and the Origin of the System). *Guanli shijie* 管理世界 (Management World), 2 (2012).

Jia Kang 賈康, and Bai Jingming 白景明. "Xian xiang caizheng jiekun yu caizheng tizhi chuangxin" 縣鄉財政解困與財政體制創新 (Resolving County- and Township-Level Government Financial Problems and Financial Institutional Innovation). *Jingji yanjiu* 經濟研究 (Economic Research Journal), 2 (2002).

Li Meng 李猛, and Shen Kunrong 沈坤榮. "Difang zhengfu xingwei dui Zhongguo jingji bodong de yingxiang" 地方政府行為對中國經濟波動的影響 (Effects of Regional Governments' Behavior on China's Economic Fluctuations). *Jingji yanjiu* 經濟研究 (Economic Research Journal), 12 (2010).

Li Shi 李實, and Ding Sai 丁賽. "Zhongguo chengzhen jiaoyu shouyilü de changqi bianduo qushi" 中國城鎮教育收益率的長期變動趨勢 (Trends of the Yield of Education of Urban China in the Long Run). *Zhongguo shehui kexue* 中國社會科學 (Social Sciences in China), 6 (2003).

Li Shi 李實, and Zhao Renwei 趙人偉. "Zhongguo jumin shouru feipei zai yanjiu" 中國居民收入分配再研究 (Further Study of the Redistribution of Income among Citizens in China). *Jingji yanjiu* 經濟研究 (Economic Research Journal), 4 (1999).

Li Ping 李萍. *Zhongguo zhengfu jian caizheng guanxi tujie* 中國政府間財政關係圖解 (Graphic Illustration of the Financial Relationships among Chinese Governments). Beijing: China Financial & Economic Publishing House, 2006.

Li Shaorong 李紹榮, and Geng Ying 耿瑩. "Zhongguo de shuishou jiegou、jingji zengzhang yu shouru feipei" 中國的稅收結構、經濟增長與收入分配 (The Effects of Tax Revenue Structure on Economic Growth and Income Distribution). *Jingji yanjiu* 經濟研究 (Economic Research Journal), 5 (2005).

Li Tao 李濤, and Huang Chunchun 黃純純. "Fenquan, difang gonggong zhichu he Zhongguo jingji zengzhang" 分權、地方公共支出和中國經濟增長 (Decentralization, Regional Public Expenditure, and China's Economic Growth). *Zhongguo Renmin Daxue xuebao* 中國人民大學學報 (Journal of Renmin University of China), 5 (2008).

Li Tao 李濤, and Zhou Ye'an 周業安. "Caizheng fenquan shijiao xia de zhichu jingzeng he Zhongguo jingji zengzhang: Jiyu Zhongguo shengji mianban ziliao de jingyan yanjiu" 財政分權視角下的支出競爭和中國經濟增長:基於中國省級面板資料的經驗研究 (Expenditure Competition and Economic Growth of China from the Perspective of Fiscal Decentralization: A Study Based on the Panel Data of Provinces in China). *Shijie jingji* 世界經濟 (The Journal of World Economy), 11 (2008).

———. "Zhongguo difang zhengfu jian zhichu jingzeng yanjiu——Jiyu Zhongguo shengji mianban ziliao de jingyan zhengju" 中國地方政府間支出競爭研究——基於中國省級面板資料的經驗證據 (Study of the Expenditure Competition among Regional Governments in China: Evidence from the Panel Data of Provinces in China). *Guanli shijie* 管理世界 (Management World), 2 (2009).

Li Xuesong 李雪松, and J. Richard Heckman. "Xuanze biancha、bijiao youshi yu jiaoyu de yizhi huibao: Jiyu Zhongguo weiguan ziliao de shizheng yanjiu" 選擇偏差、比較優勢與教育的異質回報：基於中國微觀資料的實證研究 (Choice Deviation, Comparative advantage, and the Heterogeneous Return on Education: An Empirical Analysis of the Microeconomic Data of China). *Jingji yanjiu* 經濟研究 (Economic Research Journal), 4 (2004).

Li Yongyou 李永友, and Shen Kunrong 沈坤榮. "Caizheng zhichu jiegou、xiangdui pinkun yu jingji zengzhang" 財政支出結構、相對貧困與經濟增長 (Fiscal Expenditure Structure, Relative Poverty, and Economic Growth). *Guanli shijie* 管理世界 (Management World), 11 (2007).

———. "Xiaqu jian jingzeng、celüexing caizheng zhengce yu FDI zengzhang jixiao de quyutezheng" 轄區間競爭、策略性財政政策與FDI增長績效的區域特徵 (Competition among Jurisdictions, Strategical Fiscal Policies, and Regional Characteristics of FDI's Growth Achievements). *Jingji yanjiu* 經濟研究 (Economic Research Journal), 5 (2008).

Li Yongyou 李永友, and Shen Yuping 沈玉平. "Zhuanyi zhifu yu difang caizheng shouzhi juece——Jiyu shengji mianban ziliao de shizheng yanjiu" 轉移支付與地方財政收支決策 —— 基於省級面板資料的實證研究 (Transfer Payments and Decision-Making of Regional Fiscal Expenditure and Revenue: An Empirical Study of the Panel Data of the Provincial Governments). *Guanli shijie* 管理世界 (Management World), 11 (2009).

Liao Chuhui 廖楚輝. "Zhongguo renli ziben he wuzhi ziben de jiegou ji zhengfu jiaoyu touru" 中國人力資本和物質資本的結構及政府教育投入 (Structure of Human and Physical Capital and Government Education Investment in China). *Zhongguo shehui kexue* 中國社會科學 (Social Sciences in China), 1 (2006).

———. "Zhengfu jiaoyu zhichu quyujian bupingheng de dongtai fenxi" 政府教育支出區域間不平衡的動態分析 (Dynamic Analysis of Imbalance in Government Education Expenditure in Different Regions). *Jingji yanjiu* 經濟研究 (Economic Research Journal), 6 (2004)

Liao Chuhui 廖楚暉, and Yu Ke 余可. "Difang zhengfu gonggong zhichu jiegou yu jingji zengzhang —— Jiyu Zhongguo shengji mianban ziliao de shizheng fenxi" 地方政府公共支出結構與經濟增長——基於中國省際面板資料的實證分析 (Structure of the Public Expenditure of Regional Governments and Economic Growth: Empirical Analysis of the Panel Data of Provinces in China). *Caimao jingji* 財貿經濟 (Finance & Trade Economics), 11 (2006).

Liu Xiahui 劉霞輝. "Weishenma Zhongguo jingji bushi guoleng jiushi guore?" 為什麼中國經濟不是過冷就是過熱？(Why is the Economic Fluctuation in China so High?). *Jingji yanjiu* 經濟研究 (Economic Research Journal), 11 (2004).

Liu Xiaolu 劉曉路. "Caizheng fenquan yu jingji zengzhang: Dierdai caizheng fenquan lilun" 財政分權與經濟增長：第二代財政分權理論 (Fiscal Decentralization and Economic Growth: Second Generation Fiscal Decentralization Theories). *Caimao jingji* 財貿經濟 (Finance & Trade Economics), 3 (2007).

Liu Yi 劉怡, and Nie Haifeng 聶海峰. "Jianjieshui fudan dui shouru fenpei de yingxiang fenxi" 間接稅負擔對收入分配的影響分析 (The Effect of Indirect Tax Incidence on Income Distribution). *Jingji yanjiu* 經濟研究 (Economic Research Journal), 5 (2004).

Lou Hong 婁洪. "Changqi jingji zengzhang zhong de gonggong touzi zhengce —— Baohan yiban yongjixing gonggong jichu sheshi ziben cunliang de dongtai jingji zengzhang moxing" 長期經濟增長中的公共投資政策——包含一般擁擠性公共基礎設施資本存量的動態經濟增長模型 (Public Investment Policy in Long-Run Economic Growth: General Congestion Public Infrastructure in Long-run Growth Model). *Jingji yanjiu* 經濟研究 (Economic Research Journal), 3 (2004).

Lu Ming 陸銘, and Chen Zhao 陳釗. "Chengshihua、chengshi qingxiang de jingji zhengce yu chengxiang shouru chaju" 城市化、城市傾向的經濟政策與城鄉收入差 (Urbanization, Urban-Biased Economic Policies, and Urban-Rural Inequality). *Jingji yanjiu* 經濟研究 (Economic Research Journal), 6 (2004).

Luo Chuliang 羅楚亮. "Chengzhen jumin jiaoyu shouyilü ji qi fenbu tezheng" 城鎮居民教育收益率及其分佈特徵 (Return to Education and Its Distribution in Urban China). *Jingji yanjiu* 經濟研究 (Economic Research Journal), 6 (2007).

Luo Dan 羅丹, and Chen Jie 陳潔. "Xianxiang caizheng de kunjing yu chulu —— Guanyu jiu xian (shi) ershi yu ge xiangzhen de shizheng fenxi" 縣鄉財政的困境與出路——關於9縣（市）20餘個鄉鎮的實證分析 (Financial Difficulties of County- and Township-Level Governments and The Solution: Empirical Analysis of Nine Counties and More than Twenty Townships). *Guanli shijie* 管理世界 (Management World), 3 (2009).

Ministry of Finance of the People's Republic of China. "2010 nian caizheng shouzhi qingkuang" 2010年財政收支情況 (Fiscal Expenditure and Revenue 2010), http://gks.mof.gov.cn/zhengfuxinxi/tongjishuju/201101/t20110120_421479.html.

Ping Xinqiao 平新喬, and Bai Jie 白潔. "Zhongguo caizheng fenquan he difang gonggong wupin de gonggei" 中國財政分權和地方公共物品的供給 (Fiscal Decentralization and Demand for and Supply of Public Goods in China). *Caimao jingji* 財貿經濟 (Finance & Trade Economics), 2 (2006).

Qiao Baoyun 喬寶雲. *Zengzhang yu jundeng de qushe —— Zhongguo caizheng fenquan zhengce de yanjiu* 增長與均等的取捨——中國財政分權政策研究 (The Trade-Off between Growth and Equity). Beijing: People's Press, 2002.

Qiao Baoyun 喬寶雲, Fan Jianyong 范劍勇, and Feng Xingyuan 馮興元. "Zhongguo de caizheng fenquqan yu xiaoxue yiwu jiaoyu" 中國的財政分權與小學義務教育 (Fiscal Decentralization and Compulsory Primary Education in China). *Zhongguo shehui kexue* 中國社會科學 (Social Sciences in China), 6 (2005).

Qiao Baoyun 喬寶雲, Fan Jianyong 范劍勇, and Peng Jiming 彭驥鳴. "Zhengfu jian zhuanyi zhifu yu difang caizheng nuli" 政府間轉移支付與地方財政努力 (Intergovernmental Transfer Payments and Financial Efforts of Regional Governments). *Guanli shijie* 管理世界 (Management World), 3 (2006).

Shen Kunrong 沈坤榮, and Fu Wenlin 付文林. "Shuishou jingzheng、diqu boyi ji qi zengzhang jixiao" 稅收競爭、地區博弈及其增長績效 (Tax Competition, Region Game and their Efficiency of Growth). *Jingji yanjiu* 經濟研究 (Economic Research Journal), 6 (2006).

Shen Kunrong 沈坤榮, and Sun Wenjie 孫文傑. "Touzi xiaolü, ziben xingcheng yu hongguan jingji bodong —— Jiyu jinrong fazhan shijiao de shizheng yanjiu" 投資效率，資本形成與宏觀經濟波動——基於金融發展視角的實證研究 (Investment Efficiency, Capital Formation, and Macroeconomic Fluctuations: An Empirical Analysis from the Perspective of Financial Development). *Zhongguo shehui kexue* 中國社會科學 (Social Sciences in China), 6 (2004).

Shi Youqi 石佑啟, and Yang Zhikun 楊治坤. "Lun woguo xingzheng zuzhi jiegou de youhua" 論我國行政組織結構的優化 (Optimization of the Administrative

Structure of China). *Hubei Minzu Xueyuan xuebao (zhexue shehuikexue ban)* 湖北民族學院學報（哲學社會科學版）(Journal of Hubei Institute for Nationalities(Philosophy and Social Sciences)), 1 (2010).

Shi Ji 史記. "Zhengfu guimo linian yu woguo zhengfu jigou gaige" 政府規模理念與我國政府機構改革 (Chinese Government's Concept of Size and Reform of Government Institutions). *Guojia xingzheng xueyuan xuebao* 國家行政學院學報 (Journal of China National School of Administration), 3 (2001).

Sun Qunli 孫群力. "Diqu chaju, caizheng fenquan yu Zhongguo difang zhengfu guimo" 地區差距，財政分權與中國地方政府規模 (Regional Gap, Fiscal Decentralization, and the Size of China's Regional Governments). *Caimao jingji* 財貿經濟 (Finance & Trade Economics), 7 (2009).

Sun Xueyu 孫學玉, and Wu Kaichang 伍開昌. "Dangdai Zhongguo xingzheng jiegou bianpinghua de zhanlüe gouxiang —— Yi shiguanxian tizhi wei li" 當代中國行政結構扁平化的戰略構想——以市管縣體制為例 (Strategic Concept of Contemporary China's Flat Administrative Structure: Example from the City-Level Governance of Counties). *Zhongguo xingzheng guanli* 中國行政管理 (Chinese Public Administration), 3 (2004).

Tao Ran 陶然, and Liu Mingxing 劉明興. "Zhongguo chengxiang shouru chaju、difang zhengfu kaizhi ji caizheng zizhu" 中國城鄉收入差距、地方政府開支及財政自主 (China's Urban-Rural Income Gap, Regional Government Expenditure, and Financial Autonomy). *Shijie jingji wenhui* 世界經濟文匯 (World Economic Papers), 2 (2007).

Wan Guanghua 萬廣華, Lu Ming 陸銘, and Chen Zhao 陳釗. "Quanqiuhua yu diqu jian shouru chaju: Laizi Zhongguo de zhengju" 全球化與地區間收入差距：來自中國的證據 (Globalization and Regional Income Gap: Evidence in China). *Zhongguo shehui kexue* 中國社會科學 (Social Sciences in China), 3 (2005).

Wang Haigang 王海港, Li Shi 李實, and Liu Jingjun 劉京軍. "Chengzhen jumin jiaoyu shouyilü de diqu chayi ji qi jieshi" 城鎮居民教育收益率的地區差異及其解釋 (The Differences of Rate of Return to Schooling in Urban China and an Explanation). *Jingji yanjiu* 經濟研究 (Economic Research Journal), 8 (2007).

Wang Shoukun 王守坤, and Ren Baoping 任保平. "Zhongguo shengji zhengfu jian caizheng celüexing fanying de shibie yu jiexi: 1978–2006" 中國省級政府間財政策略性反應的識別與解析：1978－2006 (The Identification and Analysis of the Effect of the Financial Competition between China's Provincial Governments between 1978 and 2006). *Guanli shijie* 管理世界 (Management World), 11 (2008).

Wang Wei 王瑋. "Caizheng fenquan yu woguo de hongguan jingji wending" 財政分權與我國的宏觀經濟穩定 (Fiscal Decentralization and Macroeconomic Stability in China). *Caimao yanjiu* 財貿研究 (Finance and Trade Research), 4 (2003).

Wang Xianbin 王賢彬, and Xu Xianxiang 徐現祥. "Difang guanyuan laiyuan、quxiang、renqi yu jingji zengzhang——Laizi Zhongguo shengzhang shengwei shuji de zhengju" 地方官員來源、去向、任期與經濟增長——來自中國省長省委書記的證據 (Reassignment and Office Term of Regional Government Officials, and Economic Growth: Evidence from the Provincial Secretaries of China). *Guanli shijie* 管理世界 (Management World), 3 (2008).

Wang Xiaolong 王小龍. "Zhongguo difang zhengfu zhili jiegou gaige: Yizhong caizheng shiejiao de fenxi" 中國地方政府治理結構改革：一種財政視角的分析 (Reform of China's Regional Governance Structure: Analysis from the Financial Perspective). *Xinhua wenzhai* 新華文摘 (Digest of Chinese Journals), 17 (2004).

———. "Xianxiang caizheng jiekun yu zhengfu gaige: Mubiao xiangrong yu lujing sheji" 縣鄉財政解困與政府改革：目標相容與路徑設計 (Solving the Financial Problems of County- and Township-Level and Government Reform: Compatibility of Goals and Roadmap). *Caimao jingji* 財貿經濟 (Finance & Trade Economics), 7 (2006).

Wang Xiaolu 王小魯, and Fan Gang 樊綱. "Zhongguo shouru chaju de zoushi he yingxiang yinsu fenxi" 中國收入差距的走勢和影響因素分析 (Income Inequality in China and Its Influential Factors). *Jingji yanjiu* 經濟研究 (Economic Research Journal), 10 (2005).

Wang Yongqin 王永欽, Zhang Yan 張晏, Zhang Yuan 章元, Chen Zhao 陳釗, and Lu Ming 陸銘. "Zhongguo de daguo fazhan daolu——Lun fenquanshi gaige de deshi" 中國的大國發展道路——論分權式改革的得失 (On China's Development Model: The Costs and Benefits of China's Decentralization Approach to Transition). *Jingji yanjiu* 經濟研究 (Economic Research Journal), 1 (2007).

Wu Jinglian 吳敬璉. *Dangdai Zhongguo jingji gaige* 當代中國經濟改革 (Economic Reform in Contemporary China). Shanghai Far East Publishers, 2003.

Xie Xuren 謝旭人. *Zhongguo caizheng gaige sanshinian* 中國財政改革三十年 (Thirty Years of Financial Reform in China). China Financial & Economic Publishing House, 2008.

Yang Canming 楊燦明, and Sun Qunli 孫群力. "Waibu fengxian dui Zhongguo difang zhengfu guimo de yingxiang" 外部風險對中國地方政府規模的影響 (The Effects of External Risk on Local Government Size of China: Theory and Evidence). *Jingji yanjiu* 經濟研究 (Economic Research Journal), 9 (2008).

Yang Jianfang 楊建芳, Gong Liutang 龔六堂, and Zhang Qinghua 張慶華. "Renli ziben xingcheng ji qi dui jingji zengzhang de yingxiang——Yige baohan jiaoyu he jiankang touru de neisheng zengzhang moxing ji qi jianyan" 人力資本形成及其對經濟增長的影響——一個包含教育和健康投入的內生增長模型及其檢驗 (Human Capital Formation and its Effects on Economic Growth). *Guanli shijie* 管理世界 (Management World), 5 (2006).

Yin Desheng 殷德生. "Zuiyou caizheng fenquan yu jingji zengzhang" 最優財政分權與經濟增長 (Optimal Fiscal Decentralization and Economic Growth). *Shijie jingji* 世界經濟 (The Journal of World Economy), 1 (2004).

Yuan Fei 袁飛, Tao Ren 陶然, Xu Zhigang 徐志剛, and Liu Xingming 劉明興. "Caizheng jiquan guocheng zhong de zhuanyi zhifu he caizheng gongyang renkou guimo pengzhang" 財政集權過程中的轉移支付和財政供養人口規模膨脹 (Transfer Payments and the Expansion of the Population of Fiscal Dependents In Fiscal Centralization). *Jingji yanjiu* 經濟研究 (Economic Research Journal), 5 (2008).

Zhang Linxiu 張林秀, Luo Renfu 羅仁福, Liu Chengfang 劉承芳, and Scott Rozelle. "Zhongguo nongcun shequ gonggong wupin touzi de jueding yinsu fenxi" 中國農村社區公共物品投資的決定因素分析 (An Analysis on the Determinants of Public Good Investment in China's Rural Communities). *Jingji yanjiu* 經濟研究 (Economic Research Journal), 11 (2005).

Zhang Gang 張鋼, and Duan Che 段澈. "Woguo difang caizheng zhichu jiegou yu difang jingji zengzhang guanxi de shizheng yanjiu" 我國地方財政支出結構與地方經濟增長關係的實證研究 (Positive Analysis on Local Fiscal Expenditure Structures and Local Economic Growth in China). *Zhejiang Daxue xuebao* 浙江大學學報 (Journal of Zhejiang University), 2 (2006).

Zhang Jun 張軍, and Gao Yuan 高遠. "Guanyuan renqi、yidi jiaoliu yu jingji zengzhang——Laizi shengji jingyan de ziliao" 官員任期、異地交流與經濟增長——來自省級經驗的資料 (Term of Office, Communications and Exchange, and Economic Growth: Experience of Provincial Governments). *Jingji yanjiu* 經濟研究 (Economic Research Journal), 11 (2007).

Zhang Qi 章奇, Mi Jianwei 米建偉, and Huang Jikun 黃季焜. "Shouru liudongxing he shouru fenpei: Laizi Zhongguo nongcun de jingyan ziliao" 收入流動性和收入分配：來自國農村的經驗資料 (Income Mobility and Income Distribution: Evidence from Rural China). *Jingji yanjiu* 經濟研究 (Economic Research Journal), 11 (2007).

Zhang Yan 張晏, and Gong Liutang 龔六堂. "Diqu chayi、yaosu liudong yu caizheng fenquan" 地區差異、要素流動與財政分權 (Interregional Disparity, Factor

Mobility, and Fiscal Decentralization). *Jingji yanjiu* 經濟研究 (Economic Research Journal), 7 (2004).

———. "Fenshuizhi gaige、caizheng fenquan yu Zhongguo jingji zengzhang" 分稅制改革、財政分權與中國經濟增長 (Tax Sharing Reform, Fiscal Decentralization, and Economic Growth in China). *Jingjixue (jikan)* 經濟學（季刊）(China Economic Quarterly), 1 (2005).

Zhao Renwei 趙人偉. "Woguo jumin shouru fenpei he caichan fenbu wenti fenxi" 我國居民收入分配和財產分布問題分析 (The Problem of Income and Asset Distribution in China). *Dangdai caijing* 當代財經 (Contemporary Finance and Economics), 7 (2007).

Zhao Wenzhe 趙文哲, and Zhou Ye'an 周業安. "Jiyu shengji mianban de caizheng zhichu yu tonghuo pengzhang guanxi yanjiu" 基於省際面板的財政支出與通貨膨脹關係研究 (Research on the Relationship between Fiscal Expenditure and Inflation Based on Provincial Panel Data). *Jingji yanjiu* 經濟研究 (Economic Research Journal), 10 (2009).

Economic Growth Frontier Subject Team (Institute of Economics, CASS). "Caizheng zhengce de gonggei xiaoying yu jingji fazhan" 財政政策的供給效應與經濟發展 (The Supply Effects of Fiscal Policy and Economic Development). *Jingji yanjiu* 經濟研究 (Economic Research Journal), 9 (2004).

———. "Guoji ziben liudong、jingji niuqu yu hongguan wending" 國際資本流動、經濟扭曲與宏觀穩定 (International Capital Flows, Economic Distortions, and Macroeconomic Stability: The Trend Analysis of Current Economic Growth). *Jingji yanjiu* 經濟研究 (Economic Research Journal), 4 (2005).

Zhou Li'an 周黎安. "Jinsheng boyi zhong zhengfu guanyuan de jili he hezuo" 晉升博弈中政府官員的激勵和合作 (The Incentive and Cooperation of Government Officials in the Political Tournaments: An Interpretation of the Prolonged Local Protectionism and Duplicative Investments in China). *Jingji yanjiu* 經濟研究 (Economic Research Journal), 6 (2004).

———. "Zhongguo difang guanyuan de jinsheng jinbiaosai moshi yanjiu" 中國地方官員的晉升錦標賽模式研究 (Governing China's Local Officials: An Analysis of Promotion Tournament Model). *Jingji yanjiu* 經濟研究 (Economic Research Journal), 7 (2007).

Zhou Li'an 周黎安, and Tao Jing 陶婧. "Zhengfu guimo, shichanghua yu diqu fubai wenti yanjiu" 政府規模，市場化與地區腐敗問題研究 (Government Size, Market Development and Corruption). *Jingji yanjiu* 經濟研究 (Economic Research Journal), 5 (2009).

Zhou Ye'an 周業安. "Difang zhengfu jingzheng yu jingji zengzhang" 地方政府競爭與經濟增長 (Local Government Competition and Economic Growth). *Zhongguo Renmin Daxue xuebao* 中國人民大學學報 (Journal of Renmin University of China), 1 (2003).

Zhou Ye'an 周業安, and Zhang Quan 章泉. "Caizheng fenquan、jingji zengzhang he bodong" 財政分權、經濟增長和波動 (Financial Decentralization, Economic Growth and Fluctuations). *Guanli shijie* 管理世界 (Management World), 3 (2008).

Zhu Hengpeng 朱恒鵬. "Fenquanhua gaige、caizheng jili he gongyouzhi qiye gaige" 分權化改革、財政激勵和公有制企業改制 (Reform of Decentralization, Financial Incentives, and Reform of Public Companies). *Shijie jingji* 世界經濟 (The Journal of World Economy), 12 (2004).

Zhuang Ziyin 莊子銀, and Zou Wei 鄒薇. "Gonggong zhichu nengfou cujin jingji zengzhang" 公共支出能否促進經濟增長 (Does Public Expenditure Boost Economic Growth? An Analysis of China's Experience). *Guanli shijie* 管理世界 (Management World), 7 (2003).

Zou Hengfu 鄒恒甫, and Gong Liutang 龔六堂. "Zhengfu huafei、shuishou、zhengfu zhuanyi zhifu he neisheng jingji zengzhang" 政府花費、稅收、政府轉移支付和內生經濟增長 (Public Expenditures, Taxes, Federal Transfer, and Endogenous Growth). *Zhongguo kexue jijin* 中國科學基金 (Bulletin of National Natural Science Foundation of China), 1 (2000).

———. "Zuiyou shuilü, zhengfu zhuanyi zhifu yu jingji zengzhang" 最優稅率, 政府轉移支付與經濟增長 (Optimal Tax Rate, Government Transfer Payments, and Economic Growth). *Shuliang jingji jishu jingji yanjiu* 數量經濟技術經濟研究 (The Journal of Quantitative & Technical Economics), 1 (2002).

English materials:

Abramovitz, Moses, and Paul A. David. "American Macroeconomic Growth in the Era of Knowledge-Based Progress: The Long-Run Perspective." In *The Cambridge Economic History of the United States*, edited by Stanley L. Engerman and Robert E. Gallman. Cambridge, New York, NY: Cambridge University Press, 2000.

Acemoglu, Daron, and James A. Robinson. "The Political Economy of the Kuznets Curve." *Review of Development Economics*, 6 (2002): 183–203.

Agell, Jonas, Thomas Lindh, and Henry Ohlsson. "Growth and the Public Sector: A Critical Review Essay." *European Journal of Political Economy*, 13 (1997): 33–52.

———. "Growth and the Public Sector: A Replay." *European Journal of Political Economy*, 15 (1999): 359–366.

Agénor, Pierre-Richard. "Infrastructure, Public Education and Growth with Congestion Costs." Working Paper, Centre for Growth and Business Cycle Research, University of Manchester, 2005.

Bibliography

Ahluwalia, Montek S., Nicholas G. Carter, and Hollis B. Chenery. "Growth and Poverty in Developing Countries." *Journal of Development Economics*, 6 (1976): 299–341.

Alesina, Alberto, Reza Baqir, and William Easterly. "Public Goods and Ethnic Divisions." *Quarterly Journal of Economics*, 114 (1999):1214–84.

Alesina, Alberto, Arnaud Devleeschauwer, William Easterly, Sergio Kurlat, and Romain Wacziarg. "Fractionalization." *Journal of Economic Growth*, 8 (2003): 155–94.

Alesina, Alberto, and Enrico Spolaore. *The Size of Nations*. MIT Press, 2003.

Alesina, Alberto, and Romain Wacziarg. "Openness, Country Size and Government." *Journal of Public Economics*, 69 (1998): 305-321.

Alt, James E., and Robert C. Lowry. "Divided Government, Fiscal Institutions, and Budget Deficits: Evidence from the States." *American Political Science Review*, 88 (1994): 811–28.

Alt, James E., David Dreyer Lassen, and David Skilling. "Fiscal Transparency, Gubernatorial Popularity, and the Scale of Government: Evidence from the State." *State Politics and Policy Quarterly*, 2 (2002); 230–50.

Anand, Sudhir, and S. M. R. Kanbur. "The Kuznets Process and the Inequality-Development Relationship", *Journal of Development Economics*, 40 (1993): 25–52.

Anselin, Luc. *Spatial Econometrics: Methods and Models*. Dordrecht: Kluwer Academic Publishers, 1988.

Anselin, Luc, and Anil K. Bera. "Spatial Dependence in Linear Regression Models with an Application to Spatial Econometrics." In *Handbooks of Applied Economics Statistics*. Springer-Verlag, 1998.

Aragon, Fernando, and Vilma Gayoso. "Intergovernmental Transfers and Fiscal Effort in Peruvian Local Governments." Working Paper, London School of Economics and Political Science, 2005.

Arcalean, Calin, Gerhard Glomm, Ioana C. Schiopu, and Jens Suedekum. "Public Budget Composition, Fiscal (De)Centralization and Welfare." IZA Discussion Paper No. 2626, 2008.

Ardagna, Silva. "Fiscal Stabilizations: When do They Work and Why?" *European Economic Review*, 48 (2004): 1047–74.

Arellano, Manuel, and Stephen Bond. "Some Tests of Specification for Panel Data: Monte Carlo Evidence and an Application to Employment Equations." *Review of Economic Studies*, 58 (1991): 277–97.

Arellano, Manuel, and Olympia Bover. "Another Look at the Instrumental Variable Estimation of Error-Components Models." *Journal of Econometrics*, 68 (1995): 29–51.

Arrow, Kenneth J., and Mordecai Kurz. *Public Investment, the Rate of Return, and Optimal Fiscal Policy*. The Johns Hopkins University Press, 1970.

Aschauer, David Alan. "Is Public Expenditure Productive?" *Journal of Monetary Economics*, 23 (1989): 177–200.

Aschauer, David Alan. "Why Is Infrastructure Important?" In *Is There A Shortfall in Public Capital Incestment?* edited by Alicia H. Munnell. Vol. 34 of *Conference Series*, 21–50. Boston: Federal Reserve Bank of Boston, 1990.

Austen-Smith, David. "Redistributing Income under Proportional Representation." *Journal of Political Economy*, 108 (2000): 1235–69.

Backus, David K., Patrick J. Kehoe, and Finn E. Kydland. "International Business Cycles: Theory vs. Evidence." *Federal Reserve Bank of Minneapolis Quarterly Review*, 17(4) (1993): 14–29

Bahl, Roy W. *Financing State and Local Government in the 1980's*. New York: Oxford University Press, 1984.

Baicker, Katherine. "The Spillover Effects of State Spending." *Journal of Public Economics*, 89 (2005): 529–44.

Bairam, Erkin I. "Level of Aggregation, Variable Elasticity and Wagner's Law." *Economics Letters*, 48 (1995): 341–44.

Baleiras, Rui Nuno. "To Fragment or to Consolidate Jurisdictions: The Optimal Architecture of Government." Working Paper, Universidade Nova de Lisboa, 2001.

Baltagi, Badi H., and Ping X. Wu. "Unequally Spaced Panel Data Regressions with AR(1) Disturbance." *Econometric Theory*, 15 (1991): 814–823.

Baqir, Reza. "Districting and Government Overspending." *Journal of Political Economy*, 110 (2002): 1318–54.

Baron, David P. "Majoritarian Incentives, Pork Barrel Programs, and Procedural Control." *American Journal of Political Science*, 35 (1991): 57–90.

Barro, Robert J. "Economic Growth in a Cross-Section of Countries." *Quarterly Journal of Economics*, 106 (1991): 407–43.

———. "Government Spending in A Simple Model of Endogenous Growth." *Journal of Political Economy*, 98 (1990): 103–26.

Barro, Robert J., and Xavier Sala-i-Martin. *Economic Growth*. Cambridge, Massachusetts: MIT Press, 1999.

———. "Public Finance in Models of Economic Growth." *Review of Economic Studies*, 59 (1992): 645–61.

Bayoumi, Tamim, and Michael W. Klein. "A Provincial View of Capital Mobility." NBER Working Paper 5115, 1995.

Bayoumi, Tamim, and Ronald McDonald. "On the Optimality of Consumption across Canadian Provinces." CEPR Discussion Paper 1030, 1994.

Benabou, Roland. "Inequality and Growth." In *NBER Macroeconomics Annual 1996*, edited by Ben S. Bernanke and Julio J. Rotemberg. MIT Press, 1996.

Bennett, John, and Huw David Dixon. "Monetary Policy and Credit in China: A Theoretical Analysis." *Journal of Macroeconomics*, 23 (2001): 97–314.

Besley, Timothy, and Anne C. Case. "Incumbent Behaviour: Vote Seeking, Tax Setting and Yardstick Competition." *American Economic Review*, 85 (1995): 25–45.

Bird, Richard M. "Wagner's Law of Expanding State Activity." *Public Finance*, 26 (1971): 1–26.

Biswal, Bagala, Urvashi Dhawan, and Hooi-Yean Lee. "Testing Wagner Versus Keynes Using Disaggregated Public Expenditure Data for Canada." *Applied Economics*, 31 (1999) 1283–91.

Blanchard, Olivier, and Andrei Shleifer. "Federalism with and without Political Centralization: China versus Russia." NBER Working Paper 7616, 2000.

Blankenau, William F., and Nicole B. Simpson. "Public Education Expenditures and Growth." *Journal of Development Economics*, 73 (2004): 583–605.

Blankenau, William F., Nicole B. Simpson, and Marc Tomljanovich. "Public Education Expenditures, Taxation and Growth: Linking Data to Theory." *American Economic Review*, 97 (2007): 393–97.

Blundell, Richard, and Stephen Bond. "Initial Conditions and Moment Restrictions in Dynamic Panel Data Models." *Journal of Econometrics*, 87 (1998): 115–43.

Bond, Stephen. "Dynamic Panel Data Models: A Guide to Micro Data Methods and Practice." *Portuguese Economic Journal*, 1(2) (2002): 141-162.

Borcherding, Thomas E., and Robert T. Deacon. "The Demand for the Services of Non-Federal Governments." *American Economic Review*, 62 (1972): 891–901.

Borck, Rainald, Marco Caliendo, and Viktor Steiner. "Fiscal Competition and the Composition of Public Spending: Theory and Evidence." IZA Discussion Papers 2428, 2006.

———. "Fiscal Competition and the Composition of Public Spending: Theory and Evidence." *FinanaArchiv (Public Finance Analysis)*, 63 (2007): 264–77.

Bordignon, Massimo, Floriana Cerniglia, and Federico Revelli. "In Search of Yardstick Competition: A Spatial Analysis of Italian Municipality Property Tax Setting." *Journal of Urban Economics*, 54 (2003): 199–217.

Brandt, Loren, and Xiaodong Zhu. "Redistribution in a Decentralized Economy: Growth and Inflation in China under Reform." *Journal of Political Economy*, 108(2) (2000): 422–39.

———. "Soft Budget Constraints and Inflation Cycles: A Positive Model of the Macro-Dynamics in China during Transition." *Journal of Development Economics*, 64 (2001): 437–57.

Brennan, Geoffrey, and James M. Buchanan. *The Power to Tax*. Cambridge: Cambridge University Press, 1980.

Bristow, John A. and Declan McDonagh. *Public Expenditure: The Key Issues*. Institute of Public Administration, 1986.

Brown, Stephen P. A., Kathy J. Hayes, and Lori L. Taylor. "State and Local Policy, Factor Markets, and Regional Growth." *The Review of Regional Studies*, 33 (2003): 40–60.

Brown, Charles C., and Wallace E. Oates. "Assistance to the Poor in a Federal System." *Journal of Public Economics*, 32 (1987): 307–30.

Bruce, Neil. *Public Finance and the American Economy*. Addison-Wesley Longman, Inc., 2001.

Brueckner, Jan K. "Strategic Interaction among Governments: An Overview of Empirical Studies." *International Regional Science Review*, 26 (2003): 175–88.

———. "Welfare Reform and the Race to the Bottom: Theory and Evidence." *Southern Economic Journal*, 66 (2000): 505–25.

Buchanan, James M., and Richard A. Musgrave. *Public Finance and Public Choice: Two Contrasting Visions of the State*. Cambridge: MIT Press, 1999.

Bucovetsky, Sam, and Michael Smart. "The Efficiency Consequences of Local Revenue Equalization: Tax Competition and Tax Distortions." *Journal of Public Economic Theory*, 8 (2006): 119–44.

Büttner, Thiess. "The Incentive Effect of Fiscal Equalization Transfers on Tax Policy." Working Paper, 2004.

Cameron, David R. "The Expansion of the Public Economy: A Comparative Analysis." *American Political Science Review*, 72 (1978): 1243–61.

Card, David, and Alan B. Krueger. "School Resources and Students Outcomes: An Overview of the Literature and New Evidence from North and South Carolina." *Journal of Economic Perspectives*, 10 (1996): 31–50.

Case, Anne C., Harvey S. Rosen, and James R. Hines, Jr. "Budget Spillovers and Fiscal Policy Interdependence: Evidence from the States." *Journal of Public Economics*, 52 (1993): 285–307.

Chen, Been-Lon. "Economic Growth with an Optimal Public Spending Composition." *Oxford Economic Paper*, 58 (2005): 123–36.

Chletsos, Michael, and Christos Kollias. "Testing Wagner's Law using Disaggregated Public Expenditure Data in the Case of Greece: 1958–93." *Applied Economics*, 29 (1997): 371–77.

Courakis, Anthony S., Fatima Moura-Roque, and George Tridimas. "Public Expenditure Growth in Greece and Portugal: Wagner's Law and Beyond." *Applied Economics*, 25 (1993): 125–34.

Creedy, John, and Norman Gemmell. "Publicly Financed Education in an Endogenous Growth Model." *Journal of Economic Studies*, 32(2) (2005): 114-131

Creedy, John, and Solmaz Moslehi. "The Optimal Composition of Government Expenditure." Research Paper 1008, The University of Melbourne, 2007.

Crucini, Mario J. "On International and National Dimensions of Risk Sharing." *The Review of Economics and Statistics*, 81(1) (1999): 73–84.

Cullison, William E. "Public Investment and Economic Growth." *Federal Reserve Bank of Richmond Economic Quarterly*, 79 (1993): 19–33.

Dahlby, Bev. "The Incentive Effects of Fiscal Equalization." Paper presented at the AIMS/MEI/FCPP Conference on "Equalization: Welfare Trap or Helping Hand?" Montreal, October 25, 2001.

Dahlberg, Matz, and Karin Edmark. "Is There a 'Race-to-the-Bottom' in the Setting of Welfare Benefit Levels? Evidence from a Policy Intervention." *Journal of Public Economics*, 92 (2008): 1193–1209.

Davoodi, Hamid R., and David A. Grigorian. "Tax Potential vs. Tax Effort: A Cross-Country Analysis of Armenia's Stubbornly Low Tax Collection." IMF Working Paper No. 07/106, 2007.

De la Croix, David, and Philippe Michel. *A Theory of Economic Growth: Dynamics and Policy in Overlapping Generations*. Cambridge University Press, 2002.

De la Fuente, Angel. "Convergence Equations and Income Dynamics: The Source of OECD Convergence, 1970-1995." *Economica*, 70 (2003): 655–71.

Devarajan, Shantayanan, Vinaya Swaroop, and Heng-fu Zou. "The Composition of Public Expenditure and Economic Growth." *Journal of Monetary Economics*, 37 (1996): 313–44.

Diebold, Francis X., and Glenn D. Rudebusch. "Measuring Business Cycles: A Modern Perspective." *Review of Economics and Statistics*, 78 (1996): 67–77.

Docquier, D., and O. Paddison. "Growth and Equality Effects of Pension Plans." *Journal of Macroeconomics*, 25 (2003): 47–71.

Driskill, R. A., and A. W. Horowitz. "Investment in Hierarchical Human Capital." *Review of Development Economics* 6 (2002): 48–58.

Easterly, William, and Ross Levine. "Africa's Growth Tragedy: Policies and Ethnic Divisions." *Quarterly Journal of Economics*, 111 (1997): 1203–50.

Easterly, William, and Sergio Rebelo. "Fiscal policy and Economic Growth: An Empirical Investigation." *Journal of Monetary Economics*, 32 (1993): 417–58.

Eberts, Randall W., and Timothy J. Gronberg. "Structure, Conduct, and Performance in the Local Public Sector." *National Tax Journal*, 43 (1990): 165–73.

Egger, Peter, Marko Köthenbürger, and Michael Smart. "Do Fiscal Transfers Alleviate Business Tax Competition? Evidence from Germany." CESifo Working Paper, 2006.

Ehdaie, Jaber. "Fiscal Decentralization and the Size of the Government: An Extension with Evidence from Cross-Country Data." Policy Research Department Working Paper, World Bank, 1994.

Elhorst, J. Paul, and Sandy Fréret. "Evidence of Political Yardstick Competition in France Using a Two-regime Spatial Durbin Model with Fixed Effects." *Journal of Regional Science*, 49 (2009): 931–51.

Ermini, Barbara, and Raffaella Santolini. "Horizontal Interaction on Local Councils' Expenditures: Evidence from Italy." Working paper, 2007.

Fan, Shenggen, Linxiu Zhang, and Xiaobo Zhang. "Growth, Inequality, and Poverty in Rural China: The Role of Public Investments." International Food Policy Research Institute, Research Report 125, 2002.

Fatás, Antonio, and Ilian Mihov. "Government Size and Automatic Stabilizers: International and Intranational Evidence." *Journal of International Economics*, 55 (2001): 3–28.

Feldstein, Martin, and Marian Vaillant. "Can State Taxes Redistribute Income?" *Journal of Public Economics*, 68 (1998): 369–96.

Feld, Lars P., Gebhard. Kirchgässner, and Christoph A. Schaltegger. "Decentralized Taxation and the Size of Government: Evidence from Swiss State and Local Governments." CESifo Working Paper No. 1087, 2003.

Feltenstein, Andrew, and Shigeru Iwata. "Decentralization and Macroeconomic Performance in China: Regional Autonomy Has Its Costs." *Journal of Development Economics*, 76 (2005): 481–501.

Figlio, David N., Van W. Kolpin, and William E. Reid. "Do States Play Welfare Games?" *Journal of Urban Economics*, 46 (1999): 437–54.

Fiva, Jon H. "New Evidence on the Impact of Fiscal Decentralization on the Size and Composition of Government Spending." *Public Finance Analysis*, 62 (2006): 250–80.

Fiva, Jon H., and Jørn Rattsø. "Local Choice of Property Taxation: Evidence from Norway." *Public Choice*, 132 (2007): 457–70.

———. "Welfare Competition in Norway: Norms and Expenditures." *European Journal Economy*, 22 (2006): 202–22.

Fölster, Stefan, and Magnus Henrekson. "Growth Effects of Government Expenditure and Taxation in Rich Countries." *European Economic Review*, 45 (2001): 1501–20.

Forbes, Kevin F., and Ernest M. Zampelli. "Is Leviathan a Mythical Beast?" *American Economic Review*, 79 (1989): 568–77.

Fortin, Nicole M. "Higher-Education Policies and the College Wage Premium: Cross-State Evidence from the 1990s." *American Economic Review*, 96 (2006): 959-987.

Gabe, Todd. "Local Industry Agglomeration and New Business Activity." *Growth and Change*, 34 (2003): 17–39.

Galí, Jordi. "Government Size and Macroeconomic Stability." *European Economic Review*, 38 (1998): 117–32.

Gamkar, Shama, and Wallace Oates. "Asymmetries in the Response to Increases and Decreases in Intergovernmental Grants: Some Empirical Findings." *National Tax Journal*, 49 (1996): 501–12.

García-Peñalosa, Cecilia, and Stephen J. Turnovsky. "Growth, Income Inequality, and Fiscal Policy: What are the Relevant Tradeoffs?" *Journal of Money, Credit and Banking*, 39 (2005): 369–94.

Gilbert, Guy, and Pierre Picard. "Incentives and Optimal Size of Local Jurisdictions." *European Economic Review*, 40 (1996): 19–41.

Gilligan, Thomas W., and John G. Matsusaka. "Deviations from Constituent Interests: The Role of Legislative Structure and Political Parties in the States." *Economic Inquiry*, 33 (2001): 383–401.

Glomm, Gerhard, and B. Ravikumar. "Opting Out of Publicly Provided Services: A Majority Voting Result." *Social Choice and Welfare*, 15 (1998): 187–99.

———. "Public Education and Income Inequality." *European Journal of Political Economy*, 19 (2003): 289–300.

———. "Public versus Private Investment in Human Capital: Endogenous Growth and Income Inequality." *Journal of Political Economy*, 100 (1992): 813–34.

Goldin, Claudia and Lawrence F. Katz. "The Legacy of U.S. Educational Leadership: Notes on Distribution and Economic Growth in the 20th Century." *American Economic Review*, 91 (2001): 18–23.

Gong, Liutang, and Heng-fu Zou. "Optimal Taxation and Intergovernmental Transfer in a Dynamic Model with Multiple Levels of Government." *Journal of Economic Dynamics and Control*, 26 (2002): 1975–2003.

Gordon, Roger H. "An Optimal Taxation Approach to Fiscal Federalism." *Quarterly Journal of Economics*, 98 (1983): 567–86.

Gramlich, Edward. M. "A Policymaker's Guide to Fiscal Decentralization." *National Tax Journal*, 46 (1993): 229–35.

———. "Federalism and Federal Deficit Reduction." *National Tax Journal*, 40 (1987): 299–313.

Greedy, John, and Norman Gemmell. "Publicly Financed Education in an Endogenous Growth Model." Working Paper No. 02/24, New Zealand Treasury, 2002.

Gregory, Allan W., Allen C. Head, and Jacques Raynauld. "Measuring World Business Cycles." *International Economic Review*, 3 (1997): 677–701.

Grossman, Philip J. "Fiscal Decentralization and Government Size: An Extension." *Public Choice*, 62 (1989): 63–69.

Gupta, Sanjeev, Luiz de Mello, and Raju Sharan. "Corruption and Military Spending." *European Journal of Political Economy*, 17 (2001): 749–77.

Häge, Frank Michael. "Determinants of Government Size: The Capacity for Partisan Policy under Political Constraints." Unpublished Diploma Thesis, Department of Politics and Mangement, University of Konstanz, 2003.

Hansen, Bruce E. "Threshold Effects in Non-Dynamic Panels: Estimation, Testing and Inference." *Journal of Econometrics*, 93 (1999): 345–68.

Hayashi, Fumio. *Econometrics*. Princeton: Princeton University Press, 2000.

Heshmati, Almas. "On the Causality between GDP and Health Care Expenditure in Augmented Solow Growth Model." *Swedish Working Paper Series in Economics and Finance*, 423 (2001).

Hess, Gregory D., and Kwanho Shin. "Intranational Business Cycles in the United States." *Journal of International Economics*, 44 (1998): 289–313.

Hines, James R., and Richard H. Thaler. "Anomalies: The Flypaper Effect." *Journal of Economic Perspectives*, 9 (1995): 217–26.

Hirschman, Albert O. *Exit, Voice, and Loyalty: Responses to Decline in Firms, Organizations, and States*. Harvard University Press, 1970.

Hocman, Oded, David Pines, and Jacques-François Thisse. "On the Optimal Structure of Local Governments." *American Economic Review*, 85 (1995): 1224–40.

Holtz-Eakin, Douglas, Whitney Newey, and Harvey S. Rosen. "Estimating Vector Autoregressions with Panel Data." *Econometrica*, 56 (1988): 1371–95.

Im, Kyung So, M. Hashem Pesaran, and Yongcheol Shin. "Testing for Unit Roots in Heterogeneous Panels." *Journal of Econometrics*, 115 (2003): 53–74.

Inman, Robert P., and Michael A. Fitts. "Political Institutions and Fiscal Policy: Evidence from the U.S. Historical Record." *Journal of Law, Economics and Organization*, 6 (1990): 79–132.

Jacoby, Hanan G. "Access to Markets and the Benefits of Rural Roads: A Nonparametric Approach." *The Economic Journal*, 110 (2000): 713–37.

Jin, Hehui, Yingyi Qian, and Barry R. Weingast. "Regional Decentralization and Fiscal Incentives: Federalism, Chinese Style." Working paper, 2001.

Jin, Jing, and Heng-fu Zou. "How Does Fiscal Decentralization Affect Aggregate, National, and Subnational Government Size?" *Journal of Urban Economics*, 52 (2002): 270–93.

Kakwani, Nanok C. "Measurement of Tax Progressivity: An International Comparison." *The Economic Journal*, 87 (1977): 71–80.

Kanbur, Ravi, and Xiaobo Zhang. "Which Regional Inequality? The Evolution of Rural-Urban and Inland-Coastal Inequality in China from 1983 to 1995." *Journal of Comparative Economics*, 27 (1999): 686–701.

Keen, Michael, and Maurice Marchand. "Fiscal Competition and the Pattern of Public Spending." *Journal of Public Economics*, 66 (1997): 33–53.

Knight, Brian. "Endogenous Federal Grants and Crowd-Out of State Government Spending: Theory and Evidence from the Federal Highway Aid Program." *American Economic Review*, 92 (2002): 71–92.

Kolluri, Bharat R., Michael J. Panik, and Mahmoud S. Wahab. "Government Expenditure and Economic Growth: Evidence from G7 Countries." *Applied Economics*, 32 (2000): 1059–68.

Kontopoulos, Yianos, and Roberto Perotti. "Government Fragmentation and Fiscal Policy Outcomes: Evidence from OECD Countries." In *Fiscal Institutions and Fiscal Performance*, edited by J.M. Poterba and J. von Hagen. Chicago: University of Chicago Press, 1999.

Kooiman, Jan. "Social-Political Governance: Overview, Reflections, and Design." *Public Management*, 1 (1999): 67–92.

Kose, M. Ayhan, Christopher Otrok, and Charles H. Whiteman. "International Business Cycles: World, Region, and Country-Specific Factors." *American Economic Review*, 4 (2003): 1216–39.

Köthenbürger, Marko. "Tax Competition and Fiscal Equalization." *International Tax and Public Finance*, 9 (2002): 391–408.

Krussel, Per, and José Víctor Ríos-Rull. "On the Size of U.S. Government: Political Economy in the Neoclassical Growth Model." *American Economic Review*, 89 (1999): 1156–81.

Krusell, Per, Lee E. Ohanian, José Víctor Ríos-Rull, and Giovanni L. Violante. "Capital-Skill Complementarity and Inequality: A Macroeconomic Analysis." *Econometrica*, 68 (2000): 1029–1053.

Kukenova, Madina, and José Antonio Monteiro. "Spatial Dynamic Panel Model and System GMM: A Monte Carlo Investigation." MPRA Paper No.14319, 2008.

Kuznets, Simon. "Economic Growth and Income Inequality." *American Economic Review*, 45 (1955): 1–28.

Lee, Jisoon. "Optimal Size and Composition of Government Spending." *Journal of the Japanese and International Economies*, 6 (1992): 423–39.

LeSage, James P. "The Theory and Practice of Spatial Econometrics." Working Paper, Department of Economics, University of Toledo, 1997.

LeSage, James P., and Robert K. Pace. *Introduction to Spatial Economics*. Taylor and Francis Group, 2009.

Li, Shi. "A Survey on China's Inequality." Paper prepared for the International Conference on Equity and Social Justice in China's Transition, Beijing, China, 2002.

Liberati, Paolo, and Agnese Sacchi. "Tax Decentralisation and Local Government Size." Working Paper, No. 123, Università degli Studi Roma Tre, 2010.

Lijphart, Arend. "Unequal Participation: Democracy's Unresolved Dilemma." Presidential Address, American Political Science Association 1996, *American Political Science Review*, 91 (1997): 1–14.

Lin, Justin Yifu, and Zhiqiang Liu. "Fiscal Decentralization and Economic Growth in China." *Economic Development and Cultural Change*, 49 (2000): 1–21.

Lloyd-Ellis, Huw. "Public Education, Occupational Choice, and the Growth-Inequality Relationship." *International Economic Review*, 41 (2000): 171–202.

Lohmann, Susanne. "Federalism and Central Bank Independence: The Politics of German Monetary Policy, 1957–1992." *World Politics*, 50 (1998): 401–46.

Lott, John R., Jr., and Lawrence Kenny. "Did Women's Suffrage Change the Size and Scope of Government?" *Journal of Political Economy*, 107 (1999): 1163–98.

Lowry, Robert C., James E. Alt, and Karen E. Ferree. "Fiscal Policy Outcomes and Electoral Accountability in American States." *American Political Science Review*, 92 (1998): 759–74.

Lucas, Robert E. "On the Mechanics of Economic Development." *Journal of Monetary Economics*, 22 (1988): 3–42.

Lundberg, Johan "Spatial Interaction Model of Spillovers from Locally Provided Public Services." *Regional Studies*, 40 (2006): 631–44.

Lyons, W. E., and David Lowery. "Governmental Fragmentation vs. Consolidation: Five Public Choice Myths about Creating Informed, Involved, and Happy Citizens." *Public Administration Review*, 49 (1989): 533–43.

Ma, Jun. *Intergovernmental Relations and Economic Management in China*. England: Macmillan Press, 1996.

Mankiw, N. Gregory, David Romer, and David N. Weil. "A Contribution to the Empirics of Economic Growth." *Quarterly Journal of Economics*, 107 (1992): 407–37.

Marlow, Michael L. "Fiscal Decentralization and Government Size." *Public Choice* 56, (1988): 259–69.

Marlow, Michael L., and Alden F. Shiers. "Do Law Enforcement Expenditures Crowd-Out Public Education Expenditures?" *Applied Economics*, 31 (1999): 255–66.

Martin, Philippe. "Public Policies, Regional Inequalities and Growth." *Journal of Public Economics* 73, (1999): 85–105.

Martínez-Vázquez, Jorge, and Robert M. McNab. "Fiscal Decentralization, Macrostability and Growth." *Hacienda Pública Española*, 179 (2006): 25–49.

Mauro, Paolo. "Corruption and the Composition of Government Expenditure." *Journal of Public Economics*, 69 (1998): 263–79.

Mayntz, Renate. "Governing Failures and the Problem of Governability: Some Comments on a Theoretical Paradigm." In *Modern Governance*, edited by Jan Kooiman. London: Sage, 1993.

McKinnon, Ronald I. "Spontaneous Order on the Road Back from Socialism: An Asian Perspective." *American Economic Review* 80, (1992): 31–36.

McKinnon, Ronald I., and Thomas J. Nechyba. "Competition in Federal Systems: The Role of Political and Financial Constraints." In *The New Federalism: Can the States be Trusted?* edited by John A. Ferejohn and Barry R. Weingast. Stanford: Hoover Institution Press, 1997.

Meltzer, Allan H., and Scott F. Richard. "A Rational Theory of the Size of Government." *Journal of Political Economy*, 89 (1981): 914–27.

Milesi-Ferretti, Gian Maria, Roberto Perotti, and Massimo Rostagno. "Electoral Systems and Public Spending." *Quarterly Journal of Economics*, 117 (2002): 609–57.

Miller, Stephen M., and Frank S. Russek. "Fiscal Structures and Economic Growth: International Evidence." *Economic Inquiry*, 35 (1997): 603–13.

Mohanty, Madhusudan S., and Fabrizio Zampolli. "Government Size and Macroeconomic Stability." *BIS Quarterly Review*, 2009.

Montinola, Gabriella, Yingyi Qian, and Barry R. Weingast. "Federalism, Chinese Style: The Political Basis for Economic Success in China." *World Politics*, 48 (1995): 50–81.

Morrison, Catherine J., and Amy Ellen Schwartz. "State Infrastructure and Productive Performance." *American Economic Review*, 86 (1996): 1095–1111.

Mulligan, Casey B., Ricard Gil, and Xavier Sala-i-Martin. "Do Democracies Have Different Public Policies than Non-Democracies?" *Journal of Economic Perspectives*, 18 (2004): 51–74.

———. "Social Security and Democracy." NBER working paper 8958, 2002.

Musgrave, Richard A. *The Theory of Public Finance*. McGraw Hill Book Company, Inc., 1959.

Niskanen, William A., Jr. *Bureaucracy and Representative Government*. Chicago: Aldine-Atherton, 1971.

Nelson, Michael A. "Decentralization of the Subnational Public Sector: An Empirical Analysis of the Determinants of Local Government Structure in Metropolitan Areas in the U.S." *Southern Economic Journal*, 57 (1990): 443–57.

Norrbin, Stefan C., and Don E. Schlagenhauf. "The Role of International Factors in the Business Cycle: A Multi-Country Study." *Journal of International Economics*, 40 (1996): 85–104.

Oates, Wallace E. "An Essay on Fiscal Federalism." *Journal of Economic Literature*, 37 (1999): 1120–49.

———. *Fiscal Federalism*. New York: Harcourt Brace Jovanovich, 1972.

———. "Searching for Leviathan: An Empirical Study." *American Economic Review*, 75 (1985): 748–57.

OECD. *Challenges for China's Public Spending: Toward Greater Effectiveness and Equity*. OECD Publishing, 2006.

Otrok, Christopher, and Charles H. Whiteman. "Bayesian Leading Indicators: Measuring and Predicting Economic Conditions in Iowa." *International Economic Review*, 4 (1998): 997–1014.

Owyang, Michael T., David E. Rapach, and Howard J. Wall. "States and the Business Cycle." *Journal of Urban Economics*, 65 (2009): 181–94.

Pauly, Mark V. "Income Redistribution as a Local Public Good." *Journal of Public Economics*, 2 (1973): 25–58.

Pereira, Alfredo M. "On the Effects of Public Investment on Private Investment: What Crowds in What?" *Public Finance Review*, 29 (2001):13–25.

Pérez Sánchez, Rafaela Mª. "Characterizing the Optimal Composition of Government Expenditures." Economic Working Papers at Centro de Estudios Andaluces E2004/81, Centro de Estudios Andaluces, 2004.

Persson, Torsten, and Guido Tabellini. "Federal Fiscal Constitutions: Risk Sharing and Moral Hazard." *Econometrica*, 64 (1996): 623–46.

———. "Federal Fiscal Constitutions: Risk Sharing and Redistribution." *Journal of Political Economy*, 104 (1996): 979–1009.

Persson, Torsten, Gérard Roland, and Guido Tabellini. "Comparative Politics and Public Finance." *Journal of Political Economy*, 108 (2000): 1121–61.

———. "Separation of Powers and Political Accountability." *Quarterly Journal of Economic*, 112 (1997): 1163–1202.

———. "Towards Micropolitical Foundations of Public Finance." *European Economics Review*, 42 (1998): 685–94.

Piancastelli, Marcelo. "Measuring the Tax Effort of Developed and Developing Countries: Cross Country Panel Data Analysis – 1985/95." IPEA Working Paper No. 818, 2001.

Piras, Romano. "Government Spending Composition in an Endogenous Growth Model with Congestion." *Metroeconomica*, 52 (2001): 121–36.

Poterba, James M. "State Responses to Fiscal Crises: The Effects of Budgetary Institutions and Politics." *Journal of Political Economy*, 102 (1994): 799–821.

———. "Budget Institutions and Fiscal Policy in the U.S. States." *American Economic Review*, 86 (1996): 395–400.

Prohl, Silika., and Friedrich Schneider. "Does Decentralization Reduce Government Size? A Quantitative Study of the Decentralization Hypothesis." *Public Finance Review*, 37 (2009): 639–64.

Prud'homme, Rémy. "The Dangers of Decentralization." *The World Bank Research Observer*, 10 (1995): 201–20.

Qian, Yingyi, and Barry R. Weingast. "Federalism as a Commitment to Preserving Market Incentives." *Journal of Economics Perspectives*, 11 (1997): 83–92.

Qian, Yingyi, and Gérard Roland. "Federalism and the Soft Budget Constraint." *American Economic Review*, 88 (1998): 1143–62.

Gomez, Juan L. "Essays on Optimal Jurisdictional Size for Local Service Delivery." Public Management and Policy Dissertations, Paper 43, Georgia State University, 2010.

Restuccia, Diego, and Carlos Urrutia. "Intergenerational Persistence of Earnings: The Role of Early and College Education." *American Economic Review*, 94 (2004): 1354–78.

Revelli, Federico. "On Spatial Public Finance Empirics." *International Tax and Public Finance*, 12 (2005): 475–92.

———. "Performance Rating and Yardstick Competition in Social Service Provision." CESifo Working Paper No. 1270, 2004.

Rhode, Paul W., and Koleman S. Strumpf. "Assessing the Importance of Tiebout Sorting: Local Heterogeneity from 1850 to 1990." *American Economic Review*, 93 (2003): 1648–77.

Riker, William H. *Federalism: Origin, Operation, Significance*. Boston: Little, Brown and Company, 1964.

Riou, Stéphane. "Transfer and Tax Competition in a System of Hierarchical Governments." *Regional Science and Urban Economics*, 36 (2006): 249–69.

Rioja, Felix K., and Gerhard Glomm. "Populist Budgets and Long-Run Growth." Unpublished, Indiana University, 2003.

Rodden, Jonathan A. "Reviving Leviathan: Fiscal Federalism and the Growth of Government." *International Organization*, 57 (2003): 695–729.

———. "The Dilemma of Fiscal Federalism: Grants and Fiscal Performance around the World." *American Journal of Political Science*, 46 (2002): 670–87.

Rodden, Jonathan A., and Erik Wibbels. "Beyond the Fiction of Federalism: Macroeconomic Management in Multitiered Systems." *World Politics*, 54 (2002): 494–531.

Rodden, Jonathan A., Gunnar S. Eskeland, and Jennie Litvack. *Fiscal Decentralization and The Challenge of Hard Budget Constraints*. Cambridge, Massachusetts: MIT Press, 2003.

Rodrik, Dani. "Why Do More Open Economies Have Bigger Government?" *Journal of Political Economy*, 106 (1998): 997–1032.

Roodman, David. "How to Do Xtabond2: An Introduction to 'Difference' and 'System' GMM in Stata." Center for Global Development Working Paper 103, 2006.

Rostow, W. W. *Politics and the Stages of Growth*. Cambridge University Press, 1971.

Salmon, Pierre. "Decentralisation as an Incentive Scheme." *Oxford Review of Economic Policy*, 3 (1987): 24–43.

Samuelson, Paul A. "The Pure Theory of Public Expenditure." *Review of Economics and Statistics*, 36 (1954): 387–89.

Saavedra, Luz Amparo. "A Model of Welfare Competition with Evidence from AFCD." *Journal of Urban Economics*, 47 (2000): 248–79.

Sanz, Ismael, and Francisco J. Velazquez. "Fiscal illusion, Fiscal Consolidation and Government Expenditure Composition in the OECD: A Dynamic Panel Data Approach." European Economy Group Working Paper, 2002.

Schaltegger, Christoph A., and Benno Torgler. "Growth Effects of Public Expenditure on the State and Local Level: Evidence from a Sample of Rich Governments." *Applied Economics*, 38 (2006): 1181–92.

Schaltegger, Christoph A., and Dominique Küttel. "Exit, Voice, and Mimicking Behavior: Evidence from Swiss Cantons." *Public Choice*, 113 (2002): 1–23.

Schiavo-Campo, Salvatore, and Pachampet Sundaram. *To Serve and to Preserve: Improving Public Administration in a Competitive World*. Manila: Asian Development Bank, 2000.

Schnellenbach, Jan. "Dezentrale Finanzpolitik und Modellunsicherheit: eine theoretische Untersuchung zur Rolle des fiskalischen Wettbewerbs als Wissen generierender Prozess." Ph.D. diss., University of St. Gallen, 2003.

Shadbegian, Ronald J. "Fiscal Federalism, Collusion, and Government Size: Evidence from the States." *Public Finance Review*, 27 (1999): 262–81.

Shah, Anwar. "Fiscal Federalism and Macroeconomic Governance: For Better or For Worse?" *World Bank Policy Research Working Paper Series*, 1999.

Shih, Victor, and Zhang, Qi. "Who Receives Subsidies: A Look at the County-Level before and after the 1994 Tax Reform." Paper presented at the conference 'Paying for Progress. Public Finance, Human Welfare, and Inequality in China,' Institute for Chinese Studies, Oxford, 2004.

Slemrod, Joel. "On Voluntary Compliance, Voluntary Taxes, and Social Capital." *National Tax Journal*, 51 (1998): 485–91.

Slemrod, Joel, William G. Gale and William Easterly. "What Do Cross-Country Studies Teach About Government Involvement, Prosperity, and Economic Growth?" *Brookings Papers on Economic Activity*, 2 (1995): 373–431.

Smart, Michael. "Taxation and Deadweight Loss in a System of Intergovernmental Transfers." *Canadian Journal of Economics*, 31 (1998): 189–206.

Stein, Ernesto. "Fiscal Decentralization and Government Size in Latin America." *Journal of Applied Economics*, 2 (1999): 357–91.

Stigler, George J. "The Tenable Range of Functions of Local Government." In *Federal Expenditure Policy for Growth and Stability: Papers Submitted by Panelists Appearing before the Subcommittee on Fiscal Policy*, Joint Economic Committee, 213–219. Washington D.C.: United States Government Printing Office, 1957.

Stine, William F. "Is Local Government Revenue Response to Federal Aid Symmetrical? Evidence from Pennsylvania County Governments in an Era of Retrenchment." *National Tax Journal*, 47 (1994): 799–816.

Stock, James H., and Mark W. Watson. "A Probability Model of the Coincident Economic Indicators." In *Leading Economic Indicators: New Approaches and Forecasting Records*, edited by Kajal Lahiri and Geoffrey H. Moore. Cambridge: Cambridge University Press, 1991.

———. "A Procedure for Predicting Recession with Leading Indicators: Econometric Issues and Recent Experience." In *Business Cycle, Indicators and Forecasting*, edited by Stock, James H., and Mark W. Watson. Chicago: University of Chicago Press for NBER, 1993.

———. "New Indexes of Coincident and Leading Economic Indicators." In *NBER Macroeconomics Annual*, edited by Olivier J. Blanchard and Stanley Fischer. Cambridge, MA: MIT Press, 1989.

Stotsky, Janet G., and Asegedech WoldeMariam. "Tax Effort in Sub-Saharan Africa." IMF Working Paper No. 97/107, 1997.

Strumpf, Koleman S., and Felix Oberholzer-Gee. "Endogenous Institutions and Policy Decentralization: Local Liquor Control from 1934–1970." Unpublished Paper, 1998.

Sturm, Jan-Egbert. "Determinants of Public Capital Spending in Less-Developed Countries." Working Paper, University of Groningen and CESifo Munich, 2001.

———. *Public Capital Expenditure in OECD Countries: The Causes and Impact of the Decline in Public Capital Spending*. Edward Elgar Publishing Limited, 1998.

Su, Xuejuan. "The Allocation of Public Funds in a Hierarchical Educational System." *Journal of Economic Dynamics and Control*, 28 (2004): 2485–2510.

Tamura, Robert F. "Income Convergence in an Endogenous Growth Model." *Journal of Political Economy*, 99 (1991): 522–40.

Tanzi, Vito. "Fiscal Federalism and Decentralization: A Review of some Efficiency and Macroeconomic Aspects." In *Annual World Bank Conference on Development Economics 1995*. The World Bank, 1996.

Tanzi, Vito, and Ludger Schuknecht. *Public Spending in the 20th Century: A Global Perspective*. Cambridge University Press, 2000.

Tanzi, Vito, and Howell H. Zee. "Fiscal Policy and Long-Run Growth." *IMF Staff Papers*, 44 (1997): 179–209.

The Netherlands Ministry of Finance Government Audit Policy Directorate (DAR). "Government Governance: Corporate Governance in the Public Sector, Why and How?" Paper presented at the 9th FEE Public Sector Conference, November 2, 2000.

Tiebout, Charles M. "A Pure Theory of Local Expenditures." *Journal of Political Economy*, 64 (1956): 416–24.

Treisman, Daniel. "Decentralization and Inflation: Commitment, Collective Action, or Continuity?" *American Political Science Review*, 94(4) (2000): 837–57.

Trueblood, Michael A., and Beth Walter Honadle. "An Overview of Factors Affecting the Size of Local Government." Staff Paper P94-7, the Department of Agricultural and Applied Economics, University of Minnesota, 1994.

Tsui, Kai-yuen. "Local Tax System, Intergovernmental Transfers and China's Local Fiscal Disparities." *Journal of Comparative Economics*, 33 (2005): 173–96.

Turnovsky, Stephen J., and Walter H. Fisher. "The Composition of Government Expenditure and its Consequences for Macroeconomic Performance." *Journal of Economic Dynamics and Control*, 19 (1995): 747–86.

Van Wincoop, Eric. "Regional Risksharing." *European Economic Review*, 37 (1995): 1545–67.

Van Zon, Adriaan, and Joan Muysken. "Health and Endogenous Growth." *Journal of Health Economics*, 20 (2001): 169–85.

Viaene, Jean-Marie, and Itzhak Zilcha. "Education Technology, Human Capital Distribution and Growth." CESifo Working Paper, 2006.

———. "Human Capital Formation, Income Inequality and Growth." In *Growth and Inequality: Issues and Policy Implications*, edited by T. Eicher and S. Turnovsky. Cambridge: MIT Press, 2003.

Visco, Ignazio. "Paying for Pensions: How Important is Economic Growth?" *BNL Quarterly Review*, 216 (2001): 73–102.

Volscho, Thomas W. "Unions, Government Employment, and the Political Economy of Income Distribution in Metropolitan Areas." *Research in Social Stratification and Mobility*, 25 (2007): 1-12.

Wallis, John Joseph. "The Political Economy of New Deal Fiscal Federalism." *Economic Inquiry*, 29 (1991): 510–24.

Wang, Lu, and Otto A. Davis. "The Composition of State and Local Government Expenditures and Economic Growth." Working Paper, Carnegie Mellon University, 2005.

Wang, Shaoguang. "The Political Logic of Fiscal Transfers in China." Working Paper, The Chinese University of Hong Kong, 2005.

Weingast, Barry R. "The Economic Role of Political Institutions: Market-Preserving Federalism and Economic Development." *Journal of Law, Economics and Organization*, 11 (1995): 1–31.

Weingast, B., Kenneth A. Shepsle, and Christopher Johnsen. "The Political Economy of Benefits and Costs: A Neoclassical Approach to Distributive Politics." *Journal of Political Economy*, 89 (1981): 642–64.

Whitehouse, Edward. "Measures of Inequality in Stata." *Stata Technical Bulletin*, 4 (1995): 1–32.

Wibbels, Erik. "Federalism and the Politics of Macroeconomic Policy and Performance." *American Journal of Political Science*, 44 (2000): 687–702.

Wibbels, Erik, and Jonathan Rodden. "Business Cycles and the Political Economy of Decentralized Finance: Lessons for Fiscal Federalism in the EU." In *Fiscal Policy Surveillance in Europe*, edited by E. Wibbels and J. Rodden. New York: Palgrave Macmillan, 2006.

Wilson, John D. "A Theory of Interregional Tax Competition." *Journal of Urban Economics*, 19 (1986): 296–315.

———. "Capital Mobility and Environmental Standards: Is There a Theoretical Basis for the Race to the Bottom?" In *Fair Trade and Harmonization: Prerequisites for Free Trade? Vol. 1*, edited by J. Bhagwati and R. Hundee. Cambridge, MA: MIT Press, 1996.

———. "Theories of Tax Competition." *National Tax Journal*, 52 (1999): 269–304.

Windmeijer, Frank. "A Finite Sample Correction for the Variance of Linear Efficient Two-step GMM Estimators." *Journal of Econometrics*, 126 (2005): 25–51.

Wößmann, Ludger. "Educational Production in East Asia: The Impact of Family Background and Schooling Policies on Student Performance." IZA Discussion Paper No 745., 2003.

Wooldridge, Jeffrey M. *Introductory Econometrics: A Modern Approach (2nd ed.)*. Thomson South-Western, 2003.

World Bank. "Sharing Rising Incomes-Disparities in China." Washington D.C., 1997.

Yang, Dennis Tao. "Urban-Biased Policies and Rising Income Inequality in China." *American Economic Review*, 89 (1999): 306–10.

Zax, Jeffrey S. "Initiatives and Government Expenditures." *Public Choice*, 63 (1989): 267–77.

Zhang, Tao, and Heng-fu Zou. "Fiscal Decentralization, Public Spending and Economic Growth in China." *Journal of Public Economics*, 67 (1998): 221–40.

Zhang, Xiaobo. "Fiscal Decentralization and Political Centralization in China: Implications for Regional Inequality." IFPRI DSGD Discussion Paper No. 21, 2005.

Zhang, Xiaobo, Shenggen Fan, Linxiu Zhang, and Jikun Huang. "Local Governance and Public Goods Provision in Rural China." *Journal of Public Economics*, 88 (2004): 2857–71.

Zhang, Zhihua, and Jorge Martinez-Vazquez. "The System of Equalization Transfers in China." International Studies Program Working Paper 03-12, Andrew Young School of Policy Studies, Georgia State University, 2003.

Zodrow, George R., and Peter M. Mieszkowski. "Pigou, Tiebout, Property Taxation, and the Underprovision of Local Public Goods." *Journal of Urban Economics*, 19 (1986): 356–70.

Zou, Heng-fu. "Dynamic Effects of Federal Grants on Local Spending." *Journal of Urban Economics*, 36 (1994): 98–115.

Index

Index

CPSIA information can be obtained at www.ICGtesting.com
Printed in the USA
LVOW03*0958300714

396646LV00005BA/68/P